CASS LIBRARY OF AFRICAN STUDIES

AFRICANA MODERN LIBRARY

No. 14

General Editor: E. U. ESSIEN-UDOM
Department of Political Science
University of Ibadan, Nigeria

BLACK SPOKESMAN

AFRICANA MODERN LIBRARY

No. 6.   Nnamdi Azikiwe
Renascent Africa   (1937)
New Impression

No. 7   Adelaide Cromwell Hill and Martin Kilson, eds.
Apropos of Africa. Sentiments of Negro American Leaders on Africa
from the 1800s to the 1950s
Original Publication

No. 8.   J. E. Casely Hayford
Ethiopia Unbound: Studies in Race Emancipation (1911)
With a new introduction by F. N. Ugonna
Second Edition

No. 9.   A. B. C. Sibthorpe (Alias Aucandu, Prince of Cucuruku, Niger, F.P.)
The History of Sierra Leone   (1886; 3rd ed. 1906)
With a new introduction by Professor Robert July
Fourth Edition

No. 10   Magnus John Sampson, ed.
West African Leadership. Public Speeches delivered by the Honour-
able J. E. Casely Hayford   (1951)
New Impression

No. 11   J. E. Casely Hayford
Gold Coast Native Institutions. With thoughts upon a healthy
imperial policy for the Gold Coast and Ashanti   (1903)
New Impression

No. 12.   James Africanus Beale Horton
Letters on the Political Condition of the Gold Coast since the Exchange
of Territory between the English and Dutch Governments, on
January 1st, 1868; together with a short account of the Ashantee
War, 1862–4, and the Awoonah War, 1866, etc.   (1870)
With a new introduction by Professor E. A. Ayandele
Second Edition

No. 13.   E. A. Ayandele
Holy Johnson. Pioneer of African Nationalism 1836–1917
Original Publication

Black Spokesman

*Selected Published Writings of
Edward Wilmot Blyden*

Edited by

HOLLIS R. LYNCH

*Professor at the Institute of African Studies,
Columbia University, New York*

FRANK CASS & CO. LTD.
1971

Published by
FRANK CASS AND COMPANY LIMITED
67 Great Russell Street, London, WC1B 3BT

ISBN 0 7146 1745 8

Printed in Great Britain by
Clarke, Doble & Brendon Ltd., Plymouth

To

Violet, Sharon, Shola
and the "Third World"

Contents

Page

INTRODUCTION   xi

PART I

Afro-America and Africa

AFRO-AMERICA AND AFRICA

1. A Voice from Bleeding Africa (1856)   7
2. An Address before the Maine State Colonization
    Society, 1862   11
3. A Letter to the *Liberia Herald*, New York, July 5th,
    1862   21
4. The Call of Providence to the Descendants of Africa
    in America (1862)   25
5. Ethiopia stretching out her hands unto God; or,
    Africa's Service to the World (1887)   35
6. The Origin and Purpose of African Colonization (1883)   39
7. The African Problem and the Method of its Solution
    (1890)   45
8. The Negro in the United States (1900)   53

PART II

Liberia—Its Role and History

LIBERIA—ITS ROLE AND HISTORY

9. Liberia as She is; and the Present Duty of her
    Citizens (1857)   63
10. A Eulogy pronounced on the Reverend John Day
    (1859)   67
11. Our Origin, Dangers and Duties (1865)   77
12. Liberia as a Means, Not an End (1867)   81
13. The Boporo Country—Boporo (1871)   85
14. Liberia—its Status and its Field (1872)   93
15. A Chapter in the History of Liberia (1892)   99
16. The Three Needs of Liberia (1908)   119

PART III

Africa—Its History and Culture

AFRICA—ITS HISTORY AND CULTURE | *Page*
17. A Vindication of the African Race (1857) | 131
18. A Chapter in the History of the African Slave-Trade (1859) | 135
19. The Negro in Ancient History (1869) | 141
20. From West Africa to Palestine (1873) | 145
21. Echoes from Africa (1878) | 159
22. African Life and Customs (1908) | 163

PART IV

Race and the African Personality

RACE AND THE AFRICAN PERSONALITY
23. On Mixed Races in Liberia (1869) | 187
24. The Return of the Exiles and the West African Church (1891) | 191
25. Study and Race (1893) | 195
26. A Letter to Booker T. Washington, *New York Age*, January 24th, 1895 | 205
27. The Jewish Question (1898) | 209

PART V

Education—Its Nature and Purpose for Africans

EDUCATION—ITS NATURE AND PURPOSE FOR AFRICANS
28. Inaugural Address at the Inauguration of Liberia College, 1862 | 219
29. The West African University (1872) | 223
30. The Aims and Methods of a Liberal Education for Africans (1881) | 231
31. Report of the President of Liberia College to the Board of Trustees (1882) | 247
32. The Lagos Training College and Industrial Institute (1896) | 253
33. The Liberian Scholar (1900) | 265

PART VI

Islam in West Africa

ISLAM IN WEST AFRICA   *Page*
34. Mohammedanism in Western Africa (1871)   273
35. Mohammedanism and the Negro Race (1875)   281
36. The Mohammedans of Nigritia (1887)   295
37. Islam in the Western Soudan (1902)   303
38. The Koran in Africa (1905)   307

PART VII

European Imperialism in West Africa

EUROPEAN IMPERIALISM IN WEST AFRICA
39. The African Problem (1895)   317
40. West Africa (1901)   323
41. Some Problems of West Africa (1903)   327
BIBLIOGRAPHY   335
INDEX   341

B

Introduction

The continuing interest in and relevance of the life and ideas of
Edward Wilmot Blyden, 1832–1912, the brilliant West Indian-born
Liberian statesman and ideologue, stems from the fact that he
attempted to grapple with the fundamental problems of his race,
problems which, albeit in a modified form, still exist today: how
to dispel the lingering myth of European peoples of the inferiority
of the Negro? how to make black Africa a respected and important
participant in the world community of nations? how to ameliorate
the condition of African peoples and their descendants in the New
World? Blyden spent his entire adult life seeking to answer these
questions, and in the process became the most outstanding black
intellectual and littérateur of the nineteenth century. It is the
purpose of this Anthology to give representative selections from
his published writing which, beginning in the 1850s, spans a period
of more than fifty years.

Knowledge about the life and ideas of Blyden has recently
increased considerably by the publication of two studies of him,[1]
and the republication by the University of Edinburgh Press of the
first edition (1887) of his influential work, *Christianity, Islam and
the Negro Race.* This is comprised of fifteen miscellaneous essays
first published between 1871 and 1887 on the themes of the influence
of Christianity and Islam on the Negro, the character and achievements of the Negro race, and the role, past and future, of New
World blacks in Africa. However, the bulk of his writings—in the
form of rare pamphlets and articles—is still largely inaccessible.
This volume seeks to remedy this. Because it also aims at giving
representative selections from all of Blyden's published writings,
I have included excerpts from six of his essays in *Christianity,
Islam and the Negro Race* drawn from the first rather than the
slightly enlarged and modified second edition (1888) because of the
more general availability of the former. A second volume will
comprise selections from Blyden's letters as also his unpublished
manuscripts.

But before Blyden is left to speak for himself, it is appropriate

[1] Edith Holden, *Blyden of Liberia. An Account of the Life and Labors of
Edward Wilmot Blyden, LL-D. As Recorded in Letters and Print,* New York
Vantage Press, 1966; and Hollis R. Lynch, *Edward Wilmot Blyden, Pan-
Negro Patriot,* 1832–1912, London and New York: Oxford University Press,
1967. The first is largely a source book of more than a 1,000 pages; the
second is an intellectual and largely thematic biography.

to provide a sketch of his career and ideas as a Liberian, a West African and pan-African figure. It is expected that readers interested in a fuller discussion will consult my biography of him. Blyden was born in St. Thomas, Virgin Islands on August 3rd, 1832, and as a youth lived also in Venezuela for two years and in the United States for seven months, but he reacted against the discrimination and disabilities which New World blacks suffered by emigrating to Liberia at the age of eighteen (January 1851) and dedicating his life to the advancement of his race. He became convinced that the only way for the Negro race to gain respect was for its members to build partially westernized new states in Africa. Initially, he believed that this could be done largely through massive emigration by black Americans who would bring with them the necessary financial resources and technological skills. He saw Liberia, the black American colony founded in 1822 and independent since 1847, as the nucleus of a West African state which he hoped would grow in size and strength with the support of New World blacks.

LIBERIAN CAREER

In Liberia, Blyden worked to prepare himself for leadership, as also to prepare Liberia for the important role he had assigned to it. He attended Alexander High School, Monrovia, and trained to be a teacher and clergyman under its Principal, Rev. D. A. Wilson, a graduate of Princeton Theological College. He studied theology, the classics, geography and mathematics, and proved to be a brilliant student.[2] In 1853 he became a lay preacher, and in 1854, a tutor at his school. In 1858 he was ordained a Presbyterian Minister and at the same time succeeded Wilson as Principal of Alexander High School. Blyden also showed himself public-spirited: he contributed regularly to the *Liberia Herald*, then Liberia's only newspaper and in 1855-6 acted as its editor. In frequent public addresses he criticized Liberians as selfish, shallow, dependent and materialistic, and urged them to devote themselves to building up a great black Republic.

Nonetheless, throughout the 1850s he remained hopeful of Liberia's future. In that decade there was an unprecedented increase in the number of emigrants to Liberia because its early years as a Republic coincided with a period of intense discrimination against

---

[2] Blyden developed into an impressively versatile scholar: linguist (he read and spoke all the romance languages as well as Arabic and Hebrew and also spoke several West African languages); classicist (he read Greek and Latin fluently), theologian, historian and sociologist.

black Americans. In these years Liberia settled more than 5,000 emigrants—as many as it had done in the previous thirty years. Blyden looked to the new emigrants to provide the human and financial resources for building a progressive Liberian nation. He himself visited the United States in the summer of 1861 and 1862 to promote black American emigration to Liberia. But the American Civil War brought all black emigration projects to a halt: Afro-Americans threw their energies in the war on the side of the North with the aim of ending slavery and securing full rights as citizens. Although disappointed that free black Americans were distracted from what he considered their racially patriotic duty of strengthening Liberia, he was confident that even if slavery was abolished, black Americans would not be treated as the equals of whites and the realization of this would once more cause them to turn their attention to the "fatherland".

In the 1860s Blyden played new and important roles as a College Professor and Secretary of State. In 1862 he was appointed Professor of Classics at Liberia College—the first secular English-speaking institution of higher learning in tropical Africa. Blyden hoped that the College would attract black scholars and students from all parts of the world and that in time it would become a University with an international reputation. In his inaugural address as Professor in January 1862, he saw the College "as a means of building us up in all those qualities which shall fit us for the discharge of various duties, and draw towards us the attention of the civilized world".[3] In 1867, in his quest to make the College increasingly more relevant to Liberia, Blyden began teaching Arabic. His aim in doing so was to train Liberians who could establish links between the Negro Republic and the Muslim states in its hinterland. Blyden had for a decade before this been identified with several attempts to open up the Liberian hinterland and to extend the Republic's jurisdiction interiorwards. In 1869 he himself visited Boporo, a centre of Muslim learning seventy-five miles from the coast. Here he found "libraries with extensive manuscripts in poetry and prose" and was able to converse with learned *ulamas.* At Boporo he established a school with an Arabic-speaking Liberian teacher who was to teach "English and western subjects". Blyden remained as a Professor at Liberia College until 1871, but his grandiose plans for it did not materialize: Liberia was in no position to support them.

Between 1864 and 1866 Blyden combined his position as Professor at Liberia College with that of Secretary of State in

[3] *Liberia's Offering,* New York, 1862, p. 96.

President Warner's Cabinet. Because of his brilliance and public-spiritedness, he had long acted as adviser to Liberian Presidents, but this was his first official position in the Liberian Government. As Secretary of State, he suceeded in 1865 in arranging for 346 highly skilled Barbadians to settle in Liberia. He had hoped to settle many more skilled West Indians who were anxious to emigrate to Liberia, and he was very disappointed that lack of funds prevented him from doing so. The second major task which Blyden set himself as Secretary of State was to terminate a protracted boundary dispute between Liberia and Sierra Leone. Blyden wished to see the poor relationship which existed between the two territories replaced by active co-operation between them; indeed, he hoped that eventually the two would become politically one. However, his efforts failed and the dispute dragged on.

Acting again in an unofficial capacity, Blyden was the major architect of reforms which President Edward James Roye, who took office in 1870, sought to institute. The programme which Roye outlined in his inaugural address was ambitious and comprehensive: it included "a thorough financial reconstruction and the establishment of a national banking system, the general education of the masses, the introduction of railroads, the improvement and incorporation of the native tribes contiguous to Liberia, and the formation of a friendly alliance with distant and powerful tribes".[4] To finance these reforms Roye borrowed £100,000 from English bankers at exorbitant rates of interests. To get sufficient time in which to implement a programme of development, Roye sought a constitutional amendment which would extend the term of the President from two to four years. Roye's ambitious and innovative programmes were strongly opposed by his political enemies comprised primarily of a powerful mulatto group. Roye and Blyden belonged to the "pure Negro" faction. In the struggle which ensued, the mulattoes triumphed: Roye was deposed and murdered, and Blyden was forced to flee Liberia. It should be noted that already by 1870, Blyden, as a result of experiences both in Liberia and in the United States, had developed a paranoid dislike of mulattoes: he claimed, with some justification, that mulattoes used "genuine" blacks but had no wish to identify with them or promote the interest of the Negro race. His hatred of mulattoes, who wielded considerable power in Liberia during most of the nineteenth century, explains in part why Blyden's career there was far from successful.

After 1871, Blyden divided his time in West Africa between

[4] American Colonization Society, *Fifty-fourth Annual Report*, Washington, 1871, p. 21.

Liberia and the British colonies of Sierra Leone and Lagos; indeed, from this time, his influence spread rapidly throughout English-speaking West Africa. However, he remained fiercely loyal to Liberia and continued to have an active career there; it is perhaps well to look at this under the convenient headings of educator, politician and diplomat before his career in the wider West African context is examined.

LIBERIAN EDUCATOR

After a two years' stay (1871–3) in Sierra Leone, Blyden returned to Liberia and resumed the Principalship of Alexander High School at Harrisburg, an interior town on the St. Paul's river. Here he was adviser and schoolmaster to all who would listen and learn: he taught manual crafts as well as academic subjects, including Arabic, in day and evening classes, and in all, earned the reputation among the mulatto élite in Monrovia of "raising up a black aristocracy on the St. Paul's River".[5] This phase of his career came to an end in 1877 after he accepted an appointment as Liberia's first ambassador to Britain.

In 1880 Blyden achieved one of his major ambitions when he was appointed President of Liberia College. As President he hoped to implement plans for making the College a pan-African agency; in his inaugural address he expressed the view that the College was "a machine, an instrument to assist in carrying forward our regular work, devised not only from intellectual ends but for social purposes, for religious duty, for patriotic ends, for racial development".[6] He was at pains to emphasize that the College was not a Liberian institution but a pan-African institution in Liberia. He appealed to West Africans as well as black Americans (during visits to the United States in 1880 and 1882) to support the College. Concerned to make the curriculum relevant, he planned to institute a chair of Arabic and West African languages. He encouraged African chiefs and Muslim scholars to visit the College and attend its ceremonies. To interest Liberians generally, he inaugurated a series of public lectures, the first of which he himself delivered on "Toussaint L'Ouverture, the Emancipator of Haiti".

And yet Blyden's attempt to establish Liberia College as a fine academic institution failed. This was so partly because the College depended almost completely for its funds on American trustees who

---

[5] Blyden to Lowrie, January 6th, 1877, Papers of the Presbyterian Board of Foreign Missions (New York), Vol. 11.

[6] *Christianity, Islam and the Negro Race*, p. 71; 2nd ed., p. 82.

did not always find Blyden's outspoken pro-Negro views (as opposed to those of mulattoes) palatable, partly because of Blyden's own deficiency of character. Although undoubtedly the most brilliant West African of his time, he was a difficult man with whom to work; he regarded himself as the "Providential Agent" of the Negro race, and was intolerant of the views and ideas of others, especially if they were mulattoes. In June 1884 after protracted wrangling with two Afro-American members of his staff, Blyden resigned, and once again Liberia College lapsed into the academic torpor which characterized its existence. In 1900 Blyden hopefully returned to Liberia College, now reorganized and deriving most of its funds from the Liberian Government itself. But he was forced to leave after six months because he taught his students the unorthodox view that polygamy and Islam were to be preferred by Africans to monogamy and Christianity. As we shall see, Blyden was also involved with plans to establish institutions of higher learning in Sierra Leone and Lagos.

LIBERIAN POLITICIAN

As we have seen, Blyden was Secretary of State in 1864–66. Between 1880 and 1882, while President of Liberia College, he again joined the Liberian Cabinet as Minister of the Interior and Secretary of Education. Once again he unsuccessfully attempted to bring the boundary dispute between Liberia and Sierra Leone to an end. The dispute was finally settled in 1885 when the British Government forced its own terms on Liberia. As Secretary of Education, Blyden drew up a comprehensive scheme for education throughout the Republic, but the chronic lack of revenue from which the Liberian Government suffered prevented its implementation.

In 1885 Blyden undertook his most ambitious political action when he contested the Liberian Presidential election. He was truly a reluctant candidate. But he had become convinced that Liberian politicians were selfish and unpatriotic, and that the only hope for an enlightened administration was by his assumption of the Presidency. His platform included an urgently needed reform: the extension of the Presidential term from two to six or eight years so as to obviate almost constant electioneering, and to provide enough time for long-term planning. (This reform eventually took place in 1900 under President Barclay, the term being extended to four years.) His plans also included the repeal of restrictive legislation against foreigners, the attraction of foreign investments, and the taking of steps to make the indigenous Africans identify completely with the Liberian state.

But unfortunately for Blyden, he possessed no flair for politics: he was too forthright—he could never pander to the prejudices of the people—too idealistic and lacking in organizing ability. The scholarly Blyden saw himself in the role of Plato's philosopher-king, wise and non-partisan, and expecting no criticisms from citizens who were not nearly so well qualified as he for the vocation of governing. He was unfortunate, too, in that he could hardly have had a more formidable opponent: Hilary R. W. Johnson, son of Elijah Johnson, one of the most illustrious early leaders of Liberia, and a haughty, hot-tempered but politically astute man. Johnson had already served one term as President, the first Liberian-born to do so, and was seeking re-election. He won easily. Blyden's defeat ended his active political career in Liberia. He saw himself, however, as the Republic's elder statesman and in his lectures, writings and letters to friends continued to give gratuitous advice as to how best Liberia could progress.

LIBERIAN DIPLOMAT

From the outset of his career, and in all his travels Blyden regarded himself as an ambassador of the Negro race. However, his first major diplomatic appointment came in 1877 when President James S. Payne named him as Liberia's Ambassador to Britain. But Africa's first resident ambassador to a foreign country assumed his appointment in rather inauspicious circumstances, for the Liberian legislature regarded a foreign embassy for the country as sheer luxury and refused to vote money for it. But Blyden felt strongly that it was essential for the self-respect and dignity of the Negro race that Liberia, as one of only two independent African countries (the other being Ethiopia), should become an active member of the world community of nations. He thus persuaded the President to appoint him directly even though this meant that he would receive neither a salary nor an allowance from the Liberian Government. As the unsalaried first African ambassador to Europe, Blyden was unique in modern diplomatic history.

Blyden had little money of his own but could rely on the help of British friends. He had visited Britain six times previously and was well known in London's highest literary, political and humanitarian circles. He also received considerable help from Edward S. Morris, a wealthy white American Quaker businessman with economic interests in Liberia. Morris acted for some time as

Blyden's secretary, to the mild consternation of the people of London who observed a relationship that was probably then unique.

Blyden remained as Liberia's ambassador to the Court of St. James until the end of 1878, and although he achieved no major diplomatic feat, he had, as a much sought-after intellectual, helped to enhance the prestige of his race. He had striven, with some measure of success, to create sympathy for and interest in Liberia among influential British.

In 1892 Blyden returned to Britain as Liberia's ambassador, this time with the approval of the Liberian legislature. At that time the territorial integrity and even the sovereignty of the weak black Republic was seriously threatened by the aggressive imperialism of the European nations. Blyden's diplomatic objective seemed to have been to get a commitment, or at least a tacit agreement from the British Government, that it would neither be a party to nor countenance the dismemberment of Liberia. Blyden spent four months in London but achieved no obvious diplomatic victories.

In 1905 Blyden, then an elderly statesman of seventy-three, was called upon for the last time to be of diplomatic service to Liberia. He was appointed by President Arthur Barclay as Envoy Extraordinary and Minister Plenipotentiary to Britain and France with the special mission of negotiating a settlement of Liberia's dispute with France over its northern boundary with the French colonies of Guinea and the Ivory Coast. Liberians believed that the French were planning to seize the Republic's potentially rich hinterland. After discussions with the British Foreign Office in late May, Blyden proceeded to Paris but found it difficult to engage the French Government in serious discussions. He finally left Paris in mid-September 1905, with his mission unaccomplished. The boundary dispute was finally settled in September 1907, again, as in the case of that with the British, to the serious disadvantage of Liberia.

But if he had failed to achieve his diplomatic objective, he had been a great social success, and characteristically, had used the opportunity to disseminate information about Liberia and West Africa. He had exchanged courtesies and visits with foreign ambassadors, and held interviews with rulers from the Middle East, among them the Shah of Persia. In Paris he also met many African and Afro-American visitors, among them Portia Washington, the daughter of the Afro-American leader, Booker T. Washington.

WEST AFRICAN NATIONALIST

By the early 1870s it had become almost clear to Blyden that the modern trans-tribal West African nation which he envisaged would not come about through any large-scale New World black emigration to West Africa. Although he continued to support the principle of "repatriation", he was disappointed by the lack of any positive response to Africa on the part of the majority of New World blacks. However, if the modern nation or nations he envisaged could not come about through the agency of New World blacks, he did not abandon that goal; indeed, his career outside Liberia could be usefully examined by his attempts to promote this goal. He sought to do so by the following means:

(*a*) fostering close links between Liberia and Sierra Leone with the hope that they would eventually unite;

(*b*) seeking to persuade the British to establish a vast protectorate over West Africa which, linked with Liberia, would eventually create a major West African nation; and, after the partition of West Africa, by giving qualified welcome to European colonial rule, which he prophesied would be temporary;

(*c*) encouraging the spread of Islam and Arabic in West Africa as unifying agencies, while seeking to foster Muslim-Christian co-operation;

(*d*) fostering cultural nationalism in West Africa based on pride in Negro history and culture and the belief that the Negro race had special attributes and a distinctive contribution to make to world civilization.

I shall elaborate on each of the above points.

Blyden thought it imperative that the two small contiguous English-speaking states of similar origin should closely co-operate. Early in his own Liberian career, he was disturbed that, in fact, there was little social intercourse between educated Africans in Sierra Leone and Liberia, and was determined to promote such intercourse. On brief visits to Sierra Leone in 1862 and 1865, he sought to persuade some of the leading Africans to emigrate to Liberia by emphasizing that it was a sovereign Republic and that opportunities for advancement there were unlimited. A thriving Liberia, he reasoned, would spur Sierra Leoneans to become independent of the British. In his two years' stay in Sierra Leone, 1871–3, Blyden excited an interest in Liberia among his new friends, including William Grant, a wealthy merchant, and a man of strong racial pride. In December 1876 Grant visited Liberia as the guest of Blyden. At a tea party which Blyden gave for him, it was resolved that "the time has arrived when there ought to be a contribution of negro talents and ability on the West Coast of Africa . . . for the elevation of our race morally, socially, politically . . . ".[7]

Blyden maintained that the boundary between Liberia and Sierra Leone was an artificial and temporary one. In a lecture delivered in Freetown in 1884, he asserted that, "The two peoples are one in origin and one in destiny, and in spite of themselves, in spite of local prejudices, they must co-operate." He lost no opportunity to promote such co-operation. Thus he saw the planned celebration of the centenary of Sierra Leone in 1887 as a good opportunity of "bringing Liberia and Sierra Leone together":[8] through his encouragement several Liberians attended the celebrations. But despite Blyden's continuous efforts, no solid community of interests developed between the two countries.

EUROPE AND THE PAN-AFRICAN GOAL

By 1871, when his hopes for large-scale New World black emigration to West Africa had all but died, Blyden looked to the British to play the nation-building role of pacifying and uniting the peoples of West Africa. While in Sierra Leone in 1871, he first sought to persuade the British to extend their jurisdiction in West Africa by appealing to their "humanitarianism" and to their "commercial instincts": a pacified West Africa under a British protectorate would not only benefit Africans but would also bring substantial pecuniary rewards to Britons through increased trade with Africans.

The British were not then interested in so ambitious and expensive an undertaking but Blyden's interest in closely linking Sierra Leone with its vast hinterland was partially rewarded when he was authorized to make two official expeditions, the first in 1872 to the pagan Kingdom of Falaba, the other in 1873 to the Muslim Kingdom of Timbo. In his letters *en route* and in his official reports Blyden again strongly but vainly urged the British to extend a protectorate over the vast hinterland of Sierra Leone on humanitarian and commercial grounds. He made his last attempt at seeking to persuade the British Government to extend its territorial jurisdiction in West Africa eight months after the end of the Berlin

[7] *West African Reporter* (Freetown), January 24th, 1877.
[8] *Christianity, Islam and the Negro Race*, p. 201.

West African Conference of 1884–5. He argued that such an expansion was immediately necessary to forestall vigorous French expansion in the Western Sudan. He recalled the long and persistent efforts of African merchants, led by such well-known figures as William Grant and Samuel Lewis, to persuade the Sierra Leone Government to bring under its protection its hinterland so as to ensure uninterrupted trade between it and the colony. He again emphasized that the new vast protectorate would provide "safe and permanent" markets for British manufactures, and would "in a short time take from the British Government the whole burden of local expenditure".

If, up to 1885, Blyden's ideal had been the creation of an English-speaking West African state and he had wished to see the influence of the French curbed with the partition of West Africa, after 1885, France became Blyden's favourite colonizing power precisely because it had done what he had been urging the British to do: the French first consolidated old claims on the coast, added as much as possible to them, then went on to conquer and control the Sudan from Senegal to Lake Chad, in the process circumscribing Liberia and the British colonies, Gambia and Sierra Leone, and to a lesser extent Nigeria and the Gold Coast (now Ghana). In this vast continuous French-controlled territory, Blyden felt, lay the seeds of one West African State. He was also very much impressed by the systematic and integrated plan for the economic development of French West Africa based on the encouragement of agriculture and the construction of roads, railroads, docks and wharves.

It is well to emphasize that Blyden himself never doubted that European political overlordship would be temporary, and that independent West African nations would emerge from the former European colonies. This optimism was based on his oft-repeated conviction that, because the climate and diseases accounted for a high mortality rate, Europeans could never successfully colonize tropical Africa. But their imperialism, with all its drawbacks, would serve to modernize Africa. He recognized that it was Europe's aim "to utilise Africa for her own purpose"[9] but he insisted that in this very process Europe was unwittingly serving Africa. His greatest fear was that through ignorance of African customs and institutions, the imperial powers would indiscriminately obliterate many which were useful. And he certainly did not wish Africa to become culturally a black replica of Europe.

[9] *Africa and the Africans*, London, 1903, p. 34.

ISLAMIC ROLE

Blyden had realized that in any plan for the formation of a West African State or States, the Muslims were bound to play an important role because of their numerical strength and widespread influence. He had been deeply impressed by the Islamic intellectual and religious movements which since the late eighteenth century had been taking place in West Africa, and which had resulted in a remarkable spread of Islam and in a new order of social and political organization in those areas brought under Muslim control. But Blyden knew that there was widespread although ill-founded Christian contempt for Muslims. He set out to dispel the prejudice against West African Muslims and to build a bridge of communication between them and the Christians.

Blyden's solution for fostering intercourse and co-operation between the Muslim and Christian communities was theoretically simple: namely, to set up schools at all levels where Muslims could learn English and western subjects, and where Christians could be taught Arabic and an appreciation of Islamic religion and literature. As we have seen, he had attempted to implement this policy in Liberia. Between 1887 and 1895 he did succeed in implementing this same policy on a private and modest scale in Sierra Leone.

His first opportunity to promote the teaching of English to Muslims in an official capacity came in 1896, when he was appointed Agent of Native Affairs in Lagos. Here, as in Sierra Leone, he was successful in dispelling the reluctance of the Muslim community to expose their children to western teaching. When he left Lagos the following year, the "western" school he founded for Muslim children was well established. The work of providing "western" education for Muslim children he carried on in Sierra Leone as Director of Muslim Education there from 1901 to 1906.

A NEW SYNTHESIS

An important means by which Blyden sought to create the consciousness of belonging to one West African community on the part of English-speaking West Africans was by fostering pride in the history and culture of the Negro race. Blyden's dilemma here was that while he believed that a certain amount of westernization could be highly beneficial to Africans, he also saw that it could have disastrous effects, creating new divisions and a sense of inferiority among them. He believed that West Africans could avoid the latter danger only if western-educated Africans retained a real pride in the basic wholesome African customs and institutions, and consciously set about selecting and integrating into a new cultural synthesis only those aspects of western culture, or modified versions of them, which they considered beneficial. For Blyden it was absolutely necessary for Africans to control this synthesizing process. As we have seen, he came to see as necessary for the creation of modern, trans-tribal West African nations the temporary political overlordship of European nations but he fervently wished Africans to retain, so to speak, their cultural independence through creative control of institutions, traditional as well as western. Blyden's first two years in Sierra Leone, 1871-3, provide an early example of his attempt to foster cultural nationalism. Starting from the premise that the Negro was endowed with special attributes, and that African customs and institutions represented a significant aspect of the character of the race, Blyden criticized foreign missionaries for seeking to completely Europeanize Africans and thus thwart the development of the "African Personality". He charged them with creating unnecessary sectarian divisions among Africans, and of disparaging and destroying African customs and institutions which were functional and compatible with the highest tenets of Christianity. To secure the "proper development" of Africans and to promote unity among them, Blyden urged the setting up of an independent, non-denominational Church, and a secular West African University controlled by Africans themselves. Many members of the Freetown educated élite, clerical as well as lay, were closely associated with Blyden's agitation, but as a group they were not large, wealthy, influential or determined enough to make important institutional changes. After Blyden left Freetown in October 1873 his nationalist agitation quickly subsided. The one tangible result from the agitation was that Fourah Bay College, a teacher training college of the Church Missionary Society, was converted in 1876 into a College of Durham University, England, but this new college was too clerical, foreign-controlled and élitist for Blyden's purposes.

A more auspicious occasion for implementing Blyden's idea of one non-sectarian West African Church came in 1890. In that year a party of C.M.S. European missionaries went out to the Niger C.M.S. mission and with fanatical ruthlessness condemned the work which Samuel Crowther, the venerable African Bishop, and his African staff had been doing for almost three decades and summarily dismissed or suspended the majority of African ministers and agents. West African Christians of all denominations were united in protesting against these high-handed actions of Europeans as "a direct insult and affront to Bishop Crowther, the whole African Church and the Negro Race".[10] Blyden, as the most prominent West African, was invited by a committee of fourteen prominent Africans of Lagos to give moral support during this crisis on the Niger. In a major pronouncement on January 2nd, 1891 Blyden unequivocally urged the setting up of an independent African church with Bishop Crowther at its head. The idea was discussed at interdenominational meetings of African clerics but no action was taken perhaps primarily because sectarianism was already too deeply entrenched among Africans. However, inspired by Blyden's advice, and disappointed by the irresolute clerical leadership, some laymen of Lagos founded the United Native African Church in August 1891, but this was a small and weak splinter falling far short of the African church which Blyden envisaged.

Blyden had also continued to advocate the establishment of a West African institution of higher learning. We have already alluded to his attempts to found a West African University in Freetown and to his work at Liberia College. He made yet another major attempt, this time in Lagos in 1896, to establish a significant educational institution. Lagos was much wealthier and seemingly more progressive than either Sierra Leone or Liberia, and Blyden was hopeful that he could win sufficient support for the establishment of an institution of higher learning offering liberal arts as well as technical subjects. Blyden discussed the idea with leading Africans who seemed amenable to it. The target was set of raising £10,000 with which to begin the institution. Blyden then discussed the idea with the Governor, Sir Gilbert Carter, who endorsed it. The Colonial Office took the stand that it was willing to support such a scheme if, in fact, the initiative in financial terms came from the Africans. The initial financial goal was not met, and this caused Blyden to express his disgust at "the lamentable incapacity of the people and their invincible apathy to anything but the accumulation . . . of money which they know not how to use".[11]

THE ROLE OF NEWSPAPERS

In attempting to create a sense of community among West Africans, Blyden saw the newspaper as an indispensable medium, and it is significant that he either helped to found or wrote for most

---

[10] J. L. Davies to Secretaries of the Church Missionary Society (London), October 24th, 1890.
[11] C.O. 147/107, Blyden to Governor Carter, November 10th, 1896.

of the important contemporary newspapers of West Africa. I have already alluded to his work on the *Liberia Herald*. In 1872 Blyden founded in Freetown the *Negro*, a weekly newspaper the aim of which was "to represent and defend the interest of . . . the Negro". About the same time, he helped to found the *Ethiopian*, a monthly journal devoted to educational matters. In 1874, the year in which the *Negro* was discontinued, Blyden helped to found, again in Free-town, the *West African Reporter*, the declared aim of which was to foster unity among English-speaking West Africans. In 1884 he helped to found the *Sierra Leone Weekly News*, which became one of the most successful newspapers of its time in West Africa. Finally, during a few years' stay in Lagos in the 1890s, Blyden was closely associated with the *Lagos Weekly Record*, another successful news-paper. All the above newspapers circulated among the English-speaking West African educated élite, and through them Blyden sought to inspire racial solidarity and initiative.

Blyden was relentless in propagating cultural nationalism. As the cultural arrogance of Europeans in West Africa grew with increasing numbers throughout the nineteenth century, so did Blyden's plea grow in urgency that Africans should never lightly discard their time-tested and functional institutions, including polygamy and secret societies, and that institutions borrowed from the West should be modified to suit African conditions and needs. He constantly urged educated Africans to study their own societies and explain them to the world. He applauded such pioneering African efforts as John Mensah Sarbah's *Fanti Customary Laws* (1897)[12] and J. E. Casely Hayford's *Gold Coast Institutions* (1903).[13] Blyden's own greatest single effort at "unfolding the African . . . through a study of the customs of his fathers" was made in 1908 with the publication of his work, *African Life and Customs*, which had first appeared as a series of articles in the *Sierra Leone Weekly News*.

Blyden's teachings and influence had led in the late 1880s to the formation of the Dress Reform Society in Freetown, the purpose of which was to encourage the educated élite to wear the traditional loose-fitting cotton garments rather than the tight woollen European suits which were ill-suited to the hot and humid climate of the West African coast. At this time, too, a number of educated Africans discarded their European names for African ones. There were similar manifestations in Lagos and the Cape Coast, but they were all short-lived because of the growing pressure to conform to western

[12] Reprinted Frank Cass, 1968.
[13] Reprinted Frank Cass, 1970.

c

cultural norms, particularly after the partition of West Africa and the establishment of European colonial rule.

To the end of his life he laid emphasis on cultural nationalism: he believed that Europeans were temporarily needed as political overlords in the carving out of new trans-tribal modern African nations: successful cultural nationalism was for him a necessary prerequisite to political independence, a view that some militant Africans during Blyden's own lifetime and subsequently have found difficult to accept. It might be said, too, that although his West African contemporaries greatly admired him for his intellectual ability, they were somewhat disappointed in him as a leader. They looked to him in vain for a sustained lead in practical matters. He produced excellent ideas but his dilettantism, impatience and lack of tact militated against the success of the ventures he undertook. He showed ambivalences which were disturbing to his admirers and would-be followers: although highly critical of Christianity in practice and extravagantly laudatory of Islam (as well as being close to West African Muslims), he remained even after he resigned from the Presbyterian Church in 1886, a non-sectarian Christian. Also, although he strongly advocated the retention of West African traditional culture and customs, he himself remained even in such externals as dress, the most westernized West African. But whatever reservations his black contemporaries had of him, they honoured and boasted of him as an international intellectual and literary figure.

PAN-AFRICAN INTELLECTUAL

Unquestionably it is primarily as a man of letters and ideas rather than as a man of action—he possessed little organizing or administrative ability—that Blyden made his greatest impact. He began writing at the age of eighteen, at first in the colonization journals of America. His writings, apart from condemning slavery and advocating the emigration of free Afro-Americans to Liberia, were concerned to prove that the Negro race had a history and culture of which it could be proud. Thus, at the outset of his career, he realized that an indispensable prerequisite to pan-African action was the creation of pride and self-esteem among Negroes.

His first pamphlet, *A Voice from Bleeding Africa*, published in Monrovia in 1856, listed some thirty blacks from Africa and the New World, including J. E. J. Capitein, the African-born author, linguist and theologian; Toussaint L'Ouverture, the celebrated general and liberator of Haiti; and his own contemporary, Frederick

Douglass, the black American leader and abolitionist; all of whom in Blyden's view, had achieved "moral and intellectual greatness". In the following year in another pamphlet, *A Vindication of the African Race*, he rebutted with cogency all the theories which purported to prove Negro inferiority. In January 1869 an article of his, "The Negro in Ancient History", appeared in *The Methodist Quarterly Review* (New York). This was the first article by a Negro in a scholarly quarterly and in it Blyden adduced evidence to prove the now academically respectable view that Negroes played "an active . . . part in early Egyptian civilization" and thus helped to transmit to posterity "the germs of . . . the arts and sciences".

In a lecture on "Africa's Service to the World", delivered in the United States in 1880, Blyden argued that the splendours of European and American civilization largely resulted from the exploitation of the Negro. Seeking to couch this unpalatable truth in language which would appeal to Negroes' pride, he asserted with hyperbole: "The political history of the United States is the history of the Negro. The commercial and agricultural history of nearly the whole of the Americas is the history of the Negro."[14]

Another important theme in Blyden's writings and one on which after the partition of Africa he constantly harped, was that, contemporary European opinion to the contrary, Africa's culture—its customs and institutions—was basically wholesome and particularly well suited to the needs of Africans. He was not opposed to African society borrowing and incorporating useful aspects of western culture, but he believed that educated Africans should be protected from becoming needlessly ashamed of their culture, a consequence of the arrogant and ethnocentric attitude of Europeans in Africa. In his book, *African Life and Customs* (1908), Blyden made his most systematic defence of African culture. Indeed, this was the first important attempt at a sociological analysis of African society as a whole. In this work he was concerned to show that there existed "an African Social and Economic System [which] was most carefully and elaborately organized, venerable, impregnable, indispensable", a thesis made famous some forty years later in Rev. Placide Tempels' book, *Bantu Philosophy*. Blyden pointed out that the African social system was socialist, co-operative and equitable—an ideal for which Europe was desperately striving as the answer to ills created by excessive individualism and unscrupulous competitiveness.

If Blyden pointed up some of the positive aspects of Negro history and culture, he was also concerned to draw attention to

[14] *Christianity, Islam and the Negro Race*, p. 119.

those influences which he believed tended to retard the progress of the Negro. He advanced the controversial thesis that one of the major retarding influences on the Negro was Christianity—not the essence but what in practice passed for Christianity. He argued that in America Christianity was used as a tool by the upholders of slavery and discrimination to foster Negro submissiveness; and that in Africa sectarianism combined with the arrogant ethnocentrism of European missionaries and teachers produced disunity and a feeling of inferiority among "westernized" Africans. On the other hand, Blyden lauded Islam as an elevating and unifying influence which did not disrupt the African social fabric; Islam, he argued, had brought Africans the benefits of a major world civilization without creating in them a sense of inferiority. This thesis was most fully developed in his *magnum opus, Christianity, Islam and the Negro Race*, first published in London in 1887. Because of its challenging and stimulating ideas, and because it was extremely well written, this book of Blyden's made a tremendous impact in Europe and America. Indeed, there were those critics who were sceptical that the book had been written by a Negro. particularly one whose formal education had not gone beyond High school.

In addition to seeking to demonstrate that the Negro race had a worthy past, Blyden asserted that it possessed unique and special attributes and had a special world mission to fulfil. This, as it were, is the basis of his negritude, which can be best understood by an examination of his concept of race.

Ironically, Blyden was led to formulate his concept of race as a result of the divisions, based largely on shades of colour, which he noticed in Liberian and American non-white society. For indeed both in the United States and Liberia light-skinned "Negroes", as part descendants of the "master race", were generally regarded and regarded themselves as superior to the blacks; invariably they comprised the "Negro" leadership. In Liberia a particularly bitter enmity developed between the educated blacks, led by Blyden who prided himself on being "pure Negro", and the mulatto ruling class, led by J. J. Roberts, Liberia's first President, who, in physical features, was indistinguishable from a white man.

This division became institutionalized socially in masonic clubs and politically into two parties: the Whig being that of the blacks and the Republican (named after the US Republican Party) being that of the mulattoes. Alexander Crummell, the sophisticated, American-born, Cambridge University-educated episcopalian clergyman, and like Blyden a leading Liberian black, wrote to a friend in March 1864: "Never have I in all my life seen such bitterness, hate and malice displayed as has been exhibited by the two factions of state."[15]

Thus Blyden's experiences both in Liberia and the United States had led him from about the early 1870s to regard light-skinned "Negroes" as a retarding influence on the progress of the Negro race and he began to question whether in fact they belonged to his race. He quickly found confirmation for his derogatory opinion of mulattoes in contemporary writings on race. For, ironically, his own concept of race was strongly influenced by the anti-Negro currents of ideas on race as enunciated by the American colonizationists and upholders of slavery; by the English school of anthropology led by James Hunt and Richard Burton; and by the writings of the Frenchman, Count Arthur de Gobineau, whose *Essays on the Inequality of the Races* has been regarded as the classic nineteenth-century statement on the subject.

The main ideas in these writings on race can be summed up as follows: there was a hierarchy of races with the Negro at or near the bottom; that there were "innate and permanent differences in the moral and mental endowments" of races; that each race had its own "talents", "instincts" and "energy", and that race rather than environmental or circumstantial factors "held the key to the history" of a people; that there exists "an instinctive antipathy among races", and that homogeneity of race was necessary for successful nation-building; that miscegenation was "unnatural", and that mulattoes were "immoral" and weak people, with "confused race instincts".[16]

Although these views were being vociferously promulgated it is certain that at the time they represented a minority opinion. And it is almost superfluous to point out that the concept of a "pure race" is now regarded as scientifically untenable; that culture is learned rather than instinctive or innate, that a people's history is largely determined by environmental and circumstantial factors, and that homogeneity of race is not at all essential for the creation of a nation.

Yet, interestingly, Blyden subscribed to all but two of the above-mentioned ideas on race. He denied that there was any "absolute or essential superiority . . . or inferiority" among races: "each race

[15] Crummell to Coppinger, March 26th, 1864, American Colonization Society Papers (Washington, D.C.), Vol. XIII.
[16] See, for instance, Count Arthur de Gobineau, *The Moral and Intellectual Diversity of Races*, Philadelphia, 1856, and James Hunt, *On the Negro's Place in History*, London, 1863.

was equal but distinct; it was a question of difference of endowment and difference of destiny".[17] In addition, he maintained that environmental and circumstantial factors did, to some extent, influence the history of a people. His own concept of race demonstrated his skill in drawing on the main current of ideas and synthesizing them in such a way to suit his own purposes. His acceptance of the theory of "mutual antipathy among races", and the idea that homogeneity was necessary for the successful creation of a nation provided him with theoretical justification for his contention, which he strongly made after 1870, that only "genuine Negroes" should be "repatriated" to Africa; just as his recognition (despite his affirmation that race largely held the key to history) that adventitious factors helped to shape a people's history, permitted him to show the circumstances which prevented the Negro race from fully developing and demonstrating its special talents.

THE AFRICAN PERSONALITY

But what, in Blyden's view, were the distinctive attributes of the Negro race, what the special contribution it could make to civilization? Blyden was very much aware of contemporary nationalist ideologies and movements, and it is probable that both in his concept of the ideal African and of the role he was to play in civilization, he was influenced by these. Such Russian nationalists as Karamazin and Dostoevsky had, in their reaction to European technological and cultural superiority, idealized the rural Slav as "perfect man", and had extravagantly prognosticated that Russia would be "the founder of a new civilization and the bearer of universal salvation".[18] Similarly, Mazzini had claimed that Italy would assume moral leadership in the regeneration of man. The German nationalists, too, influenced by their philosophers, Herder, Fichte and Hegel, saw the German people, once united, as forming the vanguard of world civilization. Blyden followed in this romantic tradition which, in each case, was intended to hurdle short-comings, dispel a feeling of inferiority and act as a spur to united, concerted action.

Thus, Blyden assumed that there was an "African Personality" (a phrase first made popular in recent times by Kwame Nkrumah) which would express itself in the execution of the special mission he believed the Negro race to possess. One of the best expressions

---

[17] *Christianity, Islam and the Negro Race*, p. 277.
[18] Hans Kohn, *Prophets and Peoples: Studies in Nineteenth-century Nationalism*, New York, 1961, Chap. 5.

of this view of his was made in a lecture, "Race and Study", delivered in Freetown, Sierra Leone, in 1893. (See Selection 26.)

Blyden portrayed the "African personality" as being the antithesis of that of the European, and serving to counteract the worst aspects of the latter. The European character, according to Blyden, was harsh, individualistic, competitive and combative; European society was highly materialistic; the worship of science and technology was replacing that of God. In the character of the African, averred Blyden, were to be found "the softer aspects of human nature"; cheerfulness, sympathy, willingness to serve, were some of its marked attributes. The special contribution of the African to civilization would be a spiritual one. There was no need for Africa to participate in the mad and headlong rush for scientific and industrial progress which had left Europe little time or inclination to cultivate the spiritual side of life, which was ultimately the most important one. Blyden did not anticipate for Africa industrialism or "any large and densely crowded cities"—which for him were merely man's "marring of God's handiwork"—the rural landscape. He defined the future relations of the African with the European as follows:

> The Northern races will take the raw materials from Africa and bring them back in such forms as will contribute to the comfort and even elegance of life . . . ; while the African in the simplicity and purity of rural enterprises will be able to cultivate those spiritual elements in humanity which are suppressed, silent and inactive under the pressures and exigencies of material progress.[19]

He saw Africa as the "spiritual conservatory of the world", and believed that it would act as a peace-maker among the ever-warring European nations, and as a "consoler" when the destructive inventions of white men led to a crisis in their civilization.

But Blyden did not claim for the Negro a monopoly of the spiritual role; he was prepared that his race would share this with the Jew. He saw a parallel in the history of the Negro and the Jew: each had a history of intense suffering and this, he argued, had served to develop the spiritual side of their natures, and fitted them to be the spiritual leaders of the world. He developed this viewpoint fully in his pamphlet *The Jewish Question* published in Liverpool in 1898. In this work he showed that he was highly conversant with contemporary Jewish thought. He expressed strong approval of "that marvellous movement called Zionism". He noted the parallel between the Jewish desire to return to their homeland

[19] *Christianity, Islam and the Negro Race*, p. 124.

and that of "thousands of the descendants of Africa in America anxious to return to the land of their fathers".

There are obvious similarities in Blyden's concept of negritude and that of the recent exponents of it: both assume certain qualities common to all Negroes—qualities of a spiritual, elemental or emotional nature: the opposite of the cold, the calculating, the mechanical; in both it is, in the words of Samuel Allen, the American Negro writer, an "endeavour to recover for his race a normal self-pride, a lost confidence in himself, a world in which he again has a sense of identity and a significant role". Finally, the negritude of both, in Jean-Paul Sartre's Hegelian terms, "is the antithesis in a dialectical progression which leads to an ultimate synthesis of a common humanity without racism". Blyden clearly and consistently maintained that the ultimate goal of the Negro was to serve humanity at large but that the most effective route to this was through dedicated service to his race. Both are open to the same criticisms, not necessarily justified, of being affective, ambivalent, racist and of doubtful necessity.

If he was an outstanding author and journalist, he also became famous as a lecturer. Dapper and dignified, learned and witty, and possessed of an excellent voice and a flair for oratory, Blyden, at the height of his powers, was in great demand as a lecturer not only in West Africa but also in Europe and America as the guest of universities, churches and learned societies. His reputation as littérateur and lecturer won him many academic awards and rare honours. He received the degree of Doctor of Law (1874) and Divinity (1884) from Lincoln University. In 1878 he was elected an honorary member of the Athenaeum, one of the most exclusive gentlemen's clubs in London; in 1880, Fellow of the American Philological Association; in 1882, honorary member of the Society of Sciences and Letters of Bengal; in 1890, honorary member of the American Society of Comparative Religion; in 1898, Corresponding Member of the newly founded American Negro Academy; in 1901, founding member and Vice-President of the African Society of London.

BLYDEN AND BLACK AMERICANS

It was partly through his published writings, partly through eight extended visits to the United States between 1850 and 1895, that Blyden's reputation among black Americans was based. He never gave up the idea that there would be a black American exodus to Africa, but from the early 1870's he came to champion only "select"

Afro-American emigration there. For Blyden, prospective emigrants should meet two criteria: they should be "blacks or very nearly blacks" and intensely race proud. Blyden worked closely with the American Colonization Society through correspondence or on visits to the United States to ensure that the 2,000 or so emigrants it sent out to Liberia in the post-Reconstruction nineteenth century met or came close to his requirements.

On his visits to the United States Blyden spoke to a large number of black audiences in both the North and South, and became acquainted with the most outstanding black American leaders, among them, Frederick Douglass, Booker T. Washington, Bishop Henry McNeil Turner, Alexander Crummell, Francis Grimke and Richard T. Greener. Although he respected all these men as individuals, all but Crummell were mulattoes, and towards these he remained ambivalent. Moreover, only Crummell, partially, and Turner, fervently, shared his views on the necessity for black American "repatriation". Crummell had been for two decades (1854–73) a colleague and friend of Blyden in Liberia during which time he favoured select emigration. However, disillusioned with Liberia, Crummell returned to the United States in 1873, and dropped his advocacy of black American emigration to Africa. Turner became the outstanding advocate of "repatriation" to Africa in the last two decades of the nineteenth and the first of the twentieth century, but was unsuccessful in organizing such a movement. Blyden's attitude towards him and his efforts was ambivalent because he did not share Turner's view of "indiscriminate" Afro-American emigration which would include light-skinned "Negroes". Blyden agreed with Booker T. Washington that the black American should give up all pretensions to political and civil rights in the United States but only because he continued to believe that the "sojourn" there of "true blacks" was temporary and that they would somehow eventually return to the "fatherland".

The other obvious black American leader with whom one would suppose Blyden might have had contact and communication is Dr. William E. B. DuBois, the Harvard-trained historian, who by the early twentieth century had already made a profound impact as a scholar, thinker and pan-African figure. Yet, although unquestionably the two men were very much aware of each other, they seemed largely to have ignored each other: I have found no evidence that they met or communicated with each other. Blyden did not attend the 1900 pan-African Conference held in London, England, at which DuBois was a leading figure, and probably boycotted it on the grounds that such a conference, dominated by such mulattoes as DuBois and Bishop Alexander Walters and held on "foreign soil" could not serve the interest of his race. Nor have I found any reference to DuBois by Blyden either in his published writings or private letters. DuBois, too, seemed to have been reticent about Blyden. His silence in print on Blyden was broken shortly before the latter's death, when as editor of the *Crisis,* DuBois referred to the Liberian as "the leading representative of the race in West Africa". An obituary in the *Crisis* two issues later described Blyden as the "Grand Old Man of West Africa" who had had "many honours bestowed on him".

Some contemporary Afro-American leaders have charged Blyden with being a divisive influence in the Afro-American community because of his hardly concealed detestation of mulattoes, his willingness to work closely with the American Colonization Society, an organization long in disrepute among the majority of black leaders, and finally his advice to give up the struggle for civil and political rights and instead prepare for an improbable repatriation. But like West Africans, whatever quarrels black Americans had with Blyden, they were glad to honour him as a supreme symbol of black intellectual ability.

POSTHUMOUS INFLUENCE

As the most articulate and brilliant vindicator of the Negro, and the staunchest advocate of cultural nationalism, Blyden has influenced both African nationalists and New World black nationalists.[20] Such stalwart West African nationalists of the twentieth century as Casely Hayford, Herbert Macaulay, Eyo Ita, Nnamdi Azikiwe and Kwame Nkrumah have all admitted deriving inspiration from his efforts. So also have such New World black nationalists and pan-Africanists as Richard Moore of Harlem, Marcus Garvey[21], the Jamaican "Black Moses" and leader of the massive Back-to-Africa Movement in the United States in the 1920s, and George Padmore, one of the great pan-African figures of the twentieth century.

By tirelessly asserting the humanity and dignity of Africans and people of African descent, by reclaiming their history and by

---

[20] See Lynch, *Edward Wilmot Blyden*, pp. 248–252.

[21] Marcus Garvey Jr., *A Talk with Afro-West Indians: The Negro Race and Its Problems*, Kingston, n.d. (circa 1915), 7 pp. Four pages of this is a direct quotation from Blyden's *Christianity, Islam and the Negro Race*, University of Edinburgh reprint, 1967, pp. 113–17. Garvey lauded Blyden as "one of our historians and chroniclers, who has done so much to retrieve the lost prestige of the race. . . ."

assigning them a special and significant future role, Blyden made his life and ideas relevant to the still continuing struggle on the part of blacks against white contempt, domination and exploitation.

*   *   *

Blyden's writings are arranged chronologically under seven broad headings: 1. Afro-America and Africa; 2. Liberia—Its Role and History; 3. Africa—Its History and Culture; 4. Race and the African Personality; 5. Education—Its Nature and Purpose for Africans; 6. Islam in West Africa; 7. European Imperialism. The sections are arranged according to a rough logic. In Blyden's pan-African dream it was important for Afro-Americans to co-operate with Africa: "repatriation" of the latter, in Blyden's early thinking at least, was a vital first step in "regenerating Africa" and re-establishing its influence. Such emigration as had taken place had resulted in Liberia and, of course, it was to play a special role on behalf of the Negro race. Yet another indispensable prerequisite for the establishment of the pan-African goal was the gaining of new confidence from a dissemination of the knowledge that African peoples did have a history and culture of which they could be proud. It was important, too, to understand the concept of race if the "African Personality" was to be properly projected. And here the educative process was all-important: its aim was to prevent Africans from indiscriminately adopting European values and institutions, and to get them to appreciate and cherish their own wholesome customs and institutions. Finally, the two last sections are intended to show his views on how foreign influences—Islam, Christianity and European imperialism—helped or hindered the pan-African goal. There is a brief introduction to each section.

Because Blyden was in great part a propagandist, and because the majority of his pamphlets had their origin in speeches and lectures, his writings tend to be repetitious and discursive. For these reasons I have omitted a few of his pieces altogether (these are indicated by asterisks in the bibliography) and I have edited the others to keep repetition and discursiveness to a minimum while taking care not to omit essential or new ideas. I have also omitted all but two pieces from newspaper sources—his famous lecture on "Study and Race" (*Sierra Leone Times*, May 27th, 1893), in which he first used the phrase "African personality", and his letter to Booker T. Washington (*New York Age*, January 24th, 1895). This is partly because many of his newspaper pieces were anonymous, though there was strong internal evidence that they were his creations, but more importantly, because his significant newspaper articles were subsequently published as pamphlets as in the case of *African Life and Customs* (1908) and the others did not contain any ideas which were not more fully developed elsewhere. For the same reason, I have also omitted short pieces (usually from one to four pages) which appeared in church and colonization journals.

To the staff of the Library of Congress, the New York Public Library, the Historical Society of Pennsylvania, and on a more personal note, to Mrs. Dorothy Porter, Librarian, Moorland Collection, Howard University Library, and to Mr. Hans Panofsky, Africana Collection, Northwestern University Library, I am grateful for providing me with copies of items of Blyden's writings. My sincere thanks are due also to Dean Otto Wirth of Roosevelt University, Chicago, for making available to me funds which helped to defray the cost of preparing the manuscript.

DR. HOLLIS R. LYNCH
April, 1970

PART I

Afro-America and Africa

PART I

Afro-America and Africa

Now that Afro-Americans are showing a new willingness to identify positively with Africa, the following selections have become topical because in them Blyden argues, essentially, that the interests of Afro-Americans and Africans are identical and that there should be close co-operation for mutual benefit. A West Indian-born Liberian, Blyden made eight visits of several months each to the United States between 1850 and 1895 during which he travelled extensively, lecturing to black American audiences and meeting with their leaders. And he maintained a keen interest in Afro-Americans until his death in 1912. The following selections tell of his own reaction to being a black man in the United States (Selection 3), comment on aspects of Afro-American life and on some leaders (Selections 2 and 8), show his efforts to create self-pride and confidence among Afro-Americans by emphasizing that they were heirs of a worthy history and culture (Selection 5), and point to the great potential of Liberia; primarily, though, they are concerned with advocating "repatriation" for racially patriotic and pioneering black Americans.

He himself emigrated to Liberia, the newly independent American-Negro-ruled Republic, in early 1851. Before this he had lived in his native St. Thomas, Virgin Islands, in Venezuela for two years and in the United States for six months. His discriminatory experiences in the United States plus the general low status of black Americans had led him to the conclusion that they would never win equality and respect in a dominant white society unless they identified positively and actively with Africa. Only the prestige and influence of progressive African nations would suffice to remove their inferior status. He believed, at least initially, that African societies needed the stimulating influence of Afro-Americans with their western ideas, technological know-how and financial resources, hence his advocacy of "repatriation". He looked upon Liberia as the nucleus of a new kind of African nation in which, ideally, there would be a synthesis of the best in African and Western cultures. All this can best be understood within the framework of his pan-African ideology: his conviction that people of African descent everywhere face common problems and should seek common solutions, and that, politically the solution lay in establishing progressive nations in Africa which would by their achievements and influence excite the pride and protect the interest also of New World Africans.

Such ideas were not original with Blyden. In the first three decades of the nineteenth century they were held and acted upon by such Afro-American leaders as Paul Cuffee, Daniel Coker, Elijah Johnson, Lott Cary and John B. Russwurm, all of whom except Cuffee died in West Africa while seeking to establish the foundations of a modern nation.[1] Among able black American contemporaries of Blyden who advocated pan-African ideas, including "repatriation", were Martin R. Delany, Henry Highland Garnet and Bishop Henry McNeil Turner.[2]

Of all these Blyden was the most outstanding as an intellectual and literary figure. His advocacy of "repatriation" spanned some sixty years during which the qualifications required of prospective "repatriates" became increasingly stringent so that towards the end of his career few would meet them. His one constant qualification was strong racial patriotism—a fervent desire to promote the welfare of the Negro race as a whole. Blyden assumed at first that this would be a common and widespread feeling among "oppressed" blacks. In the 1850s he confidently expected an "exodus" to Liberia. When, however, after the outbreak of the Civil War, it became clear that massive "repatriation" was not likely to materialize, he ascribed this to the opposition of mulatto leaders. Blyden argued that mulattoes by reason of their blood and often cultural affinity to the prestigious whites, did not wish, more than was necessary, to identify with "true" blacks: even when they emigrated to Liberia they remained aloof and apart, and took no steps to promote pan-African goals. Selection 2 is interesting as it provides the first indication of what developed into a virulently anti-mulatto attitude which, however, is much more evident in his private correspondence than in his public lectures or published writings. Thus from 1862 Blyden disqualified mulattoes as "repatriates" on the ground that they were lacking in strong "racial instincts". By the 1880s Blyden was contending further that the degrading experience even of "true" blacks in America had dulled their "natural" racial patriotism and unfitted them for any pan-African work. He had been led to this conclusion because of the failure of the most intelligent black Americans to respond positively and enthusiastically to Africa, and

---

[1] Hollis R. Lynch, "Pan-Negro Nationalism in the New World Before 1862", *Boston University Papers on Africa*, Vol. II, Jeffrey Butler, ed., Boston University Press, 1966, pp. 149–79.
[2] *Ibid.*; also Edwin S. Redkey, "Bishop Turner's African Dream", *Journal of American History*, Vol. LIV (Sept. 1967), pp. 271–90.

the further failure of Americo-Liberians to make active partners of indigenous Africans. Blyden thus came to hold an ambivalent position on "repatriation": he continued to maintain that a black "exodus" from America to Africa was inevitable, and potentially desirable, yet he was increasingly of the opinion that until black Americans acquired self-confidence and racial pride, they were useless to Africa, and could be harmful. Blyden's growing sense of the unfitness of the Afro-Americans for African work can be gauged by the following quotations of his. In 1883 (Selection 6) he wrote: "For all the work to be accomplished [in Africa] much less than one-tenth of the six millions [Afro-Americans] will be necessary." In 1890 (Selection 7) he emphasized that "Only those (few) are fit for this new work who believe in the race—have faith in its future—a prophetic insight into its destiny from a consciousness of its possibilities". In 1900 (Selection 8) he concluded that "he [the Afro-American] cannot come to Africa now. He is not yet ready for the transition". Unlike many Afro-American leaders, Blyden did not view the establishment of colonial rule in Africa in the late nineteenth and early twentieth century as a major obstacle to Afro-American "repatriation". Optimistically, and as it turned out largely correctly, he viewed this rule as temporary and felt that Afro-American emigrants both to Liberia and the new colonial territories would hasten the day of an independent black Africa. But he was concerned more than ever that only the most well-motivated Afro-Americans settle in Africa.

The "repatriation" idea and the feeling of a need to identify with Africa has persisted among some Afro-Americans. The most dramatic manifestation of this since Blyden's death has been Marcus Garvey's remarkable Back-to-Africa Movement of the 1920s which was supported emotionally and financially by millions of Afro-Americans. Interestingly, Garvey, like Blyden, favoured black Afro-Americans and detested mulattoes. If, in the post-Garvey period, there has been no major American leader advocating emigration, there has been, with the independence of African nations, a new willingness on the part of Afro-Americans to identify with Africa. These selections should help to set in historical perspective the whole question of the meaning of Africa to Afro-Americans.

D

1

A Voice from Bleeding Africa

Monrovia, 1856

LIBERIA BATTLES THE SLAVE TRADE[1]

. . . The establishment of the Colony of Liberia—a name hated and despised by the lovers of African slavery—has done more to suppress it than any other measure. . . .

But the extermination of the Slave Trade . . . would not bring about the liberation of those who were its victims; it would not undo the immense evil it has done. . . .

SLAVE-HOLDERS—"IMBECILE TYRANTS"

Many . . . reasons . . . are urged against the emancipation of the Slave. But no one who has noticed the condition of the Slave-holding states, under the operation of that "peculiar institution" can fail to perceive that the greatest barrier to immediate emancipation is the pecuniary loss which it would necessarily involve; and the necessity of eating bread by the sweat of their own brow to which it would reduce a great many of those indolent and imbecile tyrants, who have been born and nurtured on the hard and unrecompensed toil of the black man.

We conceive it to be the grossest injustice, after depriving men of their "natural and inalienable rights", and after subjecting them to a system of enormous cruelty, by which their energies are crushed, and their spirit of manliness and independence almost extinguished, to allege, as a reason for not restoring them from the influence of that system, their incapacity for enjoying and appreciating a better condition. But it is very evident that those who make this a ground for not liberating their Slaves do not themselves believe what they affirm—they do not believe that the coloured man is entirely destitute of intellectual ability. If they do, why have they made such stringent laws prohibiting the Slave from learning to read? Why do they sedulously close against him every avenue to mental development? . . . they know he *can* learn

---

[1] All the sub-headings, unless italicized, are mine [ed.].

7

what his rights and privileges as a man are—and that if he should learn them, he will be rendered altogether unfit for a state of bondage. They, therefore, debar him from all means by which men are improved and elevated above the level of the brute; and, imposing upon him the ponderous weight of a barbarous despotism, they expect him to exhibit the same intellectual and moral greatness with other men. How reasonable!

Let the Slave-holder look away from his rice and cotton plantations; let him look abroad and contemplate men of the same race as his Slave, brought up under the genial influence of freedom, and in circumstances suited to the development of their intellectual capacities, and see whether they have not distinguished themselves in every branch of science and literature. It is admitted by all candid writers, who have paid attention to the African character, that in point of intellect and capacity for improvement, the African has no superior among the races, and is in advance of some. . . .

AFRICAN GENIUSES

Among the African geniuses of the present century, one of the most remarkable was ALEXANDER PUSKIN, the poet and historian of Russia; the favourite alike of the emperor and the people. . . . Another remarkable African genius is Alexander Dumas, a citizen of France . . . a most voluminous writer of world-wide celebrity. Toussaint L'Ouverture and Petion, citizens of Haiti, are distinguished in the history of that country. Liberia, the African Republic, can boast of the late Hilary Teage, a poet and orator of brilliant talents; the late John B. Russwurm, for several years the Governor of Cape Palmas, acknowledged by competent judges to be "an able, learned and faithful man—an honour to his race"; Joseph J. Roberts, the first President of Liberia; upon whom his fellow citizens, in testimony of their appreciation of his eminent qualifications and able services, conferred the office of Chief Magistrate, four times consecutively. . . . Stephen Allen Benson, the present incumbent of the Presidential Chair, and the second President of Liberia. . . . He has filled various official and responsible stations; and in all he has discovered ability and talents that would do credit to any man, of whatever race, brought up in far more favourable circumstances. Daniel Bashiel Warner, the present Secretary of State of the Republic of Liberia, of superior literary, commercial and mechanical talent; equally at home in the counting-house, the ship-yard and the halls of diplomacy; Rev. Francis Burns and

Rev. Jas. S. Payne, ministers of the Methodist E. Church, of acknowledged ability—ornaments to the Liberian pulpit.

Among talented coloured men of the United States, we may mention Rev. J. W. C. Pennington, D.D.; Rev. Samuel R. Ward; Frederick Douglass; Rev. Alexander Crummell, B.A.; the last is now a citizen of Liberia.

In view of such examples of intellectual and moral greatness, as we have mentioned, shall such ordinary white men as the majority of American Slave-holders are, despise and insult the race from which they sprung, and allege its inferiority, in justification of their most horrible system. . . ? The fact that the souls of near three millions of men, in the land of FREEDOM AND EQUAL RIGHTS ! ! ! have been crippled, dwarfed and blinded, is no reason that they should continue to be crippled and blinded: on the contrary, it furnishes a most forcible argument for the adoption of a plan to bring about a speedy and immediate amelioration of their condition.

Immediate emancipation, we hold, as an act of justice to the despoiled African, and as a remedy for existing evils in the social, political, and moral condition of Slave-holding America, is most imperatively demanded. We know that there are some good men who believe that the immediate abolition of Slavery in America would induce a worse state of things; they contend that "the peace of society demands the breaking up of long established rights and customs shall be a gentle and gradual process; else the mischief provoked will be more calamitous than the evil we desire to redress". It is remarkable how the interests of men often, imperceptibly to themselves, give character to their arguments, shape their opinions, and control their actions. . . . It is difficult to conceive what train of reasoning, unbiased by considerations of self-interest, could lead to the conclusion that the immediate abolition of Slavery would "induce a worse state of things". What under the sun, can be worse than American Slavery, that "mystery of iniquity"? What condition can be worse to a rational being than that which deprives him of the right to exercise those powers which God has given him in such a way as he deems advantageous to himself, and makes him the tool and chattel of another man, with whom he stands equal in the eye of the great Creator? Certainly the defenders of Slavery cannot mean that the condition of the *Slave* will be rendered worse by immediate emancipation. . . ! Immediately preceding the emancipation . . . of eight hundred thousand Africans in the West Indies, great apprehensions were expressed by the enemies of freedom that such a step would prove the ruination of those islands. . . . Since emancipation [1834] the people of those islands have been more truly prosperous and happy than they had ever been. . . .

*   *   *2

The fact cannot be disguised . . . that it is the earnest desire of Liberians to see American Slavery speedily abolished. They are determined to give countenance to no act that, in their opinion, tends either directly or indirectly to strengthen or perpetuate that nefandous system; but will gladly avail themselves of every expedient that they consider, in any way, accelerative of the enfranchisement of the millions of their brethren on the other side of the Atlantic. Their object is, *the redemption of Africa, and the disenthralment and elevation of the African race* ! ! ! object worthy of the effort of every coloured man, of every Christian; a consummation glorious in itself, and pregnant with glorious results to the whole human race! !

We are aware that the minds of many of our coloured brethren in the United States are deeply imbued with prejudice against Liberia, in consequence of the opinion which has gained currency among them that the *intention* of the original movers of African Colonization was to expatriate the free coloured man from the place of his birth, without reference to his subsequent condition, in order more firmly to rivet the fetters of the Slave. . . .

. . . The coloured people of the United States should consider it of little matter, whether the motives of African Colonization were good or evil. . . .

By their exertions a free and independent nation of coloured men . . . has been established on these long-neglected shores. . . .

*   *   *

Let coloured men, then, of every rank and station, in every clime and country, in view of the glorious achievements of African Colonization, lend it their aid and influence. Let them look at the cause and not the instruments: let them behold and contemplate *results*, and not form conjectures concerning *motives* and *intentions*. . . .

---

² This is used throughout the book to indicate that one or more paragraphs have been omitted from the body of the excerpt [ed.].

2

An Address before
the Maine State Colonization Society
Portland, Maine, June 26th, 1862

New York Colonization Journal, July 1862

LIBERIA—THE FOUNDATION OF AN EMPIRE

. . . I have come tonight to bear, in general terms, my testimony
to the great good which the Society of which you are an auxiliary
branch, has done, and is doing. My residence in Liberia of eleven
years convinces me that you are engaged in a very great and a
very important work—a work which, if it were thoroughly understood by all the white and black men of this land, could not fail
to command their deepest attention, and enlist their warmest
interest. It may seem to some that the progress of Liberia has been
slow. Numerically speaking, its progress has been slow; but in
real, substantial, and solid growth—in all those elements which
are necessary in laying the foundation of empire—in building
up a nationality—its growth has been remarkably encouraging.

Those results in the moral as in the physical world, which are of
great and permanent utility, are generally of tardy development.
Ignoring this principle, the opponents of Colonization have made
themselves merry over the fact that the results, according to their
estimation, of the Colonization enterprise, have not been com-
mensurate with the labours of its supporters. . . .

The founders of Liberia looked upon the Negro as a man, needing, for his healthful growth, all the encouragement of social and
political equality. They provided for him, therefore, a home in
Africa, his own fatherland. And while a partial and narrow
sympathy was pouring out its complaints and issuing its invectives
against their operations, they were sowing the seeds of African
nationality, and rearing on those barbarous shores the spectacles
we behold of a thriving, well-conditioned, and independent Negro
State.

Many of the strong advocates for the abolition of slavery manifest
no special desire to see Negroes form themselves into an independent community. In fact, many of them do not believe that the

11

Negro is fit for any other than a subordinate position. They expect that after slavery is abolished, and the country rescued from that foul blot on its character, the Negro will find his position among the free labourers of the land. . . . He is to be, though free, always the object of pity and patronage, to be assisted and held up, never to stand alone. They do not conceive how nationality and independence can be at all objects to us. They suppose that after they have given us meat for food, houses for shelter, and raiment to cover us, there is nothing else that we desire, or are fit to enjoy. These men do not know us, or they would understand that we have souls as well as they. They would know that our hearts are made of the same material with theirs; that we feel as well as they; and that the words *nationality* and *independence* possess as much charm and music for us as for them.

The upholders of this Society show a truer appreciation of us, in aiding us to deliver ourselves from all this overshadowing and dwarfing patronage, and to enjoy a field of action where we have the whole battle to wage for ourselves, and where thousands this day feel themselves happier in the resources of their own individual industry—limited as those resources may be—than they could possibly have felt in all the provisions which could have been made for them, if they had remained in this country.

The superior advantages which our position in Liberia gives us have never been fully set forth in all the eulogiums of Colonization papers. They can never be expressed. As soon as the black man of soul lands in Liberia, and finds himself surrounded by his own people, taking the lead in every social, political educational, and industrial enterprise, he feels himself a different man. He feels that he is placed in the high attitude of an actor, that his words and deeds will now be felt by those around him. A consciousness of individual importance, which he never experienced before, comes over him. The share which he is obliged to take in the affairs of the country brings him information of various kinds, and has an expanding effect on his mind. His soul grows lustier. He becomes a more cultivated and intellectual being than formerly. His character receives a higher tone. Every sentiment which his new position inspires is on the side of independence and manliness. In a word, be becomes a full man—a distinction to which he can never arrive in this country.

When I say that the Negro can never attain in this country to the distinction of true manhood, I say so deliberately and from heart-felt conviction. I am aware there are many who are enduring their disabilities in this land with great fortitude, in view of the future. Their tranquil hearts, drilled into a most undignified contentment, are cherishing a better prospect, and reposing on the sure anticipation of happier days in this land of their thraldom. They hope that the growth of free institutions and the progress of Christian sentiment will eradicate the intolerant prejudice against them. Such advance and progress may have that effect, but by that time the Negro will have passed away, victimized and absorbed by the Caucasian.

RACIAL PREJUDICE INTENSIFYING

This feeling of prejudice seems to be intensifying, instead of decreasing. It pervades the whole national mind. And so strongly has it laid hold upon the hearts of the people, that grave and venerable legislators, in the national councils, are not ashamed to acknowledge themselves under its influence. And there is every thing to produce the conviction that it is destined to be permanent. There is every thing, both in the condition of the Negro, and in the lesson which the European daily imbibes, to perpetuate it. The condition of the Negro in this country is one of universal degradation, and of course with the characteristics inseparable from such a condition. I say this with a full knowledge of the very few honourable exceptions here and there. The occupations to which he is driven for a livelihood are of such characters as to keep him low and groveling in his aims and aspirations. He is almost universally the servant of the white man; so that, as soon as a Negro is seen, the presumption at once is that he is a menial. His colour at once associates him with that class of persons, and the general feeling is to treat him as such.

I do not wish to be understood as despising any employment by which a man honestly makes his living. But I am just speaking in accordance with what is the general experience, that where one man is a servant and the other is master—where one class of persons, as a class, are in power and authority—it matters not how well the menial class perform their part, or how ill the ruling class perform theirs—the honour, in the world's estimation, is almost sure to be given to the superior. Now, as I have said, and is everywhere evident, the Negro's condition is a menial one. In consequence of the steady stream of European immigration pouring into the country, his help in the higher department of labour is rendered unnecessary. He is confined to sordid employments. And as the immigration increases, his sphere, even in those menial occupations, is getting lower and narrower. How—I appeal to commonsense—on what ground can the Negro, driven every day to the wall by a superior force, hope to counteract these things, and elevate himself in this land? And then, as I have said, the lessons every day taught the rising generation of whites are far from favourable to the counteraction of this prejudice. Wherever the little children turn, there is everything to cause them to look upon the Negro as an inferior being, to be pitied by kind hearts, to be employed and hired, but never to be respected or honoured. They learn these lessons at home, and they are impressed upon them abroad. In the public vehicles, in the hotels, on the steamboats, they see the black man always subordinate. They see this inferiority represented in pictures by the way; they read of it in newspapers and books; they hear it pointed out in the great Congress of the nation. In all the cities which I have visited, I see the Negro carica- tured at the corners of the streets. He is held up constantly before the people in every possible light that can excite ridicule and con- tempt. Every impression which the child or the foreigner receives is unfavourable to the black man.

So generally is it taken for granted that the coloured people are the servants in this country, that Miss Leslie, in her excellent "Behaviour Book", evidently written for white people, recommends that in getting up balls, it is always advisable to secure the services of a *"respectable coloured man"* as caterer; and in all her references and allusions to coloured people in that book, they are represented as *servants*. Now, what is to prevent white children, who never come into contact with the better class of coloured people, from imbibing ideas of distance from them—from conceiving that every coloured man whom they meet of *respectable* appearance is an expert and skilful waiter? Do these learned coloured gentlemen who are so deadly opposed to emigration, suppose that when met by white people to whom they are not known, they are taken for anything more than good-looking servants.

And then, among the blacks themselves, on account of the general condition of subordination, there is no mutual respect. As a rule, every black man looks upon another as like himself—a servant—"engaged in business", as a fine-looking coloured gentle- man said to me the other day, "at the Eutaw House". (Engaged in business at such and such a place, is the new euphemism for the employment in which coloured men are engaged at the hotels.) Whenever a black gentleman comes from abroad to travel in this country, he experiences as much annoyances from the insults and slights of his own brethren in complexion, as he does from the vulgar whites. All black men, except in the limited circle where they are individually known, are on a level, both in the opinion of whites and blacks. . . .

Such, then, is the state of things with the coloured people of this country. They are pressed to the earth by the whites and by each other. And the moral effect of these things upon the masses is, that they give up all hope, and abandon themselves to the groveling influences of their condition. They see no possible chance of rising above their circumstances, and emerging into respectability. Character with them is nothing. In their desperation, they feel that they have nothing to lose. They are entirely free from any check of reputation. They exert themselves just sufficiently to supply their most urgent needs. The poorest and most ignorant Irishman or German, just arrived in this country, rapidly outstrips them, for he is urged by every possible incentive.

Now I ask again, looking at the black man under these deplorable circumstances, is it common sense, is it philanthropy, to counsel him to remain here and fight it out? What has he to fight for? As well advise McClellan to disarm his disciplined host, and march up, disrobed of weaponry, to the fortifications of Richmond!

We do not think it strange that *white* men should advise us to remain here and "fight it out", nor do we blame them, for they cannot feel on this subject as we do. The question whether we should emigrate or not is with them a question of sentiment or theory; with us it is a matter of life and death, of perpetual social and political degradation, or of respectability, influence, and power in the world. But we are particularly grieved at *coloured* men who take up the cry against Africa, under the pretence that they are opposed to Colonization.

MULATTO OPPOSITION TO EMIGRATION

But I must say here that I have not found in this land one black man (I use the term distinctively) of intelligence and standing, who is opposed to Africa. Nor do I believe that the masses of the coloured people have any hostility. All the bitter and unrelenting opposition comes from a few *half-white* men, who, glorying in their honourable pedigree, have set themselves up as representatives and leaders of the coloured people of this country, and who have no faith in Negro ability to stand alone—men who love to sit in the highest places at public gatherings and conventions held by blacks; who do all they can to identify themselves with white people; whose children are white, attend white schools, and keep as far from black people as possible—men who build houses and refuse to let them to black people, open saloons and barber-shops and refuse to accommodate the poor Negro. These are the men who rave and foam at the mouth at the idea of black men's going to Africa. These are the men who scatter their pestilential teachings with reference to Africa around the whole circle of their influence, paralyzing and poisoning every honest effort made in behalf of that country. No measure can be taken for the elevation of their motherland, but these men, like the Harpies of Virgil, must insinuate themselves and turn it all to loathesomeness. They have placed themselves at the head of the coloured people, and they are sensitively fearful that the discussion of the question of emigration will unsettle their hold upon their followers, and eventually leave none in the land low enough to do them honour. These are the men, as I have said, who are clamorous in their hostility to Africa.

And it is marvellous with what acrimony they pursue those who betake themselves to that despised country. The talent, and the eloquence, and the principle which appear to them so very respectable as long as their possessor contents himself to cling to this house of bondage, lose all their respectability and merit so soon as he goes to Africa, or gives signs of African proclivities. These men counsel the poor blacks to remain, assuring them that the prejudice will soon die out. Certainly it will in *their* case. They even now enjoy privileges from which black men are debarred. They are tolerated in places from which a black man would be spurned. . . . Shunned by the whites, and, when it can be successfully done, by his half-brother, he must fight for himself, and achieve his own destiny.

I am not by any means blaming those who, availing themselves of their complexion, can escape the indignities in this land of caste. Nature has given them that advantage, and they should use it. And those who are "blue-eyed" enough and "fair" enough with Saxon blood, should go, as many have already done, altogether with the whites. They have a right to do so. But all we beg of them is, to let us alone. Don't divide and distract the councils of coloured men. Don't keep those whom Providence is calling to do a great work in their fatherland, from responding to that call. We implore them, with tears in our eyes, to have mercy upon their motherland, even though *they* should prefer to cleave to the land which is ruled by their fathers.

Because in gratifying their hatred to Africa, they dare not give expression to the deep feelings of their heart, they conceal their malignity under the pretence that they are repelled by the word *colonization*, and frightened away by the deleterious climate. They sneer at Liberia, and cast at her all the levities of ridicule, and utter contemptuous words of her efforts, and scorn her poverty, rolling in affluence themselves, as if men who, for the most part, were slaves in this land, could take a great deal of wealth with them when they went, refugees from slavery, and from the indignities *they* so cheerfully endure, to seek an asylum on a distant shore.

Ah! there is more Negro hate in those men than they are aware of; more want of confidence and trust in their mother's blood than they are willing to admit; more dislike to go under the rule of men of their mother's race, than they give themselves credit for; more recoiling from the thought of having their "Saxon blood", so gloriously inherited, absorbed in Africa, than they would like to confess to. They cling to the side of their father. And so lost are they to all feeling of race and proper self-respect, that while the whites are doing everything for themselves, exclusively and professedly for themselves, declaring that this country belongs to white people, is ruled by them and for them, some of these coloured men, so lofty in the superiority of their benevolence, and so rich in the generosity of their hearts, are proclaiming themselves cosmopolites, as unwilling to recognize any distinction of races and countries, and are gladly welcoming and rejoicing in those abnormal and humiliating processes by which the Negro is being absorbed by the Caucasian. But it requires no profound knowledge of human nature to discover the keynote of all this exuberant philanthropy. It lies on the surface. Those persons are generally ready and willing to give away all they have who have nothing to give.

They cling, as I have said, to their father, and perhaps with reason. They have no inward consciousness and no outward demonstration of power and efficiency on the side of their mother. Everything in this country teaches them to despise their mother. Nearly all the literature of the land is anti-Negro. Even Mrs. [Harriet Beecher] Stowe is one-sided in her representations of Negro character, always representing the blacks—the Uncle Toms, Topsies, Candaces—as kind and gentle and submissive, and as showing great adaptedness and attachment to the servile condition. And the contagion is spreading to the other side of the Atlantic. Mr. Anthony Trollope, in his new work on North America, yielding to the influence of the American prejudice, gives wings to the slander against the Negro, declaring his conviction that "the full-blooded Negro is inferior, through the laws of nature, to the white man".

It is impossible, therefore, for the class of men of whom we are speaking to have escaped the conclusion to which everything drives them, and from which nothing they see in this country restrains them, that the Negro *is* inferior. We can quite believe that, under the guise of all that plausible defence they sometimes make of the Negro, there lurks a secret acquiescence in the slanders and exaggerations of the Trollopes. We cannot blame them. We say to them, Believe what you please and do what you please, only keep from distracting the councils and deliberations of those who feel the sting of degradation, and have a consciousness of innate power, under fair opportunity to stand alone.

I can see, Mr. Chairman, no other solution of the Negro question in the United States than that proposed by the Colonization Society —viz., that of transferring these people back to Africa, and building up an African empire of respectability and power. For, supposing that it were possible for black men to rise to the greatest eminence, in this country, in wealth and political distinction, so long as the resources and capabilities of Africa remained undeveloped—so long as there was no Negro power of respectability in Africa, and that continent remained in her present degradation—she would reflect unfavourably upon them. Africa is the appropriate home of the black man, and he cannot rise above her. Water cannot rise above its level; no more can the Negro above his natural home. I feel persuaded, then, that no expedient, whether of Haytien, Central or South American emigration—separate from the elevation and civilization of Africa—can counteract the general prejudice with regard to the inferiority of the Negro. If no Negro state of respectability be erected in Africa—no Negro government permanently established in that land—then the prejudice in question will make its obstinate stand against all the wealth, and genius, and skill that may be exhibited by Negroes in North or South America. The work is to be done in Africa.

REGENERATION OF AFRICA

It is certainly a great work, an arduous work, requiring time, and patience, and earnest labour to achieve it. Those tribes, now sunken in degradation, are to be raised to moral and intellectual dignity. The labour they now spend in scattering efforts at trade and agriculture, is to be organized and made productive. They are to create a demand for the products of their industry, and keep the demand regularly supplied, so as gradually to gain the confidence of the nations, and secure their custom. Through the agency of one or two millions of Africans thus working, and through the channel of that confidence and dependence on the part of the rest of the world, more will be effected than can ever be achieved by the exertions of individuals or communities in this hemisphere. But consider the influence of these things upon the moral condition of Africa. I have hitherto been urging the secular aspects and advantages of the work of the Colonization Society; but this, to the Christian, is a small part of the glory of the enterprise. Social and political influence is not the end of the labour of the Christian. It is a necessary accompaniment—an unfailing collateral. But let it never be forgotten that the great and crowning reason which justifies the Society in transferring civilized and Christian black men to Africa is the spiritual regeneration of that continent.

I have a strong belief that the evangelization of Africa is to be rapid and sudden, and it is to be brought about through the influence of Christian colonists. Of all the means that have been tried during the last four or five centuries, no other has proved so efficient in the work of African civilization as Colonization. We are only sixteen thousand civilized and Christianized coloured men in Liberia, and we influence, by means of our schools and churches, our commerce and agriculture, over one hundred thousand heathen, while over two hundred thousand are subject to our laws. Supposing, at this rate, one-fifth of the coloured population of the United States, or one million of blacks, were thrown into Africa; see what a mighty influence for good might be exerted!

The native character is not so incorrigible as some seem to imagine. They are very easily influenced. Regular intercourse with them, even for purpose of trade, without reference to their direct evangelization, may gradually bring them to a knowledge of the truth. The Mohammedan religion has attained its great development throughout Central Africa, not by any zealous and expensive, or even intentional effort on the part of the Mohammedans, but by the casual communication between the Moslem merchant pilgrims and the rude pagans through whose countries their route happens to pass. And by the same simple means, the manufactures of civilized lands, and with them Christianity and civilization, will be carried through Liberia into the heart of Africa.

This is a noble work in which this Society is engaged. It is one of the grandest philanthropic efforts of the age. I believe that there are many connected with the Colonization cause who do not appreciate its far-reaching and wide-spreading results; who look upon it only as a political measure—as a social purifying of the country, so as to secure all the land to a homogeneous race. But the Almighty has more intimately connected the civilization and evangelization of Africa with Negro slavery and degradation in America than men generally are disposed to admit. He intends, out of all this darkness, to bring great light—to rectify all these crooked things to the greater glory of his name, and to the humbling of the pride and wisdom of man. Slowly but surely he is making the wrath of man to praise him. He is never in a hurry. He inhabiteth eternity. He can afford to wait. A thousand years with him are as one day, and one day as a thousand years. We, in our finite sphere of operation, are impatient and anxious for immediate results. When urged to undertake enterprises of great benevolence, we often hesitate, because we fancy that nothing remarkable will be effected in our lifetime. But we must "learn to labour and to wait".

I look for the day when black men in this country, roused to a sense of their duty to Africa, will rush to those shores to bless that benighted continent. "Ethiopia shall soon stretch forth her hands unto God." The Almighty hath decreed it. Soon shall those beautiful valleys, now lying in melancholy loneliness, be peopled by a happy and thriving population. Soon shall those charming hilltops all over the land, now trodden by the foot of man, be crowned with temples to the Most High. The vast wilderness and the solitary places, yielding to the hand of culture, shall blossom as the rose. Genius and learning and skill shall revolutionize the land. Ethiopia, in all her length and breadth, shall be filled with the knowledge of the Lord as the waters cover the sea; for the mouth of the Lord hath spoken it.

3

A Letter to the *Liberia Herald*
New York, July 5th, 1862

New York Colonization Journal, November 1862

Mr. Editor (*Liberia Herald*):

Since I last wrote you, I have been very much pressed with business—prosecuting the duties of my mission to this country. I have preached and lectured on Africa and Liberia in all the principal cities of the North, from Washington, D.C., to Portland, Maine. In all I have been listened to with great attention. The masses of all the coloured people are favourably disposed to Liberia; but their leaders poison their feelings, and paralyse all their effort towards that country.

SOUTHWARD TO "HELL"

On arriving here, my first move was southward to Washington. And here I must say that going down South, to the coloured men in this country, is like going to that other place which Spurgeon says ministers ought not be ashamed to mention. . . .

On our way to Washington, we stopped thirty-six hours in Philadelphia, spending Sabbath in that city. Here I began to feel more keenly than I had in New York the influence of American caste, finding that no coloured person is allowed to ride in any of the street cars, and I was shocked to see tender and delicate females of education and refinement obliged to travel on foot all the distance of that city, simply because of their dark complexion; while the rudest and most vulgar white man can avail himself of the advantages of riding. Can India show anything in the line of caste to surpass this? How can coloured people have any faith in Christianity—unless God himself teaches them—when examples so contradictory to its teachings are daily set by those who claim to be its enlightened professors?

When we arrived at the railway-station to purchase tickets for Washington, we found that coloured persons, however respectable, were compelled to take their seats in the smoking-car with all sorts of ruffians and vagabonds, spitting and swearing, and doing everything but what is agreeable to gentlemen. I became indignant and

sad, and felt anxious to resign my commission and return to
Liberia. All the way to Washington, a feeling of degradation held
possession of me. I felt that I would rather be a denizen of Marmora's [African chief] town, with all its attendant disadvantages,
than be compelled, as a black man, to live in this country; that I
would rather go naked and wander among the natives interior [sic],
than occupy the position of some of the "respectable coloured
people" I see here. For then I should feel that I was in a country
of my own—untrammelled by the prejudices of "white trash", to
which many of these intelligent and respectable coloured people
so willingly submit, fondly hoping for the day when things will
be better for them.

I thought how sad it was that so many coloured people seem
disposed to cling to this land—fearing to go to Liberia, lest they
die of fever. But are they *living* in this country? Their colour is the
sign for every insult and contumely. Everybody and everything is
preferred to them. Afraid of dying! Would it not be much better
for the whole five millions of these people to leave this country,
if every one died in the process of acclimation in a land, than to
remain here in servitude at the base of society? A whole race in
degradation! The idea is horrible. If they all went and died, it
would be a noble sacrifice to liberty. Is it not better to die free
men than live to be slaves? Was it not under the influence of such
a spirit that the first settlers of this country braved the rigours and
perils of this land of savages? Was it not this spirit that nerved
the heroes of the Revolution, when every heart responded to the
noble utterance of Patrick Henry, "Give me liberty, or give me
death"? This is the spirit the Anglo Saxons everywhere exhibit.
Whenever they have been unable to strike effectually against oppression, they have escaped, at the greatest sacrifices, its crushing
influences. But the coloured American has had his soul dwarfed. It
is well, perhaps, that these Northern blacks have not rushed in
larger numbers to Liberia; they do not seem fitted to the endurance
and self-denial of founding new empires, which the southern emigrants to Liberia have manifested.

Such were the feelings in which I was indulging after I had
taken my seat in that car for Washington, and every now and then
I would give expression to some very hard remark, when I would
be set right by my friend at my side, who though suffering the
same inconveniences, would interpose his *pros* to all my *cons*—with
his true Johnsonian bluntness, "I beg your pardon, sir." "I cannot
agree with you, sir." And when indulging in pensiveness, and
getting under the influence of inexpressible *ennui*, with no inclina-

tion to talk or give my opinion on any subject whatever, my friend
constantly compelled me into conversation with his pointed "Don't
you think so, sir?"—put in that direct style, which leaves one no
chance for evasion or differing except with the alternative of getting
into a discussion—the very thing to which one feels most dis-
inclined.

WASHINGTON, D.C.—"A DISAGREEABLE PLACE"

After six hours' ride, we reached Washington, and my eyes rested
on that magnificent Capitol where so many righteous laws have
been made. The city is not what I expected. I knew it was not very
large, but I thought it was at least well built up—a compact little
city. But it looked to me like a large country town, with here and
there a magnificent and gorgeous building much above the average
wealth of the inhabitants. To me it was a very disagreeable place,
socially and physically. The streets are in a miserable condition;
when it rains, they are deluged with mud; and when it does not,
they are clouded with dust. With the exception of the Government
buildings, the Smithsonian Institute, and the Observatory, there
is nothing worth seeing. And to a coloured man, the sight of these
is not sufficient to requite him for the indignities he suffers in getting
there, and the insults he must endure while there.

*   *   *

Excepting the kindness and courtesy shown us by some of the
coloured people of Washington, my stop there was exceedingly
uncomfortable. Before I could leave, I was obliged to go to the
Provost Marshall, and get a certificate of freedom. He, after
requiring me to produce testimonials that I was from Liberia, gave
me a written "permishun"—as he spelt the word—to pass to and
from Washington. This is "The land of the free and the home of
the brave"!

*   *   *

4

The Call of Providence to the Descendants of Africa in America [1]

Liberia's Offering, New York, 1862, 67–91

Among the descendants of Africa in this country the persuasion seems to prevail, though not now to the same extent as formerly, that they owe no special duty to the land of their forefathers; that their ancestors having been brought to this country against their will, and themselves having been born in the land, they are in duty bound to remain here and give their attention exclusively to acquiring for themselves, and perpetuating to their posterity, social and political rights, not withstanding the urgency of the call which their fatherland, by its forlorn and degraded moral condition, makes upon them for their assistance.

ASHAMED OF AFRICA

All other people feel a pride in their ancestral land, and do everything in their power to create for it, if it has not already, an honourable name. But many of the descendants of Africa, on the contrary, speak disparagingly of their country; are ashamed to acknowledge any connection with that land, and would turn indignantly upon any who would bid them go up and take possession of the land of their fathers.

. . . It is theirs to betake themselves to injured Africa, and bless those outraged shores, and quiet those distracted families with the blessings of Christianity and civilization. It is theirs to bear with them to that land the arts of industry and peace, and counteract the influence of those horrid abominations which an inhuman avarice has introduced—to roll back the appalling cloud of ignorance and superstition which overspreads the land, and to rear on those shores an asylum of liberty for the down-trodden sons of Africa wherever found. This is the work to which Providence is obviously calling the black men of this country.

I am aware that some, against all experience, are hoping for the day when they will enjoy equal social and political rights in this

[1] This was Blyden's standard speech as Liberian Emigration Commissioner delivered in the main American cities of the East Coast from Washington, D.C., to Portland, Maine, in the summer of 1862 [ed.].

25

land. We do not blame them for so believing and trusting. But we would remind them that there is a faith against reason, against experience, which consists in believing or pretending to believe very important propositions upon very slender proofs, and in maintaining opinions without any proper grounds. It ought to be clear to every thinking and impartial mind, that there can never occur in this country an equality, social or political, between whites and blacks. The whites have for a long time had the advantage. All the affairs of the country are in their hands. They make and administer the laws; they teach the schools; here, in the North, they ply all the trades, they own all the stores, they have possession of all the banks, they own all the ships and navigate them; they are the printers, proprietors, and editors of the leading newspapers, and they shape public opinion. Having always had the lead, they have acquired an ascendancy they will ever maintain. The blacks have few or no agencies in operation to counteract the ascendant influence of Europeans. And instead of employing what little they have by a unity of effort to alleviate their condition, they turn all their power against themselves by their endless jealousies, and rivalries, and competition; every one who is able to "pass" being emulous of a place among Europeans or Indians. This is the effect of their circumstances. It is the influence of the dominant class upon them. It argues no essential inferiority in them. . . . They are the weaker class overshadowed and depressed by the stronger. They are the feeble oak dwarfed by the overspreadings of a large tree, having not the advantage of rain, and sunshine, and fertilizing dews.

Before the weaker people God has set the land of their forefathers, and bids them go up and possess it without fear or discouragement. Before the tender plant he sets an open field, where, in the unobstructed air and sunshine, it may grow and flourish in all its native luxuriance.

There are two ways in which God speaks to men: one is by his word and the other by his providence. He has not sent any Moses, with signs and wonders, to cause an exodus of the descendants of Africa to their fatherland, yet he has loudly spoken to them as to their duty in the matter. He has spoken by his providence. First; By suffering them to be brought here and placed in circumstances where they could receive a training fitting them for the work of civilizing and evangelizing the land whence they were torn, and by preserving them under the severest trials and afflictions. Secondly; By allowing them, notwithstanding all the services they have rendered to this country, to be treated as strangers and aliens, so as to cause them to have anguish of spirit, as was the case with the Jews in Egypt, and to make them long for some refuge from their social and civil deprivations. Thirdly; By bearing a portion of them across the tempestuous seas back to Africa, by preserving them through the process of acclimation, and by establishing them in the land, despite the attempts of misguided men to drive them away. Fourthly; By keeping their fatherland in reserve for them in their absence.

The manner from which Africa has been kept from invasion has been truly astounding. Known for ages, it is yet unknown. For centuries its inhabitants have been the victims of the cupidity of foreigners. The country has been rifled of its population. It has been left in some portions almost wholly unoccupied, but it has remained unmolested by foreigners. It has been very near the crowded countries of the world, yet none has relieved itself to any great extent of its overflowing population by seizing upon its domains. Europe, from the North, looks wishfully and with longing eyes across the narrow straits of Gibraltar. Asia, with its teeming millions, is connected with us by an isthmus wide enough to admit of her throwing thousands into that country. But, notwithstanding the known wealth of the resources of the land . . . there is still a terrible veil between us and our neighbours, the all-conquering Europeans, which they are only now essaying to lift; while the teeming millions of Asia have not even attempted to leave their boundaries to penetrate our borders. Neither alluring visions of glorious conquests, nor brilliant hopes of rapid enrichment, could induce them to invade the country. It has been preserved alike from the boastful civilization of Europe, and the effete and barbarous institutions of Asia. We call it, then, a Providential interposition, that while the owners of the soil have been abroad, passing through the fearful ordeal of a most grinding oppression, the land, though entirely unprotected, has been uninvaded. We regard it as a providential call to Africans everywhere, to "go up and possess the land"; so that in a sense that is not merely constructive and figurative, but truly literal, God says to the black men of this country, with reference to Africa: "Behold, I set the land before you, go up and possess it."

Of course it can not be expected that this subject of the duty of coloured men to go up and take possession of their fatherland, will be at once clear to every mind. Men look at objects from different points of view, and form their opinions according to the points from which they look, and are guided in their actions according to the opinion they form. As I have already said, the majority of exiled Africans do not seem to appreciate the great privilege of going and taking possession of the land. They seem to have lost all interest in that land, and to prefer living in subordinate and inferior positions in a strange land among oppressors, to encountering the risks involved in emigrating to a distant country. As I walk the streets of these cities, visit the hotels, go on board the steamboats, I am grieved to notice how much intelligence, how much strength and energy is frittered away in those trifling employments, which, if thrown into Africa, might elevate the millions of that land from their degradation, tribes at a time, and create an African power which would command the respect of the world, and place in the possessions of Africans, its rightful owners, the wealth which is now diverted to other quarters. Most of the wealth that could be drawn from that land, during the last six centuries, has passed into the hands of Europeans, while many of Africa's own sons, sufficiently intelligent to control those immense resources, are sitting down in poverty and dependence in the land of strangers— exiles when they have so rich a domain from which they have never been expatriated, but which is willing, nay, anxious to welcome them home again.

AFRICAN POWER NEEDED

We need some African power, some great centre of the race where our physical, pecuniary, and intellectual strength may be collected. We need some spot whence such an influence may go forth in behalf of the race as shall be felt by the nations. We are now so scattered and divided that we can do nothing. . . . So long as we remain thus divided, we may expect impositions. So long as we live simply by the sufferance of the nations, we must expect to be subject to their caprices.

Among the free portion of the descendants of Africa, numbering about four or five millions, there is enough talent, wealth, and enterprise, to form a respectable nationality on the continent of Africa. For nigh three hundred years their skill and industry have been expended in building up the southern countries of the New World, the poor, frail constitution of the Caucasian not allowing him to endure the fatigue and toil involved in such labours. Africans and their descendants have been the labourers, and the mechanics, and the artisans in the greater portion of this hemisphere. By the results of their labour the European countries have been sustained and enriched. All the cotton, coffee, indigo, sugar, tobacco, etc., which have formed the most important articles of European commerce, have been raised and prepared for market by the labour of the black man. . . . And all this labour they have done, for the most part not only without compensation, but with abuse, and contempt, and insult, as their reward.

Now, while Europeans are looking to our fatherland with such eagerness of desire, and are hastening to explore and take away its riches, ought not Africans in the Western hemisphere to turn their regards thither also? We need to collect the scattered forces of the race, and there is no rallying-ground more favourable than Africa. . . . *Ours* as a gift from the Almighty when he drove asunder the nations and assigned them their boundaries; and ours by peculiar physical adaptation.

An African nationality is our great need, and God tells us by his Providence that he has set the land before us, and bids us go up and possess it. We shall never receive the respect of other races until we establish a powerful nationality. We should not content ourselves with living among other races, simply by their permission or their endurance, as Africans live in this country. We must build up Negro states; we must establish and maintain the various institutions; we must make and administer laws, erect and preserve churches, and support the worship of God; we must have governments; we must have legislation of our own; we must build ships and navigate them; we must ply the trades, instruct the schools, control the press, and thus aid in shaping the opinions and guiding the destinies of mankind. Nationality is an ordinance of Nature. The heart of every true Negro yearns after a distinct and separate nationality.

Impoverished, feeble and alone, Liberia is striving to establish and build up such a nationality in the home of the race. Can any descendant of Africa turn contemptuously upon a scene where such efforts are making? Would not every right-thinking Negro rather lift his voice and direct the attention of his brethren to that land? Liberia, with outstretched arms, earnestly invites all to come. We call them forth out of all nations; we bid them take up their all and leave the countries of their exile . . . taking with them their trades and their treasures, their intelligence, their mastery of arts, their knowledge of the sciences, their practical wisdom, and everything that will render them useful in building up a nationality. We summon them from the States, from the Canadas, from the East and West Indies, from South America, from everywhere, to come and take part with us in our great work.

But those whom we call are under the influence of various opinions, having different and conflicting views of their relations and duty to Africa, according to the different standpoints they occupy. . . .

AMERICAN SPIES

. . . Spies sent from different sections of this country by the coloured people—and many a spy not commissioned—have gone to that land, and have returned and reported. . . . Most believe Africa to be a fertile and rich country, and an African nationality a desirable thing. But some affirm that the land is not fit to dwell in, for "it is a land that eateth up the inhabitants thereof", notwithstanding the millions of strong and vigorous aborigines who throng all parts of the country, and thousands of colonists who are settled along the coast; some see in the inhabitants incorrigible barbarism, degradation, and superstition, and insuperable hostility to civilization; others suggest that the dangers and risks to be encountered, and the self-denial to be endured, are too great for the slender advantages which, as it appears to them, will accrue from immigration. A few only report that the land is open to us on every hand—that "every prospect pleases", and that the natives are so tractable that it would be a comparatively easy matter for civilized and Christianized black men to secure all the land to Christian law, liberty, and civilization.

I come today to defend the report of the minority. The thousands of our own race, emigrants from this country, settled for more than forty years in that land, agree with the minority report. Dr. [Heinrich] Barth, and other travellers to the east and south-east Liberia, endorse the sentiment of the minority, and testify to the beauty, and healthfulness, and productiveness of the country, and to the mildness and hospitality of its inhabitants. In Liberia we hear from natives, who are constantly coming to our settlements from the far interior, of land exuberantly fertile, of large, numerous, and wealthy tribes, athletic and industrious; . . . *black* men, pure Negroes who live in large towns, cultivate the soil, and carry on extensive traffic, maintaining amicable relations with each other and with men from a distance.

The ideas that formerly prevailed of the interior of Africa, which suited the purposes of poetry and sensation writing, have been proved entirely erroneous. . . . The land possesses every possible inducement. That extensive and beauteous domain which God has given us appeals to us and to black men everywhere, by its many blissful and benignant aspects; by its flowery landscapes, its beautiful rivers, its serene and peaceful skies; by all that attractive and perennial verdure which overspreads the hills and valleys; by its every prospect lighted up by delightful sunshine; by its natural charms, it calls upon us to rescue it from the grasp of remorseless superstition, and introduce the blessings of the Gospel.

But there are some among the intelligent coloured people of this country who, while they profess to have great love for Africa, and tells us that there souls are kindled when they hear of the fatherland, yet object to going themselves, because, as they affirm, the black man has a work to accomplish in this land—he has a destiny to fulfil. He, the representative of Africa, like the representatives from various parts of Europe, must act his part in building up this great composite nation. It is not difficult to see what the work of the black man is in this land. The inexperienced observer may at once read his destiny. Look at the various departments of society here in the *free* North; look at the different branches of industry, and see how the black man is aiding to build up this nation. Look at the hotels, the saloons, the steamboats, the barber-shops, and see how successfully he is carrying out his destiny! And there is an extreme likelihood that such are forever to be the exploits which he is destined to achieve in this country until he merges his African peculiarities in the Caucasian.

Others object to the *climate* of Africa, first, that it is unhealthy, and secondly, that it is not favourable to intellectual progress. To the first, we reply that it is not more insalubrious than other new countries. Persons going to Africa, who have not been broken down as to their constitutions in this country, stand as fair a chance of successful acclimation as in any other country of large, unbroken forests and extensively uncleared lands. In all new countries there are sufferings and privations. All those countries which have grown up during the last two centuries, in this hemisphere, have had as a foundation the groans, and tears, and blood of the pioneers. But what are the sufferings of pioneers, compared with the greatness of the results they accomplish for succeeding generations? Scarcely any great step in human progress is made without multitudes of victims. Every revolution that has been effected, every nationality that has been established, every country that has been rescued from the abominations of savagism, every colony that has been planted, has involved perplexities and sufferings to the generation who undertook it. In the evangelization of Africa, in the erection of African nationalities, we can expect no exceptions. The man, then, who is not able to suffer and to die for his fellows when necessity requires it, is not fit to be a pioneer in this great work.

We believe, as we have said, that the establishment of an African nationality in Africa is the great need of the African race; and the men who have gone, or may hereafter go to assist in laying the foundations of empire, so far from being dupes, or cowards, or traitors, as some have ignorantly called them, are the truest heroes of the race. They are the soldiers rushing first into the breach—physicians who at the risk of their own lives are the first to explore an infectious disease. How much more nobly do they act than those who have held for years that it is nobler to sit here and patiently suffer with our brethren! Such sentimental inactivity finds no respect in these days of rapid movement. The world sees no merit in mere innocence. The man who contents himself to sit down and exemplify the virtue of patience and endurance will find no sympathy from the busy, restless crowd that rush by him. Even the "sick man" must get out of the way when he hears the tramp of the approaching host, or be crushed by the heedless and massive car of progress. . . . The world requires active service; it respects only productive workers. The days of hermits and monks have passed away. Action —work, work—is the order of the day. Heroes in the strife and struggle of humanity are the demand of the age.

With regard to the objection founded upon the unfavourableness of the climate to intellectual progress, I have only to say, that proper moral agencies, when set in operation, can not be overborne by physical causes. . . . It has not yet been proved that with the proper influences, the tropics will not produce men of "cerebral activity". . . .

. . . For my part, I believe that the brilliant world of the tropics, with its marvels of nature, must of necessity give to mankind a new career of letters, and new forms in the various arts, whenever the millions at present uncultivated shall enjoy the advantages of civilization.

Africa will furnish a development of civilization which the world has never yet witnessed. Its great peculiarity will be its moral element. . . .

. . . If the black men of this country, through unbelief or indolence, or for any other cause, fail to lay hold of the blessings which God is proffering to them, and neglect to accomplish the work which devolves upon them, the work will be done, but others will be brought in to do it, and to take possession of the country.

For while the coloured people here are tossed about by various and conflicting opinions as to their duty to that land, men are going thither from other quarters of the globe. They are entering the land from various quarters with various motives and designs, and may eventually so preoccupy the land as to cut us off from the fair inheritance which lies before us, unless we go forth without delay and establish ourselves.

* * *

Liberia, then, appeals to the coloured men of this country for assistance in the noble work which she has begun. She appeals to those who believe that the descendants of Africa live in serious neglect of their duty if they fail to help raise the land of their forefathers from her degradation. She appeals to those who believe that a well-established African nationality is the most direct and efficient means of securing respectability and independence for the African race. She appeals to those who believe that a rich and fertile country, like Africa, which has lain so long under the cheerless gloom of ignorance, should not be left any longer without the influence of Christian civilization—to those who deem it a far more glorious work to save extensive tracts of country from barbarism and continued degradation than to amass for themselves the means of individual comfort and aggrandizement—to those who believe that there was a providence in the deportation of our forefathers from the land of their birth, and that that same providence now points to a work in Africa to be done by us their descendants. Finally, Liberia appeals to all African patriots and Christians—to all lovers of order and refinement—of peace, comfort, and happiness—to those who having felt the power of the Gospel in opening up to them life and immortality are desirous that their benighted kindred should share in the same blessings. . . .

5

Ethiopia stretching out her hands unto God; or, Africa's Service to the World [1]

Christianity, Islam and the Negro Race, London, 1887, 118–21;
2nd ed., 136–9

AFRICA—FERTILIZER OF EUROPE AND AMERICA

. . . He who writes the history of modern civilization will be culpably negligent if he omit to observe and to describe the black stream of humanity, which has poured into America from the heart of the Soudan. That stream has fertilized half the Western continent. It has created commerce and influenced its progress. It has affected culture and morality in the Eastern and Western hemispheres, and has been the means of transforming European colonies into a great nationality. Nor can it be denied that the material development of England was aided greatly by means of this same dark stream. By means of Negro labour sugar and tobacco were produced; by means of sugar and tobacco British commerce was increased; by means of increased commerce the arts of culture and refinement were developed. The rapid growth and unparalleled prosperity of Lancashire are, in part, owing to the cotton supply of the Southern States, which could not have risen to such importance without the labour of the African.

The countless caravans and dhow-loads of Negroes who have been imported into Asia have not produced, so far as we know, any great historical results; but the slaves exported to America have profoundly influenced civilization. The political history of the United States is the history of the Negro. The commercial and agricultural history of nearly the whole America is the history of the Negro.

Africa, in recent times, also, has been made, incidentally, to confer an important political benefit upon Europe, and probably upon the whole of the civilized world. When, two generations ago, Europe was disturbed and threatened by the restless and uncontrollable energy of one of whom Victor Hugo has said that he put Providence to inconvenience (*il gênait Dieu*); and when the civiliza-

---

[1] This took its first form as a lecture delivered in several cities of the United States in the spring of 1880 [ed.].

tion of the whole world was in danger of being arrested in its progress, if not put back indefinitely, by a prolific and unscrupulous ambition, Africa furnished the island which gave asylum to this infatuated and maddened potentate, and, by confining to that sea-girt rock his formidable genius, gave peace to Europe, restored the political equilibrium, and unfettered the march of civilization.

EUROPEAN EXPEDITIONS TO AFRICA

And now that Europe is exhausting itself by over-production, it is to Africa that men look to furnish new markets. India, China and Japan are beginning to consume their raw material at home, thus not only shutting Europe out from a market, but cutting off the supplies of raw material. Expedition after expedition is now entering the country, intersecting it from east to west and from north to south, to find out more of the resources of a land upon which large portions of the civilized world will, in no very remote future, be dependent. In the days of the slave-trade, when the man of the country was needed for animal purposes, no thought was given to the country. . . .

But now things have changed. The country is studied with an almost martyr-like devotion, but with a somewhat contemptible indifference as to the inhabitants. In their eager search, the explorers have discovered that Africa possesses the very highest capacity for the production, as raw material, of the various articles demanded by civilized countries. English, and French, and Germans, are now in the struggles of an intense competition for the hidden treasures of that continent. Upon the opening of Africa will depend the continuation of the prosperity of Europe. . . .

Thus, Ethiopia and Ethiopians, having always served, will continue to serve the world. The Negro is, at this moment, the opposite of the Anglo-Saxon. Those everywhere serve the world; these everywhere govern the world. The empire of the one is more widespread than that of any other nation; the service of the other is more widespread than that of any other people. The Negro is found in all parts of the world. He has gone across Arabia, Persia, and India to China. He has crossed the Atlantic to the Western Hemisphere, and here he has laboured in the new and in the old settlements of America; in the Eastern, Western, Northern and Southern States; in Mexico, Venezuela, the West Indies and Brazil. He is everywhere a familiar object, and he is, everywhere out of Africa, the servant of others. And in the light of the ultimate good of the universe, I do not see why the calling of the one should be considered the result of a curse, and the calling of the other the result of special favour. . . . Africa is distinguished as having *served* and *suffered.* In this, her lot is not unlike that of God's ancient people, the Hebrews, who were known among the Egyptians as the servants of all; and among the Romans, in later times, they were numbered by Cicero with the "nations born to servitude",[2] and were protected, in the midst of a haughty population, only "by the contempt which they inspired". The lot of Africa resembles also His who made Himself of no reputation, but took upon Himself the form of a servant, and, having been made perfect through suffering, became the "Captain of our salvation". And if the principle laid down by Christ is that by which things are decided above, viz., that he who would be chief must become the servant of all, then we see the position which Africa and the Africans must ultimately occupy. . . .

[2] Renan's *Hibbert Lectures*, p. 47.

F

6

The Origin and Purpose of African Colonization

A Discourse at the Anniversary of the American Colonization Society,
January, 1883
Christianity, Islam and the Negro Race, London, 1887, 96–110;
1888 ed., 110–26

Among the agencies proposed for carrying on the work of civilization in Africa, none has proved so effective as the American Colonization enterprise. People who talk of the civilizing and elevating influence of mere trade on that continent, do so because they are unacquainted with the facts. Nor can missionaries alone do the work. We do not object to trade, and we would give every possible encouragement to the noble efforts of missionaries. We would open the country everywhere to commercial intercourse. We would give everywhere hospitable access to traders. Place your trading factories at every prominent point along the coast, and even let them be planted on the banks of the rivers. Let them draw the rich products from remote districts. We say, also, send the missionary to every tribe and every village. Multiply throughout the country the evangelizing agencies. Line the banks of the rivers with the preachers of righteousness—penetrate the jungles with those holy pioneers—crown the mountain-tops with your churches, and fill the valleys with your schools. No single agency is sufficient to cope with the multifarious needs of the mighty work. But the indispensable agency is the Colony. Groups of Christian and civilized settlers must, in every instance, bring up the rear, if the results of your work are to be widespread, beneficial and enduring.

This was the leading idea that gave birth to the Society whose anniversary we have met to celebrate. Today we have the Sixty-sixth Annual Report of the American Colonization Society. This fact by itself would excite no feeling, and, perhaps, no remark; but when we consider that, although this is but the sixty-sixth year of its existence, it has been successful in founding a colony which has now been for thirty-five years an independent nation, acknowledged by all the Powers of the earth, we cannot but congratulate the organization upon an achievement which, considering the circumstances, is unparalleled in the history of civilization, and which

39

must be taken as one of the most beautiful illustrations of the spirit and tendency of Christianity.

LIBERIA'S SPECIAL WORK

The special work which, at this moment, claims the attention of the Republic [of Liberia] is to push the settlements beyond the seaboard to the elevated and salubrious regions of the interior, and to incorporate the aborigines, as fast as practicable, into the Republic. Native chiefs are summoned to the Legislature from the different countries, and take part in the deliberations; but, as yet, only those Aborigines who conform to the laws of the Republic as to the tenure of land, are allowed to exercise the elective franchise. All the other questions which press upon independent nations, questions of education, of finance, of commerce, of agriculture, are receiving the careful attention of the people. They feel the importance of making provisions by judicious laws and by proper executive, legislative and judicial management, for the preservation and growth of the State.

In educational matters, there is daily noticeable improvement. We are developing a system of common schools, with a College at the head as a guarantee for their efficiency. The educational work is felt to be of the greatest possible importance; education, not only in its literary and religious forms, but also in its industrial, mechanical, and commercial aspects.

The effort now is to enlarge the operations and increase the influence of the College. The faculty has just been added to by the election of two new Professors in this country, young men of learning and culture. . . .[1]

It will be gratifying to the people of Liberia, as well as to their friends on this side, to observe how heartily the Press of this country, both secular and religious, has endorsed and commended this new move for the advancement of education in that land. The College now contains fifty students in the two departments, and it is hoped that the number will soon increase to hundreds, if we can only get the needed help. We have application for admission to its advantages from numerous youths in various institutions of learning in this country, who wish, on the completion of their course, to labour in Africa. Influential chiefs on the coast and in the interior are also anxious to send their sons; and we shall, before very

[1] Hugh Mason Browne, Professor of Intellectual and Moral Philosophy; and Thomas McCants Stewart, Professor of History and Law [ed.].

long, have young men from the powerful tribes in our vicinity—
Mandingoes, Foulahs, Veys, Bassas, Kroos, Greboes.

A female department has also lately been established in connection with this Institution, and a Christian lady of education
and culture, in this country [Miss Jennie E. Davis], longing to
labour in the land of her fathers, has been appointed as first
Principal. . . .

In financial matters the Republic is hopeful. The public debt is
not so large that it cannot, by the reforms now contemplated, be
easily managed and placed under such control as to give no inconvenience to the State. There are evidences of an abundance of gold
in the territory of the Republic. The precious metal is brought
to the coast from various points in the interior. But the Government
is not anxious to encourage the opening up of gold mines. We prefer
the slow but sure, though less dazzling process, of becoming a
great nation by lapse of time, and by the steady growth of internal
prosperity—by agriculture, by trade, by proper domestic economy.

In commercial matters, there is also everything to encourage.
Three lines of steamers from England and Germany, and sailing
vessels from the United States, visit the Liberian ports regularly
for trading purposes. And the natural resources of the Republic
have, in various portions of it, hardly yet been touched. Palm oil,
camwood, ivory, rubber, gold-dust, hides, beeswax, gum copal, may
be produced in unlimited quantities. For the enterprising merchants
of this country—coloured or white—there is no better field for the
investment of pecuniary capital.

The agriculture of the country is rapidly on the increase. Liberia
has been supplying the Coffee Planters of Ceylon and Brazil with
a new and superior kind of coffee for their agricultural industry.
The Liberian coffee is considered among the best in the world, and
the people are now turning their attention largely to its cultivation.
As immigrants arrive from this country, extensive farms under
their persevering industry are taking the place of the dense forests.
The new settlements, pushing out to the rich valleys and fertile
slopes of the interior, are a marvel to those who, a few years ago,
saw the country in its primitive condition; and to the Negro newcomer from this country in search of a field for his energy and
enterprise, there is no picture which, for inspiration and grandeur,
can ever equal the sight of these new proprietors of land and these
new directors of labour engaged in their absorbing and profitable
pursuits. When he sees the thriving villages, the comfortable
dwellings, the increasing agriculture, all supervised and controlled
by men just like himself, who had been more fortunate in preceding

him by a few years, a feeling of pride and gratification takes
possession of him. . . .

"CRAVING FOR THE FATHERLAND"

The general practice among superficial politicians and irresponsible coloured journalists in this country, is to ignore and deprecate
the craving for the fatherland among the Negro population. But
nothing is clearer to those who know anything of race instincts
and tendencies than that this craving is a permanent and irrepressible impulse. For some reason the American Government has never
seen its way clear to give any practical recognition to these aspirations. In vain, apparently does the American Colonization Society,
from year to year, present the cries and petitions of thousands and
hundreds of thousands who yearn for a home in the land of their
fathers. Individual philanthropists may admit that such cries deserve
respectful sympathy, but the Government takes no note of them.
It must be stated, however, that the Government is ever ready to
extend assistance to Liberia, and on the ground, partly, as often
urged in their diplomatic correspondence, that Liberia is to be
the future home of American citizens of African descent.

Has not the time come when an earnest and united effort should
be made by all sections of this great country to induce the Government to assist the thousands who are longing to betake themselves
to those vast and fertile regions to which they are directed by the
strongest impulses that have ever actuated the movements of
humanity? While it is true that there are causes of dissatisfaction
with his position in this country on the part of the Negro, still he
will be carried to Africa by a higher impulse than that which brings
millions to this country from Europe. . . .

No natural impulses bring the European hither—artificial or
economic causes move him to emigrate. The Negro is drawn to
Africa by the necessities of his nature.

We do not ask that all the coloured people should leave the
United States and go to Africa. If such a result were possible it
is not, for the present, at least, desirable; certainly it is not indispensable. For the work to be accomplished much less than one-
tenth of the six millions will be necessary. . . .

There are Negroes enough in this country to join in the return—
descendants of Africa enough, who are faithful to the instincts of
the race, and realize their duty to their fatherland. I rejoice to know
that here, where the teachings of generations have been to disparage
the race, there are many who are faithful, there are men and women

who will go, who have a restless sense of homelessness which will never be appeased until they stand in the great land where their forefathers lived; until they catch glimpses of the old sun, and moon and stars, which will shine in their pristine brilliancy upon that vast domain; until, from the decks of the ship which bears them back home, they see the visions of the hills rising from the white margin of the continent, and listen to the breaking music of the waves—the exhilarating laughter of the sea as it dashes against the beach. These are the elements of the great restoration. It may come in our lifetime. It may be our happiness to see those rise up who will formulate progress for Africa—embody the ideas which will reduce our social and political life to order; and we may, before we die, thank God that we have seen His salvation; that the Negro has grasped with a clear knowledge his meaning in the world's vast life—in politics, in science, in religion.

I say it is gratifying to know that there are Negroes in this country who will go to this great work—cheerfully go and brave the hardships and perils necessary to be endured in its accomplishment. These will be among the redeemers of Africa. If they suffer they will suffer devotedly and if they die, they will die well. And what is death for the redemption of a people? History is full of examples of men who have sacrificed themselves for the advancement of a great cause—for the good of their country. Every man who dies for Africa—if it is necessary to die—adds to Africa a new element of salvation, and hastens the day of their redemption. And when God lets men suffer and gives to pain and death, it is not the abandoned, it is not the worst or the guiltiest, but the best and the purest, whom He often chooses for His work, for they will do it best. Spectators weep and wonder; but the sufferers themselves accept the pain in the joy of doing redemptive work, and rise out of lower levels to the elevated regions of those nobler spirits—the glorious army of martyrs—who rejoice that they are counted worthy to die for men.

The nation now being reared in Africa by the returning exiles from this country will not be a reproduction of the American. The restoration of the Negro to the land of his fathers will be the restoration of a race to its original integrity, to itself; and working by itself, for itself and from itself, it will discover the methods of its own development, and they will not be the same as the Anglo-Saxon methods. . . .

7

The African Problem
and the Method of its Solution

A Discourse delivered at the 73rd Anniversary of the American
Colonization Society
Washington D.C., January 1890

African Repository, July, 1890, 65–79

I am seriously impressed with a sense of the responsibility of my
position tonight. I stand in the presence of the representatives of
the great organization which seems first of all the associations in
this country to have distinctly recognized the hand of God in the
history of the Negro race in America—to have caught something
of the meaning of the Divine purpose in permitting their exile to
and bondage in this land. I stand also in the presence of what, for
the time being at least, must be considered the foremost congregation of the land—the religious home of the President of the United
States. There are present, also, I learn, on this occasion, some of
the statesmen and law makers of the land.

My position, then, is one of honour as well as responsibility, and
the message I have to deliver, I venture to think, concerns directly
or indirectly the whole human race. I come from that ancient
country, the home of one of the great original races . . . a country
which is now engaging the active attention of all Europe. I come,
also, from the ancestral home of at least five millions in this land.
Two hundred millions of people have sent me on an errand of
invitation to blood relatives here. Their cry is, "Come over and
help us". And I find among hundreds of thousands of the invited
an eager and enthusiastic response. . . . They have for the last
seventy years been returning through the agency of the Society
whose anniversary we celebrate tonight. Some have gone every
year during that period, but they have been few compared to the
vast necessity. They have gone as they have been able to go, and
we are making an impression for good upon that Continent. My
subject tonight will be, THE AFRICAN PROBLEM, AND THE METHOD
OF ITS SOLUTION.

ABOLITIONISTS AND COLONIZATIONISTS

In the development of the Negro question in this country the
colonizationists might be called the prophets and philosophers; the

45

abolitionists, the warriors and politicians. Colonizationists saw what was coming and patiently prepared for its advent. Abolitionists attacked the first phase of the Negro problem and laboured for its immediate solution; colonizationists looked to the last phase of the problem and laboured to get both the whites and the blacks ready for it. They laboured on two continents, in America and in Africa. Had they not begun as early as they did to take up lands in Africa for the exiles, had they waited for the abolition of slavery, it would now have been impossible to obtain a foothold in their fatherland for the returning hosts. The colonizationist, as prophet, looked at the State as it would be; the abolitionist, as politician looked at the State as it was. The politician sees the present and is possessed by it. The prophet sees the future and gathers inspiration from it. The politician may influence legislation; the prophet, although exercising great moral influence, seldom has any legislative power. The agitation of the politician may soon culminate in legal enactments; the teachings of the prophet may require generations before they find embodiment in action. . . .

The first phase of the Negro problem was solved at Appomattox, after the battle of the warrior, with confused noise and garments rolled in blood. The institution of slavery, for which so many sacrifices had been made, so many of the principles of humanity had been violated, so many of the finer sentiments of the heart had been stifled, was at last destroyed by violence.

Now the nation confronts the second phase, the educational, and millions are being poured out by State governments and by individual philanthropy for the education of the freedmen, preparing them for the third and last phase of the problem, viz.: EMIGRATION.

*   *   *

It is not surprising that some of those who, after having been engaged in the noble labours of solving the first phase of the problem—in the great anti-slavery war—and are now confronting the second phase, should be unable to receive with patience the suggestion of the third, which is the emigration phase, when the Negro, freed in body and in mind, shall bid farewell to these scenes of his bondage and discipline and betake himself to the land of his fathers, the scene of larger opportunities and loftier achievements. . . .

TIME NOT RIPE FOR NEGRO EXODUS

But things are not yet ready for the solution of the third and last phase of the problem. Things are not ready in this country among whites or blacks. The industrial condition of the South is not prepared for it. Things are not yet ready in Africa for a complete exodus. Europe is not ready; she still thinks that she can take and utilize Africa for her own purposes. She does not yet understand that Africa is to be free for the African or for nobody. Therefore she is taking up with renewed vigour, and confronting again, with determination, the African problem. Englishmen, Germans, Italians, Belgians, are taking up territory and trying to wring from the grey-haired mother of civilization the secret of the ages. Nothing has come down from Egypt so grand and impressive as the Sphinxes that look at you with calm and emotionless faces, guarding their secret today as they formerly guarded the holy temples. They are a symbol of Africa. She will not be forced. She only can reveal her secret. Her children trained in the house of bondage will show it to the world. Some have already returned and have constructed an independent nation as a beginning of this work on her western borders.

It is a significant fact that Africa was completely shut up until the time arrived for the emancipation of her children in the Western World. When Jefferson and Washington and Hamilton and Patrick Henry were predicting and urging the freedom of the slave, Mungo Park was beginning that series of explorations by English enterprise which has just ended in the expedition of Stanley. Just about the time that England proclaimed freedom throughout her colonies, the brothers Lander made the great discovery of the mouth of the Niger; and when Lincoln issued the immortal proclamation, Livingstone was unfolding to the world that wonderful region which Stanley has more fully revealed and which is becoming now the scene of the secular and religious activities of Christendom. The King of the Belgians has spent fortunes recently in opening the Congo and in introducing the appliances of civilization, and by a singular coincidence a bill has been brought forward in the United States Senate to assist the emigration of Negroes to the Fatherland just at the time when that philanthropic monarch has despatched an agent to this country to invite the co-operation in his great work of qualified freedmen.[1] This is significant.

What the King of the Belgians has just done is an indication of what European Powers will do when they have exhausted them-

---

[1] The Butler Bill did not come to a vote and other efforts to promote black American 'repatriation' did not succeed. Blyden was aware of the atrocities committed against Africans in the Congo, but apparently thought that black American 'repatriation' would serve to further expose and mitigate these atrocities [ed.].

selves in costly experiments to utilize white men as colonists in Africa. They will then understand the purpose of the Almighty in having permitted the exile and bondage of the Africans, and they will see that for Africa's redemption the Negro is the chosen instrument. They will encourage the establishment and building up of such States as Liberia. They will recognize the scheme of the Colonization Society as the providential one.

The little nation which has grown up on that coast as a result of the efforts of this Society, is now taking hold upon that Continent in a manner which, owing to inexperience, it could not do in the past. The Liberians have introduced a new article into the commerce of the world—the Liberian coffee. They are pushing to the interior, clearing up the forests, extending the culture of coffee, sugar, cocoa, and other tropical articles, and are training the aborigines in the arts of civilization and in the principles of Christianity. The Republic occupies five hundred miles of coast with an elastic interior. It has a growing commerce with various countries of Europe and America. No one who has visited that country and has seen the farms on the banks of the rivers and in the interior, the workshops, the schools, the churches, and other elements and instruments of progress will say that the United States, through Liberia, is not making a wholesome impression upon Africa—an impression which, if the members of the American Congress understood, they would not begrudge the money required to assist a few hundred thousand to carry on in that country the work so well begun. They would gladly spare them from the labouring element of this great nation to push forward the enterprises of civilization in their Fatherland, and to build themselves up on the basis of their race manhood.

AN "HISTORICAL" PICTURE OF AFRICA

If there is an intelligent Negro here tonight I will say to him, let me take you with me in imagination to witness the new creation or development on that distant shore; I will not paint you an imaginary picture, but will describe an historical fact; I will tell you of reality. Going from the coast through those depressing alluvial plains which fringe the eastern and western borders of the Continent, you reach, after a few miles' travel, the first high or undulating country, which, rising abruptly from the swamps, enchants you with its solidity, its fertility, its verdure, its refreshing and healthful breezes. You go further, and you stand upon a higher elevation where the wind sings more freshly in your ears, and your heart beats fast as you survey the continuous and unbroken forests that stretch away from your feet to the distant horizon. The melancholy cooing of the pigeons in some unseen retreat, or the more entrancing music of livelier and picturesque songsters alone disturb the solemn and almost oppressive solitude. You hear no human sound and see the traces of no human presence. You decline to pursue your adventurous journey. You refuse to penetrate the lonely forest that confronts you. You return to the coast, thinking of the long ages which have elapsed, the seasons which, in their onward course, have come and gone, leaving those solitudes undisturbed. You wonder when and how are those vast wildernesses to be made the scene of human activity and to contribute to human wants and happiness. Finding no answer to your perplexing question you drop the subject from your thoughts. After a few years—a very few it may be—you return to those scenes. To your surprise and gratification your progress is no longer interrupted by the inconvenience of bridle-paths and tangled vines. The roads are open and clear. You miss the troublesome creeks and drains which, on your previous journey, harassed and fatigued you. Bridges have been constructed, and without any of the former weariness you find yourself again on the summit, where in loneliness you had stood some time before. What do you now see? The gigantic trees have disappeared, houses have sprung up on every side. As far as the eye can see the roofs of comfortable and homelike cottages peep through the wood. The waving corn and rice and sugar cane, the graceful and fragrant coffee tree, the umbrageous cocoa, orange, and mango plum have taken the place of the former sturdy denizens of the forest. What has brought about the change? The Negro emigrant has arrived from America, and, slender though his facilities have been, has produced these wonderful revolutions. You look beyond and take in the forests that now appear on the distant horizon. You catch glimpses of native villages embowered in plantain trees, and you say these also shall be brought under civilized influences, and you feel yourself lifted into manhood, the spirit of the teacher and guide and missionary comes upon you, and you say, "There, below me and beyond lies the world into which I must go. There must I cast my lot. I feel I have a message to it, or a work in it"; and the sense that there are thousands dwelling there, some of whom you may touch, some of whom you may influence, some of whom may love you or be loved by you, thrills you with a strange joy and expectation, and it is a thrill which you can never forget; forever and anon it comes upon you with increased intensity. In that hour you are born again. You hear for evermore the call ringing in your ears, "Come over and help us".

These are the visions that lie before the Liberian settler who has turned away from the coast. This is the view that exercises such an influence upon his imagination, and gives such tone to his character, making him an independent and productive man on the Continent of his fathers.

As I have said, this is no imaginary picture, but the embodiment of sober history. Liberia, then, is a fact, an aggressive and progressive fact, with a great deal in its past and everything in its future that is inspiring and uplifting.

It occupies one of the most charming countries in the western portion of that Continent. It has been called by qualified judges the garden spot of West Africa. I love to dwell upon the memories of scenes which I have passed through in the interior of that land. I have read of countries which I have not visited—the grandeur of the Rocky Mountains and the charms of the Yosemite Valley, and my imagination adds to the written description and becomes a gallery of delightful pictures. But of African scenes my memory is a treasure-house in which I delight to revel. I have distinctly before me the days and dates when I came into contact with their inexhaustible beauties. Leaving the coastline, the seat of malaria, and where are often seen the remains of the slaver's barracoons, which always give an impression of the deepest melancholy, I come to the high table-lands with their mountain scenery and lovely valleys, their meadow streams and mountain rivulets, and there amid the glories of a changeless and unchanging nature, I have taken off my shoes, and on that consecrated ground adored the God and Father of the Africans.

"REPATRIATION" SOCIETY

This is the country and this is the work to which the American Negro is invited. This is the opening for him which, through the labours of the American Colonization Society, has been effected. The organization is more than a *colonization* society, more than an emigration society. It might with equal propriety, and perhaps with greater accuracy, be called the African *Repatriation* Society; or since the idea of planting towns and introducing extensive cultivation of the soil is included in its work, it might be called the African Repatriation and Colonization Society, for then you bring in a somewhat higher idea than mere colonization—the mere settling of a new country by strangers—you bring in the idea of restoration, of compensation to a race and country much and long wronged.

Colonizationists, notwithstanding all that has been said against them, have always recognized the manhood of the Negro, and been willing to trust him to take care of himself. They have always recognized the inscrutable providence by which the African was brought to these shores. They have always taught that he was brought hither to be trained out of his sense of irresponsibility to a knowledge of his place as a factor in the great work of humanity; and that after having been thus trained he could find his proper sphere of action only in the land of his origin to make a way for himself. They have believed that it has not been given to the white man to fix the intellectual or spiritual status of this race. They have recognized that the universe is wide enough, and God's gifts are varied enough to allow the man of Africa to find out a path of his own within the circle of genuine human interests, and to contribute from the field of his particular enterprise to the resources—material, intellectual, and moral—of the great human family.

But will the Negro go to do this work?

Is he willing to separate himself from a settled civilization which he has helped to build up to betake himself to the wilderness of his ancestral home and begin anew a career on his own responsibility?

I believe that he is. And if suitable provision were made for their departure tomorrow hundreds of thousands would avail themselves of it. The African question, or the Negro problem, is upon the country, and it can no more be ignored than any other vital interest. The chief reason, it appears to me, why it is not more seriously dealt with is because the pressure of commercial and political exigencies does not allow time and leisure to the stronger and richer elements of the nation to study it. It is not a question of colour simply—that is a superficial accident. It lies deeper than colour. It is a question of race, which is the outcome not only of climate, but of generations subjected to environments which have formed the mental and moral constitution.

It is a question in which two distinct races are concerned. This is not a question then purely of reason. It is a question also of instinct. Races feel; observers theorize.

The work to be done beyond the seas is not to be a reproduction of what we see in this country. It requires, therefore, distinct race perception and entire race devotion. It is not to be the healing up of an old sore, but the unfolding of a new bud, an evolution; the development of a new side of God's character and a new phase of humanity. . . .

*　　*　　*

You can easily see . . . why one race overshadowed by another should long to express itself—should yearn for the opportunity to let out the divinity that stirs within it. This is why . . . thousands and thousands of Negroes in the South are longing to go to the land of their fathers. They are not content to remain where everything is to be done under the influence of a new racial spirit, under the impulse of new skies and the inspiration of a new development. Only those who are fit for this new work, who believe in the race— have faith in its future—a prophetic insight into its destiny from a consciousness of its possibilities. The inspiration of the race is in the race.

*　　*　　*

8

The Negro in the United States

A.M.E. Church Review, January 1900, 308–15

Africa has heard with deep regret and sorrow of the unhappy state of things which prevails in the Southern portions of the United States. Every paper recently received from America tells of horrors which seem inexplicable on any other theory than that the actors and sufferers, both black and white have, for the time being . . . "lost their heads".

Making allowance for the exaggeration of an enterprising press, there must still be a residuum of truth in the reports which represent the Negro in the South as having to endure, for alleged inhuman and villainous crimes, of which in other countries the courts take cognizance, brutalities and tortures, inflicted by irresponsible mobs, at the thought of which the soul sickens and the brain reels.

The last mail brings us intelligence that the atrocities committed upon the wretched, perhaps demented, Sam Hose,[1] have since been exceeded by the resources of a terrible ingenuity which has invented and continued to invent elaborate, nameless and blood-curdling cruelties such as no African ferocity, even when inspired and goaded by heartless and unjustifiable foreign invasion and oppression, ever yet dreamed of inflicting on its victims. It is impossible to convey to the unsophisticated, untravelled African any adequate conception of the horrors perpetrated upon his "kin beyond the sea" by the strangers in whose country they have lived and toiled for three hundred years. He can form no image in his mind of such a state of things. The hideous love of cruelty, of inflicting pain for the pleasure of beholding agony, of spending actual intellectual effort in contriving unheard of tortures, is a passion abhorrent to him. . . .

* * *

FREDERICK DOUGLASS AND BISHOP TURNER

This, of course, brings up the vast question of the presence and future of the Negro in America. It has sometimes been urged as a reproach against him by white men with whom I have conversed both in England and America on the race question, that he is

---

[1] A lynch victim of early May 1890 [ed.].

indifferent to the land of his fathers. This charge, I am happy to say, I have been in a position to repel and refute. My intercourse with the late Frederick Douglass, and with the happily still vigorous and active Bishop Turner—antipodal in their views on the subject of African emigration—as well as my own travels in the South have served to convince me of the mischievous error of two statements concerning the American Negro; viz: First, that he is dying out, and secondly, that he is opposed to returning to his ancestral home. During a never-to-be-forgotten week which I had the privilege of spending with the "Old Man Eloquent" at his elegant home in the suburbs of Washington, and where I had him all to myself, among the numerous subjects discussed was the question of the Negro's decay in the South. Referring to this, he said, with an intensity of interest which does not appear in his simple language, "I, too, used to think that the Negro was dying out until I went South, where I was entirely reconstructed on that point, for I saw a Negro boy on every rail, a black baby on every curbstone. This," he added, with unaffected and inimitable fervour, "gave me hope for the future of the race, and I felt myself enthused."

No one who has ever conversed with Mr. Douglass, especially on the race question, can ever forget the flashes of poetic imagination which adorned his utterances. He has written some of the most beautiful things in English literature; but his table talk, when he felt free to let himself go, was the most inspiring of his effusions. He spoke at times with a keen and profound pathos, and at times with exquisite humour. Tears and laughter often chased or kissed each other under the spell of the conjurer. His conversation was elevated prose, as near poetry as prose can go. He was seldom able to resist an epigram, or an alliteration, either in public or private speech, producing a picturesqueness of effect which the listener was delighted to recognize and ever after to cherish as an inspiring remembrance. The myrrh and frankincense of imperishable praise will ever embalm his memory for those who were admitted to his personal friendship. And by those who knew him only in his writings, he will be assigned no unequal or undistinguished place among the greatest of Americans who have fought for the physical, political and spiritual freedom of the race.

On the subject of the universal desire of the Southern Negro to return to the land of his fathers, Bishop Turner is my other witness. He is the embodiment of hyperbole. It is a constitutional gift. Some call it a defect. He has said to me, not once nor twice, "I could, if I had the means at command, bring millions—yes, *millions*—of Negroes from the South to Africa in a few years, so deep and widespread is the desire among them to return home. . . ."

Bishop Turner's wonderful gift, call it what we may, has served many a noble purpose, carried out many a necessary work, which, without that peculiar talent, could not have been effected. He has turned many around . . . and made them face Africa, though he could not always make them open their eyes to contemplate the attractions before them. . . .

The Negro exodus from America—gradual it may be, but, nevertheless, an exodus—is sure to come. It is an inevitable condition in the evolution of the Negro race, and Bishop Turner's part in the great work can never be eliminated from the history of that process. He has saturated with his views on emigration all the leading Southern papers. He has been persistent and consistent in his advocacy of the great cause through the evil report and the good report of nearly thirty years. The contagion of his earnestness and sympathy has inoculated thousands of minds. He is, it must be admitted, frightfully pugnacious, beyond comparison the most combative writer who controls a Negro journal or any journal in America. Where his unparalleled vocabulary does not furnish the necessary epithet, his abounding fertility is never at a loss. He coins words with a bewildering readiness to serve as vehicles for his passionate exuberance. . . .

When in company with him he has furnished a most puzzling object of study. His intellectual versatility and resourcefulness have surprised me when contrasted with his restlessness if anything is said which he cannot just fit in with his preconceived notions; his fits of irritation growing, probably, out of an uncomfortable and nervous organization, characteristic of the impetuous and intractable Eboe tribe[2] from which he sprang—a pedigree which goes far to explain, if it does not excuse, his ferocity of utterance. But, as with the Eboes, whose anger is very short madness, the clouds of wrath readily disperse and sunshine appears as if there had been no storm. There is in this character much that is generous, much that is hearty and spontaneous. In spite of his contemptuous and often abusive attitude towards adversaries; in spite of his too frequent indulgence in terms of scorn and vituperation; in spite, also, of the fact that clever people have always a *little* malice against the stupid; no man has a warmer heart or more expansive and unrestricted sympathies; none is more abundant in generosity towards the unfortunate and helpless; often with the simplicity and

[2] The Eboes, currently spelt "Ibos" are the dominant ethnic group of Eastern Nigeria.

abandon of a child he will weep with those who weep and rejoice with those who rejoice, and readily follow when led in any direction that seems to point to racial, or, I should say, human benevolence, patriotism and virtue. Chivalry is the keynote of his whole character. Therefore the fact cannot be ignored—criticize his methods as we may—that the person who, at the present moment, has the greatest, the surest, the most diffused influence over the great mass of the Negroes of the South is indisputably Henry McNeal Turner, and this because he has the most pronounced reverence for the ancestral home of at least five-sixths of the coloured population, and never ceases, with all the earnestness of prophetic insight, to warn, to admonish of present and impending dangers, and to point out with irrepressible enthusiasm to the glorious inheritance of the race—theirs by divine appointment—beyond the sea.

The *Voice of Missions* is emphatically Bishop Turner's paper—a personal production, stamped with the individuality, the image and superscription of its creative and versatile founder. In his editorial and other didactic labours, the Bishop proceeds upon the principle which in conversation with me he has often insisted upon, that a leader to be effective must be not only *intelligent* but *intelligible* to those he attempts to lead. Moreover, when hatred of oppression is to be vigorously expressed; when indolence and indifference are to be made odious; when the drowsy and lethargic preacher is to be awakened; when the call to the Fatherland is to be emphasized, it is not the oily and plausible man that is needed; it requires for the ear of the Negro just out of bondage a sound much bigger and far more trumpet-tongued than any "Voice" but that of Bishop Turner is competent to produce. Fifty years hence this "Voice" will not be needed and it will not exist then. The circumstances requiring it are local and temporary. . . . But . . . the memory of the paper will exist as that of one of the most trustworthy records of the habits and customs and the tone of thought of the American Negro during the first fifty years after his deliverance from chattel bondage. It will be studied, also, as an instructive appendage to the biography of one of the most remarkable characters produced among the Negroes of the South under, or, perhaps, in spite of, the stern discipline of the "peculiar institution".

But to return to the subject of which Bishop Turner is so important a part that the digression in which I have indulged to say a few words about him will be readily understood and excused.

The Negro in the Southern States, then, is not dying out and he is not indifferent or antagonistic to the Fatherland. But he cannot come to Africa now. He is not yet ready for the transition. Still his suffering continues without any apparent diminution. Dark and dreary are the days before him. Suffering, however, is nothing new to him and adversities have their uses. He will survive them.

But what is his duty now? The interest as well as the duty of the Southern Negro, it appears to me, is to follow the practical and sensible advice given by Mr. Booker T. Washington, in his now famous metaphor, "to drop his bucket where he is"—to use the ample, and I must add, unexampled means to put into his hands for real progress and permanent usefulness. In politics he should turn over a new leaf.

. . . The ignoring of politics by the Negroes of the South would be the most important step in the direction of genuine progress taken by the race since the Civil War.

PART II

Liberia—Its Role and History

PART II

Liberia—Its Role and History

For most of its history, particularly after its independence as a Republic in 1847, and before the independence of other black African countries, Liberia remained, if not an object of pride, a symbol of hope to pan-African nationalists. Thus in the 1920s, Marcus Garvey, the Jamaican-born American-based leader of a Back-to-Africa Movement with a massive following, looked upon Liberia as an indispensable beach-head from which to launch his planned liberation of colonial Africa. In 1934, Dr. Nnamdi Azikiwe, the American-trained Nigerian scholar and nationalist, defended Liberia against charges of stagnation and exploitation of indigenous peoples in his first book *Liberia in World Politics*. Three years later, in *Renascent Africa*, Azikiwe expressed the hope that intelligent black men would support Liberia so that it could attain "a more glorious destiny".

Such a hope was frequently expressed in the nineteenth century by pan-African nationalists. None expressed it more often or fervently than Blyden. When he emigrated there in 1851, he saw the Republic as the nucleus of a modern, progressive nation—a synthesis of the best in African and Western cultures. He developed the highest conception of the role which Liberia was to play on behalf of the entire Negro race: it was to demonstrate to the world African talents and abilities and make distinctive contributions to humanity at large. He himself had an active career in and on behalf of the Republic as an educator, clergyman, politician, diplomat and statesman. In these capacities he strove to advance Liberia's interests abroad and to bring about reforms at home, and was keenly disappointed that Liberia, because of its lack of trained manpower, financial resources and wise leaders, was never remotely in a position to play the ambitious pan-African role he assigned it. He was at once Liberia's harshest and most constructive critic. He attacked the unproductive and conspicuous consumption of the ruling class (Selection 9), and their lack of racial patriotism: he held up for their emulation the dedicated career of Rev. John Day (1799–1858), missionary, teacher and judge (Selection 10); and pleaded for constitutional reforms which included the extension of the President's term from two to six years and the establishment of an independent Civil Service (Selection 11). A mere two years

61

before his own death, he was still prescribing for Liberia's ills (Selection 16).

Because he played a highly significant role in nineteenth century Liberian history, and knew well the indigenous peoples of that black Republic and its hinterland, his historical and sociological writings are a valuable source of information to students of Liberia : his graphic description of the Muslim town of Boporo (Selection 13), his shrewd observations on the major Liberian tribes (Selection 14), and his vivid recounting of the conflicts between the migrant and indigenous groups in Grand Bassa County (Selection 15).

9

Liberia as She is; and the Present Duty of her Citizens

An Independence Day address given at Monrovia, July 27th, 1857
African Repository, November 1857, pp. 328–32.

What then . . . are the moral causes of the present evils in Liberia? . . .

. . . as a people we *have been in too much haste to be rich*. Relinquishing the pursuit of those attributes that would fit us for the faithful discharge of our peculiar duties as men, as Liberians, as an infant nation, we have used every possible measure to enhance our pecuniary importance; and in the precipitate efforts at wealth, we have not been careful as to what means we have employed. The desire to be rich, or to *appear* to be rich, pervades all classes. The love of money . . . has grown upon us to such a degree that all other avenues of distinction seem but trifling in comparison of those which lead to the acquisition of money.

To be rich seems with many "the chief end of man". Hence, no talents, no endowment of the mind, no skill or knowledge, no amount of education, is appreciated only so far as it *will pay*. . . . This fact has operated greatly in retarding the literary progress of our youth. . . .

CONSPICUOUS CONSUMPTION

Another cause of our adversity may be seen in the unjustifiable extravagance in which we indulge; in that luxury of expenditure for houses, for dress, for furniture, for food, constantly made the reprehensible remark by thinking foreigners. We are in dreadful error in regard to our country, if we suppose we are truly prosperous. Our prosperity is not real; it is false; it is fictitious. The prosperity of a nation is real when the springs of the prosperity are contained within itself, in the hands of its citizens; when it depends for its existence upon its own resources; when it is independent. But this is not the case in Liberia. We are, as a nation, upheld by foreigners. We are entirely dependent upon foreigners for our schools, for churches, for preachers, for teachers. Most of the talent of the country is in the employ and at the control of foreigners. Those thus employed must ever hold their talents and their efforts subservient, not to what they conceive to be the interests of their country, but to the desires and direction of foreign employers. . . . What we wish to bring before our minds today is the humiliating fact, that nearly all the talent of Liberia—talent not in ordinary men, but in our principal men—is supported by foreign means and controlled by foreign influence. And yet, in the face of these humbling realities, we boast of our civilization, of our prosperity, of our independence, and indulge in unjustifiable extravagance. . . .

*   *   *

. . . the money lavished upon houses, which add nothing to health and comfort; upon dress, which does not increase the dignity and beauty of personal appearance; the large sums laid out in expensive furniture, . . . the great amount consumed in the luxuries of the table would go a great way in keeping our streets clear of weeds, in felling the dense forests around us, in reclaiming the wilderness, in cultivating the soil, in civilizing our . . . brethren.

. . . Look at the numbers who . . . in order to advance to, or maintain this [extravagant] style of living, flock to the fostering arms and sheltering wings of these [foreign] societies. Thus dishonesty stalks abroad under the semblance of piety; and impiety assumes the appearance of religion for the sake of gain. And . . . this extravagant manner of living . . . are made in the minds of many the standard of respectability . . . we attach more importance to *display* than to *reality*. There is very little that is substantial about us. . . .

*   *   *

. . . It is our duty to learn that there are other objects of infinitely greater importance than wealth in our rising country. . . . A higher destiny is ours: our duty and privilege is the laying of the foundation of future empires in Africa. . . .

. . . It is our duty to curtail our superfluous expenditures. There should be retrenchment of our expenditures for splendid edifices. . . . Let our surplus means be beneficially expended; let it be vested in the improvement of our country, in placing our prosperity upon a safer and more permanent foundation—in rendering ourselves independent. . . .

. . . It is our duty to *labour*. We dwell in a country rich in resources, which with little exertion can be called forth in sufficient variety and abundance to render us comfortable and independent. But there is a fatal lack of productive industry among us. . . . The commerce of the country has always been in such articles as our citizens have had no part in producing; hence we acquire wealth from this source without helping to create it. We purchase the palm oil and camwood and ivory from the natives giving them in exchange articles of foreign production. . . . The prosperity arising from our commerce is almost as evanescent as that based on missionary appropriations. Foreigners on the one hand, and the natives on the other, are our supporters.

* * *

. . . we must either abandon our state of utter dependency upon foreigners, by creating the means of supplying our own wants, or relinquish our profession of liberty as a nation. A state of dependency is entirely incongruous with a state of liberty. . . .

. . . The . . . rich and fertile soil . . . invites us to its cultivation. Nothing should be allowed to interfere between us and the soil. . . .

10

A Eulogy pronounced on the Reverend John Day

Providence Baptist Church, Monrovia, March 2nd, 1859
Liberia's Offering, New York, 1862, 127–40

There are times in the history of nations as of individuals when they are called upon by the voice of Providence to look back upon their past, to examine their present, and to endeavour to rectify whatever is wrong, to adjust whatever is disordered, and to harmonize whatever is discordant in their social and political organization, to see whether they have not departed too far from the old landmarks, or whether, destitute of an experience sufficient for a wise eclecticism, they have not adopted principles which militate against their progress and success. And, perhaps, no occasion more naturally suggests this retrospection and introspection than when called upon, as we are called upon this evening, to recite the history and reproduce the examples of those who have occupied positions of trust and responsibility, who have made themselves useful to the community, by whose wisdom, patriotism, and energy the nation has been advanced in respectability and prosperity, but who, by the rude entrance of death, have been torn from our embraces.

And, perhaps, there never was a time in the history of Liberia when we needed more carefully to ponder our condition; when the necessity seemed greater to hold up to our view whatever was virtuous and exemplary in the character of our fathers; that by summoning to our gaze, from those pure and lofty regions, their noble spirits, there may possibly be disposted from the midst of us that selfishness and unpatriotic feeling, and that spirit of disunion which we fear are taking the place of the public spirit, the enlarged benevolence, the self-sacrificing zeal, and the spirit of unity, under the influence of which this nation was founded, and by the aid of which it has been brought thus far.

The history of the late Rev. John Day, which we now propose briefly to review, is not, it is true, marked by any of those stirring incidents, those marvellous and exciting adventures, those heroic actions which are pleasing to the minds of some. He achieved no great and remarkable exploits, which by the common and voluntary consent of mankind, place his name at once high among the great and honoured of the earth. But there are, nevertheless, points in his history, monotonous and undiversified as a history enacted for the most part in Liberia must of necessity be, from the consideration of which important lessons may be gathered. We shall attempt, therefore, on this occasion, to collect some of the materials, which render his memory dear to every Liberian, to every Christian, and which should dispose us to cherish that memory as a precious inheritance, and to transmit it as a valuable legacy to future generations.

A PRIVILEGED YOUTH

John Day was born in the northern part of the State of North Carolina, in the year 1797. His native county, bordering upon the State of Virginia, was influenced not a little by the manners and customs of Virginian life. The circumstances of his birth were favourable. Born of a family of a high degree of respectability and held in great esteem by their white neighbours, his privileges were superior to those of many of his race in that country. And in the region where he was born and brought up, as indeed over the greater portion of North Carolina and Virginia at that time, the distinction which now prevails between respectable persons of colour and white persons was not known. Nathaniel Turner had not yet achieved his magnificent failure, and abolitionism had not yet assumed its rabid and sectional character. In his youthful education Mr. Day was fortunate. He attended the best schools in the country, and sat side by side with the sons of the most aristocratic planters. He was born at a time when the spirit that engendered the American Revolution was still rife among the people; when the exciting oratory of Patrick Henry still rang in their ears; when the mighty reverberations of his "Give me liberty, or give me death!" had not yet died from the mountain-ranges of Old Virginia. Sentiments averse to oppression of every kind still pervaded the breasts of the white inhabitants, and were diffused throughout their conversation. Mr. Day, allowed freely to mingle with the immediate descendants of the Jeffersons, the Randolphs, the Henrys, caught the flame of liberty and independence. And, as he looked around, and saw the majority of his brethren in thralldom, which, by that keen foresight with which he was gifted, he saw would sooner or later affect unfavourably the condition of all persons of colour, he sighed for a land where he might not witness the degradation of his brethren. He thought of Hayti, but he thought also of its foreign language, its priestcraft, and its frequent revolutions. He formed various plans for his future life, looking forward to a time when, amid some fortunate scene, and beneath some auspicious sky, he would realize his ardent desires for the enjoyment of liberty untrammeled by the adventitious circumstance of colour.

Having been put to the trade of cabinet-making, he made such proficiency in that branch of industry that he was soon enabled to establish himself in business. By the superior finish and strength of his work, he attracted considerable custom. The most distinguished persons for miles around furnished him with work. He soon made himself a competency. But just as he was forming plans large and magnificent for his worldly aggrandizement and gratification, just as he was beginning to say with the rich man of old, "My grounds have brought forth plentifully, what shall I do?" it pleased the Great Head of the Church, by that mysterious influence whose operation is like the wind, blowing where it listeth, to transform his moral nature and make him a child of God. He found himself with new feelings and new desires, new predilections and new antipathies. He must now, therefore, form new plans. He looked abroad upon the world, and his enlarged heart took in all mankind. He felt that he had a work to do. He felt that it was his duty, as he esteemed it his privilege, to exhort others to flee from that impending wrath from which as a brand from the everlasting burnings he has been plucked. He was strongly impressed with the conviction that he should devote himself to the important business of preaching the Gospel. Having enjoyed the advantages of a good English education, he entered, through the recommendation of some friend, a theological class, whose reading was directed by Rev. Mr. Clopton, a Baptist minister of profound learning, skilful in the languages, and an adept in metaphysical science. Standing foremost in the ranks of Baptist ministers at that time, Mr. Clopton was eminently fitted for the duties of preparing young men for the ministry. Rev. Dr. J. B. Jeter, of Richmond, Virginia, then quite a young man, also frequented Mr. Clopton's study. Mr. Clopton has paid close attention to the laws of the mind, and had great facility in explaining difficulties in religious experience, which at that time frequently troubled Mr. Day. And from him, doubtless, the subject of our remarks acquired that love for metaphysical discussion and research which those who were intimate with him, or attended his preaching, could not fail to discover.

While pursuing his studies under Mr. Clopton, the colony of Liberia, as an asylum for free persons of colour, began to attract attention in that part of the country where he resided. No sooner had he heard of the place than he at once made up his mind to cast in his lot with the people who, on these far-off shores, and

H

in this insalubrious clime, were endeavouring to establish a home for themselves and their children. Coincident with the desire for a land of liberty, there was now a burning zeal to preach the Gospel to the thousands of degraded Africans who roam these forests. He diligently applied himself to the work of preparation for the Gospel ministry. But unfortunately for the intellectual advancement of Mr. Day, a circumstance transpired—a circumstance to which, even down to the day of his death, he frequently referred with expressions of unmingled regret—which obliged him to relinquish his studies before he had gone through the prescribed course, and enter upon the active duties of the calling which he had chosen.

LIBERIAN EMIGRANT

Having sacrificed his property, he embarked in December of the year 1830, with a most amiable wife, and four interesting children, for this land, which was so soon to be the grave of the affectionate group. He arrived in Liberia, entered at once upon his sacred duties, pursuing the business of cabinet-making for his support, and preaching as often as opportunity offered. He had not been long in the land before he saw his lovely companion stricken down by the relentless hand of death—a companion to whose charms and loveliness he was most keenly alive, and around whom the most ardent affections of his soul were so firmly entwined, that the great depths of his heart seemed upheaved by the severance. Then, one after another, he saw his beloved offspring wrapped in the chilling embraces of the grim monster, and conveyed to the house appointed for all living, until his whole family melted away from him, and none was left to remind him of the scenes and associations of the past. There he stood alone in a new country, amid new scenes and associations; there he stood, like some solitary oak in the dead of winter, stripped of its foliage, and exposed, dry and defenceless, to all the beatings of the northern storms. Finding himself in this grievous solitude, and entirely at a loss how to dispose of the sad and weary hours that hung so oppressively upon him, he abandoned himself to gloomy abstractions and melancholy reveries. This led to the supposition that there was some unhingement of his mental organization. But notwithstanding his deep afflictions he never murmured; was never disposed to abandon the field which he had chosen for the labours of his life. He had numerous inducements to return to the land of his birth. His relatives, in comfortable and respectable circumstances, urged him again and again to return. Several wealthy friends anxiously waited to welcome him. But he had put his hand to the plough, and he would not look back. His ardent and cherished desire was to labour for the evangelization of his heathen brethren in this land, and he would not, notwithstanding his deep bereavements, and the imminent danger in which his own life often stood, swerve from his noble purpose. Here we have an instance of the triumph of grace in the soul. Here we see true Christian benevolence, the constraining love of Christ, the new, living, and all-controlling principle implanted in every regenerate heart, rising superior to all earthly interests, forsaking father and mother, and hazarding life itself for the cause of Christ. . . .

After Mr. Day had resided here for several years, a mission was established by the Northern Baptist Board of Missions, with which he became connected, and in the service of which, for a number of years, he was abundant in labours. The principal seat of the operations of that Board was in the county of Grand Bassa. Frequently have we sat and heard him recite for hours together the interesting and instructive incidents of those laborious, painful, and hazardous tours which he repeatedly made for hundreds of miles into the interior, preaching and teaching the people. And there are now to be found scattered all over that country delightful fruits of his labours. Taking the city of Buchanan as a centre, and with a radius of sixty or seventy miles, describe a semicircle, and there is no point to which you can go within that semicircle where the name of John Day is not a household word, and at many points you will readily recognize precious evidences of his toils and efforts.

Mr. Day subsequently became connected with the Southern Baptist Convention, who have established missions throughout Liberia, at Sierra Leone, and in Central Africa. For several years, and up to the hour of his death, he filled the responsible position of superintendent of their missions in Liberia and at Sierra Leone, and prosecuted to the utmost of his ability the arduous duties of that station of trust.

PATRIOTIC CITIZEN

But Mr. Day *was patriotic*. Of this no citizen of Liberia, within the sound of my voice, needs any elaborate demonstration. Residing within the limits and being a citizen of a nation in the incipient stages of progress, he felt that, notwithstanding his arduous ministerial labours, he had a work to perform in shaping the political institutions of his country. No love of indulgence or ease, no dread of severe application, kept him from striving to qualify himself for usefulness to his country and fellow-citizens. He studied closely and patiently the science of jurisprudence and the general principles of statesmanship, so that he was fitted for usefulness in all those positions for which intelligent men are needed in rising communities. Nor were his talents and acquirements slighted by his fellow-citizens. After having filled various subordinate offices, elective and otherwise, he was, in the year 1853, placed as successor of Chief-Justice Benedict at the head of the Judiciary, which position he occupied with dignity and credit until his demise. It is said by competent judges that his charges to juries and decisions, when Judge of the Court of Quarter Sessions in the county of Grand Bassa, were most elaborate, and discovered a deep insight into legal principles. In the Legislative hall he did not very often take the floor, but whenever he did his counsels were wise and judicious. His remarks were brief, but to the point. And when he occupied leading positions on committees, where important reports and other documents had to be prepared, he showed his wisdom and skill, did justice to his subject and credit to himself.

The declaration of the Independence of Liberia, the establishment of the first Republican government on the Western Shores of Africa, did not, it is true, solve any intricate problem in the history of nations. It did not shed any new light upon mankind with reference to the science of government. It was not the result of the elaboration of any novel principle in politics. But it poured new vigour into the poor, dying existence of the African all over the world. It opened a door of hope for a race long the doomed victims of oppression. It animated coloured men everywhere to fresh endeavours to *prove* themselves men. It gave the example of a portion of this despised race, far away in the midst of heathenism and barbarism, under the most unfavourable circumstances, assuming the responsibilities and coming forward into the ranks, of nations; and it demonstrated that, notwithstanding the oppression of ages, the energies of the race had not been entirely emasculated, but were still sufficient to establish and to maintain a nationality.

When the idea of bringing to pass this mighty achievement in the history of the race was first mooted, many regarded it as chimerical, some viewed it as presumptuous, and others thought it but little less than treason. In the county in which Mr. Day then resided there was considerable opposition to the measure; but, deeply thoughtful, he saw beneficial results which were likely to accrue to the country and to the race from the assumption of Independence. He boldly advocated the measure, notwithstanding various threats from an exasperated populace. The boisterousness of the mob could not daunt him. He persevered, and rode triumphantly over the tumultuous surges. He was elected a delegate to the National Convention which assembled in this city to draft a Declaration of Independence and a Constitution for the new Republic. He was therefore among the signers of the Declaration of Independence. And here we are reminded of the melancholy fact that those distinguished men are fast passing away. . . .

But four of the twelve who sat in that memorable convention survive. This admonishes those of us who are youthful that soon the fathers will have gone forever, and it presses home to our hearts, with all the solemnity of the grave, the question: Are we preparing ourselves, by mental and moral culture, to take their places and lead on this infant nation, which they have established in weakness and in much trembling, to independence and glory?

. . . We have with regret noticed of late a growing tendency among some of the juvenile members of the community to depreciate the labours of our fathers, the pioneers of Liberia. . . . We regret it because it is doing great injustice to the heroic men who for years have struggled, in sickness and in health, in joy and in sorrow, to maintain themselves on these shores. We are tauntingly asked: "What have these men done?" And we are told that "all that has been achieved has been achieved by foreign means". What have they done? We would ask in return what have they *not* done? They have voluntarily expatriated themselves from the land of their birth; forsook the endearing scenes and associations of childhood; severed themselves from the comforts and conveniences of an advanced state of society; denied themselves the enjoyment of health, and the pleasure of civilized and enlightened influences, and gave themselves up to a living death on these barbarous shores. And for what purpose? That they might found a home not for themselves, for they knew they would not live to enjoy it, but for their posterity. Foreign means indeed! It is true they were poor men. They had no gold and silver to lavish out upon improvements; but mark their superior self-abnegation and heroism, *they gave themselves.* And what could foreign learning and foreign wealth have done without their groans, and sweat, and blood? Yes, they suffered keenly, and bore up heroically under their sufferings for us. Their work consisted in patient endurance—a task far more difficult than active exertion. Let us not, then, depreciate their sacrifices and toils, but rather let us endeavour to qualify ourselves to carry on, by labour and well-directed effort, what they have begun in intense suffering and endurance. And if we are wise to detect any faults or deficiencies in any of their doings, let us not boastingly expatiate upon them, but rather let us, taking the mantle of charity, hasten to spread it over them, lest, while we luxuriate and delight ourselves with ideas of our own superiority to them, there come over the land a physical barrenness, a mental and moral blight, because we have not accorded the reverence due to our fathers.

We are not by any means, however, asserting that it is incumbent upon us to entertain such unquestioning deference to the opinions and actions of our fathers as to re-enact their errors, and proceed, right or wrong, in the beaten track; but we are for interring with their bones the ill they may have done, encouraging the vitality of their virtuous deeds, and immortalizing their exemplary conduct. Let us emulate their noble actions. Let us not be content to live and die without doing something to ameliorate the condition of our down-trodden race. Oh! let us not be drones in the great hive of humanity.

. . . Not only was Mr. Day laborious and diligent in qualifying himself for the public duties which he was so frequently called upon to perform, but he assiduously endeavoured to fit himself for use-fulness in the more private scenes of life. In that part of Liberia where he spent the greater portion of his time, there was seldom any physician, yet there were frequently cases among the people which needed medical attention. Mr. Day, therefore gave himself, in addition to his numerous other studies, to the reading of medical works, and to the study of the natural sciences, that he might fit himself for ordinary practice. He soon acquired a sufficient know-ledge of pathological principles and of therapeutics to enable him to be a very useful practitioner among the poor of his neighbour-hood. He willingly went from house to house, administering relief to the sick, healing the diseases of the body, and endeavouring to bind up the wounds of the spirit. Not a little of his earning was expended in unwearied services among the poor and afflicted. By his well-bred gentility, the cordiality of his manners, and his sympathy with their griefs, he won the esteem and love of all around him. The sick and the afflicted, the poor and needy, were satisfied that he was their friend; and in the very humblest of their tenements he was met with exhibitions of their warmest welcome. In these private and retired acts, we have the most complete demon-stration of the greatness of his spirit.

We make a great mistake when we confine deeds of eminence to public scenes and magnificent occasions. It is often in the loneli-ness of a limited social or domestic circle, and in the discharge of the most common-place duty, that the greatest self-denial has to be exercised. Men in obscure stations, of whom the world never hears, may have the hardest tasks to perform, and the greatest sacrifices to make in the cause of God and religion. We should not lavish all our applause and admiration on such as stand foremost in the ranks of philanthropists, and whose names stand prominently forth as having done and suffered much to alleviate human suffering. We should not confine the honours of a true philanthropy to those who, in the sight and amid the applause of thousands, pour out of their abundance in the cause of charity. We conceive that he who, sequestered from the gaze of the multitude, "little and unknown", distributes daily and habitually of his earning to satisfy the needs of an indigent neighbourhood, is to the full as deserving as he whose thousands, abstracted from a large and constantly increasing heap, are bestowed in the vicinity of a newspaper-office.

Mr. Day, then, by his activity in the performance of those deeds of charity, which were far removed from the observation of men generally, which attracted no attention, showed that he was possessor of a large and expansive soul. . . .

11

Our Origin, Dangers and Duties

An Independence Day Address given at Monrovia on July 26th, 1865; published New York, 1865, 20–36

A PLEA FOR CONSTITUTIONAL REFORM

Our Constitution needs various amendments. It is of very great importance that the utmost care should be exercised in interfering with the fundamental law of the land; but we must not attach to it such mysterious and unapproachable sacredness as to imagine that it must not be interfered with at all, even when circumstances plainly reveal to us the necessity of such interference. The Constitution is only a written document, and, like all written documents . . . it has many errors and omissions. It becomes us, then, who long for the prosperity of our country, calmly and deliberately to examine and consider such defects as may exist in that most important paper, and set ourselves to the work of remedying them to the best of our ability. It is the people's Constitution, and it is the work of the people to correct its deficiencies.

The first point to which I would like to call your attention as needing amendment is that relating to the Presidential term of office. I believe that most of the thinking men in Liberia agree that the President should be elected for a longer term than two years. My own opinion is, that the Chief Magistrate should be elected for a term of six to eight years and not be immediately re-eligible. If we could bring to pass such an amendment . . . then we should doubtless get Presidents who, during their terms, would devote their attention to statesmanship—to such measures as pertain to the public weal and not electioneering expedients; and the country would be delivered from the frequent recurrence of convulsing political conflicts. In all cases where re-election is possible the magistrate in office is placed in the position of a candidate. He is tempted, especially as his term of office draws near its end, to direct his administration mainly with a view to secure popular favour. Thus, instead of statesmen we have electioneerers as Presidents. . . .

A second amendment needed in our Constitution, is one which shall involve the rescinding of the clause conferring upon the President the power of dismissing government *employees* indiscriminately at his pleasure. There are some officers that ought to be subject to his control, but they are only a few. The practice of dismissing all officials at every change of government is a most prolific source of mischief. . . .

Another mistake in our Constitution and laws is the arrangement which causes several months to elapse between the election of the President and his inauguration—from May to January—which gives his predecessor, if he be of an opposing party, a long time during which to carry out his party's views. Our arrangement is alarmingly defective, for instead of four months as in the United States, we allow fully eight months to the dissentient minority to carry out their purposes. This is a defect that calls loudly for immediate remedy.

*   *   *

These changes . . . depend upon the will of the people; but we must remember that the people cannot be browbeaten into them. They have to be reasoned with and convinced by patient and per-severing argument. The enterprise of persuading and convincing them deserves the utmost exertion of true patriots. The reward with which such efforts will be crowned is no less than the emanci-pation of the body politic from fatally injurious influences and the introduction among us of salutary conditions of national existence, under which we may go on prospering and to prosper.

*   *   *

RACE PRIDE NEEDED

If any man who has lived in Liberia two years cannot come to believe in the ability of the Negro race, under favourable circum-stances, to maintain an organized, regular and adequate govern-ment, that man has mistaken his country—he should at once pack up bag and baggages and transfer his residence to a more congenial clime. . . .

It is provoking to hear men sometimes going around and des-pising themselves and disparaging the opportunities for usefulness in the country; indulging in the most doleful prophecies of the future. Such is the very kind to kill all enterprise and to extinguish every noble aspiration. . . .

We are engaged here on this coast in a great and noble work. We cannot easily exaggerate the magnitude of the interests involved in the enterprise to which we are committed. Not only the highest welfare of the few thousands who now compose the Republic, but the character of a whole race is implicated in what we are doing. Let us then endeavour to rise up to the "height of this great argument". . . . Something has been done; but what is the little we have achieved compared to what has still to be done! The little of the past dwindles into insignificance before the mighty work of the future.

We are more eagerly watched than we have any idea of. The nations are looking to see whether "order and law, religion and morality, the rights of conscience, the rights of persons, the rights of property, may all be secured" by a government controlled entirely and purely by Negroes. Oh, let us not by any unwise actions compel them to decide in the negative.

* * *

GROWTH OF NATIONALISM

The tendency among the nations now seem to be to group themselves according to natural affinities of sentiment and race. Witness the struggles in Italy—the dreams of Mazzini and Garibaldi, with reference to the unification of that country. Germany is striving after consolidation. The same principle is at work in Hungary, and the visions of Kossuth may yet be realized. Even Poland is feeling for the same thing; and the mysterious Fenian movement is significant. In the Western World Mexico and Santo Domingo are determined to assert and protect their unity and freedom. The tendency in that direction is seen everywhere. . . .

Here is a land adapted to us . . . peculiarly ours to the exclusion of alien races. . . .

We have made a fair beginning. . . . Here we are, with all our unfavourable antecedents, still, after eighteen years of struggle, an independent nation. We have the germ of an African empire. Let us, fellow-citizens, guard the trust committed to our hands. The tribes in the distant interior are waiting for us. We have made some impression on the coast; . . . we shall make wider and deeper impressions. . . .

12

Liberia as a Means, Not an End

Independence Day Address, Monrovia, July 26th, 1867;
African Repository, November 1867, 327–39

European nations are now taking a lively interest in African
explorations and in the development of the resources of this continent. England has lately appointed a consul to reside on the Niger.
France is sending out explorers from Senegal to the heart of the
continent; and it has been predicted . . . that, in a few years European boats will keep up a regular intercourse between the great
basin of the Tchad and the Bay of Biafra; and if so, they will certainly drain the whole of the intervening country, which is extremely
rich and fertile, of its wealth. It is very clear to every thinking mind
that no prudent people should be content with the position we have
hitherto maintained. We ought not to be content to have in our
hands an effective instrument of substantial influence and live year
by year without using that instrument. It is evident that the most
effective plan for preventing the encroachment of Europeans on our
eastern borders, is to be wary and diligent in time—devoted to the
work of fraternizing with the natives. We might long since, by a
judicious policy, have had them so firmly bound to us that it would
have been impossible for any foreign influence to interfere with our
control of them.

So long as we continue the policy of adhering to the coast, and
keeping from enlarging the sphere of our influence towards the
interior, it is to no purpose that we labour and toil here to build
a nation: it is to no purpose that we get Presidents of consummate
ability, or Ministers of Finance to regulate the finances wisely, we
shall ever be impoverished and devoid of significance in the world.
Can we make a nation without the aid of the aborigines? Were
it not for them should we have any commerce worthy of the name?
any coastwise trade upon which to place restrictions? When we
went before the world to ask to be received into the family of
nations, did we not base our request upon the native population?
Was it not them that we professed to represent? Just as at that
time it was to our interest to avail ourselves of their numerical
assistance to secure national recognition, so now it is our wisest
policy, apart from philanthropic duties, to fraternize with them
in order to secure national strength and respectability. We should

court their friendship by an energetic and sympathetic intercourse with them. We should attract their children to our institutions of learning. . . . And it would not be an unwise policy, if we could have commissioners, civilized, educated and Christian men, representing our government at the principal towns—Boporo and Musadu for instance—whose duty it should be to learn the languages of the powerful tribes and instruct them in civilized practices, and form alliances with those who may be disposed to be friendly.

*   *   *

NO WHITE CITIZENS

The [present] administration has never entertained the policy of admitting white men just now to political rights in the country. Instead of looking for help to Europeans, it has steadily looked to the vast interior, by intercourse with whose teeming millions immense and mutual benefits may be conferred. We may be able to convey on them the blessings of civilization and Christianity, and they in turn give us of their wealth, which for the most part now goes to enrich others. Not that the administration has had any prejudice against foreigners, but it has felt that as a nascent Negro nation we might be overshadowed and absorbed by the superior wealth and intelligence of Europeans; and it was thought that there should be one place in the world—one spot on the continent of our fathers where the Negro should be the man. The influx of Europeans would be an effectual hindrance to such a result; the Negro element would be "rendered subdued and silent", if not altogether eliminated from any controlling influence. We dare not be liberal beyond our ability. It is often thrown up as a taunt that we exclude Europeans from our political affairs. Well, just now we cannot help it. With the history of the American Indians, the poor Caribs, the Australians, and New Zealanders before us, we shrink from the contest with that energetic race. It may be the fashion among Caucasians to be cosmopolite. But the Negro is so peculiarly circumstanced that the moment he undertakes to be cosmopolite, that moment he is stripped of a great deal which for the proper development of his manhood he ought to cherish. . . .

FOREIGN INFLUENCE OF LIBERIA INCREASED

But the administration has not neglected to cultivate friendly intercourse with foreigners. Perhaps no administration has, in the same space of time, done as much to increase the foreign influence of the Republic as the present administration. The first and most important foreign measure was to enter into relations of friendship with the small State of our own race in the Western Hemisphere. Liberia stretched her arms across the Atlantic and embraced the Republic of Haiti.

An unfortunate interruption of friendly international relations between Liberia and France, caused by the matter of the *Regina Coeli*,[1] has been happily adjusted, and an official communication sent by special conveyance from the French Minister for Foreign Affairs "expresses the interest which the Government of the Emperor continues to bear towards the State of Liberia, the desire which he entertains for the continuance of its prosperity, and his wish to maintain with it the best and most friendly relations". We are now represented by a Consul-General in France.

. . . the Spanish Government . . . has given [assurances] . . . of the most friendly feelings towards Liberia and the deepest interest in her welfare. A Liberian Consul now resides at Madrid.

Great Britain has virtually withdrawn from the controversy respecting our north-west territory, and left the whole matter to be settled by circumstances.[2]

Austria has entered into treaty stipulations with us. The nations of the far north have also given us the hand of friendship—Russia, Denmark and Sweden, and Norway.

Communications have been freely opened with the United States Government, as announced in the last message of the lamented Lincoln: and it has recently appointed to reside near our Government a diplomatic officer of very high grade.

The administration has therefore shown its interest in extending our foreign relations and evinced the high estimate which it places upon the friendship of foreigners; when it retires from power it will leave the foreign affairs of the country in a satisfactory condition—the Republic enjoying the goodwill of all the great nations of the earth.

Without pecuniary resources, and working in a net of fetters, the administration has put the internal and foreign affairs of the country in a direction and given them an impulse that must tell, if followed up, with important effect upon the development of the coming years.

The future is now before us—immeasurably in our own hands—and its character will depend upon the way we now act. If we act

[1] See Selection 18, p. 138 below.
[2] This boundary dispute was finally settled in 1885 in Sierra Leone's favour [ed.].

a judicious and patriotic part—with hearts wide enough to embrace all mankind, and at the same time so narrow as to feel for and give special attention to the wants of the Negro—if we look upon ourselves as instruments and agents for the great work in this land, the most happy effects will be felt in all the desolate regions— blessings will attend us in our ways, cries of failure and despondency will cease to be heard around us; men will cease to complain of the poverty of the Government, and the inefficiency of the Legislature. Liberia will become a political organization deeper in its foundation, wider in its scope, and loftier in its significance than it has ever been. And in our various fields of labour, instead of crippling one another through jealousy, we shall stimulate one another to zeal and activity; and we shall bring about a movement in this part of the world which the civilized world will be compelled to acknowledge. Our "experiment" on this coast will become a satisfactory demonstration.

13

The Boporo Country—Boporo

African Repository (1871), 236–42 and 258–62

The town of Boporo is situated in lat. 7° 25′ N., lon. 10° 25′ W., on a rising ground, gently sloping on the eastern side, enclosed by a circular barricade about a quarter of a mile in diameter, and entered by four gates, answering to the four principal points of the compass. It is a very ancient town, originally founded by the Golahs, once a powerful and influential people in these regions. But about sixty years ago it was captured by King Boatswain, who completely revolutionized the country and formed a new dynasty, in which Momoru Sou, the present ruler, is one of his successors, being the eldest son of Boatswain.

Boatswain was a Mandingo—his native name being Sabsu. Having by nature a restless and enterprising disposition, he founded his way in his early years to the Coast and shipped on board an English merchant vessel, where he acquired the name by which he came to be known to the Liberians and to the pagan tribe between Boporo and the Coast. After leaving the vessel, where he received some insight into civilized customs and acquired a good knowledge of the English language, he returned to his country to set himself up as a kind of factor, to furnish slaves to the Coast; but finding some difficulty, he gathered around him a large number of Comdoes, a warlike people living southeast of Boporo, and undertook in person a series of operations against the tribes in the neighbourhood. Everywhere his arms were successful. He expelled the Golahs from that part of the country, overcame their king, Bowrah, and captured their stronghold, Bamah, now called Bokoma or Boporo.[1]

By the moderation exercised by Boatswain when victorious he secured the attachment of the vanquished themselves; and several small tribes placed themselves under his sway.

"His personal qualifications were of the most commanding description. To a stature approaching seven feet in height, perfectly erect, muscular, and finely proportioned, a countenance noble, intelligent, and full of animation, he united great comprehension

---

[1] (The Mandingoes call it Bokma and the Camdoes or Boatswain people call it Boporo, both words signifying *beyond the hills*, as it is beyond the hills to persons coming from the plains on the north and east.)

and activity of mind, and, what was still more imposing, a loftiness and grandeur of sentiment—forming altogether an assemblage of qualities obviously disproportionate to the actual sphere of his ambition."[2] His son still retains the spear ordinarily used by his father, which he exhibits with evident pride to visitors. It is of unusual length and weight, so that no man of common strength can wield it. . . . Liberians have great reason to cherish a grateful respect for the memory of King Boatswain, for it was owing to his friendly interposition, . . . in behalf of the feeble few who first settled in Perseverance Island, that they were enabled to gain a foothold in this portion of Africa. . . .

* * *

After journeying four days on foot from the town of Vonswah, which is about four days travel from Monrovia, we reached Boporo. We entered the town through the western gate, preceded by a white and Liberian flags, and followed by a long train of carriers, many of whom, not at all connected with us, had joined us on the road. We were led first to the Mandingo quarter, as my mission was primarily with them, having copies of Arabic Scriptures for distribution among them. After a formal reception by some of the Imams, we were taken to the King's reception hall, a large open building, with thatched roof, about thirty feet long by sixteen wide. Chairs were brought, and Mr. [N. A.] Richardson [a Liberian] and myself were seated in the midst of a suffocating crowd. After a few minutes the King arrived with his *suite*, and, grasping me cordially by the hand, bade me welcome to his town. Taking from my desk a communication which had been forwarded to him by the President of Liberia, stating the object of my mission, and commending me to his kind attention, I handed it to him. Having by his request read and explained it to him sentence by sentence, he seemed much gratified. I then expressed to him the pleasure I felt in visiting his country, and the desire of the Liberians to be in friendship with him. He replied that he was glad to see me, and that he would do all in his power to facilitate my efforts in the prosecution of the objects of my mission. I then turned, and with his permission addressed the Mandingoes, a large number of whom were present, telling them of the great desire entertained by the Christians on the Coast . . . to be united with them, that we might become politically and religiously what we are by race and blood, *one people*: but it was necessary in order to [*sic*] an intelligent and permanent union, that we should understand each other. I had therefore

[2] The author does not give the source of this quotation [ed.].

brought them several copies of our sacred book . . . that they might get some insight into the Christian religion. I quoted in the course of my remarks several passages from the Koran in Arabic, referring to the sameness of origin of all nations and to the one overruling Providence. They manifested every now and then sympathy in an audible manner with my remarks. After an interchange of personal civilities with a few of the leading men, the king sent us to the house which he had prepared for us. Here, after washing and refreshing ourselves, we were called upon by a number of Mandingoes, who protracted their visits until nightfall, when the King himself came in with his armour-bearer and remained until bedtime.

On the following morning, January 1, 1869, with the King's Janissary as guide, we had an opportunity of walking over the town. It contains between three and four hundred houses, built closely together. The houses are for the most part circular, built of poles placed upright in the ground, and plastered inside and outside with beautiful whitish clay. They all have thatched conical roofs, projecting about a foot and a half, sometimes two feet, so as to afford a shade in the heat of the day. They are now nearly all new, as the town has been recently rebuilt, having suffered from a conflagration about three years ago.

. . . The streets are clean, not paved, but solid, consisting of hard sand and gravel, narrow and tortuous. . . .

The settled inhabitants cannot be much over two thousand, while during the period of trading activity—from December to May—there may be an additional floating population of about one thousand.

Very near the centre of the town stands the Mohammedan mosque, a circular building, about forty feet in diameter, height of wall about ten feet to the roof projection, surmounted by a lofty conical roof. In this building there is no furniture, excepting mats on the floor. About mid-way of the eastern wall is a niche, where the Imam stands to recite the prayers during worship.

Opposite the mosque is an open area, where the daily market is held. Hither persons from the agricultural villages bring their productions, and expose them for sale every morning from six to ten. . . .

We saw exposed for sale in the market clean white rice, sold by the pint, quart or gallon; excellent palm oil; dried meat, dried fish from the St. Paul's, said to be a day's walk southeast of Boporo; potatoes, cassadas, plantains, bananas, lima beans; different kinds of dyes; earthen bowls and pots etc. The articles given in exchange were tobacco and salt. A leaf of tobacco was sometimes cut into three or four parts; each part may buy a separate article. The sellers in the market were almost exclusively women.

The market area and a small square opposite the new building now in course of erection for the King—where stands the grave of King Boatswain—are the only open places for public resort. From these, several diverging streets run out, leading to the gates of the barricade.

*   *   *

. . . The atmosphere during our whole stay in the town was pleasant and moderate—the mountainous character of the country no doubt obviating oppressive heat.

KING MOMORU

With regard to the history of Momoru Sou; there is a singular tradition at Boporo. It is said that his father, being a Mandingo, preferred taking his wife from among his own people, but all his children by Mandingo women died in infancy. At length an old Mandingo priest called upon him, and said to him, "I am aware of your anxiety to have sons succeed you in this government, but as yet you have none to live. There is a Golah woman living at Sublung, near the Coast, if you could secure her for a wife, she would bear you sons to succeed to your kingdom." Boatswain followed the advice of the old priest, and the first son born of that woman was Momoru, the present ruler of Boporo; four of his sons by her still survive. Three of them have been under the training of Liberians. Mr. George R. McGill and his son, Hon. J. B. McGill, had the privilege of implanting seeds of civilization in Momoru and two of his brothers, the result of which the civilized man may now witness at Boporo and its vicinity.

Momoru is now a man near fifty years of age, of stout and compact frame, of beautiful glossy black complexion, about five feet high. He has inherited a great many of the qualities of his father, and by wars, subsidies, and marriages, has enlarged the area of political and material power left by his father.

Boatswain died somewhere about 1840, and his successors were Pakro, Pakroyah, Marvi, Gogommah, Lasanua, and Tosoru. These chiefs, though they displayed considerable energy in governing the country, never acquired the influence of Boatswain. . . .

Boatswain, before and since his accession to power, has, by several acts, won over the confidence and esteem of all the powerful chiefs under him. His knowledge of [western] civilization, though imperfect and limited, gives him and his brothers who preside over large towns, decided advantages over the other chieftains. I observed that when he and his brothers were together in the company of the other chiefs, they communicated with each other in the English language.

The territories over which he rules extend from Boporo as a centre, S.E. a day's walk to the St. Paul's [River]; N. a journey of eight days; W. to the little Cape Mount river; S. to Gebeh.

He informed me that his plan is to form family connections by inter-marriages with all the powerful chiefs of which he can hear. "By this means," he said, "I have the hand and heart of a great many kings for several days' journey into the interior. If the Liberians would lay hold of my hand in that way, you would form connection through me, as a link, with the distant tribes."

SLAVE REVOLT

He has over thirty thousand people under his sway, and a large number of slaves, his personal property, in all the towns.

To secure order, regular industry, and security among such a number of ignorant and uninstructed people, he is obliged occasionally to set examples of great severity. Two years ago, the slaves belonging to Musadoreh, a prominent Mandingo, one of his subjects, revolted and captured the town of their master, who being old and blind, was not slain, but allowed to remain in the town. The other Mandingo inhabitants had to flee to Boporo for their lives. The slaves kept the town during a period of three weeks, endeavouring to secure the co-operation of their slaves to enable them to institute a general and exterminating warfare. But their efforts not being seconded by the majority of the servile population, they were easily circumvented and captured by a treacherous chief to whom they had applied, and whom they had paid for assistance, but who, under the garb of friendship and sympathy, decoyed them from their enclosure, took them to his own town under the pretext of their making more extensive preparations for the war, and having got from them their arms, tied them, every one, and taking them to Boporo, delivered them to Momoru. They numbered sixty-five able-bodied men.

Momoru assembled a council of chiefs and tried them, allowing them an opportunity, as he informed us, to show cause why they made efforts to destroy human lives and lay waste the country. They could show no just grounds for their revolt, except the undying aspiration in every human breast to be free; a cause which no slaveholder has ever admitted is sufficient to deprive him of his property.

The unfortunate slaves were found . . . guilty, and sentenced to death. They were beheaded in the presence of Momoru and other chiefs one morning before breakfast, under two silk cotton trees, near the Marvo creek, and their bodies thrown into that stream. Their skulls are now exposed on stakes outside the eastern gate, as a warning to the servile population.

Those who would affectedly recoil in horror from this picture, must remember the awful enormities which have been perpetrated in the interest of slavery by nations and communities in other lands, professing Christianity; must recall those awful excesses which have been committed even in the alleged defence of Christianity; such as the criminal burning of witches, the fiendish tortures of the inquisition, the sanguinary persecutions of the Jews, etc. Such vigorous procedure on the part of Momoru, then, must not be attributed to the fact that he was Negro, but that he is a *man*. Such actions flow from the essence of human nature, which is virtually the same under all zones and all conditions of existence. Everywhere unenlightened and unsanctified men are alike. . . .

As a man, however, and as a ruler, Momoru is for many reasons worthy of respect, if not of admiration. He is a man of first class intellect. . . . He can converse fluently in all the languages of the tribes which he holds under his jurisdiction—nearly one dozen different and distinct languages. He speaks English readily and reads and writes a little. . . .

. . . His judicial and executive powers are astonishing. He has daily to attend to and dispose of business of various magnitude, from the quarrels of important chiefs, involving the security and peace of whole districts, to the little disagreement of neighbours in the towns. Every morning he holds long audiences in behalf of any who have grievances to redress or claims to advance. These audiences are held under trees outside the town. The reason for leaving the enclosure on such occasions, as alleged, is, that women must not hear their palavers. . . .

In cases of life and death, and in the enactment of all legislative acts intended to be permanent in their character or extensive in their operation, the leading chiefs are summoned for consultation.

Although the accession of numerous tribes enables Momoru, whenever the occasion requires it, to call into the field a far more imposing force than can be collected by any other chief for hundreds of miles around, yet his region is entirely free from any record of wasting massacres or wholesale devastation. He occasionally furnishes examples of great severity, because, as he told us, in apparent paradox, he is averse to bloodshed and opposed to war. He is sometimes severe, but never wantonly cruel.

During our visit to Boporo, he was using every means in his power to settle a dispute between two interior chiefs, which had led to open hostility between them, so as to interfere with the prosecution of trade along their borders. His great aim is to secure for his country the benefits of regular and unimpeded traffic; and to attain these he is unwearied in his efforts to keep the roads open and to suppress those tendencies to predatory warfare which are the curse of the region north and east of his country. He is continually forming plans for the improvement and adorning of his towns. He has at Toto-Korie, his favourite half town, about eight miles east of Boporo, a two-storey framed building, surrounded by a verandah, of which the materials were all prepared and put together under his personal superintendence. He is erecting at Boporo three large buildings, on an improved plan, for his own residence, and has in view the construction of a market house, for the more comfortable accommodation of vendors from the surrounding country.

Momoru enjoys the universal esteem and respect of his people. He is affable and kind to all; always has a smile for the humblest that comes to him, and often an embrace.

And then he shows considerable tact in adapting himself to the often conflicting prejudices of his heterogenous subjects. He informed us that he conforms to a great many of the customs of the country, more to conciliate and secure the goodwill of the tribes over which he rules, than because he believes in their necessity either as political or religious measures. Half Mohammedan and half pagan in his genealogy, he manifests the same hybrid characteristic in his religious demeanour. He does, to conciliate the pagan element, a great many things which the Mandingoes, from religious scruples and better knowledge, will not do. During our visit, he had his son circumcised with great pomp and ceremony, feasting and dancing, in deference to the Mohammedans; a few days after, he had the remains of a leading man, which had been interred at a distant town, in his absence, in what is called "half ground", taken up and reinterred, with all the ceremonies which the pagan customs require. This conformation to ancient customs is what has caused the King of Dahomey to be so much censured by some foreigners. That monarch is far from being the monster which he has been represented to be by interested or prejudiced men.

After the regular interment of the distinguished man, whose funeral ceremonies we have referred to above, a plate of cooked rice and other articles were brought and carefully deposited on the grave, for the use of the dead. This of course the king considers absurd, but it is in deference to an old custom. . . .

14

Liberia—its Status and its Field

African Repository, September 1872, 267–8 and October 1872, 289–96

CONSTITUTIONAL DISPUTE

At the biennial election held in May, 1869, the question of lengthening the presidential term to four years was submitted to the people. A large number voted in favour of the amendment, but the result not appearing satisfactory to the Legislature, the question was again submitted to the people in May, 1870. On the result of this second election the President and the Legislature differed. The Legislature passed a resolution declaring the amendment not carried. The President vetoed their resolution. The Legislature failing to secure a two-third vote to set aside the veto, the President and his friends held that the constitutional amendment was carried, and he refused to call the usual election in May, 1871. His opponents maintained that his course was unconstitutional, and took it upon themselves to hold an election, at which they voted, with no opposing candidate, for J. J. Roberts for President. This irregularity paved the way for numerous other irregularities, which ended in the deposition of the President.

Of course we must expect that there will be in the outside world a hue and cry against the Negro. We shall hear reiterated from the enemies of the race the charge of his incapability for self-government, as if there were no pure Negro governments in Africa over a thousand years old, conducted with a steadiness and regularity which might put to shame some of the European Governments. The people of Liberia have had many and peculiar discouragements to contend against; but they have hitherto maintained a patience and forbearance, an appreciation of liberty, a respect for order, a quickness to comprehend the nature of new institutions, and the value of new rights and obligations, at least as signal and meritorious as can be observed among many of those who are loud in proclaiming the incapacity of the Negro for freedom and self-government.

We hold that in spite of the recent proceedings in Liberia, which must be deplored by every lover of order and good government, that infant nation is on the advance. These sad events are not incompatible with the fulfilment of the noble destiny to which the

Republic is called. When, in 1847. they declared their independence, they embarked upon a political system which requires the largest experience in self-government. Democratic institutions are not the best under which to train a people who have hardly acquired the very rudiments of self-government. Hence the tendency lately to illegal violence and popular excesses. The will of the people acknowledged as supreme, will not tolerate the slowness of constitutional forms. . . . It does not even respect the privileges which, for the more efficient exercise of its own supremacy, it has itself created and transferred to a minority. The President and his Cabinet are deposed within three months of the meeting of the Legislature, because their act seems to conflict with the momentary impulses of the majority. But these irregularities are not peculiar to Liberia. We have read of wholesale *fusillades* and *noyades* in large cities much more experienced in the art of government than Liberia. But the proceedings in Liberia will no doubt be raised into prominence by foreign observers, because as an infant Negro State she has not the prestige of a much older community in Europe to veil her blunders, or the pecuniary or political influence to silence her enemies. She is bound to justify herself before the world for such acts. But Liberians, like others, must learn by experience the actual difficulties of administering a popular government. And if at this late day we are told "the French are waiting for a policy which shall insure them against military reverses and domestic misgovernment", why should the lack of administrative skill in Liberia be a matter of surprise? . . .

* * *

LIBERIAN TRIBES

The Veys extend from Gallinas, their northern boundary to Little Cape Mount, their southern boundary; and they stretch inland about two days' journey. They have invented an alphabet for writing their own language, and are enjoying the blessings of a written system, for which they are entirely indebted to their own ingenuity and enterprise. Next to the Mandingoes they are the most interesting and promising of the aboriginal population of Liberia. Some of their learned men, adepts in the traditional lore of the country, have informed us that the Veys are closely related to the Mandingoes; that they were originally inhabitants of a distant region north-east of their present country; and that, driven away from their home by war, they crossed the mountain and came to the Coast, where they carried on successful warfare against the tribes whom they found on the seaboard. Continually pressing toward the south, driving the weaker tribes before them, and forming alliance with the stronger ones, they eventually reached the banks of the St. John's river, in the Country of Grand Bassa. Having acquired an ascendant influence over the country through which they had passed, the principal men retraced their steps and settled in the region of Wakora (Grand Cape Mount), as a more delightful section of the country than any they had seen.

We are quite disposed to credit this statement. First, because the Veys, occupying the narrow extent of country between Gallinas and Little Cape Mount, are an entirely distinct people from the Mendi, on the north of them, and the Deys, on the south. The Mendi and Dey languages have no particular affinity with the Vey. Second, because the Mandingoes and all the tribes north of Liberia have a tradition of a great and widespread war in their country about the close of the seventeenth century, waged by the Foulah Mohammedans for the spread of their religion. Dr. Koelle, who lived five years at Sierra Leone, and made a collection of African stories, gives a very interesting account of those belligerent operations, gathered from the lips of intelligent natives.[1] It is possible that the Veys, unwilling to adopt the faith of Islam, and not able to resist the conquering hosts, retreated to the southwest and settled in their present locality, where . . . they have retained, amid so many incongruous elements, their tribal integrity.

*   *   *

The next tribe of importance accessible to, and under the influence of, the Liberian Republic, are the Pessehs, located about seventy miles from the Coast, and extending about one hundred miles from north to south. They may be called the peasants of West Africa. They supply most of the domestic slaves for the Veys, Bassas, Mandingoes, and Kroos. They are hard-working and industrious. It is said that the work of a Pesseh man is worth twice as much a day as that of a Vey or Bassa. The natives in the low alluvial lands of the Coast, who are given to trade, rely for the cultivation of their lands upon the skill and industry of the Pessehs who have practised agriculture on the difficult slopes of their hilly country. This people are entirely pagan. . . .

A very interesting tribe, next to the Pessehs, has recently been brought into treaty relations with Liberia by Mr. W. Spencer Anderson, namely, the *Barline*. The Barline country, about eight days' journey northeast of Monrovia, was visited in 1858 by Mr.

[1] [S.W.] Koelle's *Polyglotta Africana*, Introduction, p. 8.

James L. Sim, an intelligent young Liberian. Mr. Simms describes Palaka, the capital of Barline, as it appeared at the time as follows: "Palaka, which contained about four thousand inhabitants, half of whom were Manni-Mohammedans, and was surrounded by a clay wall nine or ten feet high, had every appearance of being a very old town. The wall in some places was in a very dilapidated condition. . . . In the centre of the town was a market place. The people were . . . most industrious, and . . . happy; it seemed as though the whole country was one immense rice farm. The Mohammedan women had several establishments for manufacturing earthen ware; while the Barline women prepared rice, palm oil, and other necessaries for market."

*   *   *

According to the account of Mr. W. Spencer Anderson, the latest explorer, there are no Mohammedans at present in the Barline country.

The next tribe, proceeding south along the coast, is that of the Bassa, occupying a coastline of over sixty miles, and extending about the same distance inland. They are the great producers of palm-oil and camwood, which are sold to foreigners by thousands of tons annually. . . .

*   *   *

The Kroomen, occupying the region of the country south of Bassa, are a large and powerful tribe, and, in many respects, more remarkable than the Bassas. They extend about seventy miles along the Coast, and only a few miles inland. They are the sailors of West Africa. They are shrewd, intelligent and manly, never enslaving or selling each other. . . .

Bordering upon the southeastern boundaries of the Kroos are the Greboes, another large and influential tribe, extending from Grand Sesters to the Cavalla river, a distance of about seventy miles. It is supposed that this people emigrated about one hundred and fifty years ago from the leeward Coast. They are said to equal the Kroomen in physical development, and to resemble them in intellectual character. Indeed, the two tribes have many points in common. The same love of freedom, the same martial qualities, the same love of maritime adventure, and the same patience of exposure and fatigue, characterize both tribes.

*   *   *

But perhaps the most interesting and promising tribe in the territory of Liberia are the Mandingoes. They are numerous, intelligent, enterprising, and not a few of them learned. They are found on the whole of the eastern frontier of the Republic, and extend back to the heart of the Soudan. Through them Liberia at no distant day may exert a considerable influence on the great and populous interior. They have books and schools and mosques in every large town. They read and write and many speak the Arabic language. They have diffused everywhere among the pagan tribes contiguous to and within the Republic, the idea of the presence and power of the Supreme Being.

. . . we learn that an ambitious young Mohammedan king, named Ibrahima Sisi, occupying a large city called Medina, has been conducting a series of warlike operations against the Kafirs in the surrounding regions to reduce them to the faith. . . . Ibrahima is an able and energetic young ruler, having under his command a vast army, terrible to the powers around him. His cavalry consists of one thousand horsemen. His organizing and direct influence in the country is said to be considerable. . . . It would be well if Liberia could secure his friendship and alliance. His capital is only about four weeks' journey from Monrovia.

We have now . . . glanced at the leading tribes composing the aboriginal population of Liberia. For the most part these people live in towns or villages of from two hundred to five thousand inhabitants, and in communities of eight or ten villages. In these communities, excepting the Mandingoes, they have no written forms of law, but are governed, as a general thing, by certain traditional usages, handed down from generation to generation. Nominally, monarchy is the only form of government acknowledged among them; but when closely scrutinized, their systems show much more of the popular and patriachal than of the monarchical element. . . .

*   *   *

The indirect influence of Liberia upon the natives has already accomplished much. . . . A new spirit has been gradually insinuating itself among them. . . . It is true that domestic slavery still exists in the interior, a circumstance which some of the friends of Liberia abroad seem to view with a degree of concern. To us, however, looking at the matter from a nearer standpoint, it is a subject of no special apprehension. It would be difficult, and perhaps impossible, for the Government of Liberia to interfere directly and effectually to any great extent with that institution. The natives all know that under the laws of Liberia every man is free. Slaves coming into the settlements or their neighbourhood, and craving Liberian protection, cannot be taken back to their masters. The evils will gradually pass away as Christian influence advances into the interior. It is well known that throughout Europe serfdom or slavery, where master and slave belonged to the same race, gradually disappeared as civilization advanced, as skill was superadded to physical strength, and as labour became more productive. Every improvement in art and science and industrial contrivance tends to diminish the value of the slave. So it must be in this country.

15

A Chapter in the History of Liberia

A.M.E. Church Review, July 1892, 48–68

It is my purpose . . . to deal with those aspects of the History of Liberia generally and of Grand Bassa County particularly, from which, at this important period in the national life, we may gather some practical and useful lessons.

It is now more than thirty years since I had the pleasure of visiting this country; and yet here was the scene of my first experiences in Liberia. Here I landed as a boy in 1851, and was initiated in the solemn mysteries of African fever, under the skilful guidance of Dr. J. S. Smith, then fresh from his studies. . . .

I was fortunate in arriving here at the time when nearly all the great men who shaped the destinies of the country and largely of the Republic survived. It was my privilege to meet and hold discourse with such men as John Day, John Hanson, William L. Weaver, Stephen Allen Benson, James Moore, John H. Cheeseman, Aaron P. Davies, Charles Henry, Matthew Rand, together with Walker Brumskine and S. S. Herring. . . .

At that time Mr. Herring, with an indomitable will and insuperable energy, was endeavouring to prove to the world, by machinery of his own invention, that the oil from the palm kernel could be made a profitable article of commerce. He succeeded, after long, painful and expensive effort, in bringing into the market an article which is now represented in the trade all along the coast by millions annually. It is not often that reformers or inventors live to witness the result of their obscure and solitary labours. Mr. Herring has been fortunate. If he has not been enriched pecuniarily, it should console him to know that the reward is in the deed itself, and that his country will reap honour and profit from his discovery.

I have often visited his workshop and watched with unflagging interest his manipulation of his new mechanical creation, and listened with pride—gathering inspiration as to the ability of the Negro—while he explained the *modus operandi*, and dwelt upon his high hopes of producing a revolution in the trade of West Africa. . . .

Liberia, insignificant as she may seem among the nations, has been instrumental in introducing into commerce two most valuable articles—viz., the palm kernel and the Liberian coffee. This coffee, brought forward by the industry and enterprise of Liberians, has been welcomed by the decaying plantations of Brazil, Central America, Natal and Ceylon, and is now cultivated in various parts of West Africa from Sierra Leone to the Gaboon.

I am confident that when this Republic comes to herself—I mean her African self . . . and understands how to co-operate with and utilize her aboriginal population, she will have many things to teach the world for the welfare and advancement of humanity.

Grand Bassa County has always held a peculiar and influential relation to the rest of Liberia. Here, from time to time, have transpired events which have had an important bearing, upon the history of the nation. It is my purpose, therefore . . . to go with you briefly over certain facts in the history of your country, so as to set up a . . . memorial for your children and your successors of the great work done . . . by our fathers. But since the history of Bassa is almost coeval with the history of Liberia, I must refer to certain dates and events preceding the actual settlement of this country which will give us a starting point. Omitting several very important circumstances connected with the sailing of the first emigrants from the United States in the ship *Elizabeth*, in February, 1820, their arrival at Sierra Leone in the following month, their removal thence to Sherbro, their sufferings and disasters in that insalubrious locality, their return to Sierra Leone and settlement at Fourah Bay, I will come to the date and the event which may be said to mark the beginning of Liberian history, viz., the month of January, 1822, when as many of the dispersed immigrants as could be collected at Freetown were brought to the Montserrado River and settled on an island at its mouth, which had been bought from the natives by Dr. [Eli] Ayres, the Agent of the American Colonization Society, in December, 1821. The island was called Perseverance Island, because it was the third spot in their fatherland which the newcomers had made an effort to occupy—which they had *persevered* in reaching, while some of their number had either died at Sierra Leone or deserted the enterprise.

Their new insular home was very circumscribed. The only shelter it afforded to the people and their stores was to be found under the decayed thatch of half-a-dozen diminutive native huts, and the place was entirely destitute of fresh water and firewood.

I will not detain you with the story of their privations and sufferings under these circumstances—how they were ill-treated by some of the aborigines, how others came to their succour and relief, and how, three months after their arrival, they began the laborious task of clearing away the heavy forest which covered the peninsula where they proposed to build their town and where now stands the city of Monrovia, the capital of the Republic.

Just as they were thinking of crossing the river and beginning preparations to occupy the heights of Montserrado, the white agent, Dr. Ayres, left for Sierra Leone and gave the superintendence of the colony into the hands of one of the colonists, Mr. Frederick James, some of whose descendants are now in Montserrado County. Mr. James, then, was the first coloured Governor of the new colony; and . . . under his counsel and example the preparations of the new habitations of the settlers advanced so rapidly as in a few weeks to present the rudiments of twenty-two dwellings, ranged in an orderly manner, on the principal street of their settlement.

The settlers were finally transferred from their narrow and inconvenient home to Cape Montserrado, in the second week in July, 1822, when the town of Monrovia may be said to have begun.

During the superintendence of Mr. James, several incidents occurred of a most trying nature, which threatened the existence of the little colony, but the settlers demeaned themselves with courage and discretion.

On the return of Dr. Ayres, the agent, with his assistant, Mr. Wiltberger, he found the settlers suffering from gloomy forebodings as to their immediate future. The store of provisions was scanty and all the other stores nearly exhausted. A storm of native hostility threatened and sickness prevailed among the people.

Under these circumstances it is not to be wondered at that the agent should have come forward with a proposal to re-embark the settlers and stores and convey them back to Sierra Leone. But a large majority of the people having entirely dissented from this proposal it was urged no further. . . .

Some of the settlers, however, availed themselves of the agent's proposal and embarked with him for Sierra Leone, leaving, exclusive of the women and children, a little force numbering only twenty-one persons capable of bearing arms.

Such was the condition of the colony when Jehudi Ashmun, who became its guide and champion, arrived. Mr. Ashmun was appointed by the United States Government as their agent to take charge of eighteen recaptured Africans to be returned to their native land. The brig *Strong* having been chartered for this service by the Government in Baltimore, the American Colonization Society took advantage of the opportunity to place on board thirty-seven emigrants with a moderate supply of stores for the new settlement, so

K

that there were fifty-five passengers on board all told. The *Strong* sailed from Hampton Roads, May 26th, 1822, but did not arrive at Monrovia until the 8th of August. Mr. Ashmun, though under commission from the United States Government, felt himself constrained by the pledge he had given the Board of Managers of the American Colonization Society, to render the colony whatever aid might be in his power. His arrival at the time he did was most opportune. He possessed all the mental and moral characteristics suited for the extraordinary labours which he was called to undergo. He was engineer, soldier, statesman, scholar, preacher, teacher, physician. He found the colony on the eve of ruin, without defence, without laws, delivered to anarchy and despair, and threatened by hostile aborigines. He fortified Monrovia, excited a military spirit in the people, became the arbiter of their quarrels, and prepared them for the fearful contest in which they were soon to engage.

So early as the 18th of August—ten days after his arrival . . . he planned the Martello tower—he employed a company of labourers to clear the ground on which it stood. He took a particular survey of the military strength and means of the settlers. Of the Americans, twenty-seven, when not sick, were able to bear arms; but they were wholly untrained to their use. There were forty muskets in store, which, with repairing, were capable of being rendered serviceable. Of one brass and five iron guns attached to the settlement, the first only was fit for service, and four of the latter required carriages. Several of these were nearly buried in the mud on the opposite side of the river. Not a yard of fencework had been constructed. There was no fixed ammunition, nor without great difficulty and delay was it possible to load the only gun which was provided with a sufficient carriage.

THE FIRST SETTLER—AFRICAN WAR

The natives, although they had been threatening the colony for several months, did not really make the attack until the settlers were in tolerably prepared condition to receive them. On the 7th of November—three months after the arrival of Mr. Ashmun—the native forces began to collect on Bushrod Island, opposite Monrovia, for an attack on the settlement. Early on the morning of the 10th, intelligence was brought to the agent that the hostile forces were crossing the Montserrado River a few miles above the settlement.

On the morning of the 11th they made their attack. They approached the small settlement, to the number of about two thousand, with savage fierceness. But they were without discipline. They suddenly presented a front of ten yards in width, at sixty distant, delivered their fire, and rushed forward with their spears to seize the post. Several of the Americans were killed or disabled by the first fire, and the remainder driven from their guns, without discharging them. Had the enemy at this instant pressed their advantage it is hardly conceivable that they should have failed of success. Their avidity for plunder was their defeat. Four houses in the outskirt of the settlement had fallen into their hands. Many rushed impetuously upon the pillage thus thrown in their way. The movement of the main body was disordered and impeded, and an opportunity afforded the agent, assisted principally by Rev. Lott Cary, to rally the broken forces of the settlers. The two central guns, with a part of their own men, and several who had been driven from the western station, were, with a little exertion, brought back into action, thirty yards in advance of the enemy.

The second discharge of a brass field-piece, double-shotted with ball and grape, brought the whole body of the enemy to a stand. That gun was well served and did great execution. The havoc would have been greater, had not the fire, from motives of humanity, been so directed as to clear the dwellings about which the enemy's force was gathered in heavy masses. These houses were known at that moment to contain more than twelve helpless women and children.

The settlers, perceiving their advantage, now regained possession of the western post, and instantly brought the long nine to rake the whole line of the enemy, eight hundred of whom were compact together, and all exposed to a gun of great power, raised on a platform, at only thirty to sixty yards distance. Every shot literally spent its force in a solid mass of human flesh! Their fire suddenly terminated. A savage yell was raised which filled the dismal forest with a momentary horror. It gradually died away and the whole host disappeared. Thus the colony escaped its first peril from an attack made by overwhelming numbers of simple barbarians, instigated by murderous foreign slave-traders. But on the part of the settlers it was soon discovered that considerable injury had been sustained. The following was the result of a return which the agent had caused to be made in the evening:

Mrs. Minty Draper, flying from her house with her two infant children, received a wound in the head from a cutlass, and was robbed of both her babes, but providentially escaped. Mrs. Ann Hawkins, who had imprudently passed the night in the house first beset by the enemy, had received thirteen wounds, and been thrown aside as dead. Mrs. Mary Tines, with the mother of five small children, finding the house in which they slept surrounded by savage enemies, barricaded the door, in the vain hope of safety. It was forced. Each of the women then seizing an axe, held the irresolute barbarians in check for several minutes longer. Having discharged their guns, the natives seemed desirous of gaining the shelter of the house previous to reloading. At length, with the aid of their spear, and by means of a general rush, they overcame their heroic adversaries, and instantly stabbed the youngest to the heart. The mother, instinctively springing for her suckling babe, which recoiled through fright and was left behind, rushed through a small window on the opposite side of the house, and providentially escaped to the lines unhurt, between two fires.

Joseph Benson, eldest son of James Benson, the father of the late President Benson, was shot dead in the beginning of the action. Thomas Spinn, mortally injured by five wounds. Billy, a native African, mortally wounded. Daniel Hawkins severely wounded through the thigh. James Benson, severely through the shoulder. There were missing two small children of Minty Draper, five children of James Benson, oldest thirteen years; one of these was the late President.

But not withstanding the signal victory achieved by the settlers, there was still sufficient ground for despondency in the following circumstances. There were not at this time, exclusive of rice, fifteen days' provisions in store. Nothing could be obtained from the country. Seven infants were in the hands of an enemy infuriated by recent losses. The ammunition of the colony was insufficient for a single hour's defence if the place were hotly attacked.

The agent, therefore, desired, if possible, to engage the kings in treaty of peace. On the 22nd of November, a message from the agent was with some difficulty got through to the council of chiefs who were engaged in debating the question of renewing hostilities at King Peter's town, a few miles northwest of Monrovia. This message expressed a desire for peace, but at the same time declared an ability and readiness to carry on the war, and with even greater vigour if the natives desired hostilities. The message left the settlement at six o'clock p.m., and at daylight the next morning an answer was received, alleging on the part of the natives certain grievances and demanding satisfaction before peace could be made. This day—the 23rd—was devoted to "humiliation, thanksgiving and prayer, both on account of recent success and losses and the actual perilous state of the settlement". Two days afterward the most pressing wants of the people were relieved by a small purchase from a transient trader touching at the Cape. On the 29th, Captain H. Brassey, an Englishman of Liverpool, touched at Monrovia, and, learning of the state of things, nearly exhausted his own stores, unasked and with no prospect of remuneration, to provide the sick and wounded with necessaries; and exerted an extensive influence acquired by a long acquaintance with the country's chiefs to disarm their hostilities. But to no purpose. They had hired a strong reinforcement from the interior and determined to make another attack, which they did with great fury and energy, and in large numbers, on the morning of December 1st.

They met with no better success, however, than on the previous occasion, but were driven back with some serious losses. . . .

But here I must refer to a circumstance not generally known by Liberians, but which is of some importance as showing the share which England took through some of her sons in the perils of the founders of Liberia. After the battle of December 1st the guards were still kept at their stations. In the dead of night, a movement discovered near one of the stations had induced the officer commanding there to open a brisk fire of musketry, accompanied with several discharges of the large guns.

The English colonial schooner *Prince Regent*, laden with military stores, and having as passengers Captain Laing, of the Royal African Light Infantry, and a prize crew, commanded by Midshipman Gordon, belonging to H.B.M. sloop-of-war *Driver*, six days from Sierra Leone, bound for Cape Coast, was at this moment in the offing and a little past the Cape. So unusual a circumstance as a midnight cannonading could not fail to attract notice, and the vessel lay by till morning. A Krooman, by whom she was then boarded, gave intelligence of the situation of the settlement. He was immediately dispatched ashore with the generous offer of any assistance in the power of the schooner to afford.

On the following morning, the officers, led by Captain Laing, landed, and, in their character as neutrals, exerted themselves to bring about peace between the colonists and the natives, which they succeeded in doing. From that time up to the present the settlements in Montserrado County have been considered entirely invincible to any native force. In each of the other counties decisive battles with the indigenous tribes, in which the colonists showed great energy and courage, have settled in the minds of the natives that they cannot attack the settlements with impunity. The repulse of the combination of Kroomen which attacked Bassa Cove in November, 1851, and the military expedition which captured and demolished their stronghold at Trade Town in 1852; the expedition to Sinoe, in 1856, to punish the tribes for the murder of certain colonists, which marched through the whole of the Sinoe and Butaw countries, capturing and destroying strongholds supposed to be impregnable; the Padee war of 1861, in which some of the most warlike tribes in Maryland County were subdued—having served to satisfy the natives within the entire territory of Liberia that it is better to live in harmony with the colonists and submit to the laws of the Republic than to pursue an opposite course.

Midshipman Gordon, brave, generous and amiable, and eleven of the crew, concluded to remain with the colonists (while their vessel continued her voyage), to guarantee the truce settled by Captain Laing. They, unhappily, were only about three weeks with the colonists, sharing in their labours and privations, when they all fell victims to their zeal and devotion to the cause of black men and laid their bodies besides those of the martyred Negro pilgrims who sacrificed themselves to lay the foundation of a home for their children. The Englishmen had no such inspiring motives. They died, not for themselves, but for others. Christians they were in deed and in truth. . . .

* * *

The character of the natives was considerably redeemed in the minds of the colonists by the treatment which they were found to have accorded to the seven hapless and tender captives. It was the first object of the native captives to place the children under the maternal care of several aged women; who, in Africa, as in most countries, are proverbially tender and indulgent. The affections of their little charges were so perfectly won in the four months of their captivity, as to oblige their own parents, at the end of that time, literally to tear from their keepers several of the youngest, amidst the most affecting demonstrations of mutual attachment. They were captured on November 11th, 1822, and returned to their parents on March 12th, 1823. Their gratuitous restoration was voted almost unanimously, in the large council of native chiefs.

The following account of his capture, as gathered from the notes of Stephen Allen Benson, may be of interest at the present time:

The party who captured him proceeded toward the present Krootown, at the base of the Cape. When about half way they halted in the forest and formed a camp. Fires were lighted in every direction. Their wounded, dying and dead, scattered around, presented a frightful spectacle, inspiring the youthful captive with indescribable sensations and fears that nothing short of his own life would satisfy their revenge. Of these anxieties he was soon relieved by their feelingly striving to offer comfort, assuring him that he should not be injured, but that, as soon as hostilities ceased, he should be restored to his family.

After a rest of two hours they turned toward the seacoast, directing their course to the St. Paul's River, the whole company walking half bent, to prevent detection by the settlers, who occupied the hill with cannon. They succeeded in reaching a native village near St. Paul's bar in the course of the day. Soon after they embarked in a canoe for Peter Bromley's Town—the site of the present settlement of Virginia, at which place they arrived the same afternoon, delivering their captive to the old chief, Peter Bromley, by whom he was kindly treated. During the four months of his captivity Stephen saw no civilized person except his brother James, who was permitted by the chief, who held him prisoner, to pay him a visit. Frequent intelligence was received from his older brothers and sisters that they were also kindly treated, thus alleviating in some degree the separation from each other.

INTERNAL IMPROVEMENTS

Peace now having been permanently established between the colony and the aborigines, Mr. Ashmun began to turn his attention to internal improvements and territorial enlargement. That able and indefatigable first Governor of the Colony, introduced in those early days nearly all the agencies of advanced and advancing civilization.

In two years he was able to report to the society complete surveys of Cape Montserrado and of the waters and contiguous lands of the Cape, of large purchases of territory on the St. Paul's, the completion of a wharf and the opening of the river-street in front of all the appropriated lands.

He could also report the existence of large public buildings, as well as a government schooner of ten tons burden, called the *St. Paul's*, built to carry on the rice trade between Monrovia and the leeward coast. In a comparatively short time fourteen boats, built by settlers, were engaged in the coasting service.

The means of maritime communication with the coast being now provided, the agent directed his attention to the acquisition of leeward territory, and in 1825 accession of territory was made in

Grand Bassa. This was the commencement of what is now the County of Grand Bassa.

On June 20th, 1826, Mr. Ashmun wrote to the Society as follows:

Our endeavours for eight months past to acquire Factory Island, the key to the Bassa district, have been crowned with success. I am more gratified with the circumstances attending this acquisition than those of any preceding one. When the proposal to purchase was first laid before the proprietor and heads of the nation, it was received with a coldness which seemed to say that though disposed to be your friends, we will never resign to you an inch of our country. We want your trade, and we value you it, but we value our country and independence more. I was satisfied, nothing could be gained, but much might be lost, by attempting to subdue, by unseasonable importunity, a reluctance apparently growing out of prudent regard to their own interests. A grant of the perpetual use of a tract of land on the south bank of the Southern Branch of the St. John's, was accordingly accepted for the present in lieu of the island. A factory was immediately established on this tract for the benefit of the colony; and James Benson (the father of the late President), a very judicious and deserving colonist, who lost the use of his arm in the battle on November 11th, 1822, was made the superintendent, with particular instructions so to conduct the business of the factory, and otherwise demean himself in all his intercourse with the people of the country, as strongly to impress them with the superiority of our characters, acts, morals and means of happiness, and with the great advantages to be expected from a settlement of civilized people.

I owe it to Mr. Benson's prudence and fidelity to state, that my views have been entirely accomplished by his manner of conducting the factory, and the management of every part of his delicate and responsible charge. The intended impression has been most effectually made.

It will appear, then, that the first Superintendent of Grand Bassa County was James Benson, the father of the President and the grandfather of the present Senator-elect from this county. In consequence of his prudent administration, Mr. Ashmun was able to effect the purchase of Factory Island, and thus secure the key to the whole Bassa country.

But for six years nothing more was done than to trade. There was no regular settlement formed until 1832, on the 18th of December, under the administration of Governor [Joseph] Mechlin, when Edina was settled by volunteers from Montserrado County. Thirty-three were first sent down from Monrovia and the other settlements as pioneers, to take possession, clear a spot for settlement, and prepare the way for the families they had left behind, and such others as might be disposed to follow. They began by opening a small space in the thick underwood, erecting their houses of rather crude construction, facing the opposite sides of a square, and then with considerable care and labour barricading their little village with a strong high fence.

For several months, they employed themselves in clearing the site upon which the town of Edina now stands, and prosecuting such work as the public good and common safety required.

The name Edina was given to the settlement in honour of the liberality of the citizens of Edinburgh, who, through Mr. Elliot Cresson, had largely contributed to the funds of the American Colonization Society, which enabled them to found the colony.

Grand Bassa seemed at once to begin to rival Montserrado in efforts for progress. But nothing great can be achieved without labour and suffering. A series of trials soon came upon the colony calculated to call out all the manhood and self-reliance of the people.

In 1835, in compliance with the repeated requests of the natives, a settlement was planted at Bassa Cove. But, in accordance with the principles of Mr. [Edward Y.] Hankinson, the white agent sent out by the society in charge of the emigrants, the settlement was not provided with the means of defence. And when the colonists complained that a hostile disposition was manifested by the natives, the agent took no measures of precaution, and even refused the proffered assistance of the people of Edina, who tendered their service to defend the colony. On the same night that this assistance was refused the natives, under King Joe Harris and his brother, King Peter Harris, attacked the settlement, murdered twenty of the defenceless inhabitants, and burnt the town. Mr. Hankinson and his wife were saved by the friendly aid of a Krooman, who concealed them and secured their escape. This murderous act was induced by a slave-trader, who, on coming to anchor in the harbour, discovered that a colony of Americans had been planted on the river, and refused to land his goods, alleging that the colonists would interrupt his trade. King Joe Harris finding that the trade in slaves was likely to be cut off resolved on the destruction of the settlement. Had the colonists been armed the attack would not probably have been made. One gun owned by a colonist, and often used by his neighbour (which fact had been noticed by some of the natives), saved both houses unmolested, and the families uninjured. The colonists who escaped were carried to Monrovia, and their wants provided for. Owing to the energetic measures adopted by Dr. [Ezekial] Skinner, the agent at Monrovia, to chastise the aggressors, the offending kings gladly accepted a peace, agreeing to abandon the slave-trade forever, to permit the interior natives to pass through their country to trade with the colony, and also to build a number of houses to replace those destroyed; and to pay for or return the property carried away.

As soon as peace was concluded Dr. Skinner laid out a town on a site which he described as healthy and beautiful, and erected buildings for the reception of the dispersed citizens.

In the early part of 1836, most of the settlers had returned to Bassa Cove. Thomas Buchanan arrived in January as special agent to take the place of Mr. Hankinson, with abundant supplies for the relief of the colony. He collected the immigrants who remained at Monrovia and brought them to Bassa.

Mr. Buchanan now selected what he considered a more eligible site for a town, at the mouth of the St. John's River, about three miles distant from that in which the first colony had located.

After completing this settlement Mr. Buchanan returned to the United States, leaving Dr. McDowell in charge of the colony, who held the agency until August, 1837, when he returned to the United States, placing the government in the hands of Dr. Wesley Johnson.

It was under Dr. Johnson that the foul murder by Kroomen of Governor [Josiah P.] Finley—the first white Governor and founder of the settlement at Sinoe—took place, between Fishtown and Bassa Cove. This outrage led to a war between the natives and the settlers of Bassa Cove, known as the Fish War of 1838.

Dr. Johnson, inexperienced in military matters, led a company of sixty men and officers to avenge the murder of Finley, but they were not prepared, either in number or with ammunition, for such an enterprise. The natives got the advantage of them and pursued them on their return up the beach until they reached Bassa Cove. The settlers having now procured ammunition, and roused to desperation by the boldness of the Fishmen, rallied and checked them for the night, with a loss on both sides. The battle was renewed in the morning and raged till three o'clock at Bassa Cove. The enemy had massed their forces on the point, when some of the brave women of Edina dragged two big guns down to the front of their settlement and by a vigorous and skilful discharge of them dislodged the Fishmen and drove them away. If Montserrado County has had its pioneer heroines so has Bassa County.

But they were making precautions for another attack, and concentrating all the native tribes in the vicinity, with the design of crushing at one blow the little band. Matters continued thus until December, when reinforcements arrived from Monrovia and the other forces of the two counties, under the command of Major W. L. Weaver, completely routed the enemy. The settlements had now some rest.

In the month of May, 1839, Governor Buchanan again arrived from the United States, quite unexpectedly, to the great joy and relief of the settlers. This sagacious philanthropist and statesman soon summoned the hostile chiefs and arranged matters on a satisfactory footing, exacting suitable indemnity for the murder of Governor Finley.

At the time of Governor Buchanan's arrival the condition of things in all the settlements was deplorable; but by the wisdom and energy of his administration he soon inspired the despondent colonists with new life and the supporters of the cause in America with confidence in the operations of the Society. All the settlements were placed under one government during his administration and formed the COMMONWEALTH OF LIBERIA.

Exhausted by the variety and abundance of his labours, he succumbed to a virulent attack of fever, at Bassa Cove, on September 3rd, 1841. The death of Liberia's last white Governor having occurred in this county, it devolved upon a committee of leading citizens [William L. Weaver, Nathaniel Harris, John Day, and Louis Sheridan] to announce the melancholy event to the Lieutenant-Governor at Monrovia, Hon. J. J. Roberts, and notify him of his succession to the responsible post. . . .

PRELUDE TO INDEPENDENCE

The . . . occurrence which thrust upon us . . . the responsibility of self-government, was only the prelude to the far more important event which took place six years afterwards—the assumption by the colony of independent nationality. Perhaps very few living here now are aware that the events which hastened on the independence of Liberia occurred chiefly in this county—events which opened the eyes of the majority of Liberians to the anomaly and helplessness of their position as a colony without a mother country.

As early as 1840, Governor Buchanan complained of the violation of the revenue laws by an English schooner, the *German*, Captain Jackson, master, who traded with Fishmen at the Cove, taking off about two thousand gallons of palm oil.

Again, in 1841, in a dispatch dated April 5th, 1841, the Governor said:

Another case of collision with our laws on the part of an English trader occurred while I was at Bassa, or rather two cases. The *African*, of Sierra Leone, refused to pay anchorage and went off without doing so. The *Ranger*, of London, also refused to pay anchorage or duties on goods she was landing. The Collector seized and detained her boats, whereupon the payment was made; but the Captain (Dring) immediately declared his intention of going down to the point and dealing with the Fishmen. He was told he would not be allowed, and was also informed of the penalties which were attached to such a violation of our laws. This, however, did not deter him, and he weighed anchor and ran down and anchored off the Cove. I ordered the Collector there to take a few men and go down and prevent his taking off or landing any property. The Collector, however, was opposed in his duty, and Dring took away, in spite of this, six puncheons of oil.

But after the death of Buchanan the foreigners became bolder in their aggressions. In the early part of 1845 the schooner *John Seys*, the property of Stephen Allen Benson, lying in the harbour of Grand Bassa, was captured by Her Britannic Majesty's sloop *Lily*, commander Newton, on "suspicion of being engaged in the slave-trade, and carried to Sierra Leone for adjudication". But the Court of Admiralty found no just cause for her detention. She was released, but, strange to say, the Court decided that the owner should pay the captor's cost, amounting to some twelve hundred dollars. Mr. Benson, of course, refused to pay the cost. The vessel was therefore sold some time afterwards by Mr. Charles Heddle for two hundred and twenty pounds sterling. Mr. Benson sustained a loss of about twelve thousand dollars, cargo inclusive. The colony being entirely nondescript, had no rights which the laws of nations could respect. These facts aroused the thinking people in the counties, especially of Montserrado and Sinoe, to the desire for an independent national existence.

In Bassa County, owing to certain misrepresentations and misconceptions, there was curiously at first a strong feeling on the part of a few against assuming an independent attitude; but there were clear-headed and able men in the county at the time, who overcame the plots of the factious and discontented.

There were resident here then Rev. John Day,[1] with his culti-

[1] See Selection 10, Part II [ed.].

vated and critical intellect; Rev. Amos Herring, with his practical commonsense and powerful oratory; Colonel Weaver, with the force and fervour of an original mind and commanding influence; Judge Hanson, with his simple, straightforward and effective eloquence; Dr. James Moore, with his impulsive ardour and impressive eccentricities; Judge Benson, with his intellectual culture and manly and patriotic sympathies; Rev. John H. Cheeseman, with his spontaneous loyalty, his scholarly instincts and fluent utterance. There were giants in those days. . . .

The trials through which the county had passed had had the effect to call forth in the settlers a degree of manliness and self-reliance which, when they saw the truth, enabled them cheerfully and intelligently to confront the dangers and responsibilities of independent nationality.

When the time arrived for the convention to form a Constitution for the new State, Bassa sent four of her strongest men to represent her in that important assembly—John Day, A. W. Gardner, Amos Herring, Ephraim Titler. The Constitution and Declaration of Independence were adopted during a session of thirty days, and on July 29th, 1847, Liberia having been proclaimed a free, sovereign and independent State, an appeal was made to the nations for recognition. The form of government adopted was republican, and the model followed was the United States. The people knew no other.

The first session of the legislature of the new republic was held in January, 1848, and the county of Grand Bassa was represented in the Senate by John Hanson and William L. Weaver; in the House of Representatives by Henry B. Whitfield, Matthew A. Rand and Edward Liles—men who made their mark upon the legislation of the country in those early days.

Grand Bassa has given to Liberia two Presidents and is about to give us a third—all of them, curiously enough, connected in some way with the legal profession. And I feel that I can extend no better wish to the President-elect than that he should emulate the example of his predecessors from this county, who for practical commonsense and constructive statemanship have had no superior in the Presidential chair.

When the lone star of Liberia was unfurled to the breeze, as the emblem of republican nationality on the coast of Africa and the harbinger of Africa's redemption, it was hailed with enthusiastic and genuine applause by the foremost nations of Europe, though they were not without misgivings as to the result of the experiment.

In the month of October, 1848, both England and France, in a most liberal and complimentary manner, gave formal recognition to the State. Soon after, the following announcement appeared in the English papers: "The Lords of the Admiralty have ordered the *Lark*, a small vessel lying at Chatham, to be fitted as a yacht, for the use of the African Republic of Liberia."

The French government gave orders to the French naval commander on the West African Station, to put at President Roberts' disposal two or three ships of war, whenever they were needed for the destruction of slave Barracoons and to promote otherwise the interests of humanity.

It is well known . . . that they both, with the ships of the American squadron on the coast, rendered efficient help in establishing the prestige of the young nation along the coast, in the eyes not only of the natives, but of foreign traders.

When by constant service the *Lark* became unseaworthy, Her Majesty's Government generously supplied her place by another splendid schooner, the *Quail*.

But for these generous services, rendered especially by Her Majesty's Government, the Republic would have suffered serious detriment from the jealousy of unprincipled foreign traders, who stimulated the aborigines to, and supplied them with the facilities for, effective rebellion against the authority of the new State. Grand Bassa County was especially exposed to the plots of these alien freebooters and aboriginal savages.

The Republic had hardly attained the fourth year of its existence when an extensive and formidable combination (referred to above) of certain sections of the Kroo and Bassa tribes threatened the extinction of the settlements in this county. In 1851, the natives, by sudden onset, massacred the Garrison at Fishtown and followed up this atrocious deed by a well-planned attack upon the settlement at Bassa Cove.

On the memorable 15th of November in that year the famous battle took place, in which the notorious Tarplan, leading an untold number of infuriated natives, made a bold, courageous and daring attack upon the settlements, and for several minutes the contest was uncertain; but the heroism of the colonists, excited to the highest point by the imminence of their peril scattered the countless multitude by skilfully managed artillery, disconcerted their leaders, captured their chief warrior and drove them in confusion down the beach.

The military expedition set on foot a few months after by the Liberian government, and which after a severe struggle captured and destroyed the stronghold of the enemy at Trade Town . . . and gave the Republic unquestioned supremacy over the whole coast. . . .

There is no other community of Christian Africans anywhere which holds the relations to the civilized world and to aboriginal Africa which Liberia sustains. Our laws regulate the proceedings of nearly two millions of people, along four hundred miles of coast, and in an indefinite interior.

But we have assumed the responsibilities of a very difficult form of government. A republican government is a highly artificial organization. It is really an ideal government, never yet fully realized anywhere. It is not natural to man as an individual to be a republican, which means all for one and one for all. . . . It is not natural to man to be willing to lose himself in the public weal. . . .

. . . Left to nature every man is an egotist—a savage—taking pleasure in achieving results by force and holding his acquisitions for his own purposes.

When men rose out of their primitive state into higher intellectuality, and began to occupy loftier moral planes, they began to see that their highest welfare could be best promoted, their deeper and more permanent well-being secured by combining, merging in one, their separate interests for the advantage of all; but still there is ever and anon manifested the natural tendency wherever there is the least opportunity to monopolize. In advanced countries, especially the United States, they try to counteract this tendency to selfish monopoly by political parties, but it is found at times that the parties themselves become a vast machine run in the interests of monopolists. They develop "bosses", who are often as autocratic as any absolute ruler. . . .

* * *

Now, in Liberia, we have a republican constitution with hardly any of the machinery for carrying on a republican government. In the early days of the colony, the people enjoyed many of the elements of growth which we now look for in vain. There were schools established with the beginning of the settlements and the first newspaper, the *Liberia Herald*, was founded in 1826, when the colony was only four years old. It was suspended for awhile, after a brief existence, but was revived by John B. Russwurm, a cultivated colonist, in 1830, and soon acquired a large circulation, not only in America but in Europe. I have seen it referred to in a letter in Paris by General Lafayette, the great friend of the United States and of the American Colonization Society. The *Herald* continued for thirty years. . . .

In Grand Bassa County, as early as 1842, a high school was in full operation on Factory Island, under the able principalship of Dr. Wesley Johnson; and at Edina there was a printing press under the management of Baptist missionaries, printing the Scriptures and the school-books in the Bassa language. . . .

*   *   *

We have been received into the family of nations. We have tried to copy the United States. It is incumbent upon us, if we would retain the respect of the nations with whom we are in treaty relations, to introduce the resources and methods of civilization. We must have improved schools, newspapers, roads, steam communication by land and water, lighthouses, revenue vessels to represent the government. In these days of "scramble for Africa" and contempt for paper rights, men laugh at our pretense to control a coast of four hundred miles on which not a single government craft appears.

In the absence of the agencies of culture for our people, we notice on the one hand a tendency to the worst forms of democracy, which is the government of the unfittest, and on the other, a disposition to the monoply of power—to an autocratic and pernicious oligarchy—by the wire-pullers of political parties. Now, it is not difficult to predict what the end must be, if there be no change. We shall become the "tool of avaricious speculation", and the victims "of grasping ambition". The country will pass out of the hands of its present rulers into those of the untrained aborigines and of foreigners.

I have been very much impressed by the following passage in one of President Roberts' messages (1849), which I think is even more applicable now than when it was delivered:

As the term of many of our civil officers will expire during the present session of the legislature, it will be my duty to nominate for your approval persons to fill such offices as may be vacant. I ask for you, gentlemen of the Senate, not to approve the nomination of any man in whose qualifications to discharge the duties to which he may be nominated you have not the utmost confidence.

As public men, you are to know neither friend nor foe: fear not resentment. I need not remind you that much depends upon the selection of proper persons to occupy the various departments of the government. In the appointment of officers intrinsic merit should be the sole rule of promotion. No time ever required more economy, industry, patriotism and true devotion to the public cause than the present.

The Republic of Liberia has so far lacked *individuality*. I mean to say that it has not shown any special or peculiar adaptation to the situation it occupies. It has not given evidence of such distinct individuality as makes a man or a nation interesting and indispensable on certain lines of work. Any European colony could have done as much and more on the line we have been pursuing.

It is a truth at which not only we ourselves, but thinking foreigners are arriving, that Africa is to be elevated and civilized by Africans—not merely because of the physical adaptation, but on account of the mental idiosyncracy of Africans; not only on account of the colour of the Negro, but because of his psychological possibilities and susceptibilities.

In some respects it might be well for us to go back in the government of this country to the aboriginal common sense of our forefathers. They did not know the names for certain political regulations, but they attained all the wholesome results which those regulations are intended to produce . . . we profess to have a government founded on political science, but we lack the practicality of the empire.

Referring to the practical knowledge of the natives, President Benson in his first inaugural address said:

If we look at the aborigines of this land, and carefully study their organizations and method of government, we cannot avoid discovering incontrovertible proof of their possessing the elements of a great nation. We are oft-times constrained to admire the facility with which most of the chiefs rule their subjects, and the cheerful and often dignified obedience and respect rendered by subjects to their chiefs and the laws; and but for the accursed slave-trade of bygone years, by which they have been greatly corrupted, and which has contributed so much to the subversion of their domestic and social happiness, those very heathens would set a pattern of governing talent and governable disposition by which several of the proud civilized nations of the earth might be profited.

As you have heard in the course of the narrative, it was fifty years on the 3rd of September—two months ago—since the government of Liberia fell into the hands of Africans. . . .

16

The Three Needs of Liberia

A lecture delivered at Lower Buchanan, Grand Bassa County, Liberia, January 26th, 1908; published London, 1908, 1–31

This year we celebrate the eighty-sixth anniversary of the founding of the city of Monrovia by the Negro settlers from America. The colony is nearly ninety years old. The Republic has just celebrated its Diamond Jubilee. Still Liberia is called by foreigners an experiment. Nothing of the kind has ever happened before in the world's history. A group of returned exiles—refugees from the house of bondage—settled along a few hundred miles of the coast of their Fatherland, attempting to rule millions of people, their own kith and kin, on a foreign system in which they themselves have been imperfectly trained, while knowing very little of the facts of the history of the people they assume to rule, either social, economic or religious, and taking for granted that the religious and social theories they have brought from across the sea must be adapted to all the need of their unexpatriated brethren.

Liberia is a little bit of South Carolina, of Georgia, of Virginia— that is to say—of the ostracized, suppressed, depressed elements of those states—tacked on to West Africa—a most incongruous combination, with no reasonable prospect of success; and further complicated by additions from other sources. We take a bit from England, a little bit from France, a little bit from Germany, and try to compromise with all. We have no definite plan, no dominating race conception, with really nothing to help us from behind—the scene whence we came—and nothing to guide us from before the goal to which we are tending or should tend. . . . We are severed from the parent stock—the aborigines—who are the root, branch, and flower of Africa and of any Negro State in Africa.

. . . Our progress will come by connection with the parent stock. The question, therefore, which we should try to study and answer is, What are the underlying principles of *African* life? Every nation and every tribe has a right to demand freedom of life, and abundance of life, because it has a contribution to make peculiar to itself toward the ultimate welfare of the world. But no nation can have this freedom of life, and make this contribution, which no other nation can make, without connection with its past, of which it must carefully preserve the traditions, if it is to understand the

119

present and have an intelligent and inspiring hope of the future.

*   *   *

. . . Now, what do we need for our relief, our deliverance, our growth and permanent success? . . . THE THREE NEEDS OF LIBERIA . . . are 1st, EMANCIPATION. 2nd, ILLUMINATION. 3rd, HARMONIZATION.

First, then, we need Emancipation. When the first Negro emigrants for Liberia left the United States in the good ship *Elizabeth* in 1820, they escaped *physical* bondage. And when Abraham Lincoln in 1863, proclaimed freedom for the Negroes throughout the United States, he delivered them from material shackles which hampered and degraded the body. The body was set free, but the soul remained in bondage. Therefore, the intellectual, social and religious freedom of the American ex-slave has yet to be achieved. When our fathers came across the Atlantic they brought with them the social, industrial, and religious trammels that bound them to the intellectual and material "fleshpots" of America. Those trammels they transmitted to us. They could not help themselves. The mere passage across the sea did not change their mental condition.

And now, we, their descendants, call ourselves Americo-Liberians or Afro-Americans, that is to say, Africans with the prejudices and predilections—the bias and aspirations—of white men: with "ideals", as Sir Harry Johnston has told us in his extraordinary *History of Liberia* (1906), "pitifully Anglo-Saxon"; and these "ideals", altogether unattainable, are nevertheless, the burden, the stumbling block and the opprobrium of this nation. They beguile us into efforts to introduce a condition of things under which Europe and America are helplessly staggering, and compel us to take upon ourselves and labour to solve the problems of a foreign climate and an alien race, which of course takes away from us the desire, the disposition and the ability to study our own problems and their solution. . . .

*   *   *

Africa, therefore, has a right to demand of Europe, in replying to its indiscriminate appeals for the demolition among us of immemorial customs, an answer to the following question: "If we abolished customs known and tried and helpful to us, and adopted yours, what shall we do with our submerged tenth, our thieves, and prostitutes?" But, alas, this is a question which Europe and America are trying in vain to answer for themselves. Then Africa must say to our would-be benefactors on these subjects: "Great and good friends, *you* grapple with *your* domestic and social problems and leave us to grapple with *ours*. In political, military, material and financial problems we need and solicit your guidance and help, but as to the subtle problems which involve the physical, physiological and spiritual or psychological well-being of the people, we deprecate your benevolent but dislocating interference. . . .

*   *   *

Owing to our false training we have been legislating as Americans in America for Americans. We have been disposing of the lands of the country and we are still disposing of them on the foreign system we have been taught. But everywhere amongst us this system has failed. We have been perpetrating the absurdity of measuring out and partitioning lands to the natives, who are the lords of the soil. In many places they laugh at us because they know that in the order of Nature these lines of demarcation must disappear. By the system we are trying to introduce we always in the long run create wildernesses instead of farms and cities. Let us then study African conditions and legislate according[ly]. . . .

*   *   *

In Liberia we have failed in Agriculture, as a permanent and successful feature in our industrial system, and shall always fail because we are trying to work the land on the gang system which we learned in America. That is not the African system. It is not the natural system. It has been introduced in Europe and America and has led to the inequalities which are producing the unrest in those countries. In England farming is complicated by three distinct interests. First, there is the owner of the land; then there is the tenant or hirer of the land; then the labourer on the land. In Africa there is only one interest and that is the people's interest. Farming is communistic, allied to and guided by a patriarchal head. The land is owned by everybody. The men, women and children all work, engage in labour as a duty they owe to themselves and to each other, and all reap equal rewards. That is unto each according to his several ability. Under the African system there can be no absolutely rich man and no absolutely poor man.

Now in coming from America with foreign ideas in our head, we have tried to reverse all this, and create the distinctions which exist in Europe and America, but we have nowhere succeeded. We have been striving to produce the independently rich man, with its opposite, the abjectly poor, but we have everywhere egregiously failed. There is not a man reputedly rich fifty years ago, who has left a single trace of his position. Not a single farmer who, thirty years ago, was at the height of prosperity, exists today. The fault is not in those who persist in breaking its laws. White men tell us of the necessity and the importance of there being class distinctions—rich men and poor men—princes and beggars—in every community, but this is not Christ's idea, and it is not the African idea. The African idea is the idea of the first Christian Church— "One for all and all for one". . . .

Now this model is in entire agreement with African instincts. Our mind runs in an entirely different channel from that of the white man. We occupy an entirely different standpoint. We cannot judge by his standards or feel with his feelings. Yet from sheer necessity we have in our Schools and Colleges been using his textbooks on moral, social and religious subjects; but as we learn more and more of African customs and study more and more the kingdom of God within us, we shall find that the political economy of the white man is not our political economy, his moral philosophy is not our moral philosophy, and far less is his theology our theology; and wherever he has been successful in forcing these upon us there has been atrophy and death.

*   *   *

You will see, then that for life and effective work in the country, the Liberians need to be *Emancipated* from the social, industrial and religious theories which they have brought with them from America. When they have been emancipated they will ". . . discern, unseen before, The path to higher destinies". They will then feel the necessity of ILLUMINATION—enlightenment as to the laws governing the true life of the African in Africa. Our people know very little of the laws which regulate and fix the course and destiny of life.

The first Pilgrim fathers, before they left America, organized a Baptist Church, in Richmond, Virginia, went on board the *Elizabeth*, as a Church, landed at Monrovia thus organized and founded the Providence Baptist Church in Monrovia. There were a few individuals of other denominations among the first immigrants but they were not organized. The Baptist Church then was the first institution of the kind in Liberia—and the only institution of any kind, which has maintained unbroken continuity for eighty-six years. This church then has a right and a claim, which it ought at once to assert, to form itself into an organization to develop the true African Religion begotten by the teachings and nourished by the pure and sincere milk of the words of Christ.

Perhaps it cannot do this now; it cannot see the pillar of cloud by day and the pillar of fire by night. . . . But the time will come— and is perhaps nearer than we think—when without effort, without struggle, the morning star on the Baptist banner will fade into the brilliant light of the Sun of Righteousness. President Barclay, in his admirable State Paper delivered to the Legislature the other day, told us that the stoppage of immigration from America has given to the Liberians the opportunity or forced upon them the necessity of studying the aborigines—the life and backbone of the country.

Our white friends in America do not now take the same interest in the emigration of Negroes to Africa that they did forty or fifty years ago. Then the politicians wished to get rid of the surplus Negro population as a burden and a menace, and the philanthropists wanted to found a nation on the American model of repatriated Africans in Africa; while the Christians wanted to establish a centre in West Africa for the evangelization of the continent. But time has changed all that. The politicians now want the blacks to remain in America to plant cotton; the philanthropists do not see why they should not be happy in the South, especially in the Black Belt, where if they do not now they will soon outnumber the whites; while the Christians are not enthusiastic over the results of their two generations of expenditure of life and treasure upon what experience and science are now telling them is a hopeless task. They now feel that the work of evangelization had better be left to the Africans themselves. The white Presbyterians and the white Baptists have retired from the scene.

Americans generally are also beginning to recognize that the manifest destiny in their country is the blending in material political and religious work of the conglomerate forces existing in the land. So far as Liberia is concerned, the aim of its leaders is to make the Republic an essentially African State. That is what is implied in the recent [1907] amendment of the Constitution substituting the word *Negro* for the word *coloured*. Liberia is, then, first and foremost a Negro State. That is its basis and that must be its superstructure. All efforts to de-Negroize it will prove abortive. To have a little bit of South Carolina, of Georgia, of Virginia, as component elements of the State is not progress. We do not want the same thing in Africa we left in America. Progress is difference. The object of the Christianity we profess is that "the thoughts of many hearts may be revealed"; it is not to suppress individuality but to develop and emphasize it.

I smile when I hear some Liberians express the apprehension that if they were to conform to the laws of Africa—the constitutions established by Nature—they would be internationally ostracized. Why I am sure that our national status would be immensely advanced and our international relations strengthened. England and France and Germany and the United States would be too pleased to welcome a new plant, if genuine, in the flora of nations. At any rate, it is better to be censured or even ridiculed for being yourself than applauded for trying to be somebody else.

*   *   *

Since we are not to get emigrants from America just now and we have emphasized by Constitutional provision the aspiration of the nation for racial distinctiveness, it is wisdom to study our surroundings and get light on the subject. The race in its integrity is in the interior. . . . We are but fragments of it; and without the rock whence are hewn we are but vanishing fragments.

The great European Powers, who, since the memorable and disreputable scramble five-and-twenty years ago, have been trying to govern the natives according to the laws of Europe, have found out their mistake, chiefly through the information imparted to them by their own travellers, who have run to and fro in Africa and have increased knowledge, Mary Kingsley[1] being in the lead. They have now understood that Africa has a social, industrial and religious system, which has been in existence for millenniums, and they are making strenuous and praiseworthy efforts to study it. They recognize that the proper function of education is to help Nature; therefore, they want to know the direction in which Nature is going that they may assist her movements. The failure of their former methods—the dislocations, disintegrations and exterminations resulting from them—show that they were wrong; that where they did not produce corpses they created apes and criminals.

The January (1908) number of the *Journal of the African Society* contains interesting articles on these efforts to study the Native and to codify Native laws by Germany and England. France has long done this. . . .

Liberia has not yet the illumination necessary on this subject. She has lately been giving attention (and we can hardly blame her for this, having regard to her foreign relations and responsibilities),

[1] An influential British propagandist who made two trips to French West Africa between 1893 and 1895 and authored two major works on West Africa: *Travels in West Africa*, London, 1897, reprinted Frank Cass, 1965; and *West African Studies*, London, 1900, reprinted Frank Cass, 1964 [ed.].

to codifying laws made on foreign models by her legislatures during the last sixty years. But recent discoveries of travel and science are revealing the fact that every race, every State, which is to lead a life of its own, has a constitution existing in the nature of things, written in "the manuscripts of God". It cannot be read at once and adopted by sudden enactment. It comes to the knowledge of the people by slow degrees, by years and years of experiment and experience. The Constitution of England has grown and continues to grow out of circumstances.

Liberia, as she stands, is racially an unconstitutional State in Africa. She has made laws for her social, industrial and religious government in conflict with the natural Constitution of the country, and she finds that in many instances her laws or so-called laws are null and void because against the established order of Nature. We need, then, you will see, *Illumination* as to the laws of African life. We must learn to occupy the standpoint of our aboriginal brother, and to believe that in his place there is no man under the sun better than or equal to him.

PART III

Africa—Its History and Culture

PART III

Africa—Its History and Culture

Blyden was primarily a propagandist. All his writings were concerned to defend, champion and inspire his race. Very seldom did he write "straight" history and sociology: almost always they were used to better the image and bolster the confidence of black men; almost always they were accompanied by expressions of hopes and fears and prescriptions for future action.

But Blyden did possess the scholar's respect for diligent and critical enquiry: there are in his writings no obvious or crude distortions. The most significant selection in this section from a scholarly point of view is that on *African Life and Customs* (1908), his single most important work apart from *Christianity, Islam and the Negro Race*. Blyden was not the first West African to produce a major work of a sociological nature. Two Ghanaians, John Mensah Sarbah, author of *Fanti Customary Laws* (1897)[1] and *Fanti National Constitution* (1906),[2] and J. E. Casely Hayford, author of *Gold Coast Native Institutions* (1903)[3] preceded him. But his was the first important attempt at sociological generalizations on the institutions and customs of West African societies. At a time when Europeans, with rare exceptions, were as yet hardly convinced that African societies deserved "scientific study", Blyden had produced a work concerned to show that there existed "an African Social and Economic System most carefully and elaborately organized, venerable, impregnable, indispensable". This work could still stand as a useful short introduction to the sociology of West Africa.

Perhaps the next most interesting Selection is (20)—his account of his visit to the Egyptian pyramids and of his conviction that they were the work "of his African progenitors". Here history blends with contemporary chronicle to make exciting reading. Selection (17) argues that Africans are not inherently inferior; in (18) he describes the Liberian efforts to end the slave trade on its coast and the French attempt in the 1850s to recruit there "voluntary" labour for their West Indian colonies; in (19) he argues plausibly that "the tribes in . . . [West] Africa lived in a condition not very different from that of the greater portion of Europe", and in (21), he

---

[1] Reprinted Frank Cass, 1968.
[2] Reprinted Frank Cass, 1968.
[3] Reprinted Frank Cass, 1970.

protests against the derogatory terms used by Europeans to refer to the Negro Race and the African continent.

These writings, together with those of a similar nature on Liberia, add up to make Blyden a not insignificant pioneer historian and sociologist of Africa.

17

A Vindication of the African Race

Liberia's Offering, New York, 1862, 55–62

AFRICAN PHYSIOGNOMY

The physiognomical character of Africans is also urged as an argument in favour of the servile destiny of the race. This being the popular opinion, the greatest unfairness is generally practiced in the representations which Caucasian naturalists and ethnologists make of African features. This may appear a small matter, but we do not deem it altogether unworthy of notice. No matter how men, in their public opinions, may ridicule as absurd arguments thus founded, yet, in their private feelings, they are to a great extent influenced by them. We have observed that, generally in geographies or books on ethnography, the heads given as proper specimens of the African are pictures of some degraded slaves of poor physical development; while to represent the Caucasian race, the head of some philosopher, or of some very beautiful female is presented as a fair specimen of that whole race. They give "the *highest* type of the European and the *lowest* type of the Negro". Now we say this is unjust. That there are irregularities in the African features, is no reason that in representing them the *very worst* should be taken as specimens. This is done, however, to carry out the idea of phrenological inferiority to the other races, at least to the Anglo-Saxon race. Hence, whenever any one of this doomed people gives evidence of superior ability and talents, the disposition is to deny his connection with the genuine Negro. No candid and unprejudiced mind can read with patience the unwarrantable description furnished by Mr. [Thomas J.] Bowen, an American missionary adventurer on this coast, of what he calls "the true or typical Negro".[1] It is a pandering to prejudices entirely unpardonable in one of his profession, whose object should be to eradicate, and not to foster the seed of error. And nothing is more instinctively ridiculous than his laboured but resultless endeavour to prove that all the interior native tribes of regular and agreeable features, and of favourable mental characteristics, are the descendants of Europeans. If such are the results of his philosophical and scientific investigations, it would have been more creditable to his reputation, and of

[1] Bowen's *Central Africa*, Chapter XXIII, pp. 280, 281.

less disservice to the cause of truth, to have confined himself to the regions of common-sense.

But the intellectual character of a race can not fairly be argued from the physical appearance of some of its individuals. The external appearance is not always the index of the intellectual man. Notwithstanding the claims and pretensions of phrenology, the old adage should not be neglected: "Judge not of things by their outward appearance."

* * *

AFRICAN "INHERENT LOVE OF SLAVERY"

Another ground of argument with some in favour of the application of Noah's malediction to Africans, and their consequent inferiority to the other races, is the preference for slavery which some emancipated slaves have shown, either refusing to be set at liberty or returning into bondage after having been liberated. But they forget that this is by no means unusual, nor peculiar to the African race. The effect of slavery is to render the mind congenial to itself. Slavery begets in the slave adaptation and attachment to slavery. It is a principle of the human mind to love that to which long familiarity has accustomed it, particularly if it has been led by any means to believe that the object to which it is accustomed is productive of benefit. . . .

* * *

Cases are not wanting of coloured people fleeing from American bondage to Liberia, who, meeting a few difficulties, and unused to the task of self-reliance, wish to return and live their former life of ease and freedom from care. Some do return, and bear back evil reports of this good land. These cases are painful, but they are not surprising; they are illustrations of the invariable effects of slavery. Nor is it to be wondered at that even in Liberia, an African government, free, sovereign, and independent, there should be . . . "a degree of deference shown to white men that is not shown to coloured". This will be the case in every African community for a long time, even after the entire abolition of slavery in the Western world. This reverence of the oppressed for the oppressor . . . is not easily shaken off. Such is the influence of the latter upon the former, that their voice on any question has the effect to hush into the profoundest silence the least murmur of dissent on the part of the former.

It is however, incumbent upon the intelligent among the African race, to discountenance as much as possible this servile feeling, and to use every means to crush it wherever it appears, for its influence on the mind and morals and general progress of the race is fearfully injurious.

THE INFLUENCE OF ASPERSIONS UPON NEGROES

If an ignorant man be calumniated, and that calumny be founded upon facts of Theology, Science, or Philosophy, branches of learning with which he is, of course, utterly unacquainted, it will not be surprising if that man, even with the facts of his consciousness before him, contradictory of such calumny, should believe it, and shape his course of conduct in accordance with its *dicta*. So has it been, generally speaking, with the African race. We have been under those whose interest it was to give credit, importance, and circulation to the current aspersions against our race : and who, having all the influence over us which education, wealth, and power can confer, have succeeded too well in working in the minds of many the belief that we are a people accursed, and that, in consequence, we are in every respect inferior to them. Hence we see many ignorant and unfortunate persons of colour under the poisoning influence of this inculcated belief, who make no effort towards improvement, believing that their state has been fixed by an irreversible decree—a state of unconditional inferiority to the Caucasian. There is among such persons a constant distrust of each other; a disposition to repose with greater confidence in persons of another race; a want of faith in any thing remarkable done or projected by their own people. . . .

It is earnestly to be hoped that in the Republic of Liberia no such feeling will exist. Nothing can be more detrimental to our progress. It will act like an incubus upon our energies. Let us, when our brethren come among us from the land of bondage, poisoned with the opinion of the inferiority of the African race, endeavour as soon as possible to eradicate the notion. And let us teach our children from their infancy, for they need to be taught—that no curse except that which every day follows the impenitent, hangs upon us; that it is the force of circumstances, induced, as we have endeavoured to show, by our iniquities, that keep us down; and that we have as much right as any other people to strive to rise to the very zenith of national glory. . . .

18

A Chapter in the History of the African Slave-Trade

Anglo-African, June 1859; *Liberia's Offering*, New York, 1862, 157–163

The close of the eighteenth century, when experience had proved the traffic (in slaves) to be at variance with the laws of God and an outrage upon humanity, witnessed the inauguration of various efforts on the part of the philanthropists in England for the destruction of its legality. Mr. Wilberforce, having introduced the motion in Parliament "that the trade carried on by British subjects for the purpose of obtaining slaves on the African coast ought to be abolished", the friends of the motion ceased not in their efforts until on February 10th, 1807, a committee of the whole House passed a bill "that no vessel should clear out for slaves from any port within the British dominions after May 1st, 1807", fifteen years after the introduction of Mr. Wilberforce's motion. The legality of the traffic being thus overthrown by England, and by other nations following in her wake, the horrors of the traffic manifestly declined, and honourable commerce could again be prosecuted with some measure of safety.

The temporary immunity of the coast from the horrors attendant upon the slave-trade, occasioned by the passage of the British "Abolition Act", furnished an opportunity to certain philanthropists in America to carry out an idea which had originated years previously, of planting on the west coast of Africa a colony of civilized Africans, but which had seemed impracticable in consequence of the unlimited and pernicious sway which the slavers held on the coast. In the year 1816 a Society was instituted under the denomination of the "American Colonization Society", for the purpose of colonizing in Africa, with their own consent, free persons of colour of the United States. In 1820, the necessary preparations having been made, the ship *Elizabeth* sailed from the United States with a company of eighty-eight emigrants for the west coast of Africa. After various trials and difficulties they landed on Cape Montserrado and succeeded in establishing themselves. But scarcely had they entrenched themselves when the slavers, a few of whom still hovered on the coast and had factories in the vicinity of Montserrado, began to manifest their hostility to the settlers, endeavouring in every possible way to break up the settlement; while the aboriginal neighbours of the colonists, finding that the presence of the colony was diminishing very considerably their gains from the unhallowed trade, indulged a lurking enmity which only awaited opportunity to develop itself. But the opportunity was not long in offering, for the colony was hardly two years old when it was desperately assailed by untold numbers of savages who came down in wild ferocity upon the feeble and defenceless company, and must have swept away every trace of them had not a merciful Providence vouchsafed deliverance to the weak. The settlers triumphed against overwhelming odds.

The slave-traders, notwithstanding the signal defeat of their native allies in the traffic, were not willing to abandon a scene which for scores of years they had unmolestedly and profitably infested. "From eight to ten, and even fifteen vessels were engaged at the same time in this odious traffic almost under the guns of the settlement; and in July of the same year (1825), contracts were existing for eight hundred slaves to be furnished in the short space of four months, within eight miles of the Cape. Four hundred of these were to be purchased for two American traders."[1] During the same year Mr. Ashmun, agent of the American Colonization Society, wrote to the Society: "The colony only wants the right; it has the power to expel this traffic to a distance, and force it at least to conceal some of its worst enormities." From this time the Society began to take into consideration the importance of enlarging the territory of the colony, and thus including within its jurisdiction several tribes, in order both to protect the settlement against the evil of too great proximity to slave-factories and to place it within the competency of the colonial authorities to "expel the traffic to a distance". But even after the limits of the colony had been greatly extended and several large tribes brought under its jurisdiction, the slavers would every now and then attempt to renew their old friendships, and frequently occasioned not a little trouble to the colonists by exciting the natives to insubordination and hostility to a colony which, as they alleged (being instructed so to think by the slavers), "was spoiling their country and breaking up their lucrative trade".

The feelings of some of the natives who had surrendered themselves to Liberian authority, became, under the guidance of the "marauding outlaws", so embittered against the colony that they more than once boldly avowed their hostile sentiments, and professed utter indifference to the laws of Liberia. This, together with the fact that every once in a while slavers would locate themselves,

[1] Gurley's *Life of Ashmun*, p. 261.

erect barracoons and purchase slaves on Liberian territory under the countenance and protection of aboriginal chiefs, rendered several wars against the latter necessary in order to convince them that Liberians had power to compel them to obedience. The last war of this character was "carried" to New-Cess in 1849, immediately after the independence of Liberia had been recognized by England and France. The condign punishment inflicted upon the slavers by that military expedition, the regular cruising of the Liberian government schooner *Lark*, and the scattering of settlements at various points, have entirely driven away the slavers from the Liberian coast. The country in consequence has enjoyed a grateful repose, and the people have been peaceably prosecuting a legitimate traffic both with Liberians and foreigners.

"THE FRENCH EMIGRATION SYSTEM"

But latterly a new element of discord has been introduced on the Liberian coast, the French emigration system. French vessels visit the coast for the ostensible object of employing labourers for the French colonies. Of course it is understood or presumed that all emigrants embarking on board of these vessels do so of their own accord; if so, the trade is as lawful as any other emigration trade. But it must be borne in mind that the aborigines are not settled along the coast in independent republican communities. They are under the most despotic rule; the king or head-man having absolute control over his subjects or "boys". All the employers of emigrants has to do, then, is to offer, which he does, liberal conditions to the chiefs for the number of labourers required. The chiefs immediately send around and compel their boys to come, or if they have not a sufficient number of their own people to answer the demand, predatory excursions are made, in which they kidnap the weak and unsuspecting, or a pretext is assumed for a war with a neighbouring tribe; cruelty, bloodshed, carnage ensue; prisoners are taken, driven down to the beach and handed over to the captain of the emigrant ship, whose business being to employ all the labourers he can get, does not stop to inquire as to the method adopted for obtaining these persons. The result is, a state of things as revolting as that occasioned by the slave-trade in its most flourishing period. The bond which it was hoped Liberia had formed for the linking together of tribe to tribe in harmonious intercourse and mutual dependence, is thus being rudely snapped asunder. The natives, according to complaints made by some of them to the Liberian government, are being agitated with reciprocal fears and jealousies, their lives and property are in danger, and a check is imposed upon all their industrious efforts.

An occurrence, however, sad indeed, but no doubt providential, has recently taken place on the Liberian coast, which has clearly developed the character of the system, and which will, in all probability, arrest its deleterious influences. In the early part of April last (1858) the *Regina Coeli*, a French ship engaged in the enlistment of labourers . . . was laying at anchor off Manna, a trading port a few leagues north-west of Monrovia, with two or three hundred emigrants on board, among whom, in consequence of some of their number being manacled, considerable dissatisfaction prevailed. During the absence of the captain and one of the officers, a quarrel broke between the cook and one of the emigrants. The cook struck the emigrant, the latter retaliated, when a scuffle ensued, in which other emigrants took part. This attracted the attention of the rest of the crew, who coming to the assistance of the cook, violently beat the emigrants, killing several of them. By this time, those emigrants who had been confined below were unshackled, and joining in the fracas killed in retaliation all the crew, save one man who fled aloft and protested most earnestly his freedom from any participation in the matter. The emigrants, recognizing his innocence, spared his life, but ordered him ashore forthwith, which order he readily obeyed.

The surviving emigrants having sole charge of the vessel, awaited the arrival of the captain to dispatch him as soon as he touched the deck. But he, learning their design, did not venture on board, but sought and obtained aid from the Liberian authorities at Cape Mount to keep the exasperated savages from stranding his vessel. The unfortunate ship was subsequently rescued by an English mail steamer, and towed into Montserrado Roads.

One very important result has accrued from this sad occurrence, and that is the one already referred to—the development of the ruinous influence of the French emigration system upon the natives from among whom the labourers are taken. There have existed apprehensions on the part of the Liberian government that the emigration was constrained; but having received official information and assurance that the system enjoyed the countenance and patronage of the French government, and that the traders were under the immediate surveillance of French officials, it could not depreciate the honesty and good intentions of that renowned and magnanimous nation.

Nearly coincident with the above circumstance, and, perhaps, in some measure the result of it, was another of a similar character, in the interior of Liberia. One or two native chiefs, it appears, had collected a number of persons and were conveying them, manacled, to the coast for the purpose of supplying the emigrant vessels. On their way they stopped, with their human load, to pass the night at a native town. During the night, one of the captives having worked himself loose, untied the others, when a revolt ensued in which the prisoners killed the kidnappers and made their escape.

19

The Negro in Ancient History [1]

Methodist Quarterly Review, January, 1869; *The People of Africa*,
New York, 1871, 21–6

But we are told that the Negroes of Central and West Africa have
proved themselves essentially inferior, from the fact, that in the
long period of three thousand years they have shown no signs of
progress. In their country, it is alleged, are to be found no indications of architectural taste or skill, or of any susceptibility of
aesthetic or artistic improvement; that they have no monuments
of past exploits; no paintings or sculptures; and that, therefore,
the foreign or American slave-trade was an indispensable agency
in the civilization of Africa; that nothing could have been done for
the Negro while he remained in his own land, bound to the practices
of ages; that he needed the sudden and violent severance from home
to deliver him from the quiescent degradation and stagnant barbarism of his ancestors; that otherwise the civilization of Europe
could never have impressed him.

In reply to all this we remark: 1st, That it remains to be proved,
by a fuller explanation of the interior that there are not architectural remains, no works of artistic skill;[2] 2ndly, If it should be
demonstrated that nothing of the kind exists, this would not necessarily prove essential inferiority on the part of the African. . . .
3rdly, With regard to the necessity of the slave trade, we remark . . .
that without the foreign slave trade Africa would have been a great
deal more accessible to (European) civilization, and would now, had
peaceful and legitimate intercourse been kept up with her from
the middle of the fifteenth century, be taking her stand next to
Europe in civilization, science and religion. When four hundred
years ago, the Portuguese discovered this coast, they found the
natives living in considerable peace and quietness, and with a certain
degree of prosperity. Internal feud, of course, the tribes sometimes
had, but by no means so serious as they afterwards became under
the stimulating influence of the slave trade. From all we can gather
the tribes in this part of Africa lived in a condition not very different
from that of the greater portion of Europe in the Middle Ages.

---

[1] Reputedly the first article by a Negro in a scholarly quarterly [ed.].
[2] It is now well known that these areas did have a high degree of artistic
achievement, best exemplified by bronze, wood and ivory carvings [ed.].

There was the same oppression of the weak by the strong; the same resistance by the weak, often taking the form of general rebellion; the same private and hereditary wars; the same strongholds in every prominent position; the same dependence of the people upon the chief who happened to be in power; the same contentedness of the masses with the tyrannical rule. But there was industry and activity, and in every town there were manufacturers, and they sent across the continent to Egypt and the Barbary States other articles besides slaves.

The permanence for centuries of the social and political states of the Africans at home must be attributed, first, to the isolation of the people from the progressive portion of mankind; and, secondly, to the blighting influence of the traffic introduced among them by Europeans. Had not the demand arisen in America for African labourers, and had European nations inaugurated regular traffic with the coast, the natives would have shown themselves as impressible for change, as susceptible of improvement, as capable of acquiring knowledge and accumulating wealth, as the natives of Europe. Combination of capital and co-operation of energies would have done for this land what they have done for others. Private enterprise (which has been entirely destroyed by the nefarious traffic), encouraged by humane intercourse with foreign lands, would have developed agriculture, manufactures, and commerce; would have cleared, drained, and fertilized the country, and built towns; would have improved the looms, brought in ploughs, steam-engines, printing-presses, machines, and the thousand processes and appliances by which the comfort, progress, and usefulness of mankind are secured. . . .

But although, amid the violent shocks of those changes and disasters to which the natives of this outraged land have been subject, their knowledge of the elegant arts . . . declined, they never entirely lost the *necessary* arts of life. They still understand the workmanship of iron, and, in some sections of the country, of gold. The loom and the forge are in constant use among them. In remote regions, where they have not intercourse with Europeans, they raise large herds of cattle and innumerable sheep and goats; capture and train horses, build well-laid-out towns, cultivate extensive fields, and manufacture earthenware and woollen and cotton cloths. . . .

VEY LITERATURE

And in our own times, on the West Coast of Africa, a native development of literature has been brought to light of genuine home-growth. The Vey People, residing half way between Sierra Leone and Cape Mesurado, have within the last thirty years invented a syllabic alphabet, with which they are now writing their own language, and by which they are maintaining among themselves an extensive epistolary correspondence. In 1849 the Church Missionary Society in London, having heard of this invention, authorized their missionary, Rev. S. Koelle, to investigate the subject. Mr. Koelle travelled into the interior, and brought away three manuscripts, with translations. The symbols are phonetic, and constitute a syllabarium, not an alphabet; they are nearly two hundred in number. They have been learned so generally that Vey boys in Monrovia frequently receive communication from their friends in the Vey country, to which they readily respond. . . .

Though "the idea of communicating thoughts in writing was probably suggested by the use of Arabic among the Mandingoes", yet the invention was properly original, showing the existence of genius in the native African who has never been in foreign slavery, and proves that he carries in his bosom germs of intellectual development and self-elevation, which would have enabled him to advance regularly in the paths of progress, had it not been for the blighting influence of the slave-trade.

20

From West Africa to Palestine

Freetown; Manchester, 1873, 89–129

ALEXANDRIA AND CAIRO

On the 10th of July, at 7 a.m., we anchored in the harbour of Alexandria. I now had before me the renowned land of Egypt. How shall I describe the emotions with which the first sight of this ancient country inspired me? How shall I select and reproduce in an order intelligible to others the thoughts which, in rapid succession, passed through my mind?

I was prepared to find a large harbour, but was greatly surprised at the presence of so large a number of vessels from nearly all parts of the world, and of three or four splendid steam corvettes belonging to the Egyptian government.

I saw in the distance the site of the ancient Pharaohs, the first great lighthouse constructed in the Mediterranean, and one of the seven wonders of the world. Immediately before me lay the city built by Alexander the Great. What a various history, political, social and religious, has it passed through! When Alexander boasted that he would here build an emporium of commerce that would surpass Tyre, which he had destroyed, and attract the shipping of the world, he little dreamed that the day would come when the most important operations carried on in this city would be by vessels from powerful nations of the west; some of them inhabiting countries then unknown to maritime enterprise. The history of Alexandria since his death has more than realized the dream of the world's conqueror.

About an hour after we anchored a steam-tug came alongside the *Nyanza*, and took off those passengers and their effects who had taken through tickets for India, China, Japan, and Australia. So far as I was concerned the responsibility of the P. (eninsular) & O. (rient) Company ceased on the arrival of the steamer at Alexandria. I was therefore obliged to hire a boat to take me ashore. On landing I was very near losing my baggage, amid the wonderful crowd of men and beasts by which I was beset—Negroes, Arabs, Turks, donkeys, camels—in terrifying rivalry for my trunks. I was not disposed to allow anyone to touch my baggage until I could

145

decide upon my destination. At length an Arab, calling himself Hamad, and representing himself as a professed dragoman, came to my assistance, and relieved me of the disagreeable pressure. He assisted me in passing through the Custom House, which was a small affair. I then hired a carriage, and had myself conveyed with my baggage to the United States Consulate-General, where, after exhibiting a letter of introduction from Mr. Adams, the American minister in London, I was most kindly received by Mr. Hale, the Consul-General, a very polite and well-educated gentleman from New England.

Learning from Mr. Hale that the next railway train from Cairo that day would start about an hour's time, I deposited my baggage in his office, and taking a letter from him to the United States Consul at Cairo, I hastened to the railway station; and, arriving just in time to get a ticket and procure a seat, I was soon whirling up the valley of the Nile at the rate of thirty miles an hour.

I looked at my ticket, and found that it was printed in Arabic characters. I felt a strong desire to retain it as a curiosity, but was obliged to give it up at the end of the journey.

After losing sight of Pompey's pillar, Cleopatra's needle, and the city of Alexandria, we came suddenly upon villages consisting altogether of mud huts. I then began to realize that I was in Egypt— the land which every Sabbath-school boy desires to see, as he reads the simple narrative of Joseph and his brethren—of Moses concealed in the ark of bulrushes—of the persecution, hard labour, and exodus of the Jews—of the haughty and tyrannical Pharaoh— and of the flight of Mary and Joseph with the infant Saviour. All these things crowded into my mind; and everything in the scenery through which we passed seemed to call up incidents in Sacred Writ.

In the vegetation which presents itself there is a pleasing and curious variety. There are palms, oranges, lemons, mulberry, pomegranate, olive, lime, grape, cactus, sycamores, gorgeous roses, and gigantic oleanders. I was so deeply interested by the novelty of everything, and at the same time its seeming familiarity—as if I had lived for years in the land—that the five hours between Alexandria and Cairo passed away almost imperceptibly.

But there was one drawback to my enjoyment—the incessant cigar-smoking kept up by my fellow passengers in the carriage.

In Egypt everybody smokes. If you are travelling in company, or visiting a friend, or a friend comes to visit you, you must either smoke or *be* smoked. Woe to the man who cannot endure the scent of tobacco! There are never any complimentary inquiries made, as in other countries, as to whether the smoke offends: everybody takes it for granted that everybody else smokes.

Mr. Palgrave tells us that among the Wahabites, Mohammedan purists in Arabia, such is the heinousness of the sin of smoking, in the view of the religious chiefs, that any man, however elevated his position, is punished with a severe beating with rods if found guilty of it. The king's brother, the heir apparent to the throne, was detected in the use of tobacco, and was publicly hoisted and beaten at his own palace gate for the offence. The Minister of Finance, who had also indulged in the practice, was beaten so severely that he died the next day. I wished a thousand times during that railway ride that the Wahabites had extended their vigorous laws and practices on the subject of tobacco into Egypt before my arrival there.

On reaching Cairo I at once, armed with a note of introduction from Rev. Dr. Schmettau, Secretary of the Evangelical Alliance in London, and with Mr. Adam's letter, repaired to the residence of Rev. Dr. Lansing, American Missionary at Cairo, by whom and his associate, Mr. David Strang, I was most hospitably received. Dr. Lansing being obliged to leave for Alexandria on the same day of my arrival, I was left in charge of Mr. Strang, who, with Miss Dales, teacher of the female school, made my stay in Cairo very pleasant.

This mission, established a few years ago by the American United Presbyterians, is doing a very important work in various needy and populous localities in Upper and Lower Egypt. Besides having the mission work carried on as usual in the mission churches and schools, both boys and girls, and among the women, and at the book depots in both Alexandria and Cairo, the members of the mission were constrained, by the urgency of the case, to form a mission-station at Osiut, one of the largest and most important towns in all Upper Egypt, and afterwards at El-Medineh, one of the most fertile and populous of all the districts in the valley of the Nile. There is a wonderfully increasing demand for books among the natives, and the spirit of inquiry is largely on the increase; so that it has been thought necessary to establish in connection with this mission a printing press to print works in the Arabic language.

VISIT TO THE PYRAMIDS

Mr. Strang kindly undertook the arrangement of all preliminaries in the way of securing donkeys, guides, etc., to enable me to visit the pyramids on the next day. After a hearty supper I retired early, so as to be up betimes the next morning to enjoy a cool ride to the wonders of Egypt. But I could not sleep. The fatigue of the railway ride, the intense heat, and the exhilarating visions of the scenes to be witnessed next day prevented me from closing my eyes. The alarm clock which Mr. Strang had set in my room for the purpose of waking me at half-past three (the time fixed for starting was four the next morning) was hardly necessary.

On the morning of the 11th of July, at half-past four o'clock, under the guidance of a young Copt, named Ibrahim, I set out for the pyramids. Owing to considerable delay in procuring a boat to cross the Nile—for the pyramids are on the other side of the river from Cairo—we did not reach our destination until eleven o'clock, under a broiling sun.

This journey will long be remembered by me, and will ever be the object of delightful reminiscences. I felt as if I were in an entirely new world. My thoughts were partly of the remote past, but mostly of the immediate future. When crossing the river, an island was pointed out to me as the spot where tradition says Moses was concealed by his mother. My interest was intense.

Half an hour after crossing the river, we caught a view of the pyramids in the distance. Here was opened to me a wide field of contemplation, and my imagination was complete "master of the situation". Though we were in an exposed plain, and my companion complained of the intense heat, I did not notice it, so eager was I to gain the pyramids, which seemed further and further to recede the longer we rode towards them. We saw them for three hours before we came up to them.

Just before reaching the pyramids we passed a small village of Arabs, who make their living, for the most part, by assisting travellers to "do" the pyramids. About a dozen of them rushed out as they saw us approaching, with goblets of water, pitchers of coffee, candles, and matches, and engraving knives. The water was very acceptable. I looked at the other articles, and wondered what could be the object of them.

The pyramids stand apparently on a hill of sand, on the borders of the Libyan desert. We had to ascend a considerable elevation—about 130 feet—before getting to the pyramid of Cheops. In the side of this apparent hill of sand, extending from the pyramids of Ghizeh to the smaller pyramids of Abusir and Sakarah, about two miles, are excavated tombs. The pyramids then are at the extremities of an immense city of the dead; they themselves forming the imperishable tombs of the mighty monarchs who constructed them.

On reaching the base of the great pyramid I tried to find the shady side, but it was impossible to find any shade. On the north side there were several large stones taken out at the base—leaving huge spaces. Into one of these Ibrahim, myself, and our donkeys entered and sheltered ourselves. The Arabs crowded about us, and kept asking question after question, suggesting the pleasure we should enjoy in ascending to the top, and the advantage to be reaped by visiting the interior. But I paid very little attention to them. They addressed me in broken English, French, and Italian. Other thoughts were crowding my mind. I thought of the continuous fatigue I had undergone, without eating anything, sustained only by the object I expected to attain in front, viz., a close inspection of the pyramids. And now that I had gained my point, and sat down to rest under the shadow of a great rock, I could not help feeling that my effort was, after all, but a forcible type of our experience in one-half the pursuits we follow through life. My enchanting dreams and fancies left me completely, as heated, and weary, and hungry, I sat down to rest. How speedily the most cursory experience of the reality often levels to the dust all the mountains built up by the imagination!

Though I cannot say that at the first view of the pyramids they fell below my expectation, still they did not exactly appear what I expected them to be. Their greatness grew upon me as I looked at them. They are something magnificent. (How inadequate that adjective to convey what I mean!)

I had read Longfellow's beautiful description:

> "The mighty pyramids of stone,
>   That, wedge-like, cleave the desert airs,
> When nearer seen and better known,
>   Are but gigantic flights of stairs."[1]

But I had supposed that his was merely poetic and ideal, referring to the layer after layer of stone or brick put up "by slow degrees, by more and more", in constructing large edifices: I did not imagine that, in reality, the pyramids were built in steps; but they are really "gigantic flights of stairs"—so that they can be ascended to the very top. Travellers frequently go up.

It is said that formerly they presented a smooth slope from the apex to the base, but the outer casing has been carefully removed, in the case of the great pyramid of Cheops wholly, and in that of Chephren to within a short distance of the summit. The casing of the lower portion of the pyramid of Chephren was a beautiful red granite, the upper portion consisting of plaster, once painted bright

[1] *St. Augustine's Ladder.*

N

vermilion, in imitation of the lower surface. Hence, while the granite has been carried off, the top still remains smooth, and retains traces of its former colour. The casing of the great pyramid was probably the grey granite of Sinai, and being brought from so great distance, and by such rude means of conveyance as most likely were then employed, would be very valuable; which may account for the whole of it having been taken away for the erection of more recent costly buildings, principally mosques, at Cairo.

After recovering myself by about an hour's rest, I suffered the Arabs to persuade me to ascend the great pyramid (Cheops). Three assisted me; one taking hold of each hand, and one supporting me from behind. Before reaching one-third of the way, however, I gave out, changed my mind, and refused to ascend those dizzy heights. The Arabs clung to me, and insisted that I should go up. I could pacify them only by promising to allow them to take me to the interior—preferring then to examine the exterior a little more closely from a less elevated and commanding, but to me a more comfortable, position.

After gazing in amazement at the outside, I made up my mind, on consultation with Ibrahim as to the safety of the enterprise, to visit the central hall in the interior. Had I known, however, that the performance required so much nerve and physical strength as I found out during the experiment, I should not have ventured. The entrance is first by a very steep and narrow passage, paved with immense stones, which have become dangerously slippery by centuries of use. There are small notches for the toes of those who would achieve the enterprise of entering, distant from each other about four or five feet, showing that they were intended for very tall men who wore no shoes. The modern traveller is obliged to make Hiawathan strides to get the toe of his boot into one of these notches, which are also wearing smooth, so as to make the hold which he gets exceedingly precarious. But for the help of these half-naked, shoeless, and sure-footed Arabs, it would be impossible for Western pilgrims generally to accomplish the feat of visiting the interior. Before entering, the Arabs lighted two candles—an operation which, I confess, somewhat staggered me, as it gave me the idea of sepulchral gloom and ghastliness. I had supposed that the interior of the pyramids was lighted in some way, though I had not stopped to think how. As we had to go down sideways, two attended me, one holding my left hand and the other my right, so that if one slipped the other would be a support. If we had slipped at once, it is difficult to imagine what would have been the result. The lighted candles were carried in advance.

In about half an hour, after descending and ascending difficult places, we gained the centre. The feeling in going up to the centre of the pyramid is akin to that which one experiences when ascending a very high hill. When we had accomplished the feat of reaching the centre, the Arabs themselves, who are not unaccustomed to the enterprise, seemed to think it a wonderful achievement, for they burst out into simultaneous boisterous hurrahs. The floor of the hall was one huge stone. On the sides were engraved the names of visitors who had been there centuries ago. But there were very few names: comparatively few travellers, it would seem, go into the pyramids. In the centre of the hall stands the large porphyry coffer in which the embalmed bodies of the kings were deposited— evidently too large to pass through the narrow passages by which we entered. How was it brought to this place? The Arabs said it was put here while the pyramid was building. "While the pyramid was building!" thought I: "that takes us back to the days of Noah—anterior to Abraham." What a wonderful sight!

Sir J. S. Wilkinson, one of the most competent authorities on all Egyptian questions, fixes the date of the construction of the pyramids at 2400 B.C. Job refers to them in chap. iii., 13, 14. "Now," says he, "should I have lain still and been quiet, I should have slept; then had I been at rest, with kings and counsellors of the earth, which built desolate places for themselves." "Desolate places", in the Arabic translation of Smith and Van Dyck, is rendered *"pyramids" (ahram)*. The Coptic version is said to give "monuments". It is clear that Job saw or knew of the pyramids. Perhaps Abraham during his sojourn in Egypt, Jacob, Joseph, and his brethren, Moses and Aaron, stood and wondered at these structures. It is certain that Homer, Thales, Solon, Pythagoras, Herodotus, Plato, and many other distinguished Greeks, who visited Egypt for purposes of study and travel, saw them.

I was amazed at the stones of immense size, placed in every possible position, by which I was surrounded. The constant wonder is, how were these stones brought hither? and how could they be arranged as they are? Instead of imagining the use of machinery now entirely unknown, may we not suppose that there were giants in those days?—that the strength of one man of those times was equal to the strength of several men in these degenerate days? Homer tells us that Diomed, in the Trojan war, hurled, with one hand, a stone at Æneas, which two men in his day would not have been able to carry. We read in Deuteronomy iii, 11: "For only Og king of Bashan remained of the remnant of giants; behold, his bedstead was a bedstead of iron. Is it not in Rabbath of the children of Ammon? Nine cubits was the length thereof, and four cubits the breadth of it."

Again, Deut. ii, 19: "I will not give thee of the land of the children of Ammon any possession, because I have give it unto the children of Lot for a possession. That also was accounted a land of giants—giants dwelt there in old times, and the Ammonites call them Zamzummims a people great and many, and tall as the Anakins."

Homer and Virgil both speak of the Cyclops—persons of huge stature and immense strength. I have often thought that the extravagant tales of the poets concerning people of enormous stature were founded on original truths; and though they are sometimes so confused that we find it very difficult to draw a correct line between truth and fable, some general ideas can be formed from them of the character of the men of remote antiquity. It is certain that the persons who introduced architecture into Greece were remarkable for their extraordinary size and great strength. Herodotus alludes to them under the name of Cadmians, and his views of their form and stature are gathered from the wonderful character of the structures which they built.

While standing in the central hall of the pyramid I thought of the lines of [Hilary] Teage, the Liberian poet, when urging his countrymen to noble deeds:

> "From pyramidal hall,
> From Karnac's sculptured wall,
> From Thebes they loudly call—
> Retake your fame."

This, thought I, is the work of my African progenitors, Teage was right; they had fame, and their descendants should strive, by nobler deeds, to "retake" it. Feelings came over me far different from those which I have felt when looking at the mighty works of European genius. I felt that I had a peculiar "heritage in the Great Pyramid"—built before the tribes of mankind had been so generally scattered, and, therefore, before they had acquired their different geographical characteristics, but built by that branch of the descendants of Noah, the enterprising sons of Ham, from whom I am descended. The blood seemed to flow faster through my veins. I seemed to hear the echo of those illustrious Africans. I seemed to feel the impulse from those stirring characters who sent civilization into Greece—the teachers of the father of poetry, history, and mathematics—Homer, Herodotus, and Euclid. I seemed to catch the sound of the "stately steppings" of Jupiter, as, with his brilliant celestial retinue, he perambulates the land on a visit to my ancestors, the "blameless Ethiopians". I felt lifted out of the commonplace grandeur of modern times; and, could my voice have reached every African in the world, I would have earnestly addressed him in the language of Hilary Teage:

"Retake your fame!"

Now that the slave-holding of Africans in Protestant countries has come to an end, and the necessity no longer exists for stripping them of the attributes of manhood, it is to be hoped that a large-hearted philosophy and an honest interpretation of the facts of history, sacred and secular, will do them the justice to admit their participation in, if not origination of, the great works of ancient civilization.

*   *   *

The heat was not so great within the pyramid as might at first be supposed; it seems to be ventilated from some quarter. Before the Arabs would consent to guide us out they insisted on receiving *bakhshish*—a present, corresponding to *dash* among the aborigines in West Africa. We had to promise them solemnly and earnestly that on gaining the open air we would satisfy all their desires. Had they left us, as they pretended to be about to do, it would have been utterly impossible for us to get out; and the idea of stumbling in the darkness, rolling down slippery places, and falling into deep holes, was harassingly frightful. We were considerably relieved, therefore, when they accepted our pledge, and, taking us upon their shoulders, carefully carried us out. . . .

On reaching the opening the Arabs sold us coffee, in very small cups, which considerably refreshed us. I felt that my perilous adventure had given me the right of inscribing my name among the hundreds which I saw engraved over and on each side of the entrance, bearing dates as early as the sixteenth century. Borrowing, or rather hiring, for I paid him a shilling for the use of it, an engraving knife from one of the Arabs, I engraved, not far from a name dated 1685, the word LIBERIA, with my name and the date— July 11th, 1866—immediately under it. There is a tolerable degree of certainty, therefore, that the name at least of that little Republic will go down to posterity.

After this I attempted to walk around the Pyramid, but I found that my strength, considerably reduced by the visit to the interior, did not allow me, especially as it was necessary to climb over a great deal of rubbish which has collected about the base. I therefore mounted my donkey and rode to the smaller Pyramid of Chephren, in front of which stands the Sphinx.

The Sphinx, which I gazed at a long while, is a most impressive spectacle. "This colossal and fanciful figure, half human, half animal, the body being that of a lion, was an emblematic representation of the king—the union of intellect and physical power. It was cut out of the solid rock, with the exception of the paws and a portion of the backbone, which are of hewn stone. Its heights to the top of the head was sixty-three feet, its length a hundred and forty-three feet, and it measured a hundred and two feet round the forehead. The head-dress is destroyed, and the face is much mutilated, so that the features, which were Egyptian in their character, are scarcely distinguishable. Below its breast and between its paws, which extend fifty feet from the chest, though now covered with sand, are the remains of a small temple and altar, the incense smoke from which ascended to its expanded nostrils."[2]

*   *   *

Having spent about three hours in the company of these wonders of antiquity, we now concluded to return to Cairo. We rode away a little distance, and then turned and took a "last lingering look"; the Arabs, unsatisfied with the pecuniary compensation they had received—which Ibrahim said was more than they usually get— still followed us, and interrupted my meditative mood by clamourously insisting upon additional *bakhshish*. The journey back to Cairo was done in a much shorter time than it took us to go. We returned in four hours.

The pyramids which I visited are the two great pyramids, known, as I have already stated, as those of Cheops and Chephren. The large pyramid—the one I entered—is about four hundred and eighty feet high, or one hundred and forty feet higher than the highest point of St. Paul's Cathedral. Its base covers thirteen acres. The solid contents have been estimated at eighty-five million cubic feet, and to contain six million tons of stone. Herodotus says that one hundred thousand men, relieved every three months, were employed about twenty years in the erection of this vast edifice.

In view of these immense structures, I do not see how the boastful spirit of the age can indulge in such unlimited panegyrics on the advancement of the present day; setting up the commonest acts of the current civilization as perfect miracles compared with the doings of the ancients. What are Atlantic telegraphs to these incomprehensible and time-defying edifices, whose authors did not invest their

[2] The author did not cite the source of this quotation [ed.].

own times with such transcendent importance as to lose all reverence for the past, and all care and forethought for the future?

*   *   *

When we arrived at the Mission House, on our return from the pyramids, the day was far spent. Though anxious to see some of the accessible curiosities of Cairo that day, as my time for sojourning in the city was spent, I was obliged to pass the whole evening in bed, on account of the fatigue of the day's exercise, which I felt for several days afterwards.

Next morning, under the guidance of Mr. Strang, I started out to "do" the lions of Cairo. It is impossible to convey to one who has not visited the east any accurate idea of the appearance presented by the streets of this thoroughly oriental city. Persons of all races and nations are met in their peculiar costumes. Carriages, and camels, and horses, and mules, and asses come into continual contact in the narrow streets—some of them so narrow that two horses or donkeys cannot walk abreast. And as they are not paved, and are of light, sandy soil, the tread of the various animals is not heard: it is necessary, therefore, for riders to warn pedestrians of their approach, which they do in a peculiar kind of shout. When the carriage of a wealthy person is approaching, the servant runs before—a proper footman—with a long stick clearing the streets, informing crowds on foot that a vehicle is coming; so that they may draw themselves up as closely as possible to the sides of the streets, or, whatever those narrow passages ought to be called. Thus he "prepares the way" of his master, and makes "his paths straight". No stranger attracts attention from the peculiarity of his dress. In the streets we met persons of all races and costumes.

THE MOSQUE OF MOHAMMED ALI

First we went to the famous mosque of the celebrated Mohammed Ali, an energetic ruler of Egypt, who lived in the early part of this century. This magnificent structure is built on a low hill to the east of the city. On presenting ourselves at the entrance of the large open square, on the eastern side of which stands the house of prayer, we were not allowed to enter until we had drawn over our shoes red slippers, with which we were provided by the door-keepers. The sacred ground must not be trodden with what has touched the common dust. But for this privilege we had to pay two shillings. We found several Moslems engaged in their devotions under a splendid dome, not excelled for beauty of interior decora-

tion by that of St. Paul's in London. Everyone we found in the
mosque was kneeling, and going through the numerous prayers and
prostrations with his face turned to the east. The ignorant Mussulmans here insist that no worship is acceptable which is not offered
with the face turned to the rising sun; while, in Syria, professors
in the same faith contend that the worshipper is disdained who does
not in his devotions turn his face towards the south. I suppose
that the pious of the sect in Persia would insist upon a westward
aspiration; while those in Mozambique would believe in a divine
afflatus from the north. And so it goes. I wonder what would be
the result of a comparison of notes by earnest and bigoted devotees
from directly opposite points of the compass. Of course, the intelligent among the Mohammedans know that the principle is that the
face of the worshipper, wherever he is, must be turned towards
Mecca, their holy city, as of old the Jews prayed towards Jerusalem. . . .

After looking around the interior of the building, and at the
tomb of Mohammed Ali, we went out and had a view of Cairo from
the citadel, said to be one of the finest views in the world. From
this elevation, through the dry, clear atmosphere of Egypt, the
greater portion of the city is distinctly seen. The numerous large
and striking buildings, patches of beautiful green, with clusters of
palm trees and sycamore, white domes of mosques and shining
minarets in every direction, present an appearance not to be
described. The view to the west is very extensive and grand, giving,
beyond the limits of the present city, the site and remains of old
Cairo, of Fostat; then the broad, placid Nile, flowing through a
wide verdant plain, fertilized by its waters. Further off, at a distance
of six miles, are seen the great pyramids of Gizeh, and the smaller
pyramids of Abusir and Sakarah, all lying in the Libyan desert,
and bounded by the range of the Libyan hills, sloping gradually
down to the Delta of the Nile. Thus the greatest structure of ancient
Egypt, and one of the finest and most costly of modern Egypt, face
each other.

From the citadel we visited "Joseph's Well", said to have been
dug by Joseph during his rule in Egypt. It is remarkable for its
great depth and the abundance of good water which it constantly
supplies. There is a passage at the side by which visitors may go
down to the bottom. We ventured about a hundred feet down, and
as we were told that we were not then half way to the bottom, we
looked through an opening in the side at the heights above and the
depths beneath, and we thought it best to retrace our steps. From
the "Well of Joseph" we visited the mosque of Sultan Hassan,

described by some travellers as, architecturally, the finest in Cairo. I confess that—probably for want of sufficiently cultivated taste in that department of art—after having visited the mosque of Mohammed Ali, I could see nothing to admire in the old dilapidated structure of Sultan Hassan. The devotees about it, however, obliged us to take off our shoes—furnishing us no slippers—before entering. I fancy that my health was not very much benefited by walking thus exposed on the cold marble pavement.

I was struck with the rigid and impressive simplicity of the interior of the mosque. There are no pews, nor chairs, nor seats of any kind; no pictures or statues. They are intended for places of prayer—not of luxurious ease—whither people go, not to gaze around or criticize, but for devotional purposes. All we saw present had, at least, the appearance of worshippers. No one man was there professedly to lead the devotions of the people, but practically —so far as many are concerned—to be their substitute in worship, while they look on as spectators paying for a weekly entertainment. The people all kneel or sit cross-legged on the floor, which is matted or carpeted. There is a pulpit, affording standing room for only one man, from which the people are sometimes addressed by the Moolah.

Around the mosque of Sultan Hassan is an open space, called the Roumaylee, a place of general resort. Here I saw the finest herd of camels I have seen in the east. The camel by itself has very little comeliness, but a drove of camels is certainly a beautiful sight.

Anxious to overtake the Russian steamer for Beyrout, which was to leave Alexandria on the afternoon of the 13th, I started by the earliest train on the following morning (the 13th), and reached Alexandria just in time to get my things on board comfortably, without enjoying the pleasure of giving the parting *salaam* to the affable consul-general, who was away at dinner when I reached his office.

I now bade adieu to the land of Egypt—land of my "father's sepulchres"—feeling more than repaid for any discomforts or privations suffered on the voyage; happy to undergo them all again, or double their number, intensified, for the sake of the instruction and enjoyment which my visit to this great country afforded.

21

Echoes from Africa

Christianity, Islam and the Negro Race, London, 1887, 138–41;
2nd ed., 159–62

*   *   *

EUROPEAN "LIBEL" AGAINST NEGROES

And here we must venture to enter our earnest protest against the
use of such phrases as "The Despised Races", which we see frequently used of late in the publications of the American Missionary
Association. . . . Such expressions as "The Despised Race" and
"The Dark Continent", applied to the Negro and his ancestral
home, have not, we fancy, the most salutary effect either upon
those who employ them or upon those to whom they refer; in the
one they often beget arrogance; in the other, servility or resentment. . . . Moreover, the whole of the rest of mankind does not
hold the European, in view of his past history, in such unqualified
admiration as to admit without serious question that he has a right
to embody in terse phrases, and to parade in the titles of books,
pamphlets, and addresses his contempt for other races. There are
those of other races who also sneer and scorn and "despise". Some
of the proceedings of [Samuel] Baker and [H. M.] Stanley in
Africa must frequently have impressed the natives with the feeling
that those energetic travellers came from much "darker continents"
than any their unsophisticated imaginations had ever before suggested to them. The African now coming forward through education
and culture cannot have unlimited respect for all the qualities of
the European races: "A people with a passion for taking away the
countries of others and dignifying the robbery as conquests; and
whose systematic cruelty has been shown for ages, in chaining, buy-
ing, and selling another race." The intelligent Negro feels that the
part of the oppressor is not less to be despised than the part of the
oppressed—that the part of the man-stealer and man-seller is far
more contemptible than the part of the man stolen and sold. And
this he will feel more and more. The brilliancy of the universal
and prolonged success which has given the European the idea that
he has a right to despise others, and to proclaim the fact—the
glories which have followed in the wake of his progress and con-

quests—are getting sadly dimmed in the light of a fuller understanding of the Gospel of Christ. Under the searching criticisms of rising intellects imbued with the essence of a Christian philosophy, and influenced by the spirit of a science properly so called, those brutal instincts which received the eulogiums of the past are finding their proper recognition as elements of character to be reprobated and suppressed. . . . Might no longer makes right. . . .

History, then, as it is read by the thinking Negro, will not diminish the vehemence of his protest against the injustice of being regarded by the European as belonging to a "despised race", nor lessen the grounds of his desire to reciprocate the disparaging sentiment. His hands are free from the blood of other men. He has not in any way oppressed other races. . . .

The Negroes on the African continent who have not read European history are divided into two classes, namely, those who have seen and had intercourse with the Europeans, and those who have never seen but only heard of them. The view taken by the former at this moment is exactly that described by Mungo Park a hundred years ago. A century has made no change. Of the impressions of the latter we have a fair specimen in one of Stanley's amusing anecdotes. Mungo Park says:

> Although the Negroes in general have a very great idea of the wealth and power of the Europeans, I am afraid that the Mohammedan converts among them think very lightly of our superior attainments in religious knowledge. The white traders in the maritime districts take no pains to counteract this unhappy prejudice. The poor Africans, whom we affect to consider as barbarians, look upon us, I fear, as little better than a race of formidable but ignorant Heathen.[1]

Mr. Stanley, describing the people on the south-western shores of Lake Tanganyika, says:

> The conduct of the first natives to whom we were introduced pleased us all. They showed themselves in a very amiable light, sold their corn cheaply and without fuss, behaved themselves decently and with propriety, though their principal men, *entertaining very strange ideas of white men*, carefully concealed themselves from view, and refused to be tempted to expose themselves within view or hearing of us.

Their doubts of our character were reported to us by a friendly young Arab as follows: "Kassanga, chief of Ruanda, says, 'How

[1] Park's *Travels*.

can the white men be good when they come for no trade, whose feet one never sees, who always go covered from head to foot with clothes? Do not tell me they are good and friendly. There is something very mysterious about them; perhaps wicked. Probably they are magicians; at any rate, it is better to leave them alone, and to keep close until they are gone.' "

22

African Life and Customs

London, 1908, preface, 10–73

The following pages have been written with the desire, if possible, of unfolding the African, who has received unmixed European culture, to himself, through a study of the customs of his fathers, and also of assisting the European political overlord, ruling in Africa, to arrive at a proper appreciation of conditions.

It is now recognized on all hands that the usefulness, true progress, and happiness of the African, and the success of the European in Africa, depend largely, if not entirely, upon the accurate knowledge on the part of the latter of the people and country which he is attempting to exploit.

* * *

There is no question now as to the human unity, but each section has developed for itself such a system or code of life as its environments have suggested—to be improved, not changed by larger knowledge. The African has developed and organized a system useful to him for all the needs of life.

* * *

The facts in this African life which we shall endeavour to point out are the following:

1st. The Family, which in Africa, as everywhere else, is the basic unit of society. Every male and female marries at the proper age. Every woman is required and expects to perform her part of the function of motherhood—to do her share in continuing the human race.

2nd. Property. The land and the water are accessible to all. Nobody is in want of either, for work, for food, or for clothing.

3rd. Social Life. This is communistic or co-operative. All work for each, and each works for all.

4th. The tribes have laws regulating every function of human life and the laws are known to all the members of the tribe, and justice is administered by the tribal chiefs in the presence of the whole people in the village or town, where any violation of tribal law may have taken place. There is no need for Standing Armies. The whole people of the village or town are jointly and severally guardians and preservers of the peace.

The foundation of the African Family is plural marriage and, contrary to the general opinion, this marriage rests upon the will of the woman, and this will operates to protect from abuse the functional work of the sex, and to provide that all women shall share *normally* in this work with a view to healthy posterity and an unfailing supply of population.

It is less a matter of sentiment, of feeling, of emotion, than of duty, of patriotism. Compulsory spinsterhood is unknown under the African system. *That* is a creation of the West. Its existence here is abnormal, anticlimatic, and considered a monstrosity . . . and is destined, wherever it seems to exist in practice, to disappear as an unscientific interference of good meaning foreign philanthropists with the natural conditions of the country.

*   *   *

. . . there is *among Africans* a regular process of education for male and female, for a period of at least three years, to prepare them for the life they are to follow, and the system under which they are to live.

In the Society for girls which goes by various names in different parts of Africa—called Bundo in our neighbourhood, and Suna further North among the Jolloffs—the teachers are women only: usually, the older women in the neighbourhood are selected for this office, but always women of experience. Instruction is given in everything which prepares a woman to act well her part in the existing social Order—everything necessary to enable the young mother to perform the function which her position involves. The women who impart these lessons are either married or aged widows, and unpaid. It is a labour which is a part of the communal work. Compare this with the system of employing paid *Spinsters* to train girls to be wives and mothers! . . .

Africa has had these institutions from time immemorial. In the Bundo Society or School, as we have said above, instruction is given in all the normal and abnormal complaints and diseases to which women are liable, especially as wives and mothers; and all the known remedies for the prevention and cure or alleviation of such diseases, are taught; so that when a girl has passed through the prescribed course of training, she is prepared without extraneous aid, everywhere and at all times, in the bush or in the town, to take care of herself in emergencies. The irregularity of males attending to females under delicate circumstances very rarely occurs.

The Bundo Society is a most ancient Order of Women, whose origin no one knows, and no one in any of the tribes can imagine a time when the Society did not exist. All its offices, as we have said, are filled, all its rites and ceremonies are performed, and all its teachings are imparted by women only. There are no male pupils or male teachers.

The Porroh Society is a similar Order of Men. Some Europeans, missionaries and laymen, in the Sierra Leone Protectorate and elsewhere, have been admitted to membership in the Porroh Society. The time may come when European females seek admission to the Bundo Society, then they will begin to understand how, from generation to generation, African mothers have produced the strong men who by their labours in the Western Hemisphere . . . and on their own continent, have helped to create the wealth of Europe, and who today do all the hard, laborious outdoor work in our settlements. East, West and South in Africa—on land and on sea— the African system of stirpiculture has furnished nearly all the physical force which has enabled Europe to assert her ascendancy on this continent—soldiers who have saturated the earth on the coast and in the interior with their blood, carrying the Union Jack and the Tricolour to victory, and have laid the foundation of the military prestige which sustains British and French authority throughout the entire Soudan.

*   *   *

. . . Every African woman, as we have said, is required and expects to perform her part of the function of motherhood—to do her share of the work of continuing the human race, but like her European sister of the present day, she objects to being simply a child-bearing machine, and she demands a period of rest in conformity to the law of reserve which is still part of the law of increase among animals. . . . This law of female reserve and recuperation which prevails everywhere in Eastern countries, the African woman has been taught by Nature and her training to follow, and she insists upon a period of three years continuous rest before taking up again the duties of motherhood. This rest in her exhausting climate preserves her physical strength and vigour, and secures like conditions in her offspring. To the Europeanized African woman these things seldom appeal, beguiled by the unnatural monopoly given to her by the Marriage Ceremony of the Church, she has come to believe that she needs no rest, that the

o

cruel imposition upon her energies is a part of the order of Nature and so clings to a state of things which she knows is fraught with evil for herself and children. . . .

When African girls have reached maturity and gone through the course of instruction to which we referred in our last, they are subjected before they leave the secret grove to the rite analogous to circumcision, which in tropical countries has an important bearing upon the welfare of mothers and their offspring. This rite is sometimes described in European medical works.

Here, then, we have a practical species of stirpiculture or eugenics, whose operation extends back over centuries producing continuously a vigorous and prolific race of men and women; and without which, in spite of what may be said or done, experience teaches that decay and death stare the African in the face.

The system of the Pagan African family differs from the Islamic system where marriages are limited to four wives, who are considered legally entitled to all conjugal rights. The Pagan system resembles more the Hebrew system, where there was no fixed limit, only the general caution "not to multiply wives".

An important social advantage also accrues from the marriage system under consideration. The girls, on leaving the school in which they associated on the most intimate terms for years, are seldom willing to separate from their companions; and, with the communistic privilege which they enjoy, they often solicit the husbands assigned them on leaving school to take their most intimate friend as a mate. It is the duty in Africa, as in Oriental countries generally, of the father of a girl on her reaching maturity to find a husband for her, and it is equally the duty of the girl to accept the husband so provided. This is so ancient a custom and so generally understood that there is seldom any friction or inconvenience; and whenever there is, the girl is always sure of a husband. She must be taken in and sheltered if the man is able to take care of her, a matter always carefully looked into before the marriage is arranged. In this way the breaking up and disintegration of Society never takes place as under the European system. . . .

INDUSTRIALISM

Just as the African has learned his eugenics from the animal kingdom—the necessity of reserve and recuperation in the female, so in his industrialism he has learned the principle of co-operation from the insects. "Go to the ant thou sluggard," said the wise man, "consider her ways and be wise." The African has had before him that wonderful insect called the termite and has watched its method and its structures. Everywhere in Africa the termitarium or "bug-a-bug hill" is an object lesson to the native, and has been for millenniums. Among them these hills are regarded as sacred. The residence which the termites build for their habitation is said to have given the idea of the Pyramids to the Egyptian architects. Similar passages traverse the internal regions of the termitaria to those seen by visitors to the interior of the great Pyramid of Cheops; leading to an open space, exactly like the Central Hall of the Egyptian monument, where the Queen bug-a-bug resides, from which she is never removed except by violence. It is said that when she has finished growing, she lays thousands and thousands of eggs every day, which the workers carry off to the nurseries; and the little grubs which hatch out of them are looked after by the workers who act as nurses and see that the little ones are fed.

The circular dwellings of the native are also derived from the termitaria. It is said that circular dwellings are found in Central and South America, only among the natives of Guiana where termitaria of large size abound. . . .

It is from this object lesson we gather that the industrial system of the African is derived. It is co-operative not egotistic or individualistic. *We*, and not I, is the law of African life. Indeed the word civilization, invented by the Romans, has its root in this idea. They adopted the maxim of Marcus Aurelius who said, "That which is not the interest of the whole swarm is not for the interest of the single bee". The word civilization derived from two Latin words *cum* and *eo*, means together or going together. This is the idea that underlies the efforts of the better class of Socialists in Europe—a socialism which says—not that all yours are mine, as a dominating and exclusive principle, but all mine are yours. . . .

By their socialistic and co-operative method in all material things, the African system avoids all this. [Such European social ills as starvation, neglect, prostitution, etc. ed.] The main business of a tribe—all the families co-operating—is to provide sufficient food, clothing, house-room, and all the conditions of a reasonably comfortable life for all—even the slaves—who are really domestic servants, children of the household. . . .

The conditions which have secured these comforts to the African from generation to generation throughout the centuries are—first, collective ownership by the tribe of all the land and water; second, the equal accessibility of these natural objects to all—man, woman, and child.

The people have free access at all times to the land and to the water, to cultivate the land for food and clothing, to hunt and to fish. All land animals, birds, and insects useful or harmful to man, are theirs to enjoy or to destroy without let or hindrance.

Everybody has the right to sail upon the river, lake, or sea and retain for his own use and benefit every thing which may be the result of his efforts in these elements. There is not law of property so sacred that any man, woman, or child would be allowed to remain and suffer either hunger or nakedness without a sufficient supply of food or clothing provided such things existed in village or community. When villages or towns become too crowded the whole population turn out and built other towns in the vacant places around. We have ourselves been witness to such improvements in the countries in the interior, where we have seen places cleared and buildings erected by the co-operative method for the accommodation of three to four hundred persons in one week.

When the full meaning to the life of the African of the two conditions we have mentioned above, as regards land and water, is understood, then it will be realized why the African everywhere fights for his land when he will hesitate to fight about anything else.

*　　*　　*

The same disasters which the competitive or egoistic system produces in England and throughout Christendom it produces in Africa even on the small scale on which it has hitherto been able to operate—happily only in the coast settlements.

These deplorable results flow from the individualistic order as naturally and regularly as showers from the clouds of summer.

If, therefore, Europe wishes to help Africa—and in her own interests she must wish to help Africa—she can do so effectively . . . only by assisting her in the maintenance and development of her own social system.

There was a time when the native African, brought up on European lines, looked upon everything European as absolutely superior; and as alone indispensable to the attainment of man's highest happiness and usefulness in this world, and even to salvation beyond the grave. He looked upon the European method of accumulating wealth, the wear and tear and excitement of trade, upon the banking system, the individualistic possession, as the *ultima Thule* of human development. But a vast, a sad, an increasing experience has provided to him, so far as happiness for himself or success for his posterity is concerned, that these things are but "broken cisterns that can hold no water".

Not one civilized native, who fifty years ago was for this country, independently rich in the European sense, has left any descendant who is not today living from hand to mouth; and there is no prospect that things will be any better in the future. The African is, therefore, rapidly arriving at a revision of his former immature ideas of the subject. There are today hundreds of so-called civilized Africans who are coming back to themselves. They have grasped the principles underlying the European social and economic order and reject them as not equal to their own as means of making adequate provision for the normal present and future—from birth all through life to death. They have discovered all the waste places, all the nakedness of the European system both by reading and by travel. The great wealth can no longer dazzle them, and conceal from their view the vast masses of the population living under what they supposed to be the ideal system, who are of no earthly use either to themselves or to others, and the great number of human beings from whom these "waste products" are recruited generation after generation. And these so-called civilized Africans are resolved, as far as they can, to save Africa from such a fate. They observe that in the social structure of Europe there are three permanent elements —Poverty, Criminality, Insanity—people who live in workhouses, prisons, and lunatic asylums. These are at the bottom of society. . . .

Above these and rising towards the surface of Society are the "submerged tenth", who live partly by work and partly by crime. Above the submerged tenth, we find the great mass of working men who can only provide for their necessities from day to day during the working years of their lives, and whom the workhouse stares constantly in the face as a final resource.

Now under the African system of communal property and co-operative effort, every member of a community has a home and a sufficiency of food and clothing and other necessaries of life and for life; and his children after him have the same advantages. In this system there is no workhouse and no necessity for such an arrangement. Although according to European ideals the people live on a lower level, still there is neither waste nor want, but always enough and to spare. They have always the power and the will for a generous hospitality. Lieutenant Cameron, who wrote *Across Africa*, told the present writer that when on his celebrated journey from the East Coast with a number of followers his supplies gave out before he had completed half the journey and he had no means to purchase food, the natives—men whom he had never seen before and whom he never expected to see again—furnished him, free of charge, with all the provisions he needed until he reached the Atlantic. Mr. H. M. Stanley tells a similar story.

These are the people whom imaginative Europeans denounce as "lazy"; but all over the continent, where they are not disturbed by the moral depredations of unappreciative foreigners, they realize and have in daily practice the reform which . . . is much needed in England.

The communistic order of African life is not the result of accident. It is born of centuries of experience and is the outcome of a philosophical and faultless logic. Its idea among all the tribes is enshrined in striking proverbs. Among the Veys, for example, a proverb runs thus, "What belongs to me is destroyable by water and fire; what belongs to us is destroyable neither by water nor by fire." Again: "What is mine goes; what is ours abides." And this proverb never fails in illustration all over Africa. Among Mohammedans the Koran comes to the help of this principle by its remarkable utterance in the chapter entitled the Spider. "Surely the frailest of all houses is the house of the spider," referring to the egotistic method of construction and purpose. . . .

*   *   *

The property laws of Africa in intention and in practice make for the widest distribution of wealth or well being and work steadily against concentrating the wealth of a community, either of land or production in the hands of a comparatively small number of individuals.

From the Family Organization and the property laws which naturally follow, the whole Social System is regularly developed. We have the village or the town, then the province or district—all of these together form the State or Tribe; and the continuity of the life of these institutions follows the general principle underlying the Family Organization. There is unity, equality, and at the same time priority or paramountcy, all the groups together composing the social system. Self-government is exercised always with the Family group; and there is also within every group recognized and acted upon this general principle, that the efforts of each and the efforts of all are and must be made for the good of each and the good of all.

Each family is responsible for the care of its own weak ones, the aged, the incurable, the helpless, and the sick. If the family fails, then responsibility falls upon the village or town, etc.

In matters of more general interest the village or town is responsible, and as the interests widen the larger and higher social groups become involved in their responsibility.

Under this system no hospitals are needed, which are necessitated by the individualistic system of Europe and America and the complications arising from foreign intervention.

Under the African system also no stealing takes place. The necessity and the habit of theft do not arise, because everybody has his rights, and everybody has enough. . . .

*   *   *

We hear of thefts and burglaries committed by aborigines in the Settlements. In their own country these people are guiltless of such crimes; they learn to indulge in them when brought into contact with the egotistic system, which everywhere furnishes both temptation and incentive to steal, and from which Europe is now endeavouring to escape.

Nothing in Native life of value is ever really destroyed by European indiscriminate interference, but everything is made weaker. Some things unrepressed by philanthropy or legislation continue to operate, albeit clandestinely, in their worst forms. The African marriage custom, for example, never abandoned, continues in its most degrading animal aspect, and a false life is assumed, poisoning the social atmosphere and undermining the moral character. The substructions of the social and moral structure being impaired, the whole building is shaky, and no man can depend on his neighbour. So much for unscientific, if good meaning intermeddling in other people's affairs.

*   *   *

This is also our complaint against the Church as it has demoralized the Social System of Africa; it has robbed us of our communistic spirit by denominational strifes and rivalries, and is helpless to supply a remedy; "it has put book into our head". as an old and prominent female member of the Church said to us last week, "and has taken love from our heart", and yet the people, owing to their spiritual aspirations and necessities cling to this Organization with a loyalty and devotion which . . . used in another connection, "amazes the outsider at the patience and inertness with which the mass of people acquiesce in what they deem to be their lot". The Church not only does not help, but imposes burdens upon the people for which there is no warrant in the system of religion as taught by Christ.

Africans living under native laws and Institutions would never co-operate with any man or company to the end that one man or company should appropriate to his or their own use and benefit the whole of the surplus wealth resulting from their joint efforts. The whole of the surplus wealth accumulated under our Native System by co-operative labour is regularly and in a most orderly manner sub-divided among all the people co-operating. "Unto each according to his several ability." Those whose efforts are worth more receive proportionately a greater share of the surplus. The internal wars of the African have been largely in defence of his Social Institutions, resisting men of his own tribe anxious to aggrandize themselves at the expense of the people. His wars against Europeans have also been in defence of his Institutions which he regards as sacred.

Our natives who have accumulated money under the individualistic system of Europe cannot go back to their tribal home because their wealth would be subjected to distribution according to native custom and law; and in view of their training it is impossible for them to submit now to such an arrangement; therefore they continue to live under the European Order and are amenable to its vicissitudes. All their wealth, sooner or later, goes back to the European, in spite of the most stringent provisions of Wills and Codicils. Men may doubt this, object to it, hate it, and think that their case will be an exception to the rule, but the law goes on all the same. It is not a rule but a law—the law of disintegration under the European competitive order.

Earnest missionaries in their innocence and goodwill strove from the very first to destroy the communistic order of African life because they saw that the whole system was based upon and grew out of the family arrangement, which, in their lack of scientific knowledge, and entire misconception of Scripture, they "abhorred". A distinguished Prelate once told the writer that the abolition of the African Family organization had done more harm to the permanent interests of the people than all the reputed cannibalism on the whole continent. . . .

*   *   *

. . . Organizations among civilized Africans, whether for Industrial, Educational, or Religious work . . . do not succeed. They have often been tried here and elsewhere on the Coast. They do not succeed because they violate the law of African life and growth. For, after all, they involve what might be called a plural egotism. They do not imply the WE of the communal life. They are competitive Organizations not only to promote their own but to circumscribe the prosperity of others. Like the Combines in Europe they threaten the life of others; and this Africa will not allow. What is *mine* goes; what is *ours* abides.

* * *

As we have said before, no African living under African laws or African institutions would help to forward any enterprise which would result in the appropriation by a few of the surplus wealth resulting from the joint efforts of the people. When this system is introduced by foreigners the African is antagonistic, and often prefers to go on strike into the primeval forest, and there, under however hard conditions, live a life of freedom from dependence on anyone for the everyday needs of even mere animal existence. Africa fights continually against a proletariat class. Under her system there must be no exploiters and no proletariat. This is why the Native sometimes appears to the unimaginative European as lazy.

Under his native institutions the African lives for the most part out of doors, and is not overburdened with clothes. He likes light and heat. He always builds his towns near water—creeks and rivers —that he may have free use of that element for purpose of ablution. He bathes in the morning before he goes to his work and in the evening when he returns, so that there is no chance of there being produced that class of wretches whom General [William] Booth[1] denounces as "a menace to public health, the source of disease, filth, and abominations"; and whom he would get rid of at any cost, whatever their innocence or guilt.

When does the African study? it may be asked. He studies every day—morning, noon, and night—from the cradle to the grave. He is ever reading the book of Nature; and there is never chapter or page in this book which he is either ashamed or afraid to look at. . . .

It is charged against the African that he is lazy, and needs a lot of wives to work for him; and yet a hundred steamers constantly dog the coast to take away his produce—created not by the help or supervision of the white man. He is lazy, yet steamers frequently lie in West African ports for days landing cargo. All this stuff must

[1] Founder in 1878 of the Salvation Army [ed.].

be presents to a lazy worthless set of men, who give nothing in return. How benevolent our kind friends in Europe must be! But let us examine the charge, looking into the daily life of the people. The man has to fell all the timber on the land, and prepare the ground for building or farming. He has to build the house for the wife. If he has six wives, he has to build a house for each of them. The women sow the seed, and the men and women reap the crop. In cloth manufacture the women spin the cotton, and the men weave. Everywhere there is this division of labour. All work. But the men everywhere always do the hardest and most exhaustive forms of labour. . . .

The African has no expensive Army or Navy or great Civil Service to maintain, so he does not need to perform unremitting work to keep up these destructive and unproductive institutions. With him work is not the object of life, but life is the object of work. He does not live to work, but he works to live. Labour with him, as with all other men, is a curse. Occupation is a blessing.

*   *   *

THE CRIMINAL IN AFRICA

. . . In nearly all the foreign periodicals that come daily to hand there is some reference to crime and the difficulties of dealing with it.

Africa has no such problem. As a rule, only the crime of murder or high treason is punished by deportation, the criminal being allowed after a term of years to return to his country. Criminals, who, after due examination, not according to individual caprice, but according to established traditional law well known to the people, are not always executed immediately, but are reserved for some appointed time when all persons proved worthy of death gathered together in some public place, where, with the sanction of religious rites, they are executed before God. . . .

Now the Africans in punishing criminals attach a sacred significance to the act. They do not regard it as their own doing, but the Lord's. The criminals and all the people are brought into the presence of the Almighty, who they feel takes cognizance of all the actions of men, and who as Judge of all the earth will by no means clear the guilty.

We often see in foreign papers great horror expressed at some public executions in Africa, which are ignorantly described as arbitrary human sacrifices and attributed to the blood-thirsty disposition of native Rulers, as if men anywhere would delight in the shedding of blood as a mere pastime.

The Africans by their penal method produce a deterrent effect upon the people, at the same time that they rid the country of the pernicious influence of the permanent criminal class, which the system in England, for example, of long or short imprisonments for certain crimes does not do. It neither deters the people from crime nor saves the community from the example, as well as the taint of criminality. . . .

The practice in Africa is to rid the country both of the crime and the criminal. Now the result of the European system is that some of the worst criminals are incarcerated for a few months and then let out to continue to poison the moral and social atmosphere. The method does not seem to be to extinguish the burglar, but to invent instruments to defeat his enterprise. Every day in England the magistrates are sending hundreds of culprits to prison, and every day hundreds are released, a large proportion of whom before that week or even before that day is ended will have again commenced a course of conflict with the law and may not impossibly be again undergoing punishment. In a word, the result of the European system of indulgence, discipline, and retribution is that Europe passes through the gaols a vast number of criminals who become as active and as dangerous an element on their release as before their capture. These men were criminals before they went to gaol and they resume the life of crime the moment they are let out, on whom, moreover, the punishment which they have just endured has had no reformatory effect, for no moral influence was brought to bear upon them during their period of incarceration.

*　　*　　*

The African system, on the other hand, while it deprives the criminal of the power of doing further mischief, safeguards the community by its effective deterrent influence.

The fact is that the African periodical "Customs" as they are called, and ascribed to inveterate barbarism and cruelty peculiar to Africa, were at one time practiced in Europe by all the nations who now lead in civilization. The practice of human sacrifice prevailed in all parts of Europe even among highly-cultured people. Men were sacrificed by the most prominent and by even the most educated individuals. At a military sedition Julius Caesar ordered two of his soldiers to be publicly killed as expiatory offerings by the High Priest and the Priest of Mars and fixed their heads before the *Regia Martis*. The Gauls sacrificed men at every important crisis at the time of Caesar and Cicero. The old Swedes every nine years, at the great National Festival, celebrated for nine days, offered nine male animals of every chief species, together with one man daily. The Danes assembling every nine years in their capital sacrificed to their gods ninety-nine horses, ninety-nine dogs, ninety-nine ducks, ninety-nine hawks, and ninety-nine men.

Among Africans these periodical customs, no longer practiced, were of the nature of sin-offerings on behalf of the whole community and thank-offering also for the national deliverance from the fact and taint of crime. We fear that no such thoughtful or pious motive enters into European executions, where the criminals are either slaughtered privately or made the sport and jest of the populace.

Of all the charges brought against the African, perhaps the most serious is that of blood-thirstiness as was supposedly exemplified in the Annual Customs which formerly took place at Ashanti, Dahomey, and Benin. The execution of large numbers of prisoners on various occasions has been generally represented as being the wanton indulgence of a natural or racial instinct in cruelty perpetrated upon innocent and harmless victims.

But the world has within the last few years—in this enlightened twentieth century—been shocked by the sanguinary proceedings in highly civilized Europe. The papers have described wholesale executions which have taken place there. The number of persons said to have been hanged at Warsaw . . . alone at one time was six hundred. We have also all read of the unprovoked massacres at Kishnieff and other places of unoffending Jews. Are we to suppose that these people were killed as a religious duty with no feeling of bitterness or revenge? Yet the method of the African in their penal arrangements has often been made an excuse by their foreign exploiters for slaughtering them wholesale, killing more natives in one day in innocent blood than the African system kills in criminals during many years. This is the way an unenlightened civilization interferes to save the natives.

Now if any executions or massacres approaching such as have occurred in Russia had taken place in Africa the news would have been heralded abroad as an example of inveterate and unmitigated savagery.

Owing to an entire misconception on the part of foreigners, a great deal has been made of what has been called the "Annual Customs", which have existed, and perhaps still exist among some of the African tribes, when the extreme penalty of the law is to be carried out.

Among some of the tribes, criminals who have forfeited their lives are reserved for a special day in the year when the Rulers of the People meet to make sacrifice for the sins of the Nation by disposing of the criminals who have been sentenced to death, under the sanction, and with the approval of the highest religious authorities. Crime is never said to be punished by the fiat of the King, but by the Judgment of God, to whom alone the people believe that vengeance belongs, and who only has the right to recompense. Compare this deliberate, calm, judicial, religious taking of life with the stories of lynching which come from the Western World or of Pogroms which come from Russia; and remember that one is the practice of benighted heathen in the European sense, and the other of enlightened Christians. If the modern superficial critic of African Customs would only read history, he would find that that great nation who gave law to the civilized world—Rome—in its most brilliant period, Virgil, Cicero and Horace had lived, and the reign of universal peace had prevailed under Augustus—practised most brutal customs; he would discover that hundreds of highly civilized people gazed periodically from the benches of the Coliseum upon the combats of men with men, between whom no enmity existed, or of men with beasts. Roman spectators encouraged men to butcher each other, not under the influence of any cause so respectable as superstition, but from a morbid love of amusement at the sight of blood. There were women among the spectators who sat and applauded, and with wild outcries urging the populace to refuse the petition of the kneeling gladiator, giving the signs of murder to the guards of the arena. If the censurer of African customs read further and came down to the time when Christianity had taken possession of Southern Europe, he would observe that among the sportive recreations of highly-cultivated Spanish Christians, was the shedding of blood, sometimes on behalf of Christianity; they would see a bull-fight in the list of amusements at Seville or an *auto-da-fé* in the square at Toledo. They would gaze at an amphitheatre thronged with spectators; the King is on the throne; Torquemada sits beside him on the dais, and the banners of the Inquisition float beside those of Aragon and Castile. The Cathedral has sent its Chapter and its Choir, the monastery, its sable or white-robed brethren; the grandees are surrounded by their suite; the beauty and the chivalry of the realm are sitting side by side; and in the outer circle is an indiscriminate crowd, eager, jubilant, and uncontrollable; the vacancy in the midst is occupied by upright stakes, on which are bound a Mohammedan, a Jew, and one who, though neither Jew nor Mohammedan, has been reading feloniously a book written fifteen hundred years before by certain fishermen of Galilee.

Now we want to ask whether Africa has ever exhibited to the world any such scenes as those described above. The religious training of the perpetrators of these deeds cannot be said to have been neglected. Their deeds cannot be ascribed to their secular in contradistinction to their religious training.

RELIGION

WHAT is Religion? Generally the answer is that which makes a man feel that he is not his own guide, judge, or ultimate authority; that he is bound to a higher and irresistible Power that created him and by whose *fiat* he will cease to live. That is religion. He may have no conception of the nature or character of the Power; and leave him to himself without external influence or the aid of books, he will never even try to define to himself what the Power is; he only knows it exists—I AM—and is sufficiently impressed by the reality of its existence, whether looking within at the workings of his own mind or without at the operations of Nature. He knows that a power not himself is working within and around him, and not to offend this power and to gain its favour, he uses various means which appeal to his untutored imagination to effect this object. All races without the Bible and even with the Bible have their own method of approaching this Being.

The African believes that the great Being can be approached through every object which he has created, whether animate or inanimate. He can conceive of nothing which is not instinct with the Creator. He is a Pantheist. . . . He never attempts to formulate any conception of the great Creator and hence he has no theology; but that he is a spiritual being all close observers of his condition admit.

*   *   *

From our standpoint, we do not believe that Africa needed the theological interference of Europe, for the Theology of Europe is derived from the conceptions of Roman, Celt and Teuton, which have modified the Semitic ideas promulgated in the Bible. European Christianity is Western Christianity—that is to say, Christianity as taught at Nazareth, in Jerusalem, and on the Mount of Beatitudes, modified to suit the European mind or idiosyncracies. What Africa does need from Europe is its Imperial and scientific help . . . and directing in the material development of the country. But for spiritual leadership in Africa, the events of a hundred years of effort do not justify her interference. . . .

* * *

It is difficult to get our philanthropic friends to understand that as a rule, the training they have been giving to the Negro with the very best intention is not the best for him; that, in many respects, it disqualifies rather than fits him for comprehending his proper relation to the outside world and his own peculiar work. They honestly give us their best and wonder that their best does not produce the best results; but their best on their line is not as good as our best on our line. There is but one way open to every man and every race for effective life and successful work; every other channel is full of difficulties and obstructions. That only way must be found out before there can be peace and harmony and progress. Among the best Imperial Administrators now of West African Colonies there is a serious and earnest effort being made to study and codify native laws on all the various subjects that affect native life. This is the method that must be pursued before any efficient education can be imparted to the natives.

The missionary work as pursued at the present day is not the same as that pursued fifty or a hundred years ago. We have now "the steamship and the railway and the thoughts that shake mankind". We have multiplication of newspapers and books that reach the native who has learned to read the English language. In former days the missionaries had what may be called a *tabula rasa*—an open and uncontested field. What he told the people remained in their mind as absolute truth, based, not only on the Word of God, but coming from a country where the people had reached the perfection almost of angels, and therefore he had a right as one of those who had "already attained" to be the guide of others. But all this is changed now. Natives frequently visit Europe and see things for themselves; and for those who remain at home the effect of what the foreign preacher says on Sunday as to religion and morality is neutralized on Monday by unsavoury reports brought by the newspapers from the country whence the teacher came. The native becomes incredulous and begins to think about the mote and the beam. Besides this, the pressure upon the time of the native; the fierce competition with foreigners on his line of work—his means of livelihood; the exigencies of the steamship and the railway, often necessitating work on Sunday; the example of lay Europeans taking their pleasure on the sacred day; all these things leave the native

no time and less disposition to listen to what the missionary is trying
to tell him. It is evident, therefore, that without a thorough revision
of missionary methods, adapting them to changed conditions,
missionary work in West Africa will become more and more
impossible.

*   *   *

Owing to the intense and increasing materialism of Europe,
especially Anglo-Saxondom, the people have lost touch with the
spirit world. This is no reason why Africans should forget the
privileges enjoyed by their fathers. The inter-communion between
the people of the earth and those in the spiritual sphere is a cardinal
belief of the African and will never be uprooted. Death is simply
a door through which men enter the life to come or the Hereafter.
This being the basis of their faith they have, like the Japanese, no
dread of death. Some years ago in our hinterland the people thought
no more of despatching one of their nearest relatives to the spirit
world than we now think of sending a messenger to a friend in one
of the neighbouring villages. At Mano-Salija before the advent of
civilization the bar of the river was considered one of the chief
entrances to the abode of the spirits. This impression still remains
amongst the people, only their spiritual leaders think that this
gateway has been polluted by the advent of strangers and strange
customs. It is said that about fifty years ago when the Vey country
was under great affliction by war from the Interior tribes, and man-
stealing by the Spaniards was at its height, the people decided to
send one of their number—of royal blood—of the lineage of the
King and Prophetess—into the world of spirits—to relate the story
of their affliction to their ancestors who in their turn would represent
it to the Supreme Being. This was also a custom among the
Japanese. It is even said that they deposited beside the corpse letters
of credit to be honoured in the next world.

We have learnt from a Vey Chief, that there are today in the
Vey Country sacred places of worship near springs and creeks and
rivers. A place called Zontomy is said to be the most wonderful
for exhibitions of specimens of the reptile kingdom which may there
be witnessed. No one finds the Zontomy unless accompanied by
the living prophetess. On the day of the Banquet of the Dead when
thousands of people go to make offerings to their ancestors (consisting of rice, flour, cassada, grain, meat, not fish) these things
are placed before the prophetess on the sandy shores of Zontomy
Creek. The visitor, who is a stranger, is alarmed when at the call
of the prophetess, a frail little woman, a huge crocodile comes to

the surface of the water in a straight line makes towards the crowd. On reaching the shore she is fed with flour in the presence of all. It is really astonishing to see a tiny old woman passing her fingers through the dreadful teeth of this monster. After this, other crocodiles come one by one as they are called by name by the prophetess. In a few minutes the whole surface of the creek is ruffled by the upward shooting of the heads of fishes and crocodiles. The food is then indiscriminately distributed over the surface of the water. The Marfah Bay, Qualu creek at Bendu, and Sugary are other sacred places. At Sugary the Sandfish family meet their sacred dead and a huge crocodile still guards the place, and the people move freely among them. At any of these places one may at any time see the prophetess going down under the surface of the water, remaining there over an hour, then coming up attired in the most gorgeous fashion, her hair plaited, beads tied all over her limbs in a most artistic manner.

At these places intercourse with the world of spirits is constantly carried on. Everywhere in Pagan Africa there is this intercourse. . . .

*   *   *

The African Religion is a matter that affects all classes of the people—men, women, and children. As a Pagan, the women assist in the functions of the State. They visit the sacred groves. The Bundo and Porroh rites act conjointly with the State in training the youth of both sexes to morality and patriotism. As in other matters, the Religion is communistic. When this system is recklessly and indiscriminately interfered with, the result is what we are witnessing everywhere in West Africa, as in Uganda—dislocations, degeneracy, death.

PART IV

Race and the African Personality

PART IV

Race and the African Personality

Partly as a reaction to European charges of Negro inferiority, partly influenced by contemporary writings on race, Blyden developed his own theory of race—the basis of his concept of negritude—in which he maintained that there was no superiority or inferiority among races, but that each of the major races did have certain inherent attributes which it was the duty of members of each race to develop for the ultimate good of humanity. The "African personality"—a phrase he seemed to have first used in 1893 (25)—was characterized by cheerfulness, sympathy and willingness to serve. It was in the spiritual and cultural sphere, he maintained, that Negroes would make their major contribution to world civilization. Note his plea for one West African non-sectarian Christian denomination doctrinally modified to suit West African conditions (24) and his letter to Booker T. Washington, the American Negro leader, asserting that spiritually the Negro was the superior of the white man (26). He opposed miscegenation as "unnatural", and developed an intense dislike of mulattoes, an attitude reflected in (23). He saw parallels between the history of Negroes and Jews, a theme he developed in (27).

Blyden's views on race have not been well known because he did not write explicitly on this; it was only in his private correspondence that he expressed himself freely. His preoccupation with racial purity stemmed from his experiences in the United States and Liberia where, among non-whites, the nearer one approximated to white physically and culturally, the higher one's social standing. In short, miscegenation had created artificial divisions among "Negroes" based at least partly on the shade of colour of one's skin. For Blyden, concerned to promote racial unity, this was deplorable. But among Africans, miscegenation has been far from common so that the question of racial purity has never greatly exercised African leaders. Nor have his racial views been popular among Afro-Americans, who, while they were aware of these divisions, showed no inclination to discuss them openly. Only one black nationalist leader from the New World, Marcus Garvey, openly agreed with Blyden on the need for "race purity" and came close to matching Blyden's own detestation of mulattoes.

However, such concepts of Blyden as negritude and the African personality, as is well known, have been subscribed to, though not necessarily as a result of direct influence, by black nationalist leaders on both sides of the Atlantic, among them Aimé Césaire of Martinique, Kwame Nkrumah, ex-President of Ghana, and Leopold Sengkor, President of Senegal.

23

On Mixed Races in Liberia

Monrovia, October 6th, 1869
Smithsonian Institute, Annual Report, 1870, 386–8

My Dear Sir:[1]

I send enclosed a catalogue of all the students who have ever been in Liberia College. It will be seen not only were they not natives (aborigines), but more than three-fourths the number have been largely mixed with Caucasian blood, and among these death and disease have made sad ravages.

The great practical difficulty in the way of succeeding with our schools is the lack of suitable teachers. It is sad to relate that notwithstanding the thousands of dollars spent annually here by the different missions for educational purposes, there are still but very few teachers to be found especially among the females, able to conduct properly an elementary school. The reason is that pains and money have been bestowed upon persons largely mixed with Caucasian blood, who, if males, have mostly died, or if females, have got married and assumed the cares of a family. It seems that the females of mixed blood, who are not obliged to put forth much exertion, and not subject to much exposure, last longer than the males. It appears, also, that mulattoes born and brought up in America, if they can pass through the acclimating process, stand the climate much better than those born here, but only by engaging in as little physical or mental labour as possible. Persons having an admixture of foreign blood are very frail, easily take cold, and seldom recover from a severe attack of illness. This will account in part for our want of enterprise and progress here. Such men have had the lead and management of things, and, by the fearful example of their disastrous inactivity, have been obstructive guides, discouraging all energy and *go-a-headitiveness*.

Before the question of race came up here, mulattoes died just as they do now, but it was not noticed. Their mortality was put down to the general unhealthiness of the climate. But since Professor Freeman,[2] in his address of July, 1868, called the attention of the

---

[1] The letter was originally sent to a Board member of the New York Colonization Society and a trustee of Liberia College [ed.].

[2] Martin H. Freeman was Professor of Mathematics and Natural Philosophy at Liberia College [ed.].

people to the startling history of mixed breeds on this coast for
the last two hundred years, the mixed classes have been watching
with alarm the numerous indication of the frail tenure of their
existence.

I have been for the last eighteen years connected with educational
matters here, and feel safe in giving it as one reason why we are
no better off in men to take charge of schools and churches, that
the attention of educators has been principally devoted to persons
of feeble constitutions.

The idea was that the presence of white blood imparted greater
aptitude for learning, and such persons were to be fitted for teachers.
Black boys of hale and hearty *physique* were left to grow up un-
noticed. Many of them have taken to sea-faring life, or gone to
reside as permanent traders among the natives, who might now be
active workers in our destitute fields. But with all the advantages
afforded to the miscegens, still the only professors for the college
yet produced in Liberia are pure Negroes; and the only man with
enterprise, energy, and talent enough to explore the interior, cal-
culate distances, and construct a map is a pure Negro;[3] and in the
future, if we have any scientific men here, botanists, mineralogists,
chemists, etc., they are sure to be pure Negroes, and perhaps from
the native tribes.

But what has become of the half and three-fourths white *pro-
tégés*? In the Alexandria high school we had Armistead, Miller,
Fleming, Melville, Augustus, Fryzon, Samuel D'Lyon, Colston,
Waring, James H. Roberts, all are dead. In Liberia College, we
have had James H. Evans, J. J. Roberts, jr., Beverly Russell, J. T.
Chambers, John Henry, J. H. Harris, Edmund J. Payne, all dead.
J. W. Leone is a raving maniac, and may die at any moment. . . .
Facts, it is said, are God's arguments. I venture to affirm that if
the names I have just cited had been Negroes, three-fourths of them
at least would have been living today; for in all that space of time
I know of only one connected with either institution who has died,
N. R. Richardson, of sunstroke.

Now, who is to blame for these things? No one in the past;
but if they are continued in the future . . . then those who continue
them must be blamed. I do not charge guilt upon any one in the
past, for I believe that these things were not done at the instigation
of wrong passions, but under the delusion of a theory. And you,
gentlemen in America, proud of your race and blood, have thought,

---

[3] Benjamin Anderson, the most noted Liberian explorer of his time; author
of *Narrative of a Journey to Musadu*, New York, 1870, to be reprinted by
Frank Cass [ed.].

perhaps, that it must, as a matter of course, endure here, when strengthened by a Negro basis, and bring to the Negro an accession of improving mental qualities. But your theory has not stood the test. So far as physical health and vigour are concerned, I would rather take my chance here as a pure Caucasian than as a mongrel. The admixture of the Caucasian and the Negro is not favoured by Providence in inter-tropical Africa, whatever may be the case in America. Let me beg you to look at this matter at once before wasting any more thousands upon an impracticable scheme. . . .

The friends of the Negro in America must learn to believe that the Negro can exist and prosper without the aid of white blood in his veins.

Now that slavery is abolished in America, and the blacks are being educated, it is to be hoped that all good men will discourage, as far as possible, the "miscegenation" doctrine. The Negro race is injured by it far more than the white, for by prejudice the nondescript progeny is consigned to our side, even if they are three-fourths or seven-eighths white, and thus involve us in an inextricable "muddle". This is certainly a vexed question. But the higher plane to which the American people have attained by the recent revolution has given them the loftier views and wide sympathies, and has furnished the means of education for the Negro, which will supply the transition process from his low estate to a more intelligent and respectable position. Respect for the Negro is becoming more and more, in the progress of events in America, the happy distinction of our age. The Negro is being taught to respect himself, and soon he will think it no honour to mingle his blood with that of the Caucasian, Indian, or Mongolian.

24

The Return of the Exiles and the West African Church

London, 1891, 24-33

PROPOSALS FOR A WEST AFRICAN CHURCH

Events now transpiring have roused thinking minds among the Christian natives along the coast to establish a Church of their own, so as to be able to deal with their own problems, with which strangers cannot safely or profitably intermeddle. The present state of things must remind every thinking African who has been abroad, of those notices on tickets sometimes issued by Railway Companies or Exhibitions—"Good for this trip only" or "Not transferable". So this present ecclesiastical arrangement, with its foreign props and support, its foreign stimulus and restraints, might be labelled—"Good for this generation only". It can neither be transmitted nor transferred. We cannot transfer or transmit that which is alien to us, however by assiduous or protracted imitation it may seem to be ours. . . . The time will come, and not in any distant future, when our foreign patrons will withhold their patronage—remove the props which have supported us; then, do you think our children will be able to maintain these alien and artificial arrangements? Will they care to keep up a complicated foreign system in which they have no extraneous assistance?

Of course, in the new movement, there will be among the more conservative here, as elsewhere, apprehensions as to the results of a change. How will it strike foreigners? How will it affect ourselves? Well, the fact is, we shall never learn to swim unless we venture into the water. Let us launch out into the deep and try the vast ocean of life, with its sweeping gales and dashing waves. If our tiny bark should be battered by storms, and we return to the port with broken spars and tattered sails, we should be learning by experience. We should learn to be careful not to spread too wide a sail before we are sure of the strength of the gale. And what if we should founder? Many a gallant ship, with able commander, has suffered that fate; but we shall not founder, if we are careful to take Him into the ship with us, whose power can calm the boisterous sea, and say to the raging waves, "Peace be still".

But to leave the figurative. I have not the slightest doubt that, in forming an independent Church, there will be at first much that is unsatisfactory. We shall probably be misgoverned; the work will be at times neglected; our finances will be mismanaged. Someone who watches on the walls may go to sleep when the hour demands unsleeping vigilance; but here again we should be learning by experience. We might be often hampered by the thought of the clumsy and blundering figure we present to the world. We might be worried by the suspicion that our enemies are marking and recording all our shortcomings. We should be certain to go through a period of difficulties, of failures, when sympathy would be with our enemies, not with us; but we should be gaining patience and experience, and acquiring by labour, by trial, by suffering, by self-denial, a possession which we can transmit as our own to our children. We should also be able to recognize those who may be to blame for our misfortunes, and be able to deal with them as we have not the power to do now with delinquents and those whose defects and vices trouble the Church and hinder her prosperity. But in this new enterprise we shall not be taking a leap altogether in the dark. There are lights and landmarks to encourage and stimulate us. Bishop Crowther and his able and persistent fellow-workers on the Niger have laid the foundation of an African Church, and have inspired throughout the Christian world the belief and hope that such a Church is possible. That institution of loftiest promise—the Native Pastorate—the Apostolic fervour and zeal and abundant labours of your James Johnson, show you the possibilities of the Native for indigenous and independent work.

But while the Church should be Native, we do not mean that it should be local. We want to drop the conventional trammels of Europe, but we do not wish to localize religion, I mean to say that we do not wish to give it any tribal colouring or bias. We want to hold up the simple teaching of Christ, and go out into the highways and hedges of our country and bring the people in, believing that there are those who are in earnest in their worship of God, needing only to have the way of salvation taught them more perfectly.

The Christian world has not yet fully grasped the teachings nor understood the example of Him who was found not only among the doctors of the Temple, but among publicans and sinners, eating and drinking with them. . . .

* * *

We must seek to bring into the Native Church the Chiefs and other men of influence. Do not expect of them the perfection which a narrow philanthropy exacts. Consider the conditions under which Europe received the Gospel. Had the hard conditions now imposed upon African Chiefs been required of European sovereigns and chiefs, Christianity might never have been permanently established on the west of the Bosphorus.

The first Christian Emperor, Constantine, was half a pagan to the end. He erected in his new capital, Constantinople, a statue of himself. At the base of this statue, it is said, he placed a fragment of what he believed to be the true Cross. In the same place he deposited the palladium, the cherished relic of Pagan Rome, which Aeneas was said to have rescued from the flames of Troy, and which Constantine himself stealthily removed to his new capital. This was his fetish, brought over from heathenism. It was the same with his legislation. Thus we find, almost side by side, promulgated within two months of each other, two Imperial decrees—the one enjoining that Sunday shall be set aside as a day of rest; the other providing that when the palace or any other public building is struck by lightning, the soothsayers shall be consulted as to the meaning of the prodigy, according to ancient custom, and the answer reported to the Emperor himself. Constantine was at one and the same time the summoner of the Nicene Council, and the chief priest of heathenism. At one moment he was preaching sermons to his courtiers, and discussing dogmas with his bishops; at the next, he was issuing orders for the regulation of some Pagan ritual. . . .

If we knew more about the history of the Church in Europe, of the compromises that had to be effected before it could gain a footing there, we should be less exacting and more charitable to our brethren in the interior, whose condition is that of Europe in her primitive times.

Not the least among the drawbacks in the influence of the agencies, secular and religious, which have operated on the coast, has been the persistent effort to ignore the peculiarities here of race and climate—to make a history for the people, and get them to enact it. The endeavour has been to introduce social forces from abroad—to allow as little as possible to racial and traditional bias, or to individual genius, forgetting that these forces in Europe were a growth, requiring time, and not a sudden inspiration; not the work of a year or a generation. The consequence is just what ought to have been expected, viz., that whatever the cleverness or industry of these foreign teachers, "the stars in their courses" fight against them, and no learning or money or valour can overcome these celestial antagonists. No; history in Africa is to be made as history everywhere else. You cannot reduce history to social formulas. The business of the foreign teacher is to impart principles which are of universal application, as all the teachings of Christ are, and to interfere as little as possible with the form they will take among the people. . . .

In one of your churches, a few sabbaths ago, a foreign missionary called attention to the unsatisfactory state of things among the Christian natives, without, however, animadverting upon the crude and unphilosophical methods which have conduced to the unfruitful results. Institutions and customs are observed among the people which strike the foreigner as incongruous and ridiculous, because they are not due to any native or spontaneous development, or even adaptation, but are rigid and slavish copies of what exists in Europe and America.

As time goes on, the philanthropic spirit which now seeks to reduce all races to a dead uniformity will find out, under the deeper teachings of science, that if they could succeed in their enterprise they would destroy elements of culture and of their own culture, as a part of humanity, and possibly the most important elements of it, without whose full play humanity must always be lame and imperfect.

The first principle of true growth is truthfulness. Now imitation often produces outward conformity without any inward agreement. Truthfulness of character lies in what we *are*, not what we *appear*, or in what we say. A man may do an act or speak a word which agrees with certain facts, but himself may be false. Truth in inward parts is the first necessity of growth. Simple outward conformity is pretence; pretence is unreality, and unreality is barren. Pretence never has produced, and never can produce, any permanent result.

The West African Church should be an African, not an English production. With Bible in hand, its framers should arrange for the suppression of whatever has hindered truthfulness in the people. The great incubus upon our development has been unreasoning imitation. This we must try to avoid. But do not run to the other extreme of avoiding what is foreign simply because it is foreign. There are many good things in foreign customs—many useful things, many precious things, not only conducive and helpful, but indispensable to a healthy Christian growth. These we must find out and cherish. We must have a Church which will have the affection of the people and the reverence of generations—in which we may feel communion with all God's saints of old, at present and to come. So that all His people we can embody in song, whether in English or Yoruba, in Ibo or Nupe . . . beautiful sentiments. . . .

25

Study and Race

A Lecture to the Young Men's Literary Association of Sierra Leone, May 19th, 1893; *Sierra Leone Times*, May 27th, 1893

TRAINING THE MIND

Gentlemen,

I am very glad to meet you this evening, as I recognize in your efforts, unobtrusive and unpretentious as they are, one of the agencies in the great work which is going on not only for the improvement of the Settlements but for the advancement of light on this continent and for the upbuilding of the race.

The rewards of a literary life are proverbially small in this country from a commercial point of view, and this is a commercial community. It is gratifying, therefore, to find that you have associated yourself together for literary pursuits, thus rising superior to the temptations—the narrow visions and restricted sympathies—around you. And if you are determined to succeed in your efforts you will find that no disadvantages of situation can prevent you from rising to usefulness if not eminence among your people.

The great point at which you should aim is not simply the information, but the *formation* of the mind. The formation of the mind being secured the information will take care of itself. Mere knowledge of itself is not power—but the ability to know how to use that knowledge—and this ability belongs only to the mind that is disciplined, *trained*, *formed*. It may be a pleasant pastime to store the mind with facts, whether of history, science or art, but if the mind is not trained to apply them, they will lie there like so much useless lumber. Moreover in this telegraphic age, with its steamships and railways—with the enormous and diversified production of the press—mental stores are continually vanishing and require to be changed like stock in a warehouse to meet the every varying demands of life. It is impossible to keep up with the rapid accumulation of facts. So if we depended upon mere knowledge we should find ourselves far behind in the race. "Of making of books there is no end," and life is not long enough to compass their contents.

The mind that is formed will be able to deal with the facts already accumulated and make them productive for the benefit of

195

other minds. Mental agility and flexibility do not come from intellectual stores but from intellectual drill. A mind properly drilled will know how to use circumstances wherever it may be thrown. Just as the blacksmith, whose muscles have been exercised and developed, will find himself at home wherever muscular energies are required.

A man who has reached eminence in any department through mental drill and energy will vindicate his superiority wherever thrown. A great clergyman, a great doctor, or a great lawyer will show greatness in whatever he puts his hands to. You have an example before you in your greatest lawyer [Samuel Lewis] becoming a successful farmer, through knowing how to utilize capital, time and energy for the work he had set before himself. It was not the reading of law—the mastering of "technicalities"—which gave him the ability—this mental alertness; but the intellectual drill which he obtained by the methods he adopted in pursuit of his legal studies.

Now, how can you in a voluntary association secure the mental discipline you so much desire? For I cannot believe that you have organized this society merely to secure from time to time an evening's recreation or amusement. But you are not in a school or college where you would be subject to discipline or restraint. You have passed school days.

Perhaps the best advice I can give, under the circumstances, couched in general terms, is, to familiarize yourself with, and endeavour to think the thoughts and live the lives of the great and good of past and contemporary times, as far as you have access to information about them. For practical purposes in your society, I think you would find it useful to select some character distinguished in Religion or Science, in Politics, Literature or Art, and devote one evening every fortnight to the study and discussion of that character. Appoint two of your number to read up carefully the life and work of the particular subject you wish to study and to present to the meeting the result of their investigations; one in the form of a carefully written essay and the other in a *memoriter* declamation. These to form, as it were, texts for a general oral discussion in which each member should be expected to take part, so that everyone would feel himself bound, during the fortnight to get, if not a special, a general knowledge of the subject.

But let the character be as nearly as possible such as would interest you, either because in some way connected with your race, with Africa, or with some work in which humanity generally is interested. It would not, for example, be of any practical interest to you to select for investigation or discussion the Mikado of Japan, or the Annexation of Hawaii to the United States. On the contrary, take, say for one evening William Wilberforce, for another, Sir Thomas Fowell Buxton, or Macaulay, Livingstone, Gladstone, Beaconsfield, Toussaint, Bishop Crowther, etc. etc., for Biography. In art, give an evening to Michelangelo, or Raphael, Titian, Mozart, Beethoven, etc. In poetry, take Shakespeare, Milton, Tennyson, Wordsworth, etc. He, I think, suits the African mind on account of his love of Nature, his simple and cordial manliness and sympathy with every interest of actual life and with every effort for freedom.

No one can read his poems without feeling what has been called their "healing power"—the indirect refreshment, the comfort, the support which every interest of life receives. It was he who, indignant at the treatment accorded by Napoleon to the Negro Toussaint, wrote the touching sonnet to his memory of which the closing words are:

> "—Thou has left behind
> Powers that will work for thee; air, earth and skies;
> There is not a breathing of the common wind,
> That will forget thee; thou has great allies;
> Thy friends are exultations, agonies,
> And love, and man's unconquerable mind."

Tennyson requires a certain kind and degree of culture to appreciate him, though there are poems of his which in their simplicity and tenderness may be understood and loved by a child. No one can fully grasp the beauty and force of Swinburne without having more than an ordinary knowledge of Latin and Greek. I never will read Byron because, brilliant as he sometimes is, he is a man of false and distempered mind.

Of American poets, Bryant, Longfellow, Lowell and Whittier, would be pleasing and edifying reading for you. Their muse did noble work for the African in the days of the Anti-slavery conflict in America.

You will find that if you pursue the course of reading and investigation in the manner I have just ventured to suggest you will, in a comparatively short time, acquire an amount of information and mental drill that will be surprising both to yourself and your neighbours.

I know that it is difficult in this community to find many valuable books; but I am acquainted with a few native gentlemen who have

Q

valuable collections, and they would no doubt under proper conditions allow you access to them. I can speak for the generosity in this respect of at least one gentleman whose name I will give to you after the meeting, if you desire it, as I am sure he would sympathize with your laudable aims.

And so long as you have good books to read you need not complain of disadvantages in having few. My own habit has been not to be ashamed of knowing little or nothing of subjects for which I have no natural aptitude, reading only what will fructify as regards my own mind; while the common fault is, not only here, but elsewhere, trying to excel or make a show in anything that appears attractive in any one else. But, remember, none but men sound in some department of literature have the courage or the confidence to say "they really do not know", for only sound men know the standard of real knowledge and the utter impossibility of comprehending everything. It is a fact, however, that men who set out intending to know only a few things well, soon find that an available knowledge of many subjects insensibly rewards for a careful and patient system of study. For instance, if you take up the life of Macaulay as a study you will at the end be master of a large variety of useful information. But never be ashamed to say in regard to anything you have not studied or have no aptitude for "I do not know". An Oxford undergraduate, a Scholar of his College, was about to go in for his final examination. He went to his tutor to talk over with him a difficult metaphysical problem. The tutor discussed it on various sides, but brought no definite solution. The pupil at last told him plainly that this was not what he wanted. "What I want is the examination answer to the question; give it me in a precise form." "I really can't," was the reply, "it is a point on which nobody can speak dogmatically. Honestly, I do not know." "Come now Mr. ——" said the other, "but you are *paid* to know." So you see that even those who are supposed to be *paid* to know are not ashamed to confess ignorance on some subjects.

But there are sources of mental discipline and culture besides books. Books were the last thing to which the Greeks resorted for information. The Athenians, we are told, spent their time in telling or hearing some new thing. They gathered their information in the streets, in the market place, in porches, by the river side, from acquaintances and strangers, from high and low, from slaves and free men.

The lack of inquisitive conversation is a great defect here. As a rule, people ask no questions except as to what immediately

concerns themselves. I have had visitors who have sat for hours—
or would have sat for hours had I allowed them—with nothing
whatever to say. They had, it seems, nothing upon which they
wished to be informed, or which they wished to communicate. Now,
this is a great bore to a busy man. We generally care to sit in
silence with those only with whom we find it interesting to
converse.

As another source of information, then, let me advise you to
cultivate the art of conversation. There is no one from whom
information of some sort may not be obtained—from the mechanic,
the farmer, the boatman, the fisherman, and especially the aborigines who come from the interior. All these are fruitful sources of
information, neglected because people do not know how to utilize
them.

You may also as a Society acquire information and mental
discipline from discussion—from debates—in which, I believe, you
engage at times. I was going to say let the object of these debates
always be to arrive at truth, not merely victory; but this would
be to presuppose the possession by you of a far higher degree of
moral force than can be found in some of the most elevated assemblies in civilized lands, where the object of speeches—many of the
political speeches I mean—seems to be to prevent men from arriving at the truth—if truth does not happen at the moment to subserve
a party purpose. But at all events, I may advise you to be earnest
and sincere in all your discussions, remembering that no man ever
really lost anything by fairness and justice.

But lastly, each man should read and study with some object in
view. Each one should consider what he reads and studies for?
What is your object? In what line can you reasonably hope to
attain the object of your wishes? I say *reasonably* hope because
some young men entertain the most extravagant and impossible
expectations.

A little Latin or a little Greek is really useful to an English
scholar. Indeed it is impossible as I have intimated above, to have
a complete or satisfactory knowledge of English without some
acquaintance with these so called dead languages. But for a man
who does not expect to go into any of the learned professions to
spend time upon these languages which might achieve some valuable
object in other branches is absurd. A young man called upon me
the other day and wanted to know whether I would take him in
Plato's Republic in the original. He presumed upon my proficiency
in Greek. I endeavoured to show him how preposterous the idea
was—with his prospects in life—of taking up the speculations

of a Greek philosopher, instead of something like Macaulay Essays.

I advised him, if he was not afraid of hard work, and was really in earnest in the desire to improve his mind, to take up Arabic. And I now recommend it to you, not only as a means of mental discipline, but as a source of intellectual pleasure and a subject of practical utility. That language alone would take you across the continent from here to Egypt. In every village and town and city you will find persons to converse with. But even here in your own settlement, you could find men from the interior and men born here with whom by means of that language you could hold literary and profitable intercourse. I am often amazed by the literary insight which I have discovered in learned Mohammedans, nothwithstanding the unspeakable platitudes which have been written about them in certain foreign periodicals. Their minds have been trained. Their acquisitions have not been merely mechanical. They have been made to think and are simply amused at the pitiful efforts made to convert them from a belief which, as Governor Fleming in his reply to their recent Address admitted, they "so sincerely and conscientiously live up to". Results like these—the power of thought—you should aim to achieve with the more complex and extensive educational machinery at your command.

AFRICAN PERSONALITY

But the principle is, to consider what course will, as Bacon says, "add to the glory of the Creator or the relief of man's estate". There are some men who heap up riches with no object whatever in view—simply for the regular satisfaction of possession—so some men heap up facts and burden themselves with stores of knowledge without any regard to health enjoyment, or even utility in their proper calling. Like the "wicked and slothful" servant in the parable they lay on their talent in a napkin. But for every one of you—for every one of us—there is a special work to be done—a work of tremendous necessity and tremendous importance—a work for the Race to which we belong. It is a great Race—great in its vitality, in its powers of endurance and its prospect of perpetuity. It has passed through the fiery furnace of centuries of indigenous barbarism and foreign slavery and yet it remains unconsumed. Well, now, there is a responsibility which our personality, our membership in this Race involves. It is sad to think that there are some Africans, especially among those who have enjoyed the advantages of foreign training, who are blind enough to the radical facts of humanity as to say, "Let us do away with the sentiment of Race. Let us do away with our African personality and be lost, if possible, in another Race."[1]

This is as wise or philosophical as to say, let us do away with gravitation, with heat and cold and sunshine and rain. Of course the other Race in which these persons would be absorbed is the dominant Race, before which, in cringing self-surrender and ignoble self-suppression, they lie in prostrate admiration. Some are really in earnest, honestly thinking that by such means they will rise to the cloudless elevation of Olympus or reach the sublime heights of Parnassus, but the verdict of spectators is that they qualify themselves for Bedlam. There is, only then, one fatal influence against all this teaching, and that is, *the whole course of nature*. Preach this doctrine as much as you like, no one will do it, for no one *can* do it, for when you have done away with your personality, you have done away with yourselves. Your place has been assigned you in the Universe as Africans, and there is no room for you as anything else. Christianity pointed out the importance and purpose of race preservation and development and provided for it. Science has recognized and accepted this truth, both as regards individuals and Races. But the world is far behind Christianity, and still in the rear of science.

What men generally have not yet found out, as they have not yet fully learned Christ, is the way to a righteous development of racial personality. One race tries to force another into its own mould and the weaker race is sometimes compelled to give way to its own detriment and the detriment of humanity.

But the duty of every man, of every race is to contend for its individuality—to keep and develop it. Never mind the teachings of those who tell you to abandon that which you cannot abandon. If their theory were carried out, it would, with all the reckless cruelty of mere theory, blot out all the varieties of mankind, destroy all differences, sacrifice nationalities and reduce the human Race to the formless protoplasm from which we are told we came.

Therefore honour and love your Race. Be yourselves, as God intended you to be or he would not have made you thus. We cannot improve upon his plan. If you are not yourself, if you surrender your personality, you have nothing left to give the world. You

[1] Blyden's lecture was in part a rebuttal of the 'unworthy' advocacy by Joseph Renner Maxwell, a Gold Coast-born lawyer, of miscegenation so as 'to combine the beauty of the Caucasian with the fine physique and physical strength of the Negro'. See Joseph Renner Maxwell, *The Negro Question or Hints for the Physical Improvement of the Negro Race*, London, 1892 [ed.].

have no pleasure, no use, nothing which will attract and charm men, for by your suppression of your individuality you lose your distinctive character.

> "Remember, every man God made
> Is *different*, has some deed to do,
> Some work to work; be undismayed;
> Though thine be humble do it too."

There is hardly anything new in a material sense, that the so-called civilized African can contribute to the world's resources, but if his individuality is preserved and developed on right or righteous lines, he will bring intellectual and spiritual contributions which Humanity will gladly welcome.

Remember, then, that these racial peculiarities are God given. For his own glory they are and were created. To neglect them, suppress them, or get rid of them is to get rid of the cord which binds us to the Creator. Try and learn the important lesson that it is God's intention for you that you should be different from all the rest of mankind—that he placed you here to reveal a phase of His character not given to others to reveal; our duty is to find out what that is.

We have not as yet as a people had the opportunity, either in these West African Settlements or in the countries of our exile, to find out our peculiar calling. But the time will come when we shall find it out, and then it will be the idea which lead our life. We shall guard it as the most precious possession. We shall carefully develop it. But not for selfish purposes. The Negro was made for service. He will put his peculiar power into vital action for the human Race.

No foreign Race need be afraid of us, in spite of the universal oppression and injustice of which we have been the victims. They need not dread the development of our personality. It will be free from any tinge of bitterness towards them or any pompous self assertion. There will be the same receptive spirit and unfailing good temper. It is not out of genuine personality that vanity or self conceit comes, but out of imitation—out of fictitious personality, out of compromise which nature abhors.

We were made for that highest of all glory, which is service for Humanity. He that will be chief let him become your servant, said the great Master. This is a different glory from that of other nations; and in human view would not be considered glory at all. "The glory of the Jew was pure conduct, and conformity to a life of religious law. The glory of the Oriental was calm, reached by putting aside all the pursuits of earth and all the passions of self. The glory of the Greek was divine harmony, the balance and proportionate subordination of all things to one another and to the best, so as to produce a perfect whole. The glory of the Roman was law, and obedience, as the worship due to law." The glory of the African thus far has been the glory of suffering—the glory of the cross—the glory of the Son of Man—the man of sorrows and acquainted with grief. But the future will have a different story to tell. The Cross precedes the Crown.

You will see, then, to give up your personality would be to give up the peculiar work and the peculiar glory to which we are called. It would really be to give up the divine idea—to give up God—to sacrifice the divine individuality; and this is the worst of suicides. We cannot compromise on this subject. But to retain Race integrity and Race individuality is no easy task in the hard, dogmatic and insurgent civilization in which we live. It has been said that the fringe of European civilization is violence. All the agencies at work, philanthropic, political and commercial, are tending to fashion us after the one pattern which Europe holds out. Society is calling upon us to be like the rest of its worshippers. All the books and periodicals we read—all the pictures we see beguile us. Every thing says to us, "Efface yourselves". Many are submerged and love to be submerged, not believing in any peculiar calling or any special work for the Negro.

Some have revelled in the prospect of hearing some fine morning of the *"last of the Negroes"*. But there is a vast future before this Race as there has been a hoary past behind it. The great mass of the race, thank God, has not been tampered with. At least 200 millions in the vast regions east and north and south of us remain intact. The contamination has affected only a few millions in the western hemisphere and a few thousands along the margin of the continent. But no pure race has ever yet been destroyed. The original races of the Eastern hemisphere have existed from the beginning and no one of them can be exterminated, as degenerate offsprings of them have been in America and the islands of the sea. Notwithstanding the injustice to which they are subject in South Africa, they are steadily multiplying. Even in the United States their rapid increase are a menace to their oppressors. The last census (1890) revealed the astounding fact that there are 6,337,980 pure Negroes in that country. There will never be of the original races any "survival of the fittest". All are fit, equally fit, for the work they will have to do, and all will continue. They are co-operating forces or forces that must co-operate in order to [sic] the progress and perfection of Humanity as a whole.

To say only the things that others have said, to repeat only what you have observed in and read of others, to speak only of knowledge which you hear outside is to say and do things with no life in them, dead things, which can impart no life to others.

The more you understand this, the more you reverence yourself as a divine offspring, the more you will reverence others—the more, because they too are personal and different from you. You will pursue after the good and the ideal which God reveals through them.

Yes, I believe that is the right way, but a way which men have not yet learned. It is a way which fulfils the Second Commandment in the Law, which Christ says is like unto the first in importance, "Thou shalt love thy neighbour as thyself". It is this personality which respects and preserves itself and respects and is anxious to preserve others. It is this which interests and awakens and has power to move the world. When it is generally understood and acted upon then will natures the most diverse harmonize and co-operate.

"The wolf also shall dwell with the lamb, and the leopard shall lie down with the kid; and the calf and the young lion and the fatling together, and a little child shall lead them." Humanity will have been revolutionized and reformed.

26

Blyden to Booker T. Washington
28th November, 1894

New York Age, January 24th, 1895

Dear Mr. Washington:

I have just been reading in the *Southern Workman* for October your most interesting letter on the industrial position and prospects of the Negro in the South. I had the privilege of making your personal acquaintance in Washington about five years ago through the courtesy of our mutual friend, Dr. [Francis] Grimke; but I had long before then heard of your intelligent, practical and successful labours for our people.

To me next in importance to the religious development of the Negro in the South is his industrial development. But I think the former depends largely on the latter. When I was a boy I used to write in copybooks, "Godliness with contentment is great gain". Godliness with contentment, if not an impossibility, has serious drawbacks.

When the Negro has attained to that industrial status which will enable him to realize to their utmost his great material possibilities he will not only, as pointed out in your letter, command the respect of the white man, but he will come nearer to God.

NEGRO'S NATURE "SPIRITUAL"

It is a small matter that the "white man has not yet advanced to the point where he will invite a Negro to his prayer meeting". Perhaps he will never advance to that point. The Negro is on a different plane, religiously, from the white man. He has a more spiritual nature; and may yet be the teacher of his master in spiritual matters. We have a symbol or foreshadowing of this in the curious and suggestive description given by Rev. T. K. Beecher in the same number of the *Southern Workman* of the address of "Brother Anderson", during which Mr. Beecher says, with genuine feeling and undisguised frankness, "my sermon seemed to shrink and fade". The Negro is even now, so to speak, a suppressed element of spiritual culture in the South. The white man feels the influence not of the masses of the Negro race but of individuals among them, even though he is not yet prepared to invite any to his prayer meeting.

I have been struck by a remark of Dr. J. H. Barrows in a recent convocation address before the University of Chicago. He said:

> Scientific study of religion is recent. One of the inevitable effects of this study will be the re-writing of Christian theology. It must have a restatement under the guiding principle of evolution and in the light of these comparative studies. Here are tasks for giants. We need not fear the results. Christ will be exalted while our conceptions of his activity are widened.

This, coming from the pastor of the First Presbyterian Church, is, to say the least, suggestive. I believe that in this "re-statement" the Negro should take a prominent part. I see that Bishop [Henry McNeil] Turner, the *Christian Advocate* and other leading coloured men have been recently suggesting a new translation of the Bible adapted to the needs of the Negro. Such a suggestion was made many years ago in *Frederick Douglass' Paper*. It is no doubt a proper aspiration. All the Christian races of Europe have their own translations: German, French, Italian, Danish, Russian, etc. But before a translation of the Scripture can be made by us for profitable use, we must produce a race of scholars able to deal with the whole question of original texts—to criticize with insight and accuracy the translation of others. The translator must bring what the Holy Spirit will reveal to him in immediate and prayerful contact with the word of God. The Bible is a vast treasury of spiritual knowledge, not to be exhausted by one race only. There are secrets of the Lord which He can unfold only to certain sections of his creatures or which only certain sections of them can grasp, though they may be before their eyes. When the Lord passes by to reveal his Name men see only that side of Him which He chooses to show. Lowell says:

> God sends his teachers unto every age
> To every clime, and every race of men,
> With revelations fitted to their growth
> And shape of mind, nor gives the realms of truth
> Into the selfish rule of one sole race.

The Negro in the Southern States cannot afford to be a politician. By this I mean that it is not in his best interest to be one. I hope I am too far away from the scene for any interested motive to be attributed to me in making that remark. Every thinking African on this side acquainted with the subject entertains the view I have just expressed. We believe that the interest of both races will be served if the Negro will eschew politics and political aspirations, where every step of the way is hampered and covered with thorns and briars. He is called to higher and nobler work. The religious and industrial sphere lie open before him, in the latter of which you have shown in your admirable letter his possibilities are unlimited. It is a pity that he should neglect the great work which he is so well fitted to do for and upon the dominant race and for himself to pursue an *ignis fatuus* which leads him away from rest and peace into all sorts of difficulties and often to death.

The African spirit is a spirit of service. I do not mean in a degrading sense, but in the highest sense, in which the Son of Man came not to be ministered unto but to minister—the sense He took upon Himself the form of a servant—slave in the original. The spirit of service in the black man is born of his spiritual genius. It is his essential characteristic; and to show you that I connect no servile or unworthy idea with this remark, I hasten to add that I believe that that spirit must lead in civilization before it can become distinctively Christian—the supple, yielding, concilliatory, obedient, gentle, patient, musical spirit that is not full of offensive resistance— how sadly the white man needs it! He will not deny this, if he thinks at all and our presence in America may help him in this matter if we avoid his politics. Let him fight the battle of government on the stump, at the polls and in the legislative halls. Our kingdom in America is not this world. We cannot compete with the Anglo-Saxon. He is so dreadfully determined, so intolerant and self assertive, intent upon carrying his point at all hazards, having good in view of course; but the wheels of his mind and understanding need oiling sadly with the oil of African good nature. If he only had a little of our disposition the terrible labour problem in America and Europe would not exist.

The Negro is a very different being from what superficial observers of him in the house of his bondage imagine him to be. It is worse than a farce to talk of the savagery of a country where such a man as Livingstone, unprotected and alone, took his little family and lived and died, not only without molestation but tenderly looked after! Think of the devotion shown to Stanley!

I can never understand the reason or necessity for lynching except on the theory that both the white man and the Negro have got out of their natural groove, or, perhaps, the white man remained in his, the Negro has got out of his.

I have read (in the London *Times*, Oct. 6th) with great satisfaction the letter of the governor of Alabama in reply to the Anti-Lynching Committee of England. The governor represents himself "as one who, in public and private station, has long been a sturdy foe of mob violence and is in thorough sympathy with the desire to overthrow it everywhere". He says further—"The people of Alabama are as mindful as those of England of the danger and brutality of mob violence, and are as firmly bent on putting an end to it in all classes of crime. . . . The laws, the efforts of the authorities, and the force of public opinion are solving the problem."

The whole civilized world has read with a feeling of relief and gratification these utterances; and there is a feeling akin to gratitude for the *gaucherie* of the Anti-Lynching Committee which elicited them. They ought to be most encouraging to the Negroes of Alabama as showing that they live under the protection of a statesmanship which will afford the opportunity of peaceful and indefinite development on industrial and religious lines. I am the more gratified by this because I believe that while there are and will continue to be intense longings on the part of many in the South for Africa, and while there will be now and then small emigrations to the Fatherland, the time for anything like a general exodus is far distant—perhaps three hundred years off—so that practically the Negro is in the United States to stay, and should adjust his relations with the white people upon a basis that will ensure peace, harmony and prosperity, at the same time that he brings his peculiar gifts to the improvement of the situation.

I will remember with great pleasure my visit to the South in the winter of 1889–90 (South Carolina, Georgia, Florida) and the kind treatment I received from the coloured and leading white people whose acquaintance it was my privilege to make. I received no insults and saw nothing offensive during my sojourn. I much regretted not to have enjoyed the opportunity of visiting you at Tuskegee, according to your very kind invitation. Owing to the pressure of business at the North and in Europe I was obliged to forgo the pleasure of complying with numerous valuable invitations. But I hope before long to be able to pay the South another and more protracted visit. Meanwhile, I bid you God's speed in your work. You are on God's line for the race. I send by this mail a copy of one of my lectures which I hope may have some interest for you.

> Yours faithfully
> EDWARD W. BLYDEN
> Sierra Leone, W. Africa, November 28th, 1894

27

The Jewish Question

Liverpool, 1898, 1–23

JEWISH INFLUENCE

I have for many years—indeed from my childhood—been an earnest student of the history of God's chosen people. I do not refer merely to the general teaching which every child brought up in the Christian religion receives in Old Testament History—those fascinating stories of the Patriarchs, of the Judges, of the Kings of Judah and of Israel; but also to that special teaching outside of books, which comes from contact with living illustrations.

I was born in the midst of Jews in the Danish island of St. Thomas, West Indies. For years, the next-door neighbours of my parents were Jews. I played with Jewish boys and looked forward as eagerly as they did to the annual festivals and feasts of their Church. I always went to the Synagogue on the solemn Day of Atonement—not inside. I took up an outside position from which I could witness the proceedings of the worshippers, hear the prayers and the reading, the singing and the sermon. The Synagogue stood on the side of a hill; and, from a terrace immediately above it, we Christian boys who were interested could look down upon the mysterious assembly, which we did in breathless silence, with an awe and reverence which have followed me all the days of this life.

In the neighbourhood in which I lived were such Jewish families as the Benjamins, Azevedos, Da Costas, Benlisas, Wolf, and other— names well known throughout the West Indies.

. . . Judah P. Benjamin, that eminent jurist and statesman, who distinguished himself both here [Britain] and in America . . . and I were born . . . in the same locality in St. Thomas, and we both left the island about the same time for the United States. I was a boy, and went with the idea of entering college in that country to complete my studies; but owing to the strong prejudices of those days admission was refused me in the institutions to which application was made. Forbidden a career in that country I went to Liberia, the newly-established African Republic in West Africa, and there I continued my studies and rose to the Principalship of the school which I entered, and afterwards to a Professorship, and to the Presidency of Liberia College.

After spending twelve years in Africa I returned to St. Thomas to visit my mother, and I remember how cordially I was received by my Jewish acquaintances. My arrival was a surprise to my mother, who was engaged in teaching a small school when I presented myself at the door. The school was, of course, at once dismissed. I had not been in the house fifteen minutes before, through the thoughtful hospitality of a Jewish neighbour living opposite, tea and other refreshments were sent in to give me a practical, and what was of course to me, a most grateful welcome.

With these early impressions, it is not surprising that when I had somewhat advanced in my studies I conceived a desire to visit the original home of the Jews—to see Jerusalem and Mount Zion, the joy of the whole earth. This desire, through the liberality of friends in America, I was enabled to carry out; and I remember how generously a little book on my travels which I published, entitled *From West Africa to Palestine*, was received by Jews in my native land.

The impressions made upon me by that visit to the land of patriarchs and prophets deepen as the years go by, so that with ever fresh interest and delight I recur to the study of the language, literature, and history of the Jews. One of the strongest wishes of my life has been to understand the Hebrew language—to read with facility the poets and prophets of the Old Testament, and the Talmud in the original. . . .

When I first entered upon the study of Hebrew, without a living teacher, as there was none accessible, I took the liberty of writing to that distinguished Hebrew scholar and divine, the late Dr. [Isidor] Kalish, informing him of my efforts and craving suggestions from him. He did me the honour of corresponding with me on the subject, and sent me his Hebrew Grammar, which have been to me a wonderful storehouse of philological, historical, and even theological information. But I am still, I regret to say, only at the threshold of the vast and magnificent temple which these works have opened before me.

ZIONISM

. . . I have taken, and do take, the deepest possible interest in the current history of the Jews—especially in that marvellous movement called Zionism. The question, in some of its aspects, is similar to that which at this moment agitates thousands of the descendants of Africa in America, anxious to return to the land of their fathers. It has been for many years my privilege and my duty to study the question from the African stand point. And as the history of the African race—their enslavement, persecution, proscription, and sufferings—closely resembles that of the Jews, I have been led also by a natural process of thought and by a fellow feeling to study the great question now uppermost in the minds of thousands, if not millions, of Jews.

In October, 1895, long before I heard of Dr. Herzl, or his "Jewish State", I delivered in the City of Washington, in America, a lecture on the "Work and Destiny of the Races", in which I discussed what at that time appeared to me the true work of my own race and that of the Jews.

Theodor Herzl has put forth ideas in his "Jewish State" which have given such an impetus to the real work of the Jews as must tell with enormous effect upon their future history. It has created an agitation which is stirring thinking minds all over the civilized world. . . .

I have been surprised to find from how many directions come evidences of the influence of that "tidal wave" from Vienna—that inspiration almost Mosaic in its originality and in its tendency, which drew crowds of Israelites to Basle in August, 1897, and has drawn them thither again in 1898.

Whenever the Jews, or any portion of the Jews, move together on any question relating to religion, the whole of humanity is affected. It shows how closely the spiritual life—that is, the only true life—of the world is connected with their special work and destiny. The spiritual life of the world now waits upon them; and it is gratifying to notice that the Zionist movement is having its effect upon the whole Jewish community, or, rather upon all the Jewish communities—both Zionists and Anti-Zionists—raising them out of an indifferent materialism into spiritual contemplation, and to a more active sense of racial privileges and responsibilities.

There is hardly a man in the civilized world—Christian, Moham-medan, or Jew—who does not recognize the claim and right of the Jew to the Holy Land; and there are very few who, if the conditions were favourable, would not be glad to see them return in a body and take their places in the land of their fathers as a great—a leading—secular power. But I believe that the majority of Christian thinkers, and many of the Jewish scholars and divines, do not believe in a literal application of those passages in the Bible, which sometimes in striking detail describe a literal repatriation.

I believe that rising Jewish scholars are disposed to recognize that the Jew has a far higher and nobler work to accomplish for humanity than establishing a political power in one corner of the earth. They believe that their race have been qualified by the unspeakable sufferings of ages to be the leaders not in politics but in religion; that to them has been entrusted the spiritual hegemony of mankind; that it is they who are to bring about the practical brotherhood of humanity by establishing, or rather, propagating, the international religion in whose cult men of all races, climes, and countries will call upon the one Lord under one Name.

* * *

It is probably true that the proscription and misappreciation of which for ages they have been the victims, have given to the Jews a timidity and a backwardness, and taught them to disparage themselves and their lofty mission. Because they nowhere hold a dominant political position, they seem to have lost self-assertion. But when this desponding and deprecating mood overtakes them, they should remember the great facts in their history, of which one of their own thinkers in terse and striking language reminds them, viz. "Twice has Judaism remodelled the world—the European world through Jesus, and the Oriental world through Islam". (James Darmesteter, *Selected Essays.*)

And it should also be remembered, that when Judaism sent forth the apostles, and the agencies of this regeneration, it had no political status—the Jews were servants to the secular power. Indeed, none of the spiritual saviours or regenerators of humanity have had, at least at the beginning of their career, either as individuals or communities, any political power. . . .

Now, the world is waiting for another upward impulse. It is immersed in materialism. Science and philosophy are the gods that men now worship. But it has been well said: "Science equips man, but it does not guide him. It illumines the world for him to the region of the most distant stars, but it leaves night in his heart. It is invincible, but indifferent, neutral, unmoral." (Darmesteter.)

* * *

It is not to be doubted that at present some great reform in religious life of the most civilized nations is needed; and I have often thought, owing, perhaps, to my complete ignorance of the subject, that the Jews do not sufficiently appreciate the duty now pressing upon them to take their place as witnesses for God—to run to and fro, that knowledge of Him may be increased. The message of the great Zionist movement to the Jews, it seems to me, is to rise from their neutrality and co-operating with or utilizing both their children—Christianity and Islam—work for the saving of mankind—the civilized from a deadening materialism and the barbarous from a stagnant and degrading superstition. This, it seems to me—I speak with great diffidence—is the work that at this moment lies before the Jews, a work that will by no means exclude the colonization of Palestine, but rather enlarge its scope. . . .

*   *   *

It is true that the persecution of ages has driven Israel to almost exclusive devotion to their own people, the almost exclusive consideration of their internal affairs. But this very introspective devotion is, it seems to me, a serious hindrance to the fulfilment of their aspirations. There is a double task laid upon Israel—to look after the sufferers and proscribed and outcast among themselves, and also to extend to other races . . . the great truths of which they are depositaries. . . .

*   *   *

Now, as an African, I hope I shall be excused if I venture to call attention to this question from the African standpoint, and in connection with that great continent. The great body of the "Dark Continent" has been apparently overlooked by the Jews. I see nothing in contemporary Jewish writings about Africa, as to its spiritual condition. . . . There is not, to my knowledge, a single synagogue in West Africa along three thousand miles of coast, and probably not two dozen representatives of God's chosen people in that whole extent of country—not a Jewish institution of any kind—either for commercial, religious or educational purposes. Have the Jews no witness to bear in inter-tropical Africa? . . .

If the world owes an immense debt to the Jews, the Jews as well as the rest of mankind owe an immense debt to Africa; for it was upon that soil that a few nomads from Western Asia settled down, and, in the furnace of affliction, as well as in the house of preservation, grew to be a nation. . . . In Africa was preserved the church to whom was to be entrusted the international or universal religion.

*   *   *

Now Europe in the great work which it believes itself called upon to do in Africa is producing conditions in which it is impossible for "souls" to "grow", and bodies can hardly survive. It is

R

introducing the material results of science; it is removing the pressure of many outward evils, dissipating harmful superstitions, and degrading prejudices. In many places the people are taught to live in better houses than their ancestors had, to wear finer clothes, to read and write and cipher. The physical obstructions, encumbrances, and inconveniences are being removed. But the value of this vast apparatus, this ponderous machinery, and these relentless appliances of civilization, is neutralized and destroyed by their effect upon the spiritual and even physical vitality of the race. The higher life of man, the moral and religious emotions, which nurse the well spring of a nobler life within, are not thought of, except in the weak attempts of a few self-denying missionaries, who owing to sectarian differences and conflicts, and to numerical insignificance, are helpless to extend the principles they inculcate. Christianity in West Africa has had only two stages—infancy and decrepitude; vigorous manhood it has never had. We look forward, therefore, with dismay to the unrestrained predominance of the purely secular agencies. . . . Science for all the really higher purposes of humanity is a dead organism of latent forces unless it is taken up by the moral nature, unless it is animated by earnest purpose and inspired by a great spiritual idea. This condition Europe is helpless to produce in Africa. . . .

* * *

Now Africa appeals to the Jew . . . to come with his scientific and other culture, gathered by his exile in many lands, and with his special spiritual endowments, to the assistance of . . . Africa. . . .

PART V

Education—Its Nature and Purpose for Africans

PART V

Education—Its Nature and Purpose for Africans

Although he played many roles, Blyden had, early in his career, conceived of his main one as being that of educator. His formal positions as an educator were as follows: in Liberia, Principal of Alexander High School, 1858–61, and again, 1874–7; Professor of Liberia College, 1862–71, and again 1900–01; President of Liberia College, 1880–4; in Lagos, as Agent for Native Affairs, 1896–7; and in Sierra Leone, as Director of Muslim Education, 1901–6.

Blyden, though conventional at first, developed into an innovative educator: he came fully to see the need for study that was relevant to African conditions and aspirations: that the curricula from Europe and America had to be greatly modified to meet African needs. His earliest ideas on education were derived largely from his Princeton-trained mentor and tutor, Rev. D. A. Wilson, Principal of Alexander High School, with whom he had studied theology, the classics, geography and mathematics. The classics became his first love, and although his views on education changed during his long career, he remained convinced of the efficacy of "ancient languages" for training the mind. He taught Latin and Greek at Alexander High School, and became a Professor of Classics at Liberia College. As yet he still uncritically accepted the conventional liberal arts College programme as suitable to Liberia needs. In his inaugural address as Professor at Liberia College in 1862 he argued against the idea that Liberia needs "a peculiar kind of education": "we have the same intellectual needs that other men have, and they must be supplied by the same means". But this was a position that he was soon to abandon. His introduction of Arabic into the University curriculum in 1867 was evidence of his growing awareness of a curriculum which answered to Liberia's peculiar needs.

By 1870, Blyden had concluded that the greatest obstacle to creative progress on the part of the black man was lack of confidence in himself and pride in his race, the result of a deleterious education received directly or indirectly from white men. In the New World the entire culture and society conspired to degrade the black man; in Africa, the influence of arrogant, sectarian missionary teachers was undermining the self-confidence and patriotism of Africans. Blyden's remedy for this, in theory, was secular educational institutions run by race-proud black educators. In 1872 Blyden strongly made this recommendation to William Grant, an African member of the Legislative Council of Sierra Leone, and John Pope Hennessy, Governor of the colony, in the first of several pleas by him for the establishment of an institution of higher learning in a British West African colony (Selection 29).

In 1881, when he made his famous inaugural address as President of Liberia College, Blyden stressed the need to modify and adapt western ideas and curricula to African conditions as well as to make the College relevant to the highest goals and aspirations of Liberia (Selection 30). Perhaps influenced by the then American vogue of "industrial education", he recommended "manual labour" for all College students as a means of helping to defray the expenses of their education; also in his report as College President at the end of 1881 he recommended the addition of "an agricultural curriculum" for "industrial and technical training" (Selection 31). Blyden had moved away from the idea of a purely liberal arts education. But Blyden's challenging plans for Liberia College were not realized partly because Liberians did not give them adequate support, partly because Blyden himself was inefficient and sometimes tactless as an administrator. After four years, he resigned as President of Liberia College.

In 1900 Blyden rejoined the Faculty of Liberia College in his last active association with an institution of higher learning. In an address in 1900 he stressed that the College should attempt to be both innovative and relevant. For him, proper fields of study were "native law, tribal organization, native languages, native religion, native politics, and the effect of all these things upon their life". But Blyden was unable to get his colleagues to support his educational ideas and he left Liberia College in 1901. To the end of his days he neglected no opportunity to discuss his "dream" University for West Africa but this never materialized.

Because of his keen concern during his long career as an educator seeking to establish educational institutions, Blyden has influenced succeeding generations of West African educators and nationalists. In the post-Blyden period, every African-initiated educational venture invoked the name and career of Blyden. As an educator, he has inspired at least two pamphlets: A. Deniga, *Blyden, the African Educationalist*, Lagos, 1932; and Julius Ojo Cole, *Dr. Edward Wilmot Blyden, an Interpretation*, Lagos, 1935.

28

Inaugural Address at the Inauguration of Liberia College, at Monrovia, January 23rd, 1862

Liberia's Offering, New York (1862), 96–123

An old and venerable custom, existing in countries where colleges and universities have been long established, requires that he who is entering upon the responsible office of Professor, should publicly express the views which he entertains of the duties devolved upon him, and the manner in which he will discharge those duties. . . .

This is an auspicious day for Liberia, and for West Africa. The first College Edifice erected on this benighted shore has been completed; and we, descendants of Africa, are assembled to inaugurate it. Perhaps this very day, one century ago, some of our forefathers were being dragged to the hold of some miserable slaver, to enter upon those horrible sufferings of the "middle passage", preliminary to their introduction into scenes and associations of deeper woe. Today, their descendants having escaped the fiery ordeal of oppression and slavery, and having returned to their ancestral home, are laying the foundation of intellectual empire, upon the very soil whence their fathers were torn, in their ignorance and degradation. Strange and mysterious providence!

It is among the most fortunate circumstances, connected with the founding of Liberia, that schools of a high order, and now a college, should be established in the early period of her history. It is impossible to maintain our national independence, or grow in the elements of national prosperity, unless the people are generally imbued with a proper sense of their duties and responsibilities, as citizens of a free government. The duties which devolve upon the citizens of Liberia, are as diversified and important as those which devolve upon citizens of larger nations and communities; and, in order to discharge those duties faithfully and successfully, we need all the fitness and qualification which citizens of larger nations possess. To say, as has been too often said, by persons abroad and by persons here, that the establishment of a college in Liberia at present is premature, is to set aside the experience of older countries, and to ignore the testimony which comes to us from a hundred communities far in advance of us, showing the indispensableness of institutions of a higher order, to send down, through

219

all the ramifications of society, the streams of wholesome and elevating influence.

I regard this, then, as an auspicious day for Liberia; hoping that there will be such a feeling of appreciation, on the part of our people, of the importance of this Institution, and such active co-operation with it, as shall render it useful as a means of building us up in all those qualities which shall fit us for the discharge of various duties, and draw towards us the attention of the civilized world.

The fear need not be entertained that a course of study in this Institution will unfit men for the practical duties of life, render them proud, and distant, and haughty, and overbearing. Such is not the effect of a true education. I am aware that there prevails with some—and perhaps not entirely without foundation—the opinion that the effect of superior education is to inflate men and render them impracticable. This is not, however, the legitimate effect of true knowledge. They are utter strangers to the genial influence of literature upon the social sentiments, who suppose that men must be distant, and haughty, and cold, in proportion as they are profound. . . .

Every country has its peculiar circumstances and characteristics. So has Liberia. From this fact, it has often been argued that we need a peculiar kind of education; not so much colleges and high schools, as other means, which are more immediately and obviously connected with our progress. But to this we reply, that if we are part of the human family, we have the same intellectual needs that other men have, and they must be supplied by the same means. It shows a painful ignorance of history, to consider the present state of things in Liberia as new and unprecedented, in such a sense as to render dispensable those most important and fundamental means of improvement, which other countries have enjoyed. Mind is every-where the same; and everywhere it receives its character and for-mation from the same elemental principles. If it has been properly formed and has received a substantial character, it will work out its own calling, solve its own problem, achieve its own destiny.

No country in the world needs, more than Liberia, to have mind properly directed. We are here isolated from the civilized world, and surrounded by a benighted people, with whom we are closely identified. And, in these circumstances, we are making the experi-ment, which, I venture to say, has never been made before, of establishing and maintaining a popular government, with a popula-tion, for the most part, of emancipated slaves. The government is thrown into the hands of the people, and they are called upon to give their opinions upon all subjects which can affect us as a nation; upon all the difficult subjects of finance, of legislation, and the most intricate points of constitutional law. Not only do they utter their opinions, but it is their right and privilege to act upon these opinions; and they do act upon them—with what success, alas! we are too well aware. And in addition to these political responsibilities, we have philanthropic duties to perform towards our aboriginal brethren—duties which require no little degree of intelligence and virtue.

De Tocqueville informs us that, before the colony that landed at Plymouth was as old as Liberia, there were laws enacted, establishing schools in every township, and obliging the inhabitants, under pain of heavy fines, to support them. Schools of a superior kind were founded in the same manner in the more populous districts. The municipal authorities were bound to enforce the sending of children to school by their parents[1] It is certainly a very remarkable fact, that, in New England, by the time the first child born in the colony had reached a proper age for admission to college, a college was established. They did not wait to have all those preparations, which some have fancied are necessary before Liberians can reap the benefit of a College. We are informed that the forests were yet standing; the Indian was still the near neighbour of the largest settlements; the colonists were yet dependent on the mother country for the very necessaries of life; and the very permanence of their settlements was as yet undecided, when they were erecting high schools and colleges. They did not regard it as too early to provide for the thorough education of their children. They had left their fatherland to seek an asylum of liberty on those distant shores, and they well knew that intelligence was indispensable to the enjoyment and maintenance of true liberty.

The people were no less eager to provide themselves with the means of education. The colony of Virginia was still struggling against the difficulties and embarrassments incident to feeble settlements, when the first efforts were made by the inhabitants to establish a college. As early as 1619, grants of land, and liberal subscriptions, were obtained for the endowment of the University of Henrico; and we may form some idea of the weak state of the colony, when we learn that the University was destroyed by an Indian massacre, and that the colony came very near being exterminated. Before the close of that century, however, the College of William and Mary was in successful operation.

Why then should not Liberia, after forty years' existence, having

[1] *Democracy in America*, Vol I, Chapter VII.

secured the confidence and respect of the aboriginal tribes, enjoy the means of superior education? The name *College*, applied to this Institution, may seem ambitious; but it is not too early in our history for us to aim at such institutions. Of course we can not expect that it will at once fulfil all the conditions of colleges in advanced countries; but it may, in time, as many American colleges have done, grow into an Institution of respectability and extensive usefulness.

It can not be denied, that the studies which shall be pursued in this Institution are of great utility to this country just now. The college course will include all those studies by which a people's mind and heart are formed. We shall have the study of language ... a study which ... aids greatly in the training and discipline of the mind.

We shall have the study of mathematics and physical science— which involves, of course, a study of the laws of nature, and the acquirement of the essential preliminary knowledge of all calculations, measurements and observations, on the sea and on the land.

We shall have—besides jurisprudence and international law—the study of intellectual and moral philosophy, by which is gained a knowledge of the mind, and the laws of thought, and of our duties to ourselves, to our fellowmen, to society, and to God.

Will any one of these studies, which I have enumerated, be superfluous in Liberia? So far from it, the course does not supply all our deficiencies.

But we need a *practical* education in Liberia. True; and so did the first settlers of North America. And does not the college course supply such an education? What is a practical education? It is not simply preparing a person specially for one sphere of life. It aims at practical results of a more important character—at imparting not simply skill in keeping accounts—in pleading at the bar—in surveying land—in navigating a vessel—but skill in exercising the intellect accurately and readily, upon any subject brought before us. The skill secured by a college education, is skill in the use of the mind.

* * *

The first College in West Africa is founded. ... We hail this institution as the precursor of incalculable blessings to this benighted land—as the harbinger of a bright and happy future for science, literature, and art, and for all the noblest interests of the African.

29

The West African University

Correspondence between Edward W. Blyden . . . , Freetown, 1872, 1–17
A Letter to the Honourable William Grant, Member of the Legislative
Council of Sierra Leone
Freetown, May 22nd, 1872

Dear Sir:

In reviewing the subjects discussed during our last interview, I
feel we traversed a wide and important field; but there was no
subject of greater importance than that relating to the establishment
in this Colony of a good Educational Institution, to be conducted
by trained and experienced Negroes—of importance, vital importance—not only to the people of this Colony, but of the whole of
the West Coast of Africa.

And it is gratifying to find that though Parents who can afford
it, send their children to Europe for education, for want of suitable
advantages at home, there is, nonetheless, in all the leading Natives,
a very strong desire for an education for their children adapted to
the peculiar necessities of the country and the people. They feel
that, somehow or other, the education received abroad does not
meet the specific wants of this country; that, except in rare cases,
by a foreign education, the mental and moral peculiarities of the
Negro are forced out of their rational relations and normal
actions.

Sierra Leone is the only place in the world where there is so
promising a basis for the erection of an educational system adapted
to our peculiar needs. Everywhere else the influences that tend to
confuse the instincts of race and diminish the proper manhood of
the Negro, are *paramount*. They cannot be counteracted. He is
obliged to shape his feelings in accordance with the prevailing tastes
around him; and therefore, wherever you find him educated in the
schools abroad, you are apt to find a man of distorted tastes, confused perceptions and defective and resultless energy. Only here and
there a man rises up in whom the race feeling is not destroyed;
and such a man, being so different from those around him, becomes
a target of the assaults of his own people and of the unsympathizing
strangers among whom he dwells; and he must consider himself
fortunate if he does not go down to a premature grave, hastened
thither by sheer grief and disappointment.

223

Not so in Sierra Leone. Here he will be surrounded by a people in whom it is possible to produce a race sentiment. No unnatural or factitious restraints growing out of the predominating presence of a foreign race can here limit investigation, experiment and expression. Under the liberal and enlightened policy of Great Britain, there has been here, as far as possible a regular, normal growth of the Negro. He has here imbibed no foul fancies, no false and pernicious notions as to his race peculiarities. He has been nearly as much at home as his ancestors were on the banks of the Niger, or in the plains of Yoruba. And if there has been any drawback it has been in proportion as he has ignored his race instincts, and has endeavoured to attain to the unnatural and artificial condition of a *Europeanized* African. A *forced* state of things is of necessity a precarious and *unpermanent* state. Hence, unless we take care, all that we are now doing—all the expense we are going to, in educating our children abroad, will end in failure, disappointment and reaction; simply because such education must necessarily divest them from their natural bent, or confuse the clearness of their native instincts. The natural and proper action of their minds is hampered or marred, and they become, as a consequence, practically useless to the race. . . .

*   *   *

. . . Youths are not sent to College in Europe and America to improve their own sakes, but expressly and specifically for the purpose of *preparing to execute the work to which their lives are to be devoted.* If this be the case, you must at once see that when a youth is sent for education from Africa to Europe, he must lose a great part of the very training for which he has been sent to school—viz., to prepare for the work of his life. The man who, in the process of his education has not imbibed a large race feeling, in whom there is not developed *pride of race*, has failed in a great part of his education. And whatever else may be acquired in Europe, it is evident that, for the Negro, race feeling must be kept in abeyance. And what is a man without this feeling? It is this strong race feeling—this pride of race—having been instilled in the mind of the Jew from his earliest infancy, which has given to that peculiar people their unquenchable vitality. Notwithstanding all the afflictions and proscriptions which barbarism and fanaticism can bring to bear upon them, whether in Roumania or Algeria, they still flourish, multiply and grow rich and influential. This undying elasticity is owing in great measure to the unrelaxing pertinacity with which they cling to the traditions of their race.

It seems, then, that a common duty devolving upon all Natives of this Colony who have any influence is to endeavour to secure for the youth the means of proper training *at home*—such a training as will conduce to the normal development of the mind and to the generation of an enlightened patriotism. This is a very important work, and I think that the attention of the Government should be called to it. . . .

Europeans sent hither to instruct us, too often labour under feeble health, and owing to physical causes, are destitute of that energy and enthusiasm which alone can properly inspire and stimulate the young. Their work is a laborious task to them; and many a distinguished teacher from abroad, fully competent to fulfil the highest function of an instructor has laboured in a network of encumbrances and limitations, until as our graveyards attest, he has been compelled to yield up his life. . . .

The establishment of an Institution here, such as you have suggested, to be conducted by earnest and well-cultivated Negro instructors, would secure to the country the presence of qualified men who would not only so far as health is concerned, be able to perform continuous and uninterrupted labours in the schools, but who would also exert a wholesome influence upon the masses and guide public opinion aright, or rather, develop and organize a public opinion, which, perhaps, does not yet exist. You may depend upon it, Sir, unless some changes are brought about in the system of educating our youth, fifty years hence will find us just where we are now—performing the arduous but resultless treadmill operation of which Lord Macaulay speaks—"always beginning again; much exertion and no progress".

Such an institution . . . deserves the encouragement of every enlightened statesman. You will find that with such an Institution here, in a short time there would be a general diffusion of that higher intelligence which originates public measures, which stimulates the people, moderates their impulses, sustains and gives weight to noble enterprises, creates and expounds a healthy public sentiment, and accelerates the moral and spiritual progress of the race.

> I remain, dear Sir,
> Very faithfully yours,
> Editor of the *Negro* newspaper.

*   *   *

Mr. Blyden to Governor Hennessy
Freetown, December 6th, 1872.

Sir:

In the interview I had the honour to have with your Excellency the other day, you expressed the opinion that a great effort should be made not only to spread the rudiments of technical and secular knowledge among the mass of the population on the coast and in the adjacent interior, but also to establish a sort of Educational Department of State for the purpose of securing to intelligent and studious Natives the advantage of instruction in the higher branches of learning.

The more I reflect upon the subject, the more I am convinced that we can have no thorough and permanent reform—no proper development and growth—without the means being afforded of a liberal education to the youth.

If in the Government of these Settlements, a native agency is to be welcomed and encouraged, and not despised, and excluded; if the people are ever to become ripe for free and progressive institutions, it must be through a system of education adapted to the exigencies of the country and race: such a system as shall prepare the cultivated youth for the responsibilities which must devolve upon them; and without interfering with their native instincts, and throwing them altogether out of harmony and sympathy with their own countrymen, shall qualify them to be efficient guides and counsellors and rulers of their people.

The system unfortunately, or want of system to which the natives of this country have been subjected in consequence of the conflicting dogmatic creeds introduced among them from abroad, has unduly biased their development and hampered their progress. All effort here. as in some other mission fields, seems to have been directed mainlv to a solution of the question of who shall be uppermost; hence denominational rivalry and the wasting of time and energy in localities already occupied instead of carrying the Gospel to "regions beyond", and proclaiming it "to every creature". Free learning has, with very few exceptions, been substituted by the narrow and dwarfing influence of ecclesiastical dogmatism. We have been torn into discordant and unprofitable sectaries by our pretending to understand the different elaborate creeds brought to us from Europe, and confusing ourselves with ecclesiastical quarrels handed down from a remote antiquity, which even in Europe only those who are learned in a particular department can grasp and comprehend.

I do not deny that the creeds brought to us from Europe rest on certain deep convictions which are present to the consciousness of the people among whom they arose and who now hold them, but I do not believe that these European formularies unmodified should be imposed upon Africa. They are constructive as records of religious growth and development in Europe and may be of great suggestive use in guiding us in the development of the African Church, which is sure to be formed in this country, if there be any natural or normal development. But it is evident that to make these creeds in all their details, authoritative in Africa, the intellectual and spiritual growth of the people must be checked or distorted by the introduction of the bitterness of theological rancour, and the harshness of conflicting sects, which have had their origin abroad and must necessarily exist in the African mind only as a *fungi.*

The future possibilities which I suggest of a new development of Christianity in this portion of Africa may excite a smile on the part of your Excellency, but if the Gospel takes root here, it must, as in other countries, assume the form adapted to the people. . . .

Now to give the people the opportunity and power of a free and healthy development—to bring out that individuality and originality of character which is one of the sure results of an advancing civilization and culture, the University is most important. The presence of such an Institution with able African teachers brought, if necessary, from different parts of the world—even a Negro Arabic Professor from Egypt, Timbuctoo or Futah—would have great influence in exposing and correcting the fallacies upon which our foreign teachers have proceeded in their utter misapprehension and, perhaps, contempt of African character.

And it occurs to me that so far as the organization of a suitable system of education for West Africa is concerned, your Excellency enjoys a noble opportunity, having—what very rarely falls to the lot of Colonial Governors— . . . an open, extensive and unencumbered field. If such a system could be organized under your Administration, or in consequence of your Administration, it would be the crown and glory of all the beneficent acts which it has been your good fortune to be instrumental in conferring upon the inhabitants of this coast and their interior neighbours.

I believe that any recommendation made by your Excellency, looking to the establishment of an educational institution here on a broad and liberal basis, would meet with the earnest sympathy and co-operation of the Government in England, and of those races which must sympathize with the Negro, as well as of all intelligent Natives on the coast.

I beg to subscribe myself, most respectfully,
Your Excellency's obedient servant,
EDWARD W. BLYDEN.

*   *   *

Mr. Blyden to Governor Hennessy
Freetown, December 11th, 1872.

Sir:

I beg to acknowledge the receipt of your Excellency's letter of yesterday and . . . that you approve the views contained in my letters.

Your letter, though brief, is particularly valuable as containing the estimates and views of a disinterested and competent foreigner who has devoted time and study to these special questions: and I am glad that you have called attention to the mistaken policy pursued in India and which proved to be so resultless, if not injurious to the people.

In the case of the Negro, the truth is, that the despotic and over-ruling method which has been pursued in his education, by good meaning but unphilosophical philanthropists has so entirely mastered and warped his mind that, in the whole civilized world, scarce any important political or social issue can be witnessed as a result of Negro training. All educated Negroes suffer from a kind of slavery in many ways far more subversive of the real welfare of the race than the ancient physical fetters. The slavery of the mind is far more destructive than that of the body. But such is the weakness and imperfection of human nature that many even of those who bravely fought to remove the shackles from the *body* of the Negro transfer them to his *mind*. . . .

Such, then, being the present condition of the Africans—mis-understood and compromised by many of their best friends, and often by themselves—it must be evident that to leave the work of initiating the education they need to "the Africans themselves" would be to put it off indefinitely. Europeans owe us a great debt, not only for unrequited physical labours we have performed in all parts of the world, but for the unnumbered miseries and untold demoralization they have brought upon Africa by the prosecution for centuries of the horrible traffic to promote their own selfish ends; and we feel that we do not simply ask it as a favour but claim it as a right when we entreat their aid as civilized and Christian Governments in the work of unfettering and enlightening the Negro mind, and placing him in a position to act well his part among the "productive agencies" of time.

We cannot expect Missionary Societies to take up and consider questions of this nature. They look upon them rather as secular and political than religious, and therefore, as part of the sphere of their operations. One only resource, under present circumstances, is to look to the Government—the Government, in the first instance of Sierra Leone.

This colony, from its peculiar circumstances, the multiplicity of African tribes genuinely represented in it, and the facilities which it has of communication with all parts of Negroland must, for the present at least, be regarded as the centre of the race: here, therefore, the special educational work at which we are aiming should be begun. To the Government of Sierra Leone, then, we look as the natural guardian of the people's interests, and the authorized disburser of the people's money for purposes best promotive of the people's welfare; and if the Government receive the support of the Natives of this Settlement in the promotion of this work of education, it will be only aiding "the Africans themselves" to carry out a most important object, supplying themselves with educational means according to the provident laws of human growth which must result in the moulding of a sober, well-disciplined and efficient African character, set free from those influences which, hitherto, have as a general thing only tended to crush or stupefy the intellect. And the dawn of a new era will be hastened in which "the Africans themselves" prepared by proper culture will come forward as the actors and prominent figures in the educational drama—to clench and rivet the nail driven by those of an alien race who had the sagacity to perceive their needs and the decision, energy and benevolence to act upon that perception.

I have the honour to be

Your Excellency's Obedient Servant,

EDWARD W. BLYDEN.

S

30

The Aims and Methods of a Liberal Education for Africans

Inaugural Address as President of Liberia College, Monrovia,
January 5th, 1881
Christianity, Islam and the Negro Race, London, 1887, 71–93;
1888 ed., 82–107

A college in West Africa, for the education of African youth by African instructors, under a Christian government conducted by Negroes, is something so unique in the history of Christian civilization, that wherever, in the civilized world, the existence of such an institution is heard of, there will be curiosity as to its character, its work, and its prospects. A college suited, in all respects, to the exigencies of this nation and to the needs of the race cannot come into existence all at once. It must be the result of years of experience, of trial, of experiment.

Every thinking man will allow that all we have been doing in this country so far, whether in church, in state, or in school—our forms of religion, our politics, our literature, such as it is—is only temporary and transitional. When we advance further into Africa, and become one with the great tribes on the continent, these things will take the form which the genius of the race shall prescribe.

The civilization of that vast population, untouched by foreign influence, not yet affected by European habits, is not to be organized according to foreign patterns, but will organize itself according to the nature of the people and the country. Nothing that we are doing now can be absolute or permanent, because nothing is normal or regular. Everything is provisional or tentative.

The College is only a machine, an instrument to assist in carrying forward our regular work—devised not only for intellectual ends, but for social purposes, for religious duty, for patriotic aims, for racial development; and when as an instrument, as a means, it fails, for any reason whatever, to fulfil its legitimate functions, it is the duty of the country, as well as the interest of the country, to see that it is stimulated into healthful activity; or, if this is impossible, to see that it is set aside as a pernicious obstruction. We cannot afford to waste time in dealing with insoluble problems under

231

impossible conditions. When the College was first founded, according to the generous conception of our friends abroad, they probably supposed that they were founding an institution which was to be at once complete in its appointments, and to go on working regularly and effectively as colleges usually do in countries where people have come to understand, from years of experience and trial, their intellectual, social, and political needs, and the methods for supplying those needs. In their efforts to assist us to become sharers in the advantages of their civilization, they have aimed at establishing institutions *a priori* for our development. That is, they have, by a course of reasoning natural to them, concluded that certain methods and agencies which have been successful among themselves must be successful among Africans. They have, on general considerations, come to certain conclusions as to what ought to apply to us. They have not, perhaps, sufficiently borne in mind that a college in a new country and among an inexperienced people must be, at least in the earlier periods of its existence, different from a college in an old country and among a people who understand themselves and their work. But, from the little experience we have had on this side of the water, we have learned enough to know that no *a priori* arrangements can be successfully employed in the promotion of our progress. We are arriving at the principles necessary for our guidance, through experience, through difficulties, through failures. The process is slow and sometimes discouraging, but, after a while, we shall reach the methods of growth that are adapted to our wants. The work of a college like ours, and among a people like our people, must be at first *generative*. It must create a sentiment favourable to its existence. It must generate the intellectual and moral state in the community which will give it not only a congenial atmosphere in which to thrive, but food and nutriment for its enlargement and growth; and out of this will naturally come the material conditions of its success.

Liberia College has gone through one stage of experience. We are, today, at the threshold of another. It has, to a great extent, created a public sentiment in its favour; but it has not yet done its generative work. It is now proposed to take a new departure and, by a system of instruction more suited to the necessities of the country and the race—that is to say, more suited to the development of the individuality and manhood of the African—to bring the institution more within the scope of the co-operation and enthusiasm of the people. It is proposed also, as soon as we can command the necessary means, to remove the College operations to an interior site, where health of body, the indispensable condition of health of mind, can be secured; where the student may devote a portion of their time to manual labour in the cultivation of the fertile lands which will be accessible, and thus assist in procuring from the soil the means for meeting a large part of necessary expenses; and where access to the institution will be convenient to the aborigines. The work immediately before us, then, is one of reconstruction, and the usual difficulties which attend reconstruction of any sort beset our first step. The people generally are not yet prepared to understand their own interest in the great work to be done for themselves and their children, and the part they should take in it; and we shall be obliged to work for some time to come, not only without the popular sympathy which we think our due, but with utterly inadequate resources.

This is inevitable in the present condition of our progress. All we can hope is that the work will go on, hampered though it may be, until, in spite of misappreciation and disparagement, there can be raised up a class of minds who will give a healthy tone to society, and exert an influence widespread enough to bring to the institution that indigenous sympathy and support without which it cannot thrive. It is our hope and expectation that there will rise up men, aided by instruction and culture in this College, imbued with public spirit, who will know how to live and work and prosper in this country, how to use all favouring outward conditions, how to triumph by intelligence, by tact, by industry, by perseverance, over the indifference of their own people, and how to overcome the scorn and opposition of the enemies of the race—men who will be determined to make this nation honourable among the nations of the earth.

We have in our curriculum, adopted some years ago, a course of study corresponding, to some extent, to that pursued in European and American colleges. To this we shall adhere as nearly as possible; but experience has already suggested, and will, no doubt, from time to time suggest, such modifications as were required by our peculiar circumstances.

NEGROES' EDUCATION "INCORRECT"

The object of all education is to secure growth and efficiency, to make a man all that his natural gifts will allow him to become; to produce self-respect, a proper appreciation of our own powers and of the powers of other people; to beget a fitness for one's sphere of life and action, and ability to discharge the duties it imposes. Now, if we take these qualities as the true outcome of a correct education, then every one who is acquainted with the facts must admit that, as a rule, in the entire civilized world, the Negro, notwithstanding his two hundred years' residence with Christian and civilized races, has nowhere received anything like a correct education. We find him everywhere—in the United States, in the West Indies, in South America—largely unable to cope with the responsibilities which devolve upon him. Not only is he not sought after for any position of influence in the political movements of those countries, but he is even denied admission to ecclesiastical appointments of importance. . . .

*   *   *

To a certain extent—perhaps to a very important extent—Negroes trained on the soil of Africa have the advantage of those trained in foreign countries; but in all, as a rule, the intellectual and moral results, thus far, have been far from satisfactory. There are many men of book-learning, but few, very few, of any *capability*—even few who have that amount, or that sort, of culture, which produces self-respect, confidence in one's self, and efficiency in work. Now, why is this? The evil, it is considered, lies in the system and methods of European training to which Negroes are, everywhere in Christian lands, subjected, and which everywhere affects them unfavourably. Of a different race, different susceptibility, different bent of character from that of the European, they have been trained under influences in many respects adapted only to the Caucasian race. Nearly all the books they read, the very instruments of their culture, have been such as to force them from the groove which is natural to them, where they would be strong and effective, without furnishing them with any avenue through which they may move naturally and free from obstruction. Christian and so-called civilized Negroes live, for the most part, in foreign countries, where they are only passive spectators of the deeds of a foreign race; and where, with other impressions which they receive from without, an element of doubt as to their own capacity and their own destiny is fastened upon them, and inheres in their intellectual and social constitution. They deprecate their own individuality, and would escape from it if they could. And in countries like this, where they are free from the hampering surroundings of an alien race, they still read and study the books of foreigners, and form their idea of everything that man may do, or ought to do, according to the standard held up in those teachings. Hence, without the physical or mental aptitude for the enterprises which they are taught to admire and revere, they attempt to copy and imitate them, and share the fate of all copyist and imitators. Bound to move on a lower level, they acquire and retain a practical inferiority, transcribing, very often, the faults rather than the virtues of their models.

Besides the result of involuntary impressions, they often receive direct teachings which are not only incompatible with, but destructive of, their self-respect.

In all English-speaking countries the mind of the intelligent Negro child revolts against the descriptions given in elementary books—geographies, travels, histories—of the Negro; but, though he experiences an instinctive revulsion from these caricatures and misrepresentations, he is obliged to continue, as he grows in years, to study such pernicious teachings. After leaving school he finds the same things in newspapers, in reviews, in novels, in *quasi* scientific works; and after a while . . . they begin to seem to him the proper things to say and to feel about his race, and he accepts what, at first, his fresh and unbiased feelings naturally and indignantly repelled. Such is the effect of repetition.

Having embraced, or at least assented, to these errors and falsehoods about himself, he concludes that his only hope of rising in the scale of respectable manhood is to strive after whatever is most unlike himself and most alien to his peculiar tastes. And whatever his literary attainments or acquired ability, he fancies that he must grind at the mill which is provided for him, putting in the material furnished to his hands, bringing no contribution from his own field; and of course nothing comes out but what is put in. Thus he can never bring any real assistance to the European. He can never attain to that essence of progress which Mr. Herbert Spencer describes as *difference*; and therefore, he never acquires the self-respect or self-reliance of an independent contributor. He is not an independent help, only a subordinate help; so that the European feels that he owes him no debt, and moves on in contemptuous indifference of the Negro, teaching him to contemn himself.

Those who have lived in civilized communities, where there are different races, know the disparaging views which are entertained of the blacks by their neighbours—and often, alas! by themselves. The standard of all physical and intellectual excellencies in the present civilization being the white complexion, whatever deviates from that favoured colour is proportionally depreciated, until the black, which is the opposite, becomes not only the most unpopular but the most unprofitable colour. Black men, and especially black women, in such communities, experience the greatest imaginable inconvenience. They never feel at home. In the depth of their being they always feel themselves strangers in the land of their exile, and the only escape from this feeling is to escape from themselves. And this feeling of self-depreciation is not diminished as I have intimated above, by the books they read. Women, especially, are fond of reading novels and light literature; and it is in these writings that flippant and eulogistic reference is constantly made to the superior physical and mental characteristics of the Caucasian race, which, by contrast, suggest the inferiority of other races—especially of that race which is furthest removed from it in appearance.

It is painful in America to see the efforts which are made by Negroes to secure outward conformity to the appearance of the dominant race.

This is by no means surprising; but what is surprising is that, under the circumstances, any Negro has retained a particle of self-respect. Now in Africa, where the colour of the majority is black, the fashion in personal matters is naturally suggested by the personal characteristics of the race, and we are free from the necessity of submitting to the use of "incongruous feathers awkwardly stuck on". Still, we are held in bondage by our indiscriminate and injudicious use of a foreign literature; and we strive to advance by the methods of a foreign race. In this effort we struggle with the odds against us. . . . The African must advance by methods of his own. He must possess a power distinct from that of the European. It has been proved that he knows how to take advantage of European culture, and that he can be benefited by it. This proof was perhaps necessary, but it is not sufficient. We must show that we are able to go alone, to carve out our own way. We must not be satisfied that, in this nation, European influence shapes our policy, makes our laws, rules in our tribunals, and impregnates our social atmosphere. We must not suppose that the Anglo-Saxon methods are final, that there is nothing for us to find for our own guidance, and that we have nothing to teach the world. There is inspiration for us also. We must study our brethren in the interior, who know better than we do the laws of growth for the race. We see among them the rudiments of that which, with fair play and opportunity, will develop into important and effective agencies for our work. We look too much to foreigners, and are dazzled almost to blindness by their exploits—so as to fancy that they have exhausted the possibilities of humanity. . . .

But there are possibilities before us not yet dreamed of. . . . Dr. Alexander Winchell, Professor in one of the American universities —who has lately written a book, in the name of Science, in which he reproduces all the old slanders against the Negro, and writes of the African at home as if Livingstone, Barth, Stanley, and Cameron had never written—mentions it, as one of the evidences of Negro inferiority, that in "Liberia he is indifferent to the benefits of civilization".[1] I stand here today to justify and commend the Negro of Liberia—and of everywhere else in Africa—for rejecting with scorn, "always and every time", the "benefits" of civilization whose theories are to degrade him in the scale of humanity, and of which such sciolists as Dr. Winchell are the exponents and representative elements. We recommend all Africans to treat such "benefits" with even . . . decided "indifference". . . . Those of us who have travelled in foreign countries, and who witness the general results of European influence along this coast, have many reasons for misgivings and reserves and anxieties about European civilization for this country. Things which have been of great advantage to Europe may work ruin to us; and there is often such a striking resemblance, or such a close connection between the hurtful and the beneficial, that we are not always able to discriminate. I have heard of a native in one of the settlements on the coast who, having grown up in the use of the simple but efficient remedies of the country doctors, and having prospered in business, conceived the idea that he must avail himself of the medicines he saw used by the European traders. Suffering from sleeplessness he was advised to take Dover's powders, but, in his inexperience, took instead an overdose of morphine, and next morning he was a corpse. So we have reason to apprehend that in our indiscriminate appropriations of European agencies or methods in our political, educational, and social life, we are often imbibing overdoses of morphine, when we fancy we are only taking Dover's powders!

And it is for this reason, while we are anxious for immigration from America and desirous that the immigrants shall push as fast as possible into the interior, that we look with anxiety and concern at the difficulties and troubles which must arise from their misconception of the work to be done in this country. I apprehend that in their progress towards the interior there will be friction, irritations and conflicts; and our brethren, in certain portions of the United States, are, at this moment, witnessing a state of things among their superiors which they will naturally want to reproduce in this country, and which, if reproduced here, will utterly extinguish the flickering light of the Lone Star, and close forever this open door of Christian civilization into Africa. . . .

[1] *Pre-Adamite Man*, p. 265.

*   *   *

In the prosecution of the work of a college for the training of youth in *this* country, the aim, it occurs to me, should be to study the causes of Negro inefficiency in civilized lands; and, so far as it has resulted from the training they have received, to endeavour to avoid what we conceive to be the sinister elements in that training.

In the curriculum of Liberia College, therefore, it will be our aim to increase the amount of purely disciplinary agencies, and to reduce to its minimum the amount of those distracting influences to which I have referred, as hindering the proper growth of the race.

The true principle of mental culture is perhaps this: to preserve an accurate balance between the studies which carry the mind out of itself, and those which recall it home again. When we receive impressions from without we must bring from our own conscious-ness the idea that gives them shape; we must mould them by our own individuality. Now, in looking over the whole civilized world I see no place where this sort of culture for the Negro can be better secured than in Liberia—where he may, with less interruption from surrounding influences, find out his place and his work, develop his peculiar gifts and powers; and for the training of Negro youth upon the basis of their own idiosyncracy, with a sense of race-individuality, self-respect, and liberty, there is no institution so well adapted as Liberia College with its Negro faculty and Negro students. . . .

PROPOSALS FOR "CORRECT" EDUCATION

. . . I propose now to sketch the outlines of a programme for the education of the students in Liberia College, and, I may venture to add, of the Negro youth everywhere in Africa who hope to take a leading part in the work of the race and of the country. I will premise that, generally, in the teaching of our youth, far more is made of the importance of imparting information than of training the mind. Their minds are too much taken possession of by mere information drawn from European sources. . . .

*   *   *

We shall devote attention principally, both for mental discipline and information, to the earlier epochs of the world's history. It is decided that there are five or six leading epochs in the history of civilization. . . . First, there was the great permanent, stationary system of human society, held together by a religious belief, or by social custom growing out of that belief. This has been called the Theocratic state of society. The type of that phase of civilization was the old Eastern empires. The second great type was the Greek Age of intellectual activity and civic freedom. Next came the Roman type of civilization, an age of empire, of conquest, of consolidation of nations, of law and government. The fourth great system was the phase of civilization which prevailed from the fall of the Roman Empire until comparatively modern times, and was called the Mediaeval Age, when the Church and Feudalism existed side by side. The fifth phase of history was that which began with the breaking-up of the power of the Church on the one side, and of feudalism on the other—the foundation of modern history, or the Modern Age. That system has continued down to the present; but, if sub-divided, it would form the sixth type, which is the Age since the French Revolution—the Age of social and popular development, of modern science and industry.

We shall permit in our curriculum the unrestricted study of the first four epochs, but especially the second, third and fourth, from which the present civilization of Western Europe is mainly derived. There has been no period of history more full of suggestive energy, both physical and intellectual, than those epochs. Modern Europe boasts of its period of intellectual activity, but none can equal, for life and freshness, the Greek and Roman prime. No modern writers will ever influence the destiny of the race to the same extent that the Greeks and Romans have done.

We can afford to exclude, then, as subjects of study, at least in the earlier college years, the events of the fifth and sixth epochs, and the works which, in large numbers, have been written during those epochs. I know that during these periods some of the greatest works of human genius have been composed. I know that Shakespeare and Milton, Gibbon and Macaulay, Hallam and Lecky, Froude, Stubbs and Green, belong to these periods. It is not in my power, even if I had the will, to disparage the works of these masters; but what I wish to say is, that these are not the works on which the mind of the youthful African should be trained. It was during the sixth period that the transatlantic slave-trade arose, and those theories—theological, social, and political—were invented for the degradation and proscription of the Negro. This epoch continues to this day, and has an abundant literature and a prolific authorship. It has produced that whole tribe of declamatory Negrophobists, whose views, in spite of their emptiness and impertinence, are having their effect upon the ephemeral literature of the day—a literature which is shaping the life of the Negro in Christian lands. His whole theory of life, quite contrary to what his nature intends, s being influenced, consciously and unconsciously, by the general conceptions of his race entertained by the manufacturers of this literature—a great portion of which, made for today, will not survive the next generation.

I admit that in this period there have been able defences of the race written, but they have all been in the patronizing or apologetic tone. . . .

It is true that culture is one, and the general effects of true culture are the same; but the native capacities of mankind differ, and their work and destiny differ, so that the road by which one man may attain to the highest efficiency, is not that which would conduce to the success of another. The special road which has led to the success and elevation of the Anglo-Saxon is not that which would lead to the success and elevation of the Negro, though we shall resort to the same means of general culture which has enabled the Anglo-Saxon to find out for himself the way in which he ought to go.

The instruments of culture which we shall employ in the College will be chiefly the Classics and Mathematics. By Classics I mean the Greek and Latin languages and their literature. In those languages there is not, as far as I know, a sentence, a word, or a syllable disparaging to the Negro. He may get nourishment from them without taking in any race-poison. They will perform no sinister work upon his consciousness, and give no unholy bias to his inclinations.

*   *   *

A great deal of misapprehension prevails in the popular mind as to the utility, in a liberal education, of the so-called dead languages, and many fancy that the time devoted to their study is time lost; but let it be understood that their study is not pursued merely for the information they impart. If information were all, it would be far more useful to learn the French and German, or any other of the modern languages, during the time devoted to Greek and Latin; but what is gained by the study of the ancient languages is that strengthening and disciplining of the mind which enables the student in . . . life to lay hold of, and, with comparatively little difficulty, to master, any business to which he may turn his attention. . . .

But we shall also study Mathematics. These, as instruments of culture, are everywhere applicable. A course of Algebra, Geometry, and Higher Mathematics must accompany, step by step, classical studies. Neither of these means of discipline can be omitted without loss. The qualities which make a man succeed in mastering the Classics and Mathematics are also those which qualify him for the practical work of life. Care, industry, judgment, tact, are the elements of success anywhere and everywhere. The training and discipline, the patience and endurance, to which each man must submit in order to succeed; the resolution which relaxes no effort, but fights the hardest when difficulties are to be surmounted—these are qualities which boys go to school to cultivate, and these they acquire, in a greater or less degree, by a successful study of Classics and Mathematics. The boy who shirks these studies, or retires from his class because he is unwilling to contend with the difficulties they involve, lacks those qualities which make a successful and influential character.

It will be our aim to introduce into our curriculum also the Arabic, and some of the principal native languages—by means of which we may have intelligent intercourse with the millions accessible to us in the interior, and learn more of our own country. We have young men who are experts in the geography and customs of foreign countries; who can tell all about the proceedings of foreign statesmen in countries thousands of miles away; can talk glibly of London, Berlin, Paris, and Washington; know all about Gladstone, Bismark, Gambetta, and Hayes; but who knows anything about Musahdu, Medina, Kankan, or Sego—only a few hundred miles from us? Who can tell anything of the policy or doings of Fanfidoreh, Ibrahima Sissi, or Fahqueh-queh, or Simoro of Boporu—only a few steps from us? These are hardly known. Now as Negroes, allied in blood and race to these people, this is disgraceful; and as a nation, if we intend to grow and prosper in this country, it is impolitic, it is shortsighted, it is unpatriotic; but it has required time for us to grow up to these ideas, to understand our position in this country. In order to accelerate our future progress, and to give to the advance we make the element of permanence, it will be our aim in the College to produce men of ability. Ability or capability is the power to use with effect the instruments in our hands. The bad workman complains of his tools; but, even when he is satisfied with the excellence of his tools, he cannot produce the results which an able workman will produce, even with indifferent tools.

If a man has the learning of Solomon, but, for some reason, either in himself or his surroundings, cannot bring his learning into useful application, that man is lacking in ability. Now what we desire to do is to produce ability in our youth; and whenever we find a youth, however brilliant in his powers of acquisition, who lacks common sense, and who, in other respects, gives evidence of the absence of those qualities which enable a man to use his knowledge for the benefit of his country and his fellow-man, we shall advise him to give up books and betake himself to other walks of life. A man without common sense, without tact, as a mechanic or agriculturist or trader, can do far less harm to the public than the man without common sense who has had the opportunity of becoming, and has had the reputation of being, a scholar.

I trust that arrangements will be made by which girls of our country may be admitted to share in the advantages of this College. I cannot see why our sisters should not receive exactly the same general culture as we do. I think that the progress of the country will be more rapid and permanent when the girls receive the same general training as the boys; and our women, besides being able to appreciate the intellectual labours of their husbands and brothers, will be able also to share in the pleasures of intellectual pursuits. We need not fear that they will be less graceful, less natural, or less womanly; but we may be sure that they will make wiser mothers, more appreciative wives, and more affectionate sisters.

In the religious work of the College, the Bible will be our text-book, the Bible without note or comment—especially as we propose to study the original language in which the New Testament was written; and we may find opportunity, in connection with the Arabic, to study the Old Testament. . . .

Christianity is not only not a local religion, but it has adapted itself to the people wherever it has gone. No language or social existence has been any barrier to it; and I have often thought that in this country it will acquire wider power, deeper influence, and become instinct with a higher vitality than anywhere else. When we look at the treatment which our own race and other so-called inferior races have received from Christian nations, we cannot but be struck with the amazing dissimilitude and disproportion between the original idea of Christianity, as expressed by Christ, and the practice of it by his professed followers.

The sword of the conqueror and the cries of the conquered have attended or preceded the introduction of this faith wherever carried by Europeans, and some of the most enlightened minds have sanctioned the subjugation of weaker races—the triumph of Might over Right—that the empire of civilization might be extended; but these facts do not affect the essential principles of the religion. We must gather its doctrines not from the examples of some of its adherents but from the sacred records. . . .

Now this is the influence which is to work that great reformation in our land for which we hope. This is the influence which is to leaven the whole country and to become the principle of the new civilization which we believe is to be developed on this continent. It has already produced important changes, notwithstanding its slow and irregular growth, notwithstanding the apparent scantiness and meagreness of its visible fruits; and it shall be the aim of this College to work in the spirit of the great Master who was manifested as an example of self-sacrifice to the highest truth and the highest good—that spirit which excluded none from his converse, which kept company with publicans and sinners that he might benefit them, which went anywhere and everywhere to seek and to save that which is lost. We will study to cultivate whatsoever things are true, whatsoever things are honest, whatsoever things are just, whatsoever things are pure, whatsoever things are lovely, whatsoever things are of good report. If there be any virtue, and if there be any praise, we will endeavour to think on these things.

Our fathers have borne testimony to the surrounding Heathen of the value and superiority of Christianity. They endeavoured to accomplish what they saw ought to be accomplished; and, according to the light within them, fought against wrong and asserted the right. Let us not dwell too much on the mistakes of the past. Let us be thankful for what good has been done, and let us do better if we can. We, like our predecessors, are only frail and imperfect beings, feelers after truth. Others, let us hope will come by-and-bye and do better than we—efface our errors and correct our mistakes, see truths clearly which we now see but dimly, and truths dimly which we do not see at all. The true ideal, the proper work of the race, will grow brighter and more distinct as we advance in culture.

Nor can we be assisted in our work by looking back and denouncing the deeds of the oppressors of our fathers, by perpetuating race antagonism. It is natural, perhaps, that we should at times feel indignation in view of past injustice, but continually dwelling upon it will not help us. It is neither edifying nor dignified to be forever declaiming about the wrongs of the race. Lord Beaconsfield once said in the House of Commons that Irish members were too much in the habit of clanking their chains on rising to speak. Such a habit, when it ceases to excite pity, begets contempt and ridicule. What we need is wider and deeper culture, more intimate intercourse with our interior brethren, more energetic advance to the healthy regions.

As those who have suffered affliction in a foreign land, we have no antecedents from which to gather inspiration.

All our traditions and experiences are connected with a foreign race. We have no poetry or philosophy but that of our taskmasters. The songs that live in our ears and are often on our lips are the songs which we heard sung by those who shouted while we groaned and lamented. They sang of their history, which was the history of our degradation. They recited their triumphs, which contained the records of our humiliation. To our great misfortune, we learned their prejudices and their passions, and thought we had their aspirations and their power. Now, if we are to make an independent nation—a strong nation—we must listen to the songs of our unsophisticated brethren as they sing of their history, as they tell of their traditions, of the wonderful and mysterious events of their tribal or national life, of the achievements of what we call their superstitions; we must lend a ready ear to the ditties of the Kroomen who pull our boats, of the Pessah and Golah men, who till our farms; we must read the compositions, rude as we may think them, of the Mandingoes and the Veys. We shall in this way get back the strength of the race. . . .

And this is why we want the College away from the seaboard—with its constant intercourse with foreign manners and low foreign ideas—that we may have free and uninterrupted intercourse with the intelligent among the tribes of the interior; that the students, even from the books to which they will be allowed access, may conveniently flee to the forests and fields of Manding and the Niger, and mingle with our brethren and gather fresh inspiration and fresh and living ideas.

It is the complaint of the intelligent Negro in America that the white people pay no attention to his suggestions or his writings; but this is only because he has nothing new to say—nothing that they have not said before him, and that they cannot say better than he can. Let us depend upon it, that the emotions and thoughts which are natural to us command the curiosity and respect of others far more than the showy display of any mere acquisitions which we have derived from them, and which they know depend more upon our memory than upon any real capacity. What we must follow is all that concerns our individual growth. Let us do our own work and we shall be strong and worthy of respect; try to do the work of others, and we shall be weak and contemptible. There is magnetism in original action, in self-trust, which others cannot resist. . . .

We have a great work before us, a work unique in the history of the world, which others who appreciate its vastness and importance, envy us the privilege of doing. The world is looking at this

Republic to see whether "order and law, religion and morality, the rights of conscience, the rights of persons and the rights of property", may all be secured and preserved by a government administered entirely by Negroes.

Let us show ourselves equal to the task.

The time is past when we can be content with putting forth elaborate arguments to prove our equality with foreign races. Those who doubt our capacity are more likely to be convinced of their error by the exhibition, on our part, of those qualities of energy and enterprise which will enable us to occupy the extensive field before us for our own advantage and the advantage of humanity— for the purposes of civilization, of science, of good government, and of progress generally—than by any mere abstract argument about the equality of races. The suspicions disparaging to us will be dissipated only by the exhibition of the indisputable realities of a lofty manhood as they may be illustrated in successful efforts to build up a nation, to wrest from Nature her secrets, to lead the van of progress in this country, and to regenerate a continent.

T

31

Report of the President of Liberia College to the Board of Trustees

December, 1881 (1882), 4–12

I am happy to be able to state that since your last meeting the cause of education has received encouraging impetus throughout Liberia. The conviction is spreading and deepening that education for Liberia is far more than it is for any other civilized country. Our circumstances are peculiar. There are internal and external reasons that make universal education among us essential and indispensable. We need it for healthful inward growth as a republican constitutional government, and for healthful outward growth —as we advance into the interior—safely to absorb and assimilate the aboriginal elements.

Liberia College has passed through great trials, but they have not been peculiar. In other countries, far in advance of ours, colleges and universities, having all external conditions favourable to their growth, have had serious difficulties to contend against; and they have succeeded only by fighting their way through. Harvard did not develop into what it is now without repeated criticisms and reforms. Even during the present year three prominent American colleges have had serious trials. The whole governing body of Yale has been sharply assailed. At Dartmouth and Cornell the trouble has been with the Faculty. At Cornell the chief complaint (a most serious one) was that the number of students was rapidly and greatly decreasing, that the best professors had left it and that their places were taken by men of inferior standing; but there was enough vital power in these institutions, and enough appreciation of education in the surrounding communities, to enable them to overcome these difficulties. So we may feel confident that Liberia College, with the aid of a sympathizing community, is now overcoming the obstacles which have impeded its progress.

You will be gratified to learn that the government, more than ever before, has taken an active interest in the work of the College. When we began our labours of instruction in February last we found that the College building was hardly habitable for want of repairs. This inconvenience became greater and more apparent as the rainy season advanced. About the middle of the rains the

Executive Committee took in hand the work of repairs, the government and citizens coming liberally to their aid. Among the citizens who have generously contributed to this work I may mention Gabriel Moore, Esq., R. A. Sherman, Esq., and Mayor T. C. Fuller. The building (with the exception of the roof, which ought to be of galvanized iron) and the roads leading to it, are now in such an improved state as has not be witnessed since 1862, when the building was dedicated. I am happy to state in this connection that one of our fellow-citizens from the leeward, who visited the building a few days ago, has promised one hundred dollars in draft or produce towards the purchase of an iron roof.

At the opening of the first term this year, in February last, eight students were enrolled in the Collegiate Department, who either paid the fee for the term or gave their note to the treasurer for the amount. These were divided into Freshmen and what we called Sub-freshmen. The Sub-freshmen did not pass the required examination for the regular Freshman Class. At the opening of the first term of 1882 they will enter as regular Freshmen, with four or five who will come from the Alexander High School. The College will then contain a larger number of students than in any one year before. We do not find that the exaction of tuition fees has at all interfered with the interests of the institution, except for the better— providing us with a fund, however small, to assist in meeting current expenses.

The Executive Committee at their regular meeting in October elected Mr. Benjamin Anderson (the explorer of Musahdu, and government surveyor) as tutor of mathematics, to give special instruction to the advanced students in practical surveying, plotting, and the use of instruments. The importance of an accurate knowledge of surveying on the part of our young men increases as our settlements advance to the interior, and as landed property on the banks of the rivers becomes more valuable.

Circumstances, I regret to state, during the year caused us to lose in the Preparatory Department the services of Mr. Arthur Barclay; but the Department has been continued with undiminished interest by another graduate of the College, Rev. Robert B. Richardson. On account of having but a single teacher the Executive Committee thought proper to limit the number of scholars in this department to thirty. Twenty-eight have been in regular attendance during the year, all of whom have paid their own expenses. We have had assistance from the New York State Colonization Society this year for only one student, a Freshman in the College. From the number of applications now on hand for admission to the Preparatory Department, it is thought that the accessions next year will exceed the limit fixed by the Committee and the ability of the teacher. I would suggest, therefore, that the Board of Trustees authorize the employment of an assistant teacher, and request the Government to bear the expense of his salary. Of aborigines there have been in this department three Bassas, one Congo, one Kroo; all of whom have maintained a respectable grade in their studies, attendance, and behaviour.

There are three students in the Collegiate Department and one in the Preparatory looking forward to the ministry. The three in the College are Presbyterians; the other, who expects to enter College next term, is a Baptist.

The annual examinations of the two departments were attended this year by an unusual number of visitors from the city and the St. Paul and Mesurado rivers.

The Mandingo youth[1] whom I had engaged at Sierra Leone as teacher of Arabic and Native Languages having been prevented from coming, I have opened a class for the teaching of the Arabic language. To this class, persons not connected with the College are admitted.

In the month of September I was visited by a learned Mohammedan Iman from Musahdu, now the presiding officer of the mosque at Vonswah. He came with four of his pupils. I gave them apartments in the College building, where he instructed his scholars daily. He had with him an elementary treatise on arithmetic in Arabic, from which he gave lessons. On his departure I presented him with a large Arabic Bible (the Beirut translation) with which he was highly pleased.

THE LIBRARY

The Library is far from adequate to the present needs and purposes of the College. It consists of about four thousand volumes, but few works of reference less than twenty-five years old. The nucleus of this library was collected in the United States in 1862. It might be well to dispose at public auction of at least fifty per cent of the volumes now on our shelves, and use the proceeds to procure a few works of more immediate and practical importance.

During the year we have received from the Trustees of Donations two consignments of valuable text-books, all new and of the latest editions. Of these we have sold some to the students, but we have

[1] Muhammed Wakka, Assistant Arabic writer to the Government of Sierra Leone.

generally lent them out to be returned for the use of other students. We are also in the regular receipt, through the Trustees of Donations, for the Library of the College, the *Princeton Review*, the *International Review*, and the New York *Nation*. I have ordered during the year elementary text-books from England, and a few works in general literature to be paid for by the Trustees of Donations.

We need books of reference and textbooks in Greek and Roman . . . in English language, history, and literature, and in Arabic. We need also modern textbooks in mathematics and the natural sciences.

Through the kindness of Hon. John Eaton, United States Commissioner of Education, of Col. W. K. Rogers, late private secretary to the President of the United States, and Professor Baird of the Smithsonian Institution, the College library has received during the year a valuable supply of the official publications of the United States Government, and of the Smithsonian Institution.

Among individual donors I may mention Mrs. Olivia Phelps Atterbury of New York, Rev. Thomas Gallagher of Lagrange, Missouri, and Hon. John H. Smyth, United States Minister-Resident at Monrovia.

We are in particular need of Chairs in the department of the Physical and Moral Sciences and Modern Languages, including those of leading aboriginal tribes.

We must not lose sight of the importance of a removal of the College operations to an interior site, where we may have wider scope. We ought to have a workshop connected with the College, in which a knowledge of the use of carpenter's and other tools may be acquired, especially for the training of youth from the interior. I should consider this sort of pursuit as by no means an unprofitable distraction from the bookwork of the place. Even in highly civilized communities the question is now beginning to be seriously considered and discussed whether the knowledge gained in the workshop is not, after all, a proper element in a liberal education, and ought not to find a place in the curriculum of a public school.

We need room also for agricultural pursuits. It is clear that this is to be largely an agricultural country. We cannot compete in manufacturing industry with the advanced nations. Our material and political success is much more dependent upon the wisdom with which we regulate and foster the culture of the soil than upon our skill in shipbuilding or progress in the knowledge of the railway or telegraph. I do not hesitate, then, to recommend that with the study of languages, mathematics, and natural science, we provide as soon as possible an agricultural curriculum which will be applicable in its arrangements and instruction to all classes of our citizens, at the same time providing the opportunity of self-help to indigent students and a growing income to the institution. For this industrial and technical training we need more land, and to get more land we must transfer the operations of the institution to the interior. Two or three hundred or a thousand acres of land would not be too much.

It is our desire and purpose to teach not so much knowledge of useful things as useful knowledge. By useful knowledge I mean such knowledge as shall serve as a stepping-stone to other knowledge—knowledge, the process of acquiring which will so strengthen, form, and enlarge the mind as to enable it to grasp and utilize the knowledge of such things as shall be useful in the development of the moral and intellectual, as well as material resources of the country. Culture for us will be whatever gives not only mental strength, but wide views of duty in this country and for this race.

It has been objected that it is too early in the life of this Republic to aim at the extensive culture of the youth of the land; but if we are an independent nation, not only having international duties and engagements to fulfil with the most cultured nations of the earth, but having also the delicate and in some respects perilous responsibility of absorbing and controlling thousands and millions of our brethren suffering from ages of darkness, it is certainly not too early to qualify ourselves for the lofty and arduous duties before us; and for the sake of the common schools of the country we need the higher education of the College. It is said that "important as the parish schools of Scotland have been, they would have been a poor affair without her universities. Potent has been the influence of the primary schools in New England, but they derived the breath of life from the colleges established by the Puritan fathers."

It must not be forgotten that we are not now coloured people living under a superior race, who discharge for us all the most important functions of national life, leaving us only the irresponsible and comparatively insignificant parts to perform. We are a Negro nation, having a new and important role to play in the world's history, and in the history of this great continent. If, as Mr. Swinburne says, "freedom is holy, but heavy to carry", what shall we say of freedom and empire combined—the *imperium et libertas*—which to a certain limited but important extent it is our privilege to enjoy? That we have not had advantages of culture will furnish no excuse for us when we show incompetence in dealing with great national questions. The consequences of political errors are indelible and cannot be overlooked. Lord Granville [British Foreign Secretary] will not excuse Secretary Gibson if he blunders in dealing with our Northwest Boundary question or with the annexation of interior kingdoms. The nation and the millions allied to us at home and abroad suffer the consequences of incompetence all the same if President Gardner is not able to understand and fulfil the functions of an independent and responsible ruler. It will not be said that the time has not yet come in the history of that nation when they may be expected to know these things. The time had come in 1847, when we declared ourselves an independent nation and were received as such by the nations of the earth; and so our friends in America felt when they took measures at once to assist us in establishing a college. Nay, the time had come when in 1821 the first Pilgrims landed on these shores, refugees from the house of bondage, to found a home for themselves and their children. . . . These are serious considerations, gentlemen, and I am glad to know that you not only appreciate their importance yourselves but that you are endeavouring to impress it upon the community.

* * *

A suspicion, born of ignorance and conscious inferiority in educational advantages, makes us dread at times that the country will be overrun by alien influences; but if we fortify our children with the advantages of culture we need fear no foreign race. If they come with the prestige of the Caucasian or Anglo-Saxon on their side, the African has the climate and the physical conditions of the country on his side. Make them equal in culture, and the balance must be in favour of the Negro. No foreigners have yet attempted violent entrance into Africa without finding that they had sown the wind to reap the whirlwind.

The Negro mind, perhaps more than that of any other race, needs all the help to be secured from disciplinary agencies. We have been the victims not only of ages of barbarism, but the most advanced of us have been the victims of what is far more pernicious—namely, foreign oppression; and our faults and failings, partly the result of remote influences of the past, but chiefly the result of our immediate antecedents, are often made the subject of unappreciative remark by those of our foreign teachers who know us only in exile.

32

The Lagos Training College
and Industrial Institute

Lagos, 1896, 1–18

Dr. Blyden to Governor [Gilbert T.] Carter
Department of Native Affairs
Lagos, May 14th, 1896

Sir:

Referring to the conversation which I had the honour to have with your Excellency on the morning of the 11th instant on the unsatisfactory results which, as a rule, have thus far been produced upon African youth by their foreign training and availing myself of the permission you gave me to address you on the subject, I beg to submit the following:

WEST AFRICAN STUDENTS IN ENGLAND

The practice of sending their children to Europe for education by West African Natives was introduced among them by Mr. Zachary Macaulay, father of the historian, when Governor of Sierra Leone, near the close of the last or the beginning of the present century.

In Knight's Memoir of Rev. Henry Venn, late Honorary Secretary of the Church Missionary Society, it is said, "several of the leading natives of Sierra Leone had been persuaded by Mr. Zachary Macaulay to entrust their sons to his care for education in England, and an establishment was formed for their reception at Clapham. Eight of these boys were subsequently baptized at Clapham Church by Mr. Venn's father in 1805". I believe that over one dozen were sent and it is said that only one was fortunate enough to return home; the rest fell victims to the rigours of the English climate. But in spite of this melancholy beginning parents able to do so have continued up to the present time to send their children to England for intellectual and other training in the hope of furnishing for their country not only intelligent and learned but good men—men of sober, prudent, and virtuous habits. But in the century that has elapsed, during which they have been going to

253

this expense, they have experienced nothing but disappointment in every case. I had the honour with other Africans, while at Sierra Leone in 1872, to address several letters to Governor Hennessy on the subject of advanced education for African youth in Africa,[1] which he forwarded with his own comments to Lord Kimberley, then Secretary of State for the Colonies. His Lordship sympathized with the views expressed in the correspondence; but the people of Sierra Leone were not then prepared to undertake the initiation of the Institution recommended, as suggested by Governor Hennessy in his letter to me, dated December 10th, 1872, and the Government did not feel justified, without the assumption of some such responsibility by the natives, in inaugurating any scheme for Higher Education.

Time, however, the course of events and additional untoward experiences have, I believe, made leading natives willing to come to the assistance of the Government; and I am of [the] opinion that here in Lagos when the matter is put before them in a practical form with a probability of its being sanctioned by the Secretary of State and becoming a part of the Government policy, they will be liberal in their contributions.

They now consider that a sufficient period has elapsed during which both time and money have been spent to very little purpose and they are anxious to have the means for the thorough training of their youth on the spot.

It is an obvious peril to young men in the most critical years of their lives to be away from their own country among strangers of an entirely different race, subject to no useful or effectual control either from their parents or other relatives; and provided they are too often absent from recitations, suffered to do as they please, read what they please, and spend as they please money with which too indulgent parents supply them. The lamentable results upon the youth who have been under such training or lack of training have proved to their unfortunate parents or guardians the extravagant folly of thus exposing their children to influences which not infrequently affect even Europeans unfavourably.

Owing to the serious inconvenience which this state of things has entailed, parents are beginning to see the absurdity of the practice introduced by Mr. Macaulay a hundred years ago and persisted in to the present time—for which, however, they are not to be altogether blamed, considering that no provisions have existed or now exist on the spot for the advanced intellectual training of youth.

[1] See above *The West African University*, pp. 223–29 [ed.].

FOUNDING OF INDIAN UNIVERSITIES

The Natives of India very soon found out the necessity for facilities at home for educating their children in Western learning. Sixty years ago, 1836, a College was founded for his people by a wealthy native gentleman, and the Universities of Calcutta, Madras and Bombay from which so many able and useful natives have come for the public service and for literary work were incorporated forty years ago.

Moral character, principles or character in general are formed not only—perhaps not mainly—by precepts inculcated at School, but by the unconscious imitation and adoption of the maxim and practices that prevail around us, and the assimilation of manners and sentiments which result from this almost irresistible contagion. African youth residing in England for education have almost unrestricted intercourse with persons outside their schools; for some reason or other that intercourse is not regulated as in the case even of English boys. Of course we cannot expect for many years to come to have any demand for the higher training which is given to natives of India; but I have a very deep conviction of the importance of placing the means of a liberal education within the reach of the promising and specially gifted youth—few and far between in any community—and of extending the means of elementary education to as large a portion of the population as possible, and consequently of the care to be bestowed upon those arrangements by which the time and the money necessary for such instruction, may be best economized and with a view to the best results.

TECHNICAL INSTITUTE

The Botanic Station at Ebute Metta where the space is now too limited for the purposes of the Government would be a splendid site for carrying out the industrial features of the scheme which must be a necessary part of it, not only for improving the industrial capacities of the population but for training workmen for the public service. I am persuaded that many persons, who are now discouraged by the results of foreign training and are becoming indifferent to learning, would renew their interest if they found that such facilities of training were on the spot as give the practical as well as the theoretical side of education.

If your Excellency will be good enough to give me briefly your views on this important subject, I may be able to propound some

simple scheme for the inauguration of the work, which I venture
to hope may be carried into effect before the close of the present
century, the first institution of its kind in West Africa; and that
it may be a standing Memorial of an Administration which was
able to add the provision for the inestimable blessing of a sound
liberal education for the Natives to the great material benefits which
it was fortunate enough to confer upon the Colony.

> I have the honour to be,
> Your Excellency's abdt. humble servant,
> EDWARD W. BLYDEN.

*　　*　　*

> *Dr. Blyden to Governor Carter*
> *Department of Native Affairs*
> *Lagos, May 21st, 1896.*

Sir:

I have the honour to acknowledge the receipt of your Excellency's
letter of the 18th instant, and I am glad to remark that you have
long thought that a thoroughly good training Institution for
Africans in Africa is the great educational need of the race. Yes;
it is not too much to say "of the race"; not of West Africa only
but of the whole Negro Race; and I am persuaded that such an
Institution established here and properly conducted would attract
aspiring Negro youth from all parts of the coast and probably from
across the Atlantic; for nowhere is the civilized Negro, who thinks
of the race at all, satisfied with either the method or the results
of his training under the prevailing systems. He finds himself by
them alienated from himself and from his countrymen. He is neither
African in feeling nor in aim. He does not breathe African air
through any of the lessons he has imbibed. The smell of African
ground is not in them, but everything is Europe and European, and
in some instances for the sake of gratifying the artificial and unnatural tastes he has contracted, he would annihilate his sisters to
produce a new race. This is among the saddest of the results produced by training the African away from his country and his
countrymen.

The new educational departure suggested is not incompatible
with a full appreciation of the past labours of the Missionaries
nor is it by any means intended to disparage or conflict with their
present operations. The good work they have done for Africa in
the past can not be lost sight of; and I am glad to be able to record
it as my opinion that by their labours and sufferings they have

conferred inestimable benefits upon the cause of Africa and her people.

In the first place, it was owing to their philanthropic and persistent efforts that in the days when universal indifference to Africa prevailed, public attention in Europe was attracted to and fixed upon the continent, and information was diffused about the people, their languages, and their social and political condition, in a manner in which the traveller, the trader, or even Government officials, as birds of passage, could not be expected to emulate. They, more than any other class of men, changed the public opinion of Europe as to the character of Africa and Africans; showed that the country was made not only as an arena of slave raiding and the source of hardworking slaves, but that the land and its people had a vital connection with the rest of mankind and a serious relationship and solemn import to all ages and to every nation. It is something—and something for which the African can not be too grateful to the memory of those self-denying men—to have secured, in days when, so far as the outside world understood, darkness covered the land and gross darkness the people, the sympathies and genius and labours and pecuniary influence of really deep and earnest thinkers and influential leaders of public opinion and to have brought Africa within the range of the scientific as well as political consideration of Europe.

But there has been marked advancement in all departments of life since they performed those great and necessary labours, and Africans for the work they now have to do need a different—a wider and deeper—training industrially and intellectually than the limits of the sphere and resources of the Missionaries allow them to give. With gratitude for the past, therefore, we are trying to take courage to face and deal with the unknown and what appears to us pregnant future.

The scheme for the proposed Institution, which I would suggest and which I venture to think is simple enough is as follows: The site for the building or buildings should be away from the town of Lagos, across the Lagoon, at Ebute Metta, if possible, and should consist of sufficient land to give ample scope for industrial training and for practical illustrations of the scientific teaching.

CURRICULUM

There should be two departments, the industrial and the literary. The curriculum of the industrial department should include the usual mechanical trades and scientific and practical agriculture.

Every student should be required to devote a certain number of hours in each week to the performance of such industrial work, either mechanical or agricultural, as his taste may select and as will give the necessary physical training and manual dexterity.

In the literary department, the curriculum should include such studies as shall lead to the acquisition of good intellectual habits and exercises. My experience and observation as a teacher of youth for many years have taught me that, after reading and writing—about the fundamental necessity and precedence of which no rational man will dispute—it is a matter of indifference to what branch of study the attention of boys is primarily directed or in pursuit of what knowledge they acquire habits of spontaneous and continued attention, self-control, and reflection, habits which it is indispensable that African youth, just from primitive conditions, should acquire if they are to become capable and useful members of the society in which they are to move.

Without entering at all into the idle dispute as to the uses and advantages of classical learning in general, I may be permitted to state that all experience has shown that the most effective of disciplinary studies are the ancient Languages and Mathematics. As to the ancient languages it is true that a knowledge of them is not apparently of any practical use. They do not seem to be indispensable for most of the many pursuits of life; and it is also true that many youth who study them for years never acquire any comfortable use of them and have, apparently, but little pleasure or profit in the knowledge they have been trying to acquire. But then, in the course of their laborious and apparently unsuccessful efforts, they have almost always acquired those habits of methodical observation, of self-command, of memory, of abstraction and generalization and even in some degree of taste, judgment and invention, which are not only useful but in reality indispensable for any serious occupation, whether as Judge on the bench, merchant at the desk or farmer in the field. As I have intimated above, the main benefit of education consists in the acquisition of these habits, and whatever teaches them most effectually is the best course of education.

Moreover, the proper study of Greek and Latin is not limited to a mere acquaintance with words in a foreign language, but necessarily involves a good deal of historical and geographical and even religious knowledge and a pretty extensive acquaintance with the best models of reasoning and eloquence, unequalled by anything to be found in modern European literature. . . .

Mathematics should be included in the curriculum—not what

is called Higher Mathematics, but those branches of the subject which shall be sufficient for disciplinary and practical purposes: for the survey of land, the erection of bridges, the construction of maps, fixing of latitude and longitude, etc. The African will not need more. He may be thoroughly qualified for his work without a knowledge of the differential or integral calculus. Many men eminent in literature have been ignorant of even elementary Mathematics. The sphere in which the Negro will be most useful and most successful will be literature. It is not his to measure the distance of the planets and mark their courses. He has not to plough unknown seas and find his way across trackless waters. That work has been assigned to another race. But if given a fair opportunity, I do not believe that in classics and languages he would be inferior to others; and he might from his vision bring forward new translations of the classics and of the Bible which would both astonish and instruct Europeans.

There are branches of science, however, which will be useful to him. He should get an insight into Botany, Mineralogy, Geology, and become to some extent at least acquainted with the laws of the moral and physical world as they are being unfolded by contemporary discoveries.

In objecting to denominational or dogmatic teaching in the Institute, it must not be understood that it is proposed to neglect religious teaching. The religious instinct is strong in the African; and for him all manly education must be based on religion; it is essential for him to a normal development, and all attempts at African education, without this, must fail of the highest end. But there are two parts of religion that can be taught without introducing distracting dogmatic views or fostering denominational prejudices; and those parts the Founder of Christianity Himself gave as alone fundamental and indispensable, namely; the love of God and the love of Man. "Thou shalt love the Lord thy God" etc., and "thou shalt love thy neighbour as thyself"; on these two commandments hang all the law and prophets. It is hardly necessary for me to add that success in these teachings—both the secular and the religious—will depend upon the general spirit of diligence and good sense with which both on the part of teacher and pupil the work is carried out.

As this letter has reached an almost undue length I will reserve for my next further details as to the Initiation and Management of the scheme.

* * *

Dr. Blyden to Governor Carter
Department of Native Affairs
Lagos, June 3rd, 1896.

Sir:

With reference to the Initiation and Management of the proposed Lagos Literary and Industrial Institute I beg most respectfully to submit the following.

In dealing with this important subject it is possible of course only to sketch outlines as far as they can be determined without practical experience under the actual conditions, leaving specific details to be filled up when some responsible body are authorized to deal with the subject.

I have laid the Correspondence, which has passed between us thus far, including all of the present communication which follows this paragraph, before two meetings of some prominent citizens of Lagos,[2] and the following after full and free discussion, are the results reached.

"POLITICAL" PLAN OF INSTITUTE

The constitution of the governing body or what may be termed the political as distinguished from the literary and industrial portion of the plan, was first considered.

1. The Government of the Institute shall be vested in a Board of Trustees with the Governor of the Colony as President *ex officio*.

2. There shall be fifteen members of the Board, six to be appointed by the Governor and nine to be elected by the contributors to the scheme. Three of the members shall be European and twelve Natives. Ten shall constitute a quorum. No Native shall be a member of the Board who shall not have contributed towards the initiation of the scheme the sum of at least £5. Each member shall hold office for five years, but may at the expiration of his term be re-appointed by the Governor, if the Governor's appointee, or re-elected by the contributors if originally chosen by them.

The Board shall meet semi-annually for the consideration of the general affairs of the Institute.

3. The Executive Government is vested in a Council or Executive Committee of five members of the Board, one to be a European and four Natives. Four shall constitute a quorum. The members of this

[2] Among those who participated were: J. J. Thomas, James Johnson, Henry Johnson, R. B. Blaize, J. S. Leigh, J. A. Otunba Payne, J. A. Savage, Mojola Agbebi, C. J. Lumpkin, H. A. Caulcrick, G. A. Williams, E. Bickersteth and John P. Jackson.

committee to be elected semi-annually by the Board. It is to meet monthly, and to choose all teachers or professors, to fix their salaries, to superintend, suspend and remove them, and conduct the financial and general affairs of the Institute; in short, to perform all the functions of persons called Visitors in England.

4. The Board of Trustees shall elect a person not a member of the Board as General Secretary, who shall record in a book kept exclusively for that purpose, all the proceedings of the Board. He shall take charge of all Books and papers of the Board, make all reports connected with the business of the Institute and discharge all such duties as the Board shall determine to lie within his sphere of work. His salary shall be fixed by the Board, payable monthly. He shall engage to serve the Board by written contract for a specified period with the understanding that he may be re-appointed if at the close of the period the Board thinks it expedient; and if the engagement is to be terminated at or before the specified time, three months' notice to be given by either side.

5. All moneys, deeds, or other securities belonging to the Institute to be deposited in the local Bank of British West Africa. The Bank shall attend, under the direction of the Executive Committee, to the financial affairs of the Institute, keep all accounts, receive all moneys and disburse the same only by order of the Committee.

6. The Executive Committee shall report its proceedings for revision to the Board of Trustees at each semi-annual meeting, and a copy of said report after its consideration by the Board shall be sent to the Governor for his sanction and approval.

7. Persons sending in donations of sums not less than £5 at once, and before the erection of buildings, shall be considered founders and shall be entitled to vote at the semi-annual meetings. The Honorary Treasurer *pro tem* will be R. B. Blaize, Esq., to whom all donations of contributions must be sent.

THE FACULTY

1. The Faculty of the Institute shall consist of the professors or teachers in the two departments, who shall elect from their own number a Principal to supervise the literary and industrial work of the Institute and to preside at all the Board of Trustees. Every thing relative to the studies to be pursued, text books to be used, and academical discipline to be under the control of the Faculty.

2. The Governor of the Colony as *ex officio* President of the Institute may appoint any member of the Board of Trustees to preside at the semi-annual meetings of the Board and at the

monthly meetings of the Executive Committee, in case of his inability to attend.

3. The Principal shall make quarterly reports to the Executive Committee on the literary and industrial condition of the Institute, number and demeanour of students in attendance, and suggest any measures which may appear to him necessary for the progress and welfare of the Institution. A copy of each report shall be forwarded to the Governor by the Secretary.

4. Pending further arrangements the meetings of the Board of Trustees and of the Executive Committee may be held in the Glover Memorial Hall. The meetings of the Faculty shall be held once a week in the buildings of the Institute.

It is hoped that as soon as possible after the scheme has received the sanction of the Secretary of State a good substantial building may be erected by Public contributions at the Botanic Station at Ebute Metta, if it is found convenient for the Government to give those premises for the purpose of the Institute, and that operations may be commenced on the completion of the building by the employment at a moderate salary of a competent teacher to be paid by the Government, to do preparatory work. It is further hoped that when matters have reached this stage and there is a prospect of competent instructors being secured for the industrial and literary work the Governor will see his way to recommend to the Secretary of State the Grant to the Institute of such an annual sum as shall suffice for the payment of teachers and for the establishment of half a dozen or more scholarships to be bestowed upon indigent and promising youths (a scholarship being £15 per year) and for the further development of the scheme, the principle always being that intellectual life and culture must go side by side with industrial training and physical activity. From the establishment of such an Institute in our own country and under our own eyes, we look forward to the following economic or material results viz.:

1. Saving of the money of our youth.
2. Saving of the time of our youth.
3. Saving of the health and life of our youth.

From these must follow important consequences.

1. Saving of the intellect of our youth.
2. Saving of the character of our youth.
3. Saving of the Racial integrity and instincts of our youth.

In conclusion, I beg to say that the public are looking forward with great interest and anxiety to the action of the Government on the important subject which I have ventured to bring to the notice of your Excellency in these letters; and I have the honour to enclose herewith extracts from leading West African papers viz.:

> *The Sierra Leone Weekly News,*
> *The Lagos Standard,*
> *The Lagos Weekly Record,*
> *The Lagos Echo,*

showing the drift of Public sentiment on the coast on the educational necessity of the present time.

* * *

Dr. Blyden to Governor Carter
Department of Native Affairs
Lagos, June 15th, 1896.

Sir,

I have the honour to acknowledge the receipt of your letter of the 8th instant with the supplementary communication made to me orally on the 10th instant.

If your Excellency will forward to the Secretary of State the extracts from recent West African papers which I enclosed in my letter of the 3rd instant, the Right Honourable gentleman will see that there is a very general and very strong desire on the coast for improved means of education, growing out of the deep conviction that the existing facilities are inadequate; and as one of the proofs that this desire has existed among leading Natives for a long time and that the necessities have been evident to leading British officials, the Secretary may be referred to Governor Hennessy's Despatch to Lord Kimberley on the subject, dated at Sierra Leone, December 28th, 1872, a copy of which I left with your Excellency on the 10th instant. There are not at present in West Africa and there have never existed facilities for the work which it is desired to accomplish by the establishment of the Lagos Training College. The industrial instruction imparted by the Hussey Charity is of the most elementary character and confined to only one or two handicrafts. Moreover, the area within which the operations of that Institution are carried on are too limited even for horticultural training, so that nothing like practical agriculture on anything like a useful scale can be taught here. It is thought that it would be a distinct gain to the colony if the site of the Charity could be removed to the mainland and placed in the neighbourhood of the proposed Training College, if not actually connected with it.

It has been decided that the President of the Board of Trustees shall have the right to vote with the ordinary member on any question in which he is not personally concerned, in addition to the usual casting vote in case of a tie. I hope to forward to you tomorrow a copy of the Prospectus which it is proposed to issue as a preliminary advertisement and Appeal to the public for any further suggestion which your Excellency may wish to make in relation to it. I enclose herewith a copy of the oral communication made to me by your Excellency on June 10th which was a continuation or postscript to your letter of June 8th.

33

The Liberian Scholar

An Address Delivered on the Occasion of the Inauguration of the
President-elect of Liberia College, February 21st, 1900
Liberia Bulletin (1900), 11–22

REORGANIZATION OF LIBERIA COLLEGE

The present reorganization of Liberia College is a notable event in
the history of Liberia. It is not therefore surprising that the Chief
Magistrate of the nation should turn aside from the cares of state—
that busy men and women, foreigners and natives, should leave
their usual occupations—to assist in the ceremonies of today.

We have all been pleased to listen to the statesmanlike words—
the words of wisdom—which have fallen from the lips of President
Coleman; and it is a most striking and interesting fact which his
presence here on this occasion and the part he has taken in these
proceedings suggest, namely, that the man who becomes one of
the most distinguished friends and patrons of learning which the
Republic has produced is a man who in his youth was denied its
advantages; but as a man of strong common sense he seems to
recognize on general grounds, as a practical man, that the public
good requires the advancement and diffusion of knowledge, and
he has never ceased, from his first assumption of the high office
he holds, to urge upon the legislature and people of Liberia the
importance of re-establishing the means of public education. The
results of his efforts we witness today.

We who are responsible for the proceedings of today are all
Africans, all members of the great Hamitic race, pledged to study
and promote to the best of our ability the highest interests of the
Negro.

*   *   *

Liberia is not only a *youthful* nation, only fifty years old, but a
new nation, with a new work, a peculiar work, and a difficult work
before it. There is no other community in the world which has
before it exactly the work we have to do.

. . . What we need is applicability to our surroundings. There
is much that is superfluous in the foreign ideas that we have
imbibed, much that is deficient, much that is injurious. Hence the

necessity of the means of thorough culture at home to produce, not the European scholar, not the American scholar, but the Liberian scholar. It matters not how well born or high born a man may be, he needs training . . . to enable him to do well and effectively the work for which he is adapted and to which by circumstances he is called.

* * *

. . . Liberia College under proper management . . . will revolutionize the thoughts not only of the citizens of the Republic about themselves, but of other Africans, and of foreigners with regard to Africans. It will produce the Liberian scholar, who will study and comprehend . . . Africa, who, with that insight which a genuine sympathy gives, will understand the African in his native state, and know how to give the world a correct knowledge of him; who will be able to study from a scientific standpoint native *law*, tribal organization, native languages, native religion, native politics, and the effect of all these things upon their life. There is much in what we call their crudeness and superstitions that is *educative*. There is much in their government, in their religion, in their social customs, which we must study and understand and take advantage of in order to live in this country.

* * *

The tendency among us—a tendency which considering our antecedents, is natural enough—is to imitate things which are sources of strength to Europe and America, but which for us are sources of disaster, of shame, and of death. I shall refer to one example. Our true policy lies not in securing from abroad expensive armaments, which in our present condition are both unnecessary and incongruous. The true policy of Liberia lies in opening roads to the interior, in establishing and fostering alliances with the great tribes around us, and in teaching them to utilize the resources of their country, to suppress their belligerent tendencies, and cultivate the arts of agricultural and commercial industry. We should aim, not only to *bring out* merchandise from Europe, which is attended with many and serious drawbacks, but to *bring in* goods and produce from the interior. It is to this policy that the present administration points, and if it is thoroughly carried out we shall cease to hear of our poverty, of our inability to discharge our pecuniary obligations, to carry out necessary improvements, and take full possession of our great heritage.

It is to enable us to adjust our relations to the country, as preliminary to the great exodus, that we need the trained intellect—Liberian scholar—and for this work he is to be subjected to a special culture, such culture as is given in colleges, where there is, as a rule, collected the aggregate experience and wisdom of a nation. The instruments of genuine culture are not the monopoly of any one race or nation. For this culture Greece sat at the feet of Egypt—Socrates, Plato, Pythagaros, Aristotle, all drank at the Egyptian fountain—and Egypt is in Africa. Rome got it from Greece, and the rest of Europe from Greece and Rome. The earnest, industrious, and ambitious student will be supplied here with the best facilities for thoroughly mastering what Europe and America have gathered in any particular department, whether of law, theology, religion, or science, and by the aid of the intellectual discipline which he will have acquired from his studies be able to make discoveries in the vast field which lies before him in his fatherland.

*   *   *

There is a great work to be done in Africa by the Africans in independent co-operation with the agencies of western civilization, and Liberia is the only field where the conditions will allow him to find out his work and undertake it without alien interference or control, and Liberia College, as an unsectarian, independent institution, is the only place where the youth can receive the necessary preparation. The Liberian scholar has to add to the store of human knowledge not only what pertains specifically to the African race, but what will be of interest and profit to other races also.

The legislature in its recent action with regard to Liberia College has solved an important problem. As long as others[1] were responsible for the support of the institution, so long they had the right to suggest, if not to shape, the mould in which our opinions should be formed, and so forestall our views and prevent progress. "Progress", one of the leading philosophers of Europe has said, "is difference." We are here a new nation to unfold a new bud in the garden of nationalities. In the course of our development laws will have to be made not known to Greek or Roman legislators; unheard of by Blackstone, Chitty, or Kent; which Napoleon never conceived, which Webster nor Clay ever expounded. And thinkers both in Europe and America will gladly help us in this work. They are never too proud to accept light—provided it is genuine light—from any quarter. They do not want things to be shaped after their

[1] Financial support for the College had derived mainly from the Boston and New York Boards of Trustees [ed.].

mould. The world would gain nothing by having the European reproduced in Africa. . . .

*   *   *

There is a great work, then, before this nation, and there is no doubt that in grappling with it, if we do so earnestly and intelligently, we shall have the sympathy and co-operation of enlightened foreigners. This is already indicated by the practical interest which those residents among us have taken in the re-opening of Liberia College. I am glad to see them so well represented here today, and I heartily believe that in the future they with us will reap the fruits of the generous culture which we hope will be imparted in this institution. . . .

PART VI

Islam in West Africa

PART VI

Islam in West Africa

In much of his writings after 1870 Blyden harshly criticized European sectarian missionary influences which he regarded as dividing Africans and creating a sense of inferiority among them. On the other hand, Blyden was highly sympathetic to Islam in West Africa because he saw it as an elevating influence bringing the Arabic language and literature to Africans, and a unifying one cutting across ethnic lines. He greatly deplored the fact that many Europeans, particularly missionaries, and their African protégés, tended to despise and belittle Muslims. It was one of his goals in West Africa to eliminate the traditional hostility between Muslims and Christians and to build a bridge of communication between them. He sought to do this not only by writing sympathetically about West African Muslims but by encouraging Muslim youths to learn English and English-speaking Africans to learn Arabic. This last he did both privately and in his official capacities as Agent for Native Affairs in Lagos, 1896–7 and as Director of Muslim Education in Sierra Leone, 1901–6.

It is not surprising that Blyden paid special attention to Islam in West Africa. From the late eighteenth century Islam had become a dominant new influence in West African history. The jihadic and conquest movements led by such scholars, warriors and statesmen as Usuman dan Fodio, Al Hajj Omar, Seka Ahmadu and Samori Toure, had resulted not only in the extension of the sway of Islam over large areas but in an intellectual and religious renaissance as well as in important new political, economic and social changes. Of these events and changes, much of which took place in his own lifetime, Blyden was the most important non-Muslim historian and chronicler of his time.

Blyden first began studying Arabic in the early 1860s. In 1866 he spent the summer in Egypt and the Middle East improving his Arabic. In 1867 he was proficient enough to teach it at Liberia College. Later, Blyden completely mastered Arabic, speaking and reading it fluently. In 1869 he visited Boporo, an important Muslim centre of learning in the hinterland of Liberia, and was impressed with its Koranic schools and its "extensive manuscripts in poetry and prose". These findings inspired him to write his first article on "Mohammedanism in West Africa" (Selection 34) in which he advanced the view that contrary to the propaganda of European missionaries and their African protégés, the influence of Islam there was "most salutary": it fostered egalitarism, brotherhood, industry and learning, and broke down tribalism. In 1871 and 1873, as a result of expeditions to Falaba and Timbo respectively, Blyden gained first-hand knowledge of the Muslim communities in the hinterland of Sierra Leone. And in his frequent travels along the coast of West Africa, he became well acquainted with the various Muslim communities.

In "Mohammedanism and the Negro Race" (Selection 35), written in 1876, Blyden again emphasized the salutory impact of Islam on Africans, and effectively contrasted this with the deleterious effects of Christianity on Africans both in the New World and Africa: to him Christianity was the main instrument used to create a sense of inferiority and servility. Writing in 1887, Blyden kept the world informed of the exploits of the great Muslim warrior, Samore Toure, who since the 1870s had conquered a vast area in the Upper Niger (36). In Selection 37, written in 1902, Blyden, now Director of Muslim Education in Sierra Leone, was seeking to persuade the new British colonial régimes in West Africa that Islam was "the most effective educational force in Negro-land". In his last article on Islam (Selection 38), written in 1905, he was concerned to show that "Negro Muslims claim a share in some of the most celebrated achievements of Islam".

Although he himself never became a Muslim, Blyden so closely identified with them that his name is still well known and highly regarded among West African Muslims. His goal of removing the antipathies between Muslims and Christians was taken up vigorously by such disciples of his as Herbert Macaulay and Nnamdi Azikiwe of Nigeria, and has been largely realized.

34

Mohammedanism in Western Africa

Methodist Quarterly Review, January, 1871
Christianity, Islam and the Negro Race, London, 1887, 173–87; 1888 ed.,
199–216

The object of the present paper is to inquire briefly into the condition and influence of Mohammedanism among the tribes of Western Africa . . . many of these tribes have received the religion of Islam without it being forced upon them by the overpowering arm of victorious invaders. The quiet development and organization of a religious community in the heart of Africa has shown that Negroes, equally with other races, are susceptible of moral and spiritual impressions, and of all the sublime possibilities of religion. The history of the progress of Islam in this country would represent the same instances of real and eager mental conflict, of minds in honest transition, of careful comparison and reflection, that have been found in other communities where new aspects of truth and fresh considerations have been brought before them. . . .

. . . all careful and candid observers agree that the influence of Islam in Central and West Africa, has been, upon the whole, of a most salutary character. As an eliminatory and subversive agency, it has displaced or unsettled nothing as good as itself. If it has introduced superstitions, it has expelled superstitions far more mischievous and degrading. And it is not wonderful if, in succeeding to a debasing Heathenism, it has, in many respects, made compromises, so as occasionally to present a barren, hybrid character; but what *is* surprising, is that a religion quietly introduced from a foreign country, with so few of the outward agencies of civilization, should not, in process of time, have been altogether absorbed by the superstitions and manners of barbarous Pagans. But not only has it not been absorbed—it has introduced large modifications in the views and practices even of those who have but a vague conception of its teachings.

Mungo Park, in his travels seventy years ago, everywhere remarked the contrast between the Pagan and Mohammedan tribes of interior Africa. One very important improvement noticed by him was *abstinence from intoxicating drinks*. "The beverage of the Pagan Negroes", he says, "is *beer and mead*, of which they often drink to excess; the Mohammedan convert drinks *nothing but* water".[1] Thus throughout Central Africa there has been established a vast *Total Abstinence Society*; and such is the influence of this society that where there are Muslim inhabitants even in Pagan towns, it is a very rare thing to see a person intoxicated. Thus they present an almost impenetrable barrier to the desolating flood of ardent spirits with which traders from Europe and America inundate the coast. . . .

Wherever the Moslem is found on the coast, whether Jalof, Foulah, or Mandingo, he looks upon himself as a separate and distinct being from his Pagan neighbour, and immeasurably his superior in intellectual and moral respects. He regards himself as one to whom a revelation has been "sent down" from heaven. He holds constant intercourse with the "Lord of worlds", whose servant he is. In his behalf, Omnipotence will ever impose in times of danger. Hence he feels that he cannot indulge in the frivolities and vices which he considers as by no means incompatible with the character and professions of the Kafir or unbeliever. . . . But there are no caste distinctions among them. They do not look upon the privileges of Islam as confined by tribal barriers or limitations. They are constantly making proselytes. As early as the commencement of the present century, the elastic and expansive character of their system was sufficiently marked to attract the notice of Mr. Park. "In the Negro country", observed that celebrated traveller, "the Mohammedan religion has made *and continues to make*, considerable progress. . . ." From Senegal to Lagos, over two thousand miles, there is scarcely an important town on the seaboard where there are not at least one mosque, and active representatives of Islam, often side by side with the Christian teachers. And as soon as a Pagan, however obscure and degraded, embraces the Moslem faith, he is at once admitted as an equal to their society. Slavery and the slave-trade are laudable institutions, provided the slaves are Kafirs. The slave who embraces Islam is free, and no office is closed against him on account of servile blood.

The Pagan village possessing a Mussulman teacher is always found to be in advance of its neighbours in all elements of civilization. The people pay great deference to him. He instructs their children, and professes to be the medium between them and Heaven, either for securing a supply of their necessities, or for warding off or removing calamities. . . . The Mohammedan, then, who enters a Pagan village with his books, and papers, and rosaries, his frequent ablutions and regularly recurring time of prayers and prostrations, in which he appears to be conversing with some in-

[1] Park's *Travels*, Chapter II.

visible being, soon acquires a controlling influence over the
people. . . .

To the African Mussulman, innocent of the intellectual and
scientific progress of other portions of the world, the Koran is all-
sufficient for his moral, intellectual, social and political needs. It
is to him far more than it is to the Turk or Egyptian, upon whom
the light of European civilization has fallen. It is his code of laws,
and his creed, his homily, and his liturgy. He consults it for direction on every possible subject; and his pagan neighbour, seeing
such veneration paid to the book, conceives even more exaggerated
notions of its character. The latter looks upon it as a great medical
repository, teaching the art of healing diseases, and as a wonderful
storehouse of charms and divining power, protecting from danger
and foretelling future events. . . . He therefore never fails to resort,
in times of extremity, to the Mohammedan for direction, and pays
him for charms against evil. These charms are nothing more than
passages from the Koran, written on slips of paper, and enclosed in
leather cases about two or three inches square—after the manner
of the Jewish phylactery—and worn about the neck or wrist. The
passages usually written are the last two chapters of the Koran,
known as the "Chapters of Refuge". . . . In cases of internal complaint, one or both of these chapters are written on certain leaves,
of which a strong decoction is made, and the water administered
to the patient. We have seen these two chapters written inside a
bowl at Alexandria for medicinal purposes.

The Moslems themselves wear constantly about their persons
certain texts from the Koran, called *Ayat-el-hifz*, verses of protection or preservation, which are supposed to keep away every species
of misfortune. The following are in most common use: "God is
the best *protector*, and He is the most merciful of those who show
mercy."[2] "And God compasseth them behind. Verily it is a glorious
Koran, written on a *preserved* tablet". . . .

The Koran is almost always in their hand. It seems to be their
labour and their relaxation to pore over its pages. They love to
read and recite it aloud for hours together. They seem to possess
an enthusiastic appreciation of the rhythmical harmony in which
it is written. But we cannot attribute its power over them altogether
to the jingling sounds, word-plays, and refrains in which it abounds.
These, it is true, please the ear and amuse the fancy, especially
of the uncultivated. But there is something higher, of which these
rhyming lines are the vehicle; something possessing a deeper power
to rouse the imagination, mould the feelings, and generate action.

[2] Sura XII, 64.

Gibbon has characterized the Koran as a "tissue of incoherent rhapsodies".[3] But the author of the *Decline and Fall* [of the Holy Roman Empire] was, as he himself acknowledges, ignorant of the Arabic language, and therefore incompetent to pronounce an authoritative judgment. Mr. Hallam, in a more appreciative vein, speaks of it as "a book confessedly written with much elegance and purity", containing "just and elevated notions of the Divine nature and moral duties, the gold ore that pervades the dross".[4] The historian of the Middle Ages, a most conscientious investigator, had probably read the book in the original—had been charmed with its *sense* as well as *sound*. Only those who read it in the language of the Arabian author can form anything like an accurate idea of its unapproachable place as a power among unevangelized communities for moulding into the most exciting and the most universal harmonies the feelings and imaginations. A recent and able critic says: "The Koran suffers more than any other book we think of by a translation, however, masterly. The grandeur of the Koran consists, its content apart, in its diction. . . ."[5] The African Moslem forms no exception among the adherents of Islam in his appreciation of the sacred book. It is studied with as much enthusiasm at Boporo, Misadu, Medina and Kankan,[6] as at Cairo, Alexandria, or Bagdad. In travelling in the exterior of Liberia,[7] we have met ulemas, or learned men, who could reproduce from memory any chapter of the Koran, with its vowels and dots, and other grammatical marks. The boys under their instruction are kept at the study of the books for years. First they are taught the letters and vowel marks, then they are taught to read the text, without receiving any insight into its meaning. When they can read fluently, they are taught the meaning of the words which they commit to memory; after which they are instructed in what they call the "Jalaleyn", a running commentary on the Koran. While learning the Jaleleyn, they have side studies assigned them in Arabic manuscripts, containing the mystical traditions, the acts of Mohammed, the duties of fasting, prayer, alms, corporal purification, etc. Young men who intend to be enrolled among the ulemas take up history and chronology, on which they have some fragmentary manuscripts. Before a student is admitted to the ranks of the learned, he must pass an examination, usually lasting seven days, conducted by a Board consisting

[3] Chapter I.
[4] *Middle Ages*, Chapter VI.
[5] Emmanuel Deutsch, in the *Quarterly Review* (London) for October 1869.
[6] Mohammedan towns, from seventy-five to three hundred miles east and north-east of Monrovia.
[7] See Part 2, Selection 13: "The Boporo Country" [ed.].

of imams and ulemas. If he is successful, he is led around the town on horseback, with instrumental music and singing. . . . After this the candidate is presented with a sash or scarf, usually of fine white cloth, of native manufacture, which he is henceforth permitted to wind round his cap, with one end hanging down the back, forming the Oriental turban. This is a sort of Bachelor of Arts diploma. The men who wear turbans have read through and recited the Koran many hundred times; and you can refer to no passage which they cannot readily find in their apparently confused manuscripts of loose leaves and pages, distinguished not by numbers, but by catchwords at the bottom. Carlyle tells us that he has heard of Mohammedan doctors who had read the Koran seventy thousand times.[8] Many such animated and moving concordances to the Koran may doubtless be found in Central and West Africa.

But the Koran is not the only book they read. We have seen, in some of their libraries, extensive manuscripts in poetry and prose. One showed us at Boporo, the *Makamat* of Hariri, which he read and expounded with great readiness, and seemed surprised that we had heard of it. . . . Dr. Barth tells us that he saw, in Central Africa, a manuscript of those portions of Aristotle and Plato which had been translated into Arabic, and that an Arabic version of Hippocrates was extremely valued. The splendid voweled edition of the New Testament and Psalms recently issued by the American Bible Society, and of which . . . we have been enabled to distribute a few copies among them, is highly prized.

We have collected, in our visit to Mohammedan towns, a number of interesting manuscripts, original and extracted. . . .

* * *

We have been surprised to notice that the manuscripts which we receive generally from Boporo, Misadu, and Kankan are much better written, and are of a much more edifying character, than those we have seen from the Gambia and that region of the country. Some of the latter consisting of childish legends and superstitious details, are often curious philologically, being mixtures of Arabic and the vernacular dialect. It is said also by those who have seen Mohammedan worship conducted by the Jalofs and Foulahs about the Gambia and Senegal, and have witnessed similar exercises among the Mandingoes in the region of country east of Liberia, that the latter exhibit in their bearing and proceedings during their religious services greater intelligence, order, and regularity than the former.

[8] *Heroes and Hero Worship*, p. 80.

X

During a visit of three weeks to Boporo in the Mohammedan month of Ramadhan (December and January 1868–69), we had an opportunity of seeing the Mandingo Moslem at home. It being the sacred months of fasting and religious devotedness, we witnessed several religious performances.

As in all Moslem communities, prayer is held five times a day. When the hour for prayer approaches, a man appointed for the purpose, with a very strong and clear voice, goes to the door of the mosque and chants the *adhan*, or the call to prayer. This man is called the Muëddin.[9] There was a simple and solemn ceremony in the chant at that still hour, which, after it had ceased, still lingered pleasantly on the ear, and often, despite ourselves, drew us out to the mosque. . . . At Boporo and other African towns we have visited, this call is made three times within the half-hour immediately preceding worship. Before the third call is concluded the people have generally assembled in the mosque. Then the Imám proceeds with the exercises, consisting usually of certain short chapters from the Koran and a few prayers, interspersed with beautiful chanting. . . .

The Mandingoes are an exceedingly polite and hospitable people. The restraints of their religion regulate their manners and control their behaviour. Both in speech and demeanour, they appear always solicitous to be *en regle*—anxious to maintain the strictest propriety; and they succeed in conforming to the natural laws of etiquette, of which they seem to have an instinctive and agreeable appreciation. In their salutations they always strive to exceed each other in good wishes. . . .

Those who speak Arabic speak the Koranic or book Arabic, preserving the final vowels of the classical language—a practice which, in the hurry and exigencies of business life, has been long discontinued in countries where the language is the vernacular; so that in Egypt and Syria the current speech is very defective, and clipped and corrupted. . . .

The introduction of Islam into Central and West Africa has been the most important, if not the sole, preservative against the desolations of the slave-trade. Mohammedanism furnished a protection to the tribes who embraced it by effectually binding them together in one strong religious fraternity, and enabling them by their united

[9] The first Moslem crier was an Ethiopian negro, Bilah by name, "a man of powerful frame and sonorous voice". He was the favourite attendant of Mohammed. Mr. Irving informs us that on the capture of Jerusalem he made the first *adhan*, "at the Caliph Omar's command, and summoned the true believers to prayers with a force of lungs that astonished the Jewish inhabitants".—Irving's *Successors of Mahomet*, p. 100.

effort to baffle the attempt of powerful Pagan slave-hunters. Enjoying this comparative immunity from sudden hostile incursions, industry was stimulated among them, industry diminished their poverty; and, as they increased in worldly substance, they also increased in desire for knowledge. Gross superstition gradually disappeared from among them. Receiving a degree of culture from the study of the Arabic language, they acquired loftier views, wider tastes, and those energetic habits which so pleasingly distinguished them from their Pagan neighbours.

Large towns and cities have grown up under Mohammedan energy and industry. Dr. Barth was surprised to find such towns and cities as Kanó and Sokoto in the centre of Africa—to discover the focus of a complex and widely-ramified commerce, and a busy hive of manufacturing, in a region which most people believed to be a desert. And there are towns and cities nearly as important farther west, to which Barth did not penetrate. . . . Mr. Benjamin Anderson, the enterprising Liberian traveller, who has recently visited Misadu, the capital of the Western Mandingoes, about two hundred miles east of Monrovia, describes that city as the centre of a considerable commerce, reaching as far north as Senegal and east as far as Sokoto.

The African Moslems are also great travellers. They seem to travel through the country with greater freedom and safety than any other people, on account, probably of their superior intelligence and greater usefulness. They are continually crossing the continent to Egypt, Arabia and Syria. We met a few weeks ago at Toto-Coreh, a town about ten miles east of Boporo, a lad who informed us that he was born at Mecca while his parents were in that city on a pilgrimage. We gave him a copy of the New Testament in Arabic, which he read with unimpeded fluency, and with the Oriental accent and pronunciation. . . .

. . . Already some of the vernaculars have been enriched by expressions from the Arabic. . . . They have received terms regarding the religion of one God, and respecting a certain state of civilization, such as marrying, reading, writing, and the objects having relation thereto, sections of time, and phrases of salutations and of good breeding; then the terms relating to dress, instruments, and the art of warfare, as well as architecture, commerce, etc.[10]

[10] See Barth's *Collection of Central African Vocabularies*, Part I, p. 29.

35

Mohammedanism and the Negro Race

Fraser's Magazine, November, 1875
Christianity, Islam and the Negro Race, London, 1887, 4–21;
1888 ed., 5–25

NORTH AFRICAN INFLUENCE

Three streams of influence have always penetrated into Negroland:
one from Egypt, through Nubia, to Bornou and Hausa; another,
from Abyssinia to Yoruba and Ashantee; the third, from the Barbary States across the desert to Timbuktu. By the first two, Egypt
and Arabia exchanged their productions for the raw materials of
the Soudan. By the third, the ports of the Mediterranean, through
the Great Desert, having Timbuktu as a centre, became outlets for
the wealth of Nigritia. Even in the days of Herodotus there appears
to have been intercourse between the region of the Tsad and the
Mediterranean, and the valuable products collected at various
centres by the itinerant traffic, which still flourishes in the interior,
shared by numerous caravans, found their way by means of
Phoenician ships to different countries of Europe and the Levant.

Central Africa has never been cut off commercially from European and Asiatic intercourse. But it was not until the ninth century
of the Christian era that any knowledge of the true God began
to penetrate into Negroland. To Akbah, a distinguished Muslim
general, belongs the credit or discredit of having subdued North
Africa to Islam. He marched from Damascus at the head of ten
thousand enthusiastic followers, and in a short time spread his
conquests along the shores of North Africa, advancing to the very
verge of the Atlantic, whose billows alone checked his westward
career.[1] But the energy which could not proceed westward turned
northward and southward. In its southern progress it crossed the
formidable wastes of the Sahara, penetrated into the Soudan and
established the centre of its influence at Timbuktu. In less than
a century from that time several large Nigritian tribes had yielded
to the influence of Islam; and it shaped so rapidly the ideas, the
manners, and the history of those tribes, that when in the Middle
Ages Ibn Batoutah, an Arab traveller, visited those regions, he
found that Islam had taken firm root among several powerful

---

[1] Gibbon's *Decline and Fall*, Chapter LI.

peoples, had mastered their life and habits, and dominated their whole social and religious policy. Among the praiseworthy qualities which attracted his attention as a result of their conversion, he mentions their devotion to the study of the Koran. . . .

MUSLIMS ENTERPRISING

Mohammedanism in Africa counts in its ranks the most energetic and enterprising tribes. It claims as adherents the only people who have any form of civil policy or bond of social organization. It has built and occupies the largest cities in the heart of the continent. Its laws regulate the most powerful kingdoms—Futah, Masina, Hausa, Bornou, Waday, Darfur, Kordofan, Senaar, etc. It produces and controls the most valuable commerce between Africa and Foreign countries; it is daily gaining converts from the ranks of Paganism; and it commands respect among all Africans wherever it is known, even where the people have not submitted to the sway of the Koran.

No one can travel any distance in the interior of West Africa without being struck with the different aspects of society in different localities, according as the population is Pagan or Mohammedan. Not only is there a difference in the methods of government, but in the general regulations of society, and even in the amusements of the people. The love of noisy terpsichorean performances, so noticeable in Pagan communities, disappears as the people come under the influence of Mohammedanism. It is not a fact that "when the sun goes down, all Africa dances", but it might be a fact if it were not for the influence of Islam. Those who would once have sought pleasure in the excitement of the tom-tom, now repair five times a day to the mosque, where they spend a quarter of an hour on each occasion in devotional exercises. After the labours of the day they assemble in groups near the mosque to hear the Koran recited, or the Traditions or some other book read. In traversing the region of country between Sierra Leone and Futah Jallo in 1873, we passed through populous Pagan towns; and the transition from these to Mohammedan districts was striking. When we left a Pagan and entered a Mohammedan community, we at once noticed that we had entered a moral atmosphere widely separated from, and loftier far than, the one we had left. We discovered that the character, feelings, and conditions of the people were profoundly altered and improved.

It is evident that, whatever may be said of the Koran, as long as it is in advance of the Shamanism or Fetichism of the African tribes who accept it—and no one will doubt that Islam as a creed is an enormous advance not only on all idolatries, but on all systems of purely human origin—those tribes must advance beyond their primitive condition.

The Koran is, in its measure, an important educator. It exerts among a primitive people a wonderful influence. It has furnished to the adherents of its teachings in Africa a ground of union which has contributed vastly to their progress. Hausas, Foulahs, Mandingoes, Soosoos, Akus, can all read the same books and mingle in worship together, and there is to all one common authority and one ultimate umpirage. They are united by a common religious sentiment, by a common antagonism to Paganism. Not only the sentiments, but the language, the words of the sacred book are held in the greatest reverence and esteem. And even where the ideas are not fully understood, the words seem to possess for them a nameless beauty and music, a subtle and indefinable charm, incomprehensible to those acquainted only with European languages. It is easy for those not acquainted with the language in which the Koran was written, and therefore, judging altogether as outsiders, to indulge in depreciation of its merits.[2] Such critics lose sight of the fact that the Koran is a poetical composition of the earliest and most primitive kind, and that therefore its ideas and the language in which they are conveyed cannot well be separated. The genuine poet not only creates the conception, but the word which is its vehicle. The word becomes the inseparable drapery of the idea. Hence the highest poetry cannot be translated. We see this in the numerous versions by which it has been sought in every age to reach the sense of the poetical portions of the Bible. No words yet furnished by Greek, Roman, or Teutonic literature have been fully adequate to bring out the subtle beauties of the Semitic original. Among Mohammedans, written or printed translations of the Koran are discouraged. The Chinese, Hindoos, Persians, Turks, Mandingoes, Foulahs, etc., who have embraced Islam, speak in their "own tongues wherein they were born", but read the Koran in Arabic.

* * *

To the outside world, easily swayed by superficial impressions, and carried away by matters of mere dramatic interest, there may

[2] The case cited by Dr. Mühleisen Arnold, in his work on Islam, of an Arab philosopher and unbeliever in Mohammed, who lived in the eighth century, depreciating the literary merits of the Koran, is no more in point as an argument against the book, it appears to us, than if a Mohammedan controversialist were to quote from Voltaire or Tom Paine against the Bible.

be nothing attractive in the progress of Islam in Africa, because, as far as known to Western readers, the history of African Mohammedanism is deficient in great characters and in remarkable episodes. There has been, it is supposed, no controlling mind developed, which has moved great masses of men. . . .

. . . To those acquainted with the interior of Africa—to the Mohammedan world of North Africa and Arabia—it is well known that numerous characters have arisen in Africa—Negro Muslims—who have exerted no little influence in the military, political, and ecclesiastical affairs of Islam, not only in Africa, but in the lands of their teachers. In the biographies of Ibn Khallikan are frequent notices of distinguished Negro Mohammedans. Koelle, in his Polyglotta Africana, gives a graphic account of the proceedings of the great Fodio,[3] whose zeal, enthusiasm, and bravery spread Islam over a large portion of Nigritia.

One of the most remarkable characters who have influenced the history of the region of country between Timbuktu and the West Coast was a native of Futah Toro, known as the Sheikh Omaru Al-Hajj. He is said to have been a Waleeu,[4] a man of extraordinary endowments, of commanding presence, and great personal influence. He was educated by the Sheikh Tijani, a Muslim missionary from Arabia. Having spent several years under the instruction of this distinguished teacher, visiting Mecca in the meanwhile, he became profoundly learned in the Arabic language. After the death of his master, he went twice to Mecca on pilgrimage. On his return to his country the second time, he undertook a series of proselytising expeditions against the powerful pagan tribes on the east and southeast of Futah Toro. He conquered several powerful chiefs and reduced their people to the faith of Islam. He banished Paganism from Sego and purified the practices of several Mohammedan districts which had become imbued with heathenish notions. He thus restored Jenne, and Hamd-Allahi, and was on his way to Timbuktu, about ten years ago, when, through the treachery of the Arabs of that region, he was circumvented and killed at a town in Masina. One of his sons, Ahmadu, is now King of Sego, another rules over Hamd-Allahi, two of the largest cities in Central Africa.

[3] Usuman dan Fodio (1754–1817), erudite Muslim theologian and mystic, and leader of the Sokoto Jihad [ed.].
[4] This word is used by the Mohammedans of Negroland in a peculiar sense. It means one called of God, and endowed with special gifts to exercise authority in ecclesiastical and sometimes political matters, inferior in official rank—according to their estimation—only to a prophet. Such men have, from time to time, arisen among African Mohammedans, and have carried out important reforms in Church and State.

Al-Hajj Omaru wrote many Arabic works in prose and poetry. His poems are recited and sung in every Mohammedan town and village, from Foulah-town, in Sierra Leone to Kano. His memory is held in the greatest respect by all native students, and they attribute to him many extraordinary deeds, and see in his successful enterprises, literary and military, proofs of divine guidance.[5]

We have heard of numerous instances of these "half-military, half-religious geniuses", as Mr. Bosworth Smith calls them, "which Islam always seems capable of producing".[6]

To the Mohammedans of Negroland, far away from the complex civilization of European life, with its multifarious interests, the struggle for the ascendancy of Islam is the one great object which should engage the attention of a rational being. It is a struggle between light and darkness, between knowledge and ignorance, between good and evil. The traditional enthusiasm of their faith makes them utterly indifferent to the sufferings of any who stand in the way of the dissemination of the truth, and patient of any evils they may have to endure in order to ensure the triumph of their cause. "Paradise is under the shadow of swords", is one of their stimulating proverbs.

BLACK CHRISTIANS SERVILE

There is one passage in Mr. Bosworth Smith's book of which we do not think that the author, who, as it seems, has not himself been in Africa, perceived the full import, but which the Christian world, it appears to us, would do well to ponder. It is as follows:

Christian travellers, with every wish to think otherwise, have remarked that the Negro[7] who accepts Mohammedanism acquires at once a sense of the dignity of human nature not commonly found even among those who have been brought to accept Christianity.[8]

[5] Report on the Expedition to Timbo made to the Governor of Sierra Leone, 1873. See also the *African Sketch Book*, by Winwood Reade, Vol. I, p. 317.
[6] The article, from which this excerpt comes, was originally an extended review of Bosworth Smith, *Mohammed and Mohammedanism* (London: 1874) [ed.].
[7] Mr. Bosworth Smith writes this word with a small "n"; but we do not see why, if it is used to designate one of the great families of man, it should not be entitled to the same distinction as such words as Indian, Hindoo, Chinaman, &c. Why give more dignity to the specific than to the general? Why write Ashantee, Congo, Mandingo, with capitals, and Negro, the generic appellation with a small "n"? Is not this in deference to the sort of prejudice against which Mr. B. Smith himself protests?
[8] Lecture I, p. 32.

Having enjoyed exceptional advantages for observation and comparison in the United States, the West Indies, South America, Egypt, Syria, West and Central Africa, we are compelled, however reluctantly, to endorse the statement made by Mr. B. Smith. And we are not surprised at his seizing hold, in his researches, of this most important fact and giving it such prominence—a prominence it richly deserves—in the discussion. Wherever the Negro is found in Christian lands, his leading trait is not docility, as has been often alleged, but servility. He is slow and unprogressive. Individuals here and there may be found of extraordinary intelligence, enterprise and energy, but there is no Christian community of Negroes anywhere which is self-reliant and independent. Haiti and Liberia, so-called Negro Republics, are merely struggling for existence, and hold their own by the tolerance of the civilized powers.[9] On the other hand, there are numerous Negro Mohammedan communities and states in Africa which are self-reliant, productive, independent and dominant, supporting, without the countenance or patronage of the parent country, Arabia, whence they derived them, their political, literary and ecclesiastical institutions. In Sierra Leone, the Mohammedans, without any aid from Government—Imperial or local—or any contributions from Mecca or Constantinople, erect their mosques, keep up their religious services, conduct their schools, and contribute to the support of missionaries from Arabia, Morocco, or Futah when they visit them. The same compliment cannot be paid to the Negro Christians of that settlement. The most enlightened native Christians there look forward with serious apprehension —and, perhaps, not without good grounds—to the time when, if ever, the instructions and influence from London will be withheld. . . . In the recent Ashantee war the most trustworthy Negro troops were the Haussas, who are rigid Mohammedans. The West India Christian Negro troops were not relied on to the same extent.

Now, what has produced this difference in the effects of the two systems upon the Negro race? In reply, we remark generally that the difference must be attributed to the difference in the conditions under which the systems came to those of the Negro race who embraced the one or the other. Mohammedanism found its Negro converts at home in a state of freedom and independence of the teachers who brought it to them. When it was offered to them they were at liberty to choose for themselves. The Arab missionaries, whom we have met in the interior, go about without "purse or

---

[9] The *Official Journal*, dated May 1st, 1875, contained intelligence of a [Haitian] conspiracy which had been suppressed, and a Presidential decree banishing forty of the conspirators.

scrip", and disseminate their religion by quietly teaching the Koran. The native missionaries—Mandingoes and Foulahs—unite with the propagation of their faith active trading. Wherever they go, they produce the impression that they are not preachers only, but traders; but, on the other hand, that they are not traders merely, but preachers. And, in this way, silently and almost unobtrusively, they are causing princes to become obedient disciples and zealous propagators of Islam. Their converts, as a general thing, become Muslims from choice and conviction, and bring all the manliness of their former condition to the maintenance and support of their new creed.

When the religion was first introduced it found the people possessing all the elements and enjoying all the privileges of an untramelled manhood. They received it as giving them additional power to exert an influence in the world. It sent them forth as the guides and instructors of their less favoured neighbours, and endowed them with the self-respect which men feel who acknowledge no superior. While it brought them a great deal that was absolutely new, and inspired them with spiritual feelings to which they had before been utter strangers, it strengthened and hastened certain tendencies to independence and self-reliance which were already at work. Their local institutions were not destroyed by the Arab influence introduced. They only assumed new forms, and adapted themselves to the new teachings. In all thriving Mohammedan communities, in West and Central Africa, it may be noticed that the Arab superstructure has been superimposed on a permanent indigenous substructure; so that what really took place, when the Arab met the Negro in his own home, was a healthy amalgamation, and not an absorption or an undue repression.

The Oriental aspect of Islam has become largely modified in Negroland, not as is too generally supposed, by a degrading compromise with the Pagan superstitions, but by shaping many of its traditional customs to suit the milder and more conciliatory disposition of the Negro. As long as Timbuktu, which was but a continuation of Morocco, retained its ascendancy, Islam kept up its strictly Arabian aspect; but since the seat of literary activity and ecclesiastical influence has been transferred to Kuka, and since Kano has become the commercial centre—two purely Negro cities grown up under Muslim influence—and since the religion has taken root among the large indigenous communities near the source of the Niger, it has been largely affected by the geographical and racial influences to which it has been exposed. The absence of political pressure has permitted native peculiarities to manifest themselves, and to take an effective part in the work of assimilating the new elements.

Christianity, on the other hand, came to the Negro as a slave, or at least as a subject race in a foreign land. Along with the Christian teaching, he and his children received lessons of their utter and permanent inferiority and subordination to their instructors, to whom they stood in the relation of chattels. Christianity took them fresh from the barbarism of ages, and forced them to embrace its tenets. The religion of Jesus was embraced by them as the only source of consolation in their deep disasters. In their abject miseries, keen anguish, and hopeless suffering they seized upon it as promising a country where, after the unexampled sorrows of this life, "the wicked cease from troubling, and the weary are at rest". It found them down-trodden, oppressed, scorned; it soothed their sufferings, subdued their hearts, and pointed them, in its exhaustless sympathy, to the "Man of Sorrows, and acquainted with grief". In their condition of outcasts and pariahs, it directed their aspirations to a heavenly and eternal citizenship; it put new songs in their mouths— those melodies inimitable to the rest of the world—which, from the lips of emancipated slaves, have recently charmed the ears and captivated the hearts of royalty and nobles in Europe by a tenderness, a sweetness, an earnestness, and a solemnity, born of adversity, in the house of bondage. . . . These are great and precious advantages; but, nevertheless, owing to the physical, mental and social pressure under which the Africans received these influences of Christianity, their development was necessarily partial and one-sided, cramped and abnormal. All tendencies to independent individuality were repressed and destroyed. Their ideas and aspirations could be expressed only in conformity with the views and tastes of those who held rule over them. All avenues to intellectual improvement were closed against them, and they were doomed to perpetual ignorance.

Mohammedanism and learning to the Muslim Negro were coeval. No sooner was he converted than he was taught to read, and the importance of knowledge was impressed upon him. The Christian Negro came in contact with mental and physical proscription and the religion of Christ, contemporaneously. If the Mohammedan Negro had at any time to choose between the Koran and the sword, when he chose the former, he was allowed to wield the latter as the equal of any other Muslim; but no amount of allegiance to the Gospel relieved the Christian Negro from the degradation of wearing the chain which he received with it, or rescued him from the political and, in a measure, ecclesiastical proscription which he still undergoes in all the countries of his exile.[10] Everywhere in Christian lands he plays, at the present moment, the part of the slave, ape or puppet. Only a few here and there rise above the general degradation, and these become targets to their unappreciative brethren. Is it any wonder, then, that "Christian travellers, with every wish to think otherwise", in commenting upon the difference between Christian and Mohammedan Negroes, with respect to true manliness, must do so to the disadvantage of the former?

"GODS IN OWN . . . IMAGE"

Another reason for the superior manliness and *amour propre* of Negro Mohammedans may be found in the fact that, unlike their Christian brethren, they have not been trained under the depressing influence of Aryan art. . . . The Second Commandment with Mussulmans as with Jews, is construed literally into the prohibition of all representations of living creatures of all kinds; not merely in sacred places but everywhere.[11] Josephus tells us that the Jews would not even tolerate the image of the emperor, which was represented on the eagles of the soldiers.[12] The early Christian Fathers believed that painting and sculpture were forbidden by the Scriptures, and that they were therefore wicked arts. Among the Mohammedans of Negroland it is considered a sin to make even the rudest representation of any living thing on the ground or on the side of a house. We shall never forget the disgust with which a Mandingo from Kankan, who was, for the first time, visiting the seaboard at Monrovia, turned from a marble figure in the cemetery through which we were showing him, exclaiming, "Amâl Shaitân! amâl Shaitân!"—the work of Satan.[13]

No one can deny the great aesthetic and moral advantages which have accrued to the Caucasian race from Christian art, through all its stages of development, from the Good Shepherd of the Catacombs to the Transfiguration of Raphael, from rough mosaics to the inexpressible delicacy and beauty of Giotto and Fra Angelico.[14] But to the Negro all these exquisite representations exhibited only the physical characteristics of a foreign race; and, while they tended to quicken the tastes and refine the sensibilities

[10] For an interesting discussion of this subject from the pen of a Negro, see Tanner's *Apology for African Methodism in the United States.*
[11] Mischat ul-Masabih, Vol. II, p. 368.
[12] Antiq. xviii–iii, I, etc.
[13] See Koran, v. 92.
[14] See a paper on the Roman Catacombs, etc., read by Dean Stanley before the Royal Institution, May 29th, 1874.

of that race, they had only a depressing influence upon the Negro, who felt that he had neither part nor lot, so far as his physical character was concerned, in those splendid representations. A strict adherence to the letter of the Second Commandment would have been no drawback to the Negro. To him the painting and sculpture of Europe, as instruments of education, have been worse than failures. They have really raised barriers in the way of his normal development. They have set before him models for imitation; and his very effort to conform to the canons of taste thus practically suggested, has impaired, if not destroyed, his self-respect, and made him the weakling and creeper which he appears in Christian lands. It was our lot not long since to hear an illiterate Negro in a prayer-meeting in New York entreat the Deity to extend his "lily white hands" and bless the waiting congregation. Another,[15] with no greater amount of culture, preaching from I John, iii, 2, "We shall be like Him", etc. etc., exclaimed, "Brethren, imagine a beautiful white man with blue eyes, rosy cheeks, and flaxen hair, and we shall be like him". The conceptions of these worshippers were what they had gathered from plastic and pictorial representations as well as from the characteristics of the dominant race around them. The Mohammedan Negro, who is not familiar with such representations, sees God in the great men of his country. The saying is attributed to an ancient philosoper[16] that if horses, oxen, and lions could paint they would certainly make gods in their own image. . . .

This is no doubt true, and the Negro who grew up normally would certainly not be inferior to lions, horses, and oxen. The Christian Negro, abnormal in his development, pictures God and all beings remarkable for their moral and intellectual qualities with the physical characteristics of Europeans, and deems it an honour if he can approximate—by a mixture of his blood, however irregularly achieved—in outward appearance, at least, to the ideal thus forced upon him of the physical accompaniments of all excellence. In this way he loses that "sense of the dignity of human nature" observable in his Mohammedan brother.

A third very important influence which has retarded the development of the Christian Negro may be found in the social and literary pressure which he has undergone. It is not too much to say that the popular literature of the Christian world, since the discovery of America, or at least for the last two hundred years, has been

---

[15] The putting forward of thoroughly illiterate men to expound the Scriptures among the Negro Christians has been another great drawback to their proper development.

[16] Xenophanes of Colophon (six centuries B.C.).

anti-Negro. The Mohammedan Negro has felt nothing of the withering power of caste. There is nothing in his colour or race to debar him from the highest privileges, social or political, to which any other Muslim can attain. The slave who becomes a Mohammedan is free.[17] Mohammedan history abounds with examples of distinguished Negroes. The eloquent Azan, or "Call to Prayer", which to this day summons at the same hours millions of the human race to their devotions, was first uttered by a Negro, Bilâl by name, whom Mohammed, in obedience to a dream, appointed the first Muezzin, or Crier.[18] And it has been remarked that even Alexander the Great is in Asia an unknown personage by the side of this honoured Negro. Mr. Muir notices the inflexible constancy of Bilâl to the faith of Islam under the severest trials.[19] Ibn Khallikan mentions a celebrated Negro Khalif, who reigned at Bagdad in the ninth century.[20] He describes him as a man of great merit, and a perfect scholar. None of the sons of Khalifs spoke with greater propriety and elegance, or composed verses with greater ability. The following lines were addressed to him by a contemporary poet:

Blackness of skin cannot degrade an ingenious mind, or lessen the worth of the scholar or the wit. Let blackness claim the colour of your body; I claim as mine your fair and candid soul.

The poet Abu Ishak Assabi, who lived in the tenth century, had a black slave named Yumna, to whom he was greatly attached, and on whom he wrote some remarkable verses, which are much quoted by Muslims. Notice the following:

The dark-skinned Yumna said to one whose colour equals the whiteness of the eye, "Why should your face boast its white complexion? Do you think that by so clear a tint it gains additional merit? Were a mole of my colour on that face it would adorn it; but one of your colour on my cheek would disfigure me."

Here is another:

Black misbecomes you not; by it you are increased in beauty; black is the only colour princes wear. Were you not mine, I should purchase you with all my wealth. Did I not possess you, I should give life to obtain you.[21]

---

[17] Ockley's *History of the Saracens*, 6th edition, London, 1871, p. 14.
[18] Muir's *Life of Mahomet*, Vol. III, p. 54.
[19] Ibid., Vol. II, p. 129.
[20] *Biographies of Ibn Khallikan*, translated by Baron de Slane, Vol. I, p. 18.
[21] *Ibn Khallikan*, Vol. I, p. 32.

Ibn Muslimeh, an enthusiastic lover, exclaims, "If a mole be set in an ugly cheek it endows it with beauty and grace; how then should the heart-stricken be blamed for looking upon his mistress as a mole all over?"[22]

Mr. Gifford Palgrave, whose travels in Eastern countries have no doubt diminished the sensitiveness of his Western prejudices, concludes his brilliant Essays on Eastern Questions with a poem composed by a Negress in memory of her celebrated semi-Arab son, who had perished in one of his daring adventures.

Now, it must be evident that Negroes trained under the influence of such a social and literary atmosphere must have a deeper self-respect and higher views of the dignity of human nature than those trained under the blighting influence of caste, and under the guidance of a literature in which it has been the fashion for more than two hundred years to caricature the African, to ridicule his personal peculiarities, and to impress him with a sense of perpetual and hopeless inferiority. Christian literature has nothing to show on behalf of the Negro comparable to Mohammedan literature; and there is nothing in Mohammedan literature corresponding to the Negro—or "nigger", as even a liberal clergyman like Mr. Haweis will call him[23]—of Christian caricaturists. . . . No one will charge the Negro Mohammedans with giving ground for the notion, put forward recently from a very distinguished source, that the African entertains "a superstitious awe and dread of the white man". Ibn Batoutah, cited before, though a Mohammedan, experienced no greater respect among the Muslims of Negroland on account of his colour, than a Negro in the same position would have received. He complains of the cool and haughty bearing of a certain Negro prince towards himself and a number of European and Arab traders who appeared in the royal presence. "It was then", he says, "that I regretted having entered the country of the Negroes on account of their bad education, and the little regard they had for white men". And what was the evidence of this "bad education and little regard for white men"? The chief chose to speak to them through a third party, "although they were very near him". "This was done", observes the sensitive traveller, "solely on account of his contempt" for them. Réné Caillié, the French traveller, who made the journey from West Africa to Morocco, via Timbuktu, was compelled to travel in strict disguise as a poor Muslim. His sojourn in Timbuktu was of only fourteen days; and, as he was in constant danger of

---

[22] *The Assemblies of Al-Hariri*, translated by Thomas Chenery; Williams and Norgate, 1870. This work is also called the *Makamat*, etc.
[23] *Music and Morals*, p. 550.

being discovered, he could neither move about freely nor note down all that he wished. Even Barth was obliged, for a short time, to adopt the character of a Muslim. . . . We admit that the Negro in Christian lands, and all along the Coast where he has been under the training of the white man, exhibits a cringing and servile spirit; but this as we have endeavoured to show, is the natural result of that habit of mind which it was the interest of his masters to impress upon him. . . .

Another very important element which has given the Mohammedan Negro the advantage over his Christian brother is the more complete sympathy which has always existed between him and his foreign teacher. . . . Long prior to the rise of Islam, as we have seen above, the Arab merchant had been in communication with the interior of Africa, and had opened the way for the Arab missionary. When, therefore, the Muslim missionary came as the propagator of a higher religion than any that had been known, he did not enter the country as a stranger. The political and social institutions of the Arabs had already been tried and found suitable to the wants and tastes of the Negro tribes; indeed, the two peoples, if not of cognate origin, have by protracted intercommunications, and by the similarity of the physical influences which have, for ages, operated upon them, become similar in tastes; and it was not difficult for the Arabs to conform to a great extent to the social and domestic customs of the Africans. The Muslim missionary often brought to the aid of his preaching the influence of social and domestic relationships—an influence which in all efforts to convert a people is not to be entirely ignored. "The conversion of the Russian nation", we are told by Dean Stanley, "was effected, not by the preaching of the Byzantine clergy, but by the marriage of a Byzantine princess."[24] So the Arab missionaries often entered into the bonds of wedlock with the daughters of Negroland,[25] and by their teaching, by their intelligence, by their intermarriages with the natives, by the trade and generosity of their merchants, they enlisted so many interests and such deep sympathies, that they rapidly took abiding root in the country. Some of the highest names in the annals not only of Islamitic but of pre-Islamitic literature, are those of the descendants of Arabs and Africans. One of the authors of the Muallakat, for instance, was half Arab and half Negro.

[24] *Eastern Church*, p. 34.
[25] Mr. Palgrave tells us that intermarriages between Arabs and Negroes have been at no period rare or abnormal; to such admixtures, indeed, the East owes not a few of her best celebrities—*Essays on Eastern Questions*, p. 337.

The sympathy, therefore, between the Arab missionary and the African is more complete than that between European and the Negro. With every wish, no doubt, to the contrary, the European seldom or never gets over the feeling of distance, if not of repulsion, which he experiences on first seeing the Negro.[26] While he joyfully admits the Negro to be his brother, having the same nature in all its essential attributes, still, owing to the diversity in type and colour, he naturally concludes that the inferiority which to him appears on the surface must extend deeper than the skin and affect the soul. Therefore, very often in spite of himself, he stands off from his African convert, even when, under his training, he has made considerable advance in civilization and the arts. And especially is this the case in West Africa, where, living among large masses of his countrymen, the African Christian, who from the pressure of circumstances has been forced into European customs, presents very often to the foreign observer, in contrast with his native brethren, an artificial and absurd appearance. And the missionary, looking from a comfortable social distance, surveys the Europeanized native, sometimes with pity, sometimes with dismay, seldom with thorough sympathy. . . . The African convert, under such practical teaching, looking upon his instructor as superior to himself—or at least apart from himself, not only in spiritual and temporal knowledge, but in every other respect—acquires a very low opinion of himself, learns to depreciate and deprecate his own personal characteristics, and loses that "sense of the dignity of human nature" which observant travellers have noticed in the Mohammedan Negro.

[26] Bishop Heber, in one of his letters written on his first arrival in India, says: "There is, indeed, something in a Negro which requires long habit to reconcile the eye to him, but for this the features and hair, far more than the colour, are responsible."—*Life of Heber*, by Taylor, 2nd edition, p. 147. And what this distinguished prelate experienced and so candidly avowed, must be experienced in a still greater degree by minds of less calibre and less culture than his. "The more ignorant the white are", says Dr. Charles Hodge of Princeton, N.J., "the more violent and unreasonable are their prejudices on this subject".—Hodge's *Essays and Reviews*, p. 519.

36

The Mohammedans of Nigritia

Christianity, Islam and the Negro Race, London, 1887, 306–32;
1888 ed., 350–78

In the present discussion, by Nigritia must be understood all the
region of West Central Africa embraced between Lake Tchad on
the east, and Sierra Leone and Liberia on the west, and between
Timbuktu on the north, and the Bight of Benin on the south, including the Niger from its source to its mouth. The European travellers
who have described various portions of this country are Mungo
Park, Denham and Clapperton, the Landers, Laing, Caillie, and
more recently, Richardson, Barth, Overweg, Vogel, and Winwood
Reade; the Liberian travellers are Benjamin Anderson, James L.
Simms, and George L. Seymour.

The country east of Lake Tchad to the Red Sea is occupied
largely by Mohammedans; but we will deal only with the countries
west of Lake Tchad, in which are situated the well-known cities
of Kano, Sokoto, Illorin, Timbuktu, Sego, Kankan, Timbo,
Musardu.

This part of Africa, although so near to Europe, seems to have
been shut out from the knowledge of Europeans, until the publication of the travels of Mungo Park, about one hundred years ago.

His descriptions are characterized by a marvellous fidelity and
accuracy. It is a remarkable fact that the accounts of the earlier
African travellers are, as a rule, more trustworthy than the statements of more recent adventures. . . . For the Nigritian country,
therefore, we would recommend Mungo Park's *Travels*; and, after
his, those of Denham and Clapperton, Caillie and the Landers.
The modern traveller is hampered by a commercial exigency. He
is under the necessity of making a book that will sell; and he is
more anxious to conform to, and perpetuate popular notions, than
to give a faithful portraiture of what he sees, for he would then
have to walk in the old groove. He must bring forth something new,
something original, something sensational. . . . In the days of Park,
Denham and Clapperton, the countries which they visited were
chiefly Pagan. They are now, through the energy and zeal of Negro
converts to Mohammedanism, all under the rule of Islam. They
enjoy a settled constitution, a written code of laws, and a regular
government.

Mohammedanism was not quite half a century old when it was introduced into North-western Africa. Its conquest swept like a whirlwind over the northern portion of the continent, from Egypt to the Atlantic. . . .

THE JIHADS

After the first conquests of the Muslims in North Africa, their religion advanced southward into the continent, not by arms, but by schools, and books, and mosques, by trade and inter-marriage. They could not have brought a force sufficient to subjugate the people for they had to deal with large, powerful and energetic tribes. . . .

. . . It was after the great tribes had been peaceably converted to Islam that we hear of Jihads—military expeditions to reduce Pagans to the faith. This religious propagandism, conducted by native warriors, has been carried on with wonderful activity and success during the last fifty years. Thirty years ago, a religious devotee and military genius—a native of Futah Toro, Al-Hajj Omaru—reduced large districts on the Upper Niger to the faith of Islam. He received the title, "Al-Hajj", "The Pilgrim" after he had performed the pilgrimage to Mecca. He was well versed in the Arabic language and literature, and wrote a number of books on his travels and on religious subjects, which are in circulation throughout Nigritia.[1]

He has had several successors in the work of disseminating the Mohammedan creed; and they are rapidly bringing the whole of Africa north of the equator under the influence of the Crescent. The most important kingdoms in this portion of the continent which are still subject to Paganism are, Dahomey and Ashantee. . . . There is, at this moment, an energetic promoter of the Jihad, having under his command scores of thousand of zealous Mohammedans anxious for the spoils of time and the rewards of eternity. By means of these, he is reducing to the faith the most warlike and powerful tribes. His name is Samadu, born about forty years ago, in the Mandingo country, east of Liberia. His fame has gone far beyond Nigritia, all through the Soudan. It has crossed the Mediterranean to Europe, and the Atlantic to America. A narrative of his proceedings now lying before us, written in Arabic, by a native chronicler, contains an interesting account of his method and

---

[1] A sketch of Al-Hajj Omaru's life is given by Lieutenant Mage, in his *Voyage d'Exploration dans le Soudan Occidental*.

achievements. The introductory chapters we translate as follows:

> This is an account of the Jihad of Imam Ahmadu Samadu, a Mandingo, an inhabitant of the town of Sanankodu, in the extreme part of the Konia country. God conferred upon him His help continually after he began the work of visiting the idolatrous Pagans, who dwell between the sea and the country of Wasulu, with a view of inviting them to follow the religion of God, which is Islam.
>
> Know all ye who reads this—that the first effort of the Imam Samadu was at a town named Fulindiyah. Following the Book and the Law, and the Traditions, he sent messengers to the King at that town, Sinidudu by name, inviting him to submit to his government, abandon the worship of idols, and worship one God, the exalted, the True, whose service is profitable to his people in this world and in the next; but they refused to submit. Then he imposed a tribute upon them, as the Koran commands on this subject; but they persisted in their blindness and their deafness. The Imam then collected a small force of about five hundred men, brave and valiant, for the Jihad, and he fought against the town, and the Lord helped him against them, and gave him the victory over them, and he pursued them with his horses until they submitted. Nor will they return to their idolatry, for now all their children are in schools, being taught the Koran, and a knowledge of religion and civilization. Praise be to God for this.
>
> Alimami Samadu then went to another idolatrous town called Wurukud, surrounded by a strong wall, and skilfully defended, etc.

The same course was adopted as with the former town, and this is the method pursued in all his operation. Large and powerful states which, two years ago, were practicing . . . Paganism, are now under the influence of schools and teachers, and the regular administration of law. In 1872, the present writer visited Falaba, the capital of the Soolima country, two hundred and fifty miles east of Sierra Leone, as Special Commissioner to the King from the British Government. He found the King and his people intelligent, warlike, brave, and energetic, but determined Pagans. For fifty years, the Foulah Mohammedans, by annual expeditions, had striven to bring them over to the faith of Islam, but they had always successfully resisted every attack. Today, however, Falaba is Mohammedan, having fallen two years ago, before the troops of

Samadu, under the melancholy circumstances detailed in the following letter, addressed to us by the Government Interpreter of Sierra Leone:

> *Freetown, Sierra Leone*
> *October 30th, 1884.*

Dear Sir:

I am sure you will be sorry to hear that Falaba is taken. As you have visited that region of country on two occasions, I know that you must take a deep interest in it. The King, Royal Family, and principal men, were killed; and the rest of the inhabitants hurried into slavery, in countries above and below Falaba, by the captors, under the command of Alfa Samadu and Mahmudi Daranii. The latter is reported to have since died. It is reported that when Sewah, King of Falaba (well known to you), found that he could do no more to save his capital, together with its inhabitants, and numerous villages, from being taken by the armed Mohammedans, he invited the whole Royal family, and many of the principal persons, into a large house, where he had a large quantity of gunpowder, and addressed them in the following words:

"Falaba is an ancient country, and never has been conquered by any tribe; it has always been ruling, and never has been ruled. I will never submit to Mohammedanism. If any of you choose to become Mohammedans you are at liberty to do so." All unanimously replied "They would rather die than become Mohammedans".

The King then threw a lighted torch into the powder, which immediately caught fire, and the whole place and people were burnt to death. Thus was Falaba taken by the great Mohammedan war, now coming to the coast. It is reported that Suluku, the chief of Big Boumba in the Limba country, has surrendered and taken a new name, Ahmadu Sofala. Should I learn anything further, I will inform you. With kind regards,   I remain, dear Sir,

> Your obedient Servant,
> THOMAS G. LAWSON,

Dr. E. W. Blyden   *Govt. Interpreter.*

This letter was published in the *West African Reporter* (November 22nd, 1884), upon which the Editor remarked as follows:

> The capture of Falaba, the capital of the Soolima country, by the troops of Alfa Samadu, will form an important epoch in the history of the Western Soudan. . . . For more than three months, Falaba successfully resisted the forces of Samadu, commanded

by three distinguished generals—Fode Daranii, Infalli and Bilâl. These men believed themselves to be fighting for the establishment of the true religion, and for the freedom and security of trade. Falaba felt itself fighting for national life. The strife was exacerbated by fanaticism on the one hand, and the phrensy [*sic*] of personal peril and menaced independence on the other. At length Samadu gave orders to cease active operations, and having a large number of men and vast resources, established a siege, which he maintained with relentless vigour, for several months, until the fatal surrender. Starvation did what the troops could not do.

The troops of this energetic commander are now moving westward towards the Atlantic. He has no quarrel with Christians, whom he treats with consideration and respect, and he would be an important auxiliary in the interior operations of Christian Governments on the coast, if only they knew how to utilize him. He displays in all his dealings a soldierly, as well as fatherly, heroism; so that he has the art as a rule, without carnage, of making his iconoclastic message acceptable to the sympathies of the Pagans whom he summons to the faith. In every town taken, either by force of arms, or its own voluntary submission, he plants a mosque and schools, and stations a teacher and preacher. He lays great stress upon education. He trusts to the Koran and to the schools far more than to the sword, as instruments for the determination of the great moral and political controversy between him and the Pagans, and for the general amelioration. Indeed, throughout Mohammedan Africa, education is compulsory. A man might now travel across the continent, from Sierra Leone to Cairo, or in any direction, from Lagos to Tripoli, sleeping in a village every night, except in the Sahara, and in every village he would find a school. There is a general epistolary communication throughout this region in the Arabic language—sometimes in the vernacular, written in Arabic characters. Bishop Crowther informed us that he received a letter at Lagos, which had come across the continent from Tripoli.

The book chiefly taught in the schools, and with a view to the elucidation of which all other books are studied, is the Koran. It is called *Alkitab*, "The Book", *par excellence*, just as the Bible is by us. It is composed in the purest Arabic, and offers many difficulties to those not acquainted with the idiom of the Desert Arabs, who alone speak the language in its perfection. The books which, beside the Koran, are taught in all the schools, are various theological treatises and the Moallakat—the six poems, which, in a literary contest of all Arabia, before the days of Islam, carried off the prize for grammatical excellence, purity and style. One of these poems was written by a Negro, and won the special admiration of Mohammed. Another work which is much studied is the *Makamat or Assemblies of Hariri*, which are said, in fifty books or parts, to contain the whole Arabic language. This work is the result of the literary system of a period in which not only the sciences, but the useful arts of life, were sacrificed by the ingenious and studious of a great nation to a profound grammatical research into the structure and resources of their own most copious language. . . .

The African Mohammedans are still in that period in which devotion to the one divine book, and to whatever serves to illustrate it, supersedes every other feeling. Great attention is paid to grammatical analysis; indeed, the language is said to have been first reduced to a system by Abu'l Aswad, Father of the Black of African extraction.[2] Nearly every Mandingo, or Foulah trader, or itinerant teacher, carries among his manuscripts the *Alfiyeh* of Ibn Malik, the most complete and celebrated of the Arabic grammatical poems. . . . There are numerous native authors who have written in the Arabic, Foulah, Mandingo, and Jalof languages; but great reverence is paid to Arabic; it is the language of devotion, of civil and ecclesiastical law, of inspiration. . . .

*   *   *

. . . It is our privilege, as we write this—one we rarely enjoy —to have the company, almost daily of such a character. He is a man, not much over thirty, of the Mandingo tribe, now visiting the coast for the first time. He is learned in all the theological, controversial and political literature of Arabia and of his native country; is himself the author of several small treatises, speaks Arabic fluently and several native languages, and is now taking English lessons. . . .

*   *   *

. . . there is an irrepressible activity—intellectual, commercial, political and religious—among the adherents of the creed in Nigritia. They pursue an extensive agriculture; they spin, weave, sew, work in the metals, engage in the craft of the potter and the tanner. Dr. Barth (1849–1855) travelled through a large portion of this country. He describes certain districts as abounding in rich pastures, in valleys of very fertile land, and in mountains clothed to the summits with noble trees. The towns and cities were walled

---

[2] *Biographies of Ibn Khallikan*; Vol. I, p. 662.

and respectably built; the markets were numerously attended, and a considerable trade carried on. He found commerce radiating from Kano, the great emporium of Central Africa, and spreading the manufactures and the productions of an industrious region over the whole of Western Africa. The fixed population of this city he estimated at 30,000; but on the occasion of the great fairs, at 60,000.

The principal commerce of Kano consists in native produce; namely, the cotton cloth woven and dyed here, or in neighbouring towns, in the form of tobes; turkedi, or the oblong piece of dress of dark-blue colour worn by the women; the zenne, or plaid of various colours. There is also a large trade in sandals and tanned hides, and in the cloth fabrics manufactured at Nupe. Throughout these districts a large variety of European goods may be seen. Arabic books, printed at Morocco and Fez, in red morocca binding, form an important article of traffic. The *Koran*, the *Traditions of Bochari*, the *Commentaries*, etc., are exchanged by Moorish traders for the fine cloth manufactures by the Nigritians, and for the gold dust and gold trinkets.

There is in this country an activity not suspected by the outside world. . . .

37

Islam in the Western Soudan

Journal of the African Society, 1902, 11–31

There is at present probably no question of deeper practical interest to the European powers, who for political and commercial objects have partitioned Africa among themselves, than the question of Islam in Soudan, both Eastern and Western. . . . Public attention has been attracted to that important region recently brought within the British Empire.

*   *   *

The books of the greatest value on Islam in Africa and most easily accessible are in the French language. The works of Idrisu, Ibn Batuta; Leo Africanus, written in Arabic from 300 to 1,000 years ago, have been translated into French and are still standard authorities on the subject. The *Tarik e Soudan*, an Arabic work of Soudanic authorship, which has recently come into the field, perhaps the most exhaustive on the history of Islam in Negroland, because the work of the native themselves, is not generally known to English-speaking people, and was, until recently, inaccessible through any European language. It is due to the learning, zeal, and energy of the distinguished French Orientalist, M. Houdas, that European scholars can now become acquainted with one of the most important works ever produced in Negroland. The eminent Professor, with prodigious labour and complete success, triumphed over almost insuperable difficulties to give us this valuable work in an admirable French translation. "The *Tarik e Soudan*," says M. Dubois,[1] "is conceived upon a perfectly clear and logical plan, according to the most correct rules of literary composition. . . . It forms, with the exception of the holy writings, the favourite of the Negro, and is known to the farthest extremity of Western Africa, from the shores of the Niger to the borders of Lake Tchad. Barth discovered fragments of it at Gando, and I heard it spoken in Senegal."

*   *   *

Islam is the most effective educational force in Negroland. A system of common schools prevails throughout Islamic Africa by

[1] *Timbuctoo the Mysterious*, pp. 312–315.

which every child is taught to read the Koran in the original and to commit to memory what has been taught. Thousands learn the Koran in this way and thus acquire a familiarity with an immense number of Arabic words, which serve as a bond of union and produce a solidarity of views and of interests which extends from the Atlantic to the Red Sea, and from the Mediterranean to the Equator. And when it is considered that five times a day millions in those latitudes repeat in their devotions the same words, it will be seen what a mighty force they form on the continent—Mandingoes, Foulahs, Jalofs, Hausas, Yorubas, and all the vast variety of tribes whose names are not known to Europe, speak each its own vernacular, but when they meet all prostrate themselves before the great Creator with the same words of adoration and self-extinction— *Allahu akbar*, and grasp each other by the hand with the same language of salutation, in the spirit of the Koran. . . .

MUSLIM MUNIFICENCE

African Muslims live only for Islam. The wealthy ones—and there are seldom any paupers among them—use their means for the promotion of intellectual and spiritual education. I was present in 1894 at the dedication of a magnificent mosque erected at Lagos at an expense of £5,000 by a wealthy native Mohammedan. The Governor of the Colony, Sir Gilbert Carter, presided, and there was present the Sheikh-ul-Islam, Quilliam, appointed by His Majesty the Sultan, Abdul Hamid Khan to represent him at the ceremony and to invest with a Turkish Order the devoted and patriotic builder.

Six months ago, during a visit which I made to the French colony of Senegal, I saw numerous evidences of the practical interest which the Native Muslims take in Education. One of the largest and most important of the mosques in St. Louis, a two-storey building, 60 feet by 48 feet, with tiled roof was erected, I was informed, by private beneficence. Prayers are held in the lower storey. The upper storey is used for literary gatherings, lectures and discussions. It is surrounded by nine small comfortable dwelling houses, constructed of similar materials, of one storey, erected by the same liberal builder of the mosque for the poor, where respectable indigent persons too poor to own or rent houses are given shelter for life. The benefactor, whose name is Ahmad Gouray, I did not have the pleasure of seeing. He had left a few weeks before my arrival on pilgrimage for the second time to Mecca.

The skill of these people in the Arabic language and literature
is often marvellous. They not unfrequently surpass in culture their
Oriental co-religionists. I have seen Arabs and Moors sit in perfect
amazement and as outsiders while listening to the reading and
exposition of Arabic books—not excepting the Koran—by Natives
of West Africa. M. Felix Dubois says: "The Soudanese doctors
were enabled to add the works of their own authors to the books
of Bagdad, Cairo, Granada, which formed the foundations of their
libraries. . . . A celebrated jurist of Hedjaz (Arabia) arriving in
Timbuctoo with the intention of teaching, found the town full of
Sudanese scholars. Observing them to be his superiors in knowledge, he withdrew to Fez, where he succeeded in obtaining employment."[2]

During my visit to Senegal referred to above, through the kindness of His Excellency M. Roume, the Governor-General, to whom
I had a letter of introduction from Sir C. A. King-Harman, the
Governor of Sierra Leone, and the obliging courtesy of M. Decazes,
Director of Native Affairs, I enjoyed exceptional opportunities for
studying the situation as it relates to Mohammedans. The chief
Government Interpreter, Al Hajj Ahmed Sek, a Jalof, thoroughly
educated in French and Arabic, and who has performed the pilgrimage to Mecca, was placed at my disposal. Among other places
of interest this gentleman took me to the Mohammedan Court,
over which Alkadi (Judge) Bakai Ba, a Native, presides—a man
much above the ordinary size, of splendid physique and commanding presence, severe, though dignified of aspect, with a voice of
masculine and impressive strength. He sat at his desk surrounded
by Arabic law books printed and in manuscript. He conversed
with equal ease in French and Arabic, and in Foulah and Mandingo,
with the interpreters, Mohammed Sanusi and Momodu Wakka,
whom I took with me from Sierra Leone. His decisions, I was told
by the Governor-General, in all civil and religious cases affecting
his co-religionists, are final.

Islam in the Soudan is propagated by self-supporting missionaries
without supervision or emolument from any recognized or directing
centre. I have often seen these missionaries in remote and sequestered pagan towns and villages, away from the public eye, earnestly
teaching and preaching the Unity of God and the Mission of His
Apostle, and the teaching of children and youth. . . .

Islam in Soudan is protective in its influence and permanent in
its conquests. When the Muslim missionary has once brought a
community within the pale of Islam, it is for ever sheltered from

[2] *Timbuctoo the Mysterious*, pp. 285 and 302.

the blighting influence of foreign trade and commerce. This the religion from Europe has nowhere done and cannot do.

All the representatives of His Majesty at present administering the affairs of the West African Colonies agree in their testimony as to the preservative and uplifting influence of Islam.

The inhabitants of Northern Nigeria are mostly Mohammedans and they have compelled the Government to legislate against the introduction of liquor by the practical argument of refusing to purchase it.

38

The Koran in Africa

Journal of the African Society, 1905, 160–166

The traders who visit Sierra Leone and Liberia during the dry season, from the distant interior, gather in groups in various parts of the Mohammedan quarter, in the cool of the afternoon, after the labours of the day, to read the sacred book, one of the company acting as expounder and commentator on difficult passages. In various parts, too, in the British settlement are seen boys and girls in classes, morning and afternoon, studying the one book. The Christians around them have very little idea of the intellectual activity of these simple and apparently uninstructed people from the country. . . .

* * *

The African Muslim pays less regard to tradition than to the words of the sacred text. They are proud of the name Muslim, which means a follower of Islam. Islam is from a root that means to deliver up oneself, to surrender. Applied to the religion, it means resignation to God and to his service. It is the name given by Mohammed to the religion which, he asserted, Abraham and all the prophets taught and which Mohammed restored—the foundation of which was the unity of God.

Intelligent Muslims in Africa become indignant when told that Mohammed was the author of the religion they profess. He was, they affirm, only a messenger—an Apostle of God—*Rasul-Allahi*—sent to proclaim Islam. They therefore strongly object to being called Mohammedans, such a description of them being, as they insist, forbidden in the Koran.

It is a remarkable fact that Mohammed is mentioned by name only four times in the Koran, and his name Ahmad occurs only once; while the name of Moses occurs one hundred and thirty-four times; of Abraham, sixty-nine times; of Jesus, twenty-five times.

They reject the name of *Mohammedan*, applied to a follower of their faith, as an invention of Europeans, who, they say, are fond of glorifying men. None of the prophets, they affirm, or any of their true followers ever encouraged the using of their names in connection with or as descriptive of the system they taught. The Negro Muslims claim a share in some of the most celebrated achievements of Islam, and their exploits are recognized in all the great Arabian works, not excepting the Koran. There is a chapter in that sacred book inscribed to a Negro, in which his wisdom and piety are especially dwelt upon and pointed out as the direct gifts of God. This is the 31st chapter entitled *Loqman*. . . .

No Muslims, whether Arab, Turk, or Indian, can read the 31st chapter of the Koran, given, according to their belief, by direct inspiration of God, and separate the Negro from participation in the privileges of God's elect. Mohammed had as his right-hand man in the incipient stages of his religion a Negro slave; and it shows the high estimate which he placed upon such persons, and the high degree of respect entertained for *Loqman* in Arabia during the time of the Prophet, that he did not believe that any slur would be cast upon the new religion connecting the Koran with the name of that remarkable slave. . . .

It is said that this recognition of the African in the Koran was natural, because the Prophet of Islam was descended in part from an African woman; and throughout the history of the religion the exploits of great Africans have been celebrated. In the military history of Islam a Negro slave distinguished himself at two turning points in the early struggles of the faith; at the battle of Ohud, when Medina, the refuge of the exiled Prophet, was threatened, in desperate combat he killed Hamzah, Mohammed's uncle, but one of his bitterest enemies and leader of the opposition. Afterwards, with the same lance with which Wahshi (for that was his name) had killed Hamzah, he slew in a sanguinary battle the imposter "Museilama, the liar", who claimed to be the equal and rival of Mohammed.[1]

Among the poets of pre-Islamic days, the Negro Antarah held a high position. He was the author of one of the celebrated prize poems—The Muallakat—and was so admired by Mohammed that the Prophet lamented that he had never seen him.[2] When I visited Futa Jallo many years ago (1873) on behalf of the British Government, a man of the colour of *Loqman* was pointed out to me as possessing a prodigious memory. He was not only a Hafiz, i.e. one who knows the whole Koran by heart, but he was called a walking dictionary. It was said that he could name every word in the Arabic language beginning with any letter from *Alif* to *Ya* or from A to Z. . . .

Dubois, speaking of literature among the blacks of the Sudan, mentions, among other, "the very learned and pious Sheik Abu

---

[1] Steinglass' translation of *The Assemblies of Hariri*, Vol. II, p. 245..
[2] Chinery's translation of *The Assemblies of Hariri*, p. 317.

Abdallah, who had no property; all his goods went to succour the poor and the unhappy, and he bought slaves that he might give them their liberty. His house had no door, everyone entered unannounced, and men came to see him from all parts and at all hours, especially on Fridays after the two o'clock prayer. Moors and Arabs flocked to him in crowds as soon as they learned his virtues.

"The Marabuts, who devoted themselves to the study of law, administered justice according to the precepts of the Koran and the decisions contained in the most important works of the Arabian jurists. They also made inventories of property, determining its succession and generally fulfilling the position of lawyer."

"During their sojourns in the foreign universities of Fez, Tunis, and Cairo, they astounded the most learned men of Islam by their erudition. That these Negroes were on a level with the Arabian *savants* is proved by the fact that they were installed as professors in Morocco and Egypt. In contrast to this, we find that the Arabs were not always equal to the requirements of Sudanic scholarship."

"A cerebral refinement was thus produced among certain of the Negro population, which has had surprising results, and which gives the categoric lie to the theorists who insist upon the inferiority of the black races."[3]

Besides this, there are thousands of native Africans as black as *Loqman*, who are blood relations to Mohammed, and are, in consequence, eligible to the highest post in the secular or spiritual affairs of Islam. A few days ago, a pure Arab missionary—an itinerant teacher in the Protectorate of the Colony . . . visited the Department of Mohammedan Education, attended by twenty of his pupils, all native blacks, and he introduced two of them to the present writer as Sharifs, i.e. descendants of the Prophet. He also presented his brother, who in colour and features would be taken for a West African, while my visitor was of the usual Arab complexion and look. I asked, "How is this"? Seeing that I referred to the difference of colour, he answered with a quotation from the Koran: "Among his signs are the creation of the Heavens and of the Earth and the variety of *your colours*. Herein truly are signs for all creatures." How can such a man fail to exert irrepressible influence among the Sudanese whom he teaches?

Another element in the consolidating influence of Islam in Africa

[3] *Timbuktoo the Mysterious*, Chapter XIII.

z

is the *lingua franca* which Arabic supplies. Every instructed Sudanese Muslim can make himself understood in not less than two languages—Arabic and his own vernacular. In most cases, he speaks three or four, Arabic always being one. English and French will become for the Sudan the language of commerce—of Government officials, civil and military—but never of the streets. Arabic will always be the language of literary intercourse and diplomacy, uniting all the various tribes from the Atlantic to the Red Sea and from the Mediterranean to the Congo. The various vernaculars will supply the medium of intercourse for the markets and the streets. At Lagos the language of the streets is Yoruba; the official language is English, but the sacred language of the majority is Arabic. There are connected with the Department of Mohammedan Education in Sierra Leone four schools, with more than eight hundred pupils on the roll being taught according to Western methods. But the first sounds these children hear in the early morning when they recite to their Alfas or religious teachers, and the last sounds they hear at night, are the sounds which twelve hundred years ago first came to the Sudan from the deserts of Arabia.

Another custom which has helped to keep up the unity and sympathy among African Mohammedans is the rigid annual fast of Ramadhan. This fast, lasting for thirty days, during which is the most self-denying abstinence from food and drink in the day-time, is, as a sanitary arrangement, not to be despised in a tropical climate. If there were a railway from West Africa to the Red Sea, and you wished to avail yourself of it to journey to Egypt during the fast month (you might perhaps accomplish the journey in seven days), you would, during those seven days, pass through a region where you would find every man, woman, and child in good health observing the fast. On the entire *route*—four thousand miles—you would notice that the fires were out in the day-time. Sixty millions of people fasting at the same time! I believe that more than one-half of these are Negroes. The Negroes of any other religion are divided. The paganism of the Temne country is not the same as the paganism of the Yoruba country, and both differ from the paganism of the Congo country; so that these people have no common observances or institutions which bring them together. Among Christian Negroes there are various denomination. . . . Often in small struggling Christian communities on this continent there are found three branches of Methodists, two of Baptists, besides Catholics and Church of England. These divisions, while each contend for his peculiarities, must bring weakness upon the people; and they must be helpless for any great comprehensive movement which requires for its success earnest co-operation and unbroken unity.

At the close of the fast comes the celebration of the festival of Bairam, called also the Id-al-Fitri, or the feast of breaking of the fast. On that occasion sixty millions of people bow together in prayers and thanksgiving to the Most High, and renew their vows and their offerings for pushing the conquests of Islam over the pagan portions of the country. . . .

PART VII
European Imperialism in West Africa

PART VII

European Imperialism in West Africa

Essentially, Blyden viewed the extension of European influence in Africa as a necessary stimulant in bringing Africa on to the world stage as an active participant. Before 1870 he had hope that black emigrants from the New World would provide the primary catalyst that he felt African society needed for creative and progressive development, with European influence playing a secondary role. After 1870, by which time he had given up hopes of a massive New World Negro emigration to Africa, and before the partition, Blyden looked primarily to the British to pacify, unite and westernize West Africa. Repeatedly did Blyden urge the British to establish a vast protectorate over West Africa. In this he was generally supported by the westernized African élite for both economic and political reasons: a peaceful protectorate would lead to a vast increase in trade; secondly, the educated élite saw themselves as allies of the British, playing an important part in governing the Protectorate.

Blyden was disappointed that the British had not acted on his advice but, as the three Selections, written between 1895 and 1903 show, he gave qualified welcome to the establishment of new colonial governments in West Africa. It should be emphasized that Blyden was fully aware that European colonial rule, characterized by greed and arrogance, was full of hazards for Africans. But he maintained that whatever suffering and humiliations Africans endured under colonial rule would in the long run be worthwhile: Europeans, he insisted, could never successfully colonize tropical Africa, and her political overlordship was bound to be temporary; once a sufficient number of Africans had acquired those aspects of European culture that they could beneficially utilize, at that point would Africans assert their political independence of Europe.

This view Blyden maintained to the end of his life. But it was a view which, by the end of the nineteenth century when colonial rule was being fully established, was finding less and less support among educated West Africans. They felt keenly the blatant discriminations against them which the new colonial régimes brought and were disposed to show their anger in political protest, of which Blyden disapproved as being premature.

Despite his willingness to co-operate with European imperialists,

315

and despite his disapproval of political agitation as premature, Blyden, who placed his greatest emphasis on cultural nationalism, did succeed in inspiring succeeding generations of West African nationalists: to this four of the most distinguished of these have testified: Herbert Macaulay and Dr. Nnamdi Azikiwe of Nigeria, and Casely Hayford and Dr. Kwame Nkrumah of Ghana.[1]

[1] Lynch, *Edward Wilmot Blyden, Pan-Negro Patriot*, 1832–1912, p. 241 and pp. 248–50.

39

The African Problem

North American Review, 1895, 327–39

EUROPEAN IMPERIALISM IN AFRICA

The African problem in Africa, which has puzzled a hundred generations of Europeans, is now engaging the earnest attention and taxing the energies of all the powers of Europe. The decision of the Berlin Conference, ten years ago, has placed Europe in relations to Africa such as never before existed between these continents. Every power of Europe, including Russia, has established or is seeking to establish interests in Africa.

*　　*　　*

Fifty years ago there was no part of the world of which less was known than the interior of Africa, and in which less interest was taken. When the Landers [Richard and John] had achieved their great exploit of proving by actual observation that the Niger had an outlet to the sea and that its banks on both sides were occupied by vast and active populations, their discoveries were not received with half the interest which is now aroused by excavations in the valley of the Euphrates or on the banks of the Nile. *The Edinburgh Review* of that day (July, 1832), rebuked the "very rigid parsimony" of a government which rewarded the labours of the enterprising travellers by a gratuity of *one hundred pounds*; but those labours were the prelude of all the modern activity in African exploration and exploitation. The English, as the first of commercial nations, could not rest without ascertaining the natural capacities of a country known to be populous, and without endeavouring to open new and easier routes of communication with it. For the series of explorations which has, within the last thirty or forty years, filled up the larger part of what used to be blank spaces in our maps of Africa, we are indebted almost altogether to the intelligence and enterprise of British travellers—from Livingstone in 1849, to Captain Lugard in 1895. But the conferences of the great powers at Berlin in 1884–5, and at Brussels in 1890, assumed for Europe the continent of Africa as its special field of operation. The "scramble" is over, and now the question is how to utilize the plunder in the interests of civilization and progress.

France has taken the lead by military operations. England has begun her work through chartered companies destined to end in protectorates. Germany has blended the military with the commercial régime. But each is proceeding cautiously and learning the best methods by daily experience. They are gradually repairing the waste places and teaching the natives to make the best possible use of their own country, by fitting it up for their own prosperity and preparing it for the exiles in distant lands who may desire to return to the ancestral home.

The task which Europe has imposed upon itself is a vast one— surpassing the labours of Hercules. But intelligence, energy and science will cleanse the Augean stables—the swamps and morasses which disfigure and poison the coast regions. They will destroy the Lernean hydra of African fever. They will bring the golden apples from the hidden gardens of the wealthy interior.

France, in the conquest of Dahomey, has performed a task which civilization has long needed. She has freed a great country from the cruel savagery of ages and thrown it open to the regenerating influence of enlightened nations. The king, who was bound hand and foot by the sanguinary superstitions of his fathers, was relieved by the military energy of the French from his blood-thirsty responsibility, and is now ending his days in bloodless luxury and quiet in the French colony of Martinique, supported like a king at the expense of his captors and deporters. Abomey, his capital, closed for hundreds of years against civilizing agencies, is now the centre of stable rule, of educational and industrial impulse. Mohammedan missionaries, formerly refused admission for religious work, are now directing the attention of besotted pagans to the "Lord of the universe".

The French are assiduous in the administration of the affairs of the countries which, by the decision of the Berlin conference, have fallen within their "sphere of influence". When, by conquest or treaty, they have acquired any territory, they spare no pains in its exploitation and development. The sons of powerful chiefs whom they have conquered in what is now called French Soudan are sent to France or North Africa for education to fit them on their return to take charge of their respective countries and govern them under French supervision in the interest of order and progress. Several Mohammedan youth, the sons of chiefs, were sent last year from Senegal to the Moslem College at Kairawan for education. Natives of intelligence and capacity are promoted to high official positions, and have the Legion of Honour conferred upon them

England is entering upon her part of the work, not as a stranger. For more than a hundred years she has been engaged in direct recuperative work, having provided Sierra Leone, after abolishing the slave trade, as an asylum for recaptured slaves. In this colony, as well as in those of Gambia, the Gold Coast and Lagos, she has expended vast amounts of money and sacrificed numberless English lives. She has very recently increased her political responsibilities in Western Soudan by taking within her jurisdiction the powerful kingdom of Ashantee, with which she has waged such frequent and expensive wars with results by no means discreditable to her native antagonists. Under the name of the Niger Coast Protectorate, England has also taken the whole of the Niger delta through which flow the great Oil Rivers or estuaries of Benin, Brass, Bonny, Opobo, New Calabar and Old Calabar. There is one feature in which the Niger may defy competition from any other river, either of the old or new world. This is the grandeur of its delta, which is probably the most insalubrious region in all of West Africa. Along the whole coast, from Benin to Old Calabar, a distance of about 300 miles, the Niger makes its way to the Atlantic through the various estuaries just enumerated. Had this delta, like that of the Nile, been subject only to periodical inundations, leaving behind a layer of fertilizing slime, it would have formed the most fruitful region on earth, and might have been almost the granary of a continent. But the Niger rolls down its waters in such excessive abundance as to convert the whole into a dreary swamp. This is covered with dense forests of mangrove and other trees of spreading and luxuriant foliage. The equatorial sun, with its fiercest rays, cannot penetrate these dark recesses; it only draws forth from them pestilential vapours, which render this coast more fatal than any other. There is not, however, the slightest doubt, now that British enterprise under government protection has access to that region, that in the course of time those forests will be levelled, those swamps drained, and the soil covered with luxuriant harvests.

Sir Claude Macdonald, to whom was entrusted four or five years ago the duty of establishing the Niger Coast Protectorate, of organizing regular government and enforcing order in that region, has performed his difficult task with admirable ability. He has in that short time created a revenue which more than suffices for the work of administration. He has abolished barbarous customs and suppressed marauding practices. The natives, he has discovered, have a perfect knowledge and appreciation of the immense industrial resources of their country, and a readiness to take advantage of them, together with an aptitude for imitation and a desire for instruction, which are most hopeful indications of progress. They are encouraged to spontaneous activity, and to a love of achievement from which important results must before long accrue. The progress has been rapid as well as steady; and may be measured from month to month, almost from day to day.

The Royal Niger Company, which has brought within British influence vast and important territories, will now, probably, like the British East Africa Company, pass into the hands of the British Government.[1] As this company has been governed by strictly commercial principles, it is feared, from recent occurrences, that the welfare of the native population may be sacrificed to the interest of the shareholders. Perhaps it may be best for all concerned that the regions in question should come under the strict control of a Protectorate, if not formed into a Crown colony.

Germany, considering her inexperience in colonial matters, is developing astounding ability and resources as a colonizing power. Her recent decided step, on behalf of native protection, in the punishment of Herr Leist for his abuse of official power in maltreating the natives at Cameroon, has satisfied the people as to her intentions and aims.

Every one has confidence in the philanthropic aims and political and commercial efforts of the King of the Belgians in the arduous and expensive enterprise he has undertaken on the Congo. But none of these powers has any idea of making Africa a home for its citizens. They know that European colonists cannot live in that country. Nature has marked off tropical Africa as the abiding home of the black races. I have met no European agent, either political, commercial or industrial, who thinks that there is any chance for Europeans to occupy inter-tropical Africa. All that Europe can do is to keep the peace among the tribes, giving them the order and security necessary to progress; while the emissaries of religion, industry and trade teach lessons of spiritual and secular life. The bulk of the continent is still untouched by Western civilization, notwithstanding the fact that Africa has been partitioned among the European powers—on paper.

It is an interesting fact that Liverpool, which, in the days of the slave trade, took so prominent a part in the nefarious traffic, is doing more than any other city to push the enterprises of reconstruction into the continent. Her steamship companies and her Chamber of Commerce are the most potent of the European agencies in the work of African regeneration. And both are doing

[1] This took place in 1899 [ed.].

all in their power to bring the natives forward and assist them to develop and take care of their own country. . . .

*   *   *

The able and experienced officers now administering the government of the British Colonies in West Africa—notably Col. Frederic Cardew, of Sierra Leone, and Sir Gilbert Carter, of Lagos—are earnestly recommending the construction of railways from the coast to the interior, their travels to the hinterland having convinced them that vast resources may soon be developed by increased facilities of intercourse and transportation. A few weeks ago a deputation from the Manchester, Liverpool, and London Chambers of Commerce waited upon the Secretary of State for the Colonies to urge upon Her Majesty's Government the immediate establishment of railways to meet the growing demands of the trade. Of all this valuable and increasing commerce the voluntary industry of the natives is the only basis.

40

West Africa

Address delivered before Liverpool Chamber of Commerce, September, 1901;
West Africa Before Europe, London, 1905, 10–18

GREAT BRITAIN IN WEST AFRICA

. . . Great Britain has been the most strenuous and self-denying of
the political agencies, but, owing to climatic hindrances, which have
not been friendly to a continuity of policy, based upon an accurate
apprehension of things, the British Government has not achieved
the results which a hundred years of contact ought to have effected.
The policy, for the most part, has been one of *laissez faire*. The fact
is, that during the greater part of the century which has just expired,
time and money and lives were devoted to getting the slave trade
out of the way, and counteracting its disintegrating effects. When
that diabolical system had been destroyed both by British naval
enterprise and the downfall of slavery in America, both the great
English political parties came to the conclusion that the policy of
England should look to a gradual withdrawal from West Africa,
excepting probably Sierra Leone, leaving the natives to the government of themselves.

This decision was owing also to the expectation that the extinction of slavery in America would lead—as was indeed suggested
in one of President Lincoln's Messages—to a wholesale emigration
of deported blacks from America to the fatherland, and the idea
in the minds of these statesmen probably was to place no hindrance
in the way of this influx of repatriates. But when it was found that
the peculiarities and exigencies of American politics would detain
the blacks in the land of their exile for time indefinite, and when
the "earth hunger" referred to by Lord Ripon the other day began
to take possession of certain Continental powers, compelling Bismarck . . . to suggest an international conference to discuss the
situation in that vast "no man's land", as it was called; and when,
as a result of that conference, a partition of Africa was made on
the map, then England began to realize the mistake of her *laissez
faire* policy, and to awake to her rights and duties in connection
with West Africa. Within the last few years a great statesman
[Joseph Chamberlain] has come to the front at the Colonial Office
who, impatient of the slumber of years . . . has brought unaccus-

tomed, we may say abnormal, activity to the "development of that portion of the estates of the Empire", which has lain fallow for generations, nay for thousands of years. Then the pendulum, having swung too far to the left, was made, for a time, to swing too far to the right. But it is now happily regaining its normal oscillation, and fruitful and beneficent are the prospects before England and the native owners of these "undeveloped estates". Next to England in protracted political work in West Africa is France.

FRANCE IN WEST AFRICA

France has a peculiar work to do for West Africa—a work much needed, and suited to the genius of the Celtic race. It was my privilege a few months ago to visit the French Ivory Coast—regions which, before the Franco-Liberian Treaty of 1892, were in Liberian territory, and I was not only satisfied, but delighted with the results so far of French administration upon the life and prospects of the natives. I made careful enquiries of civilized native traders from Sierra Leone and other settlements on the Coast who came on board the steamer from the various trading stations, as to their condition and opportunities under French rule. They all emphasized the fact of the encouragement and assistance afforded them in the prosecution of their enterprise by the local authorities. I was at first somewhat sceptical as to the result on the native population of the transfer of those territories from Liberia to France, but after actual observation all my doubts were removed. France is doing her part to pacify West Africa, to improve her material condition, and to give an opportunity for permanent progress to the sons of the soil.

The contribution of the French to the civilization of Africa evidently springs not only from what they have in common with all mankind, but from what is special to themselves. France is France, England is England. France can do for Africa what England cannot do, and England can do for Africa what France cannot do. This all thinking Africans recognize, and all gladly co-operate with each nation according to the measure in which their systems accord with native ideas and native customs and traditions. And there seems to be more of this conformity in the French methods than in the more rigid and unimaginative system of the Anglo-Saxon. Whatever there is among the natives of original, racy, or romantic interest is not perishing under French administration, therefore Miss Kingsley chose, as the proper field for her researches into West African life and character, the French settlements. And to the credit of the French this must be said: that Miss Kingsley should have been able to suffer the physical discomforts, the social and intellectual inconveniences, and the mental strain inseparable from the effort to acquire that wide and profound knowledge which she exhibited of the religion of the natives and the meaning of their customs, was owing not less to the French régime than to her own unique and incomparable genius.

The next important political agency in West Africa is comparatively a newcomer.

GERMANY IN WEST AFRICA

The Germans have only recently entered the field, but, as apt pupils, have already mastered the situation. They are taking their part with intelligence, energy, and capital. In commercial thoroughness and success only the English are their superiors. Their steamers are found in every inlet and outlet along the Coast. Their settlements in Togoland, adjoining the Gold Coast Colony, are becoming important centres of trade. Not long ago these settlements were only clusters of native huts. Little Popo is rapidly increasing in material position. In March last, when I visited it, I saw large buildings of recent construction, or in progress of construction, in the latest European style of beauty and solidity, but adapted to the climate. They are chiefly Government buildings, for offices and official residences, a few trading factories, with groups of native houses interspersed, and extensive groves of cocoanut trees in the background. There are two churches here, and a large, commodious, abundantly equipped hospital, with ample grounds for cattle, and a fine vegetable garden. A skilful physician of many years' experience on the Coast presides. I counted from the deck of the steamer between forty and fifty head of cattle grazing near the hospital. Hither come invalids from the neighbouring settlements for rest, attention, and recuperation. There are as yet visible no signs of segregation. Lome, the other German settlement of importance in these parts, has a similar development and gives a similar promise. I learnt that the experiments in cotton culture by American experts was being vigorously prosecuted. There are other though smaller German settlements in Togoland, all proving by the activity visible in them that Germany is in West Africa to stay, and come to give her desirable quota to its development and prosperity.

WHERE THE SAFETY OF AFRICA LIES

I have briefly called attention to the work in which the three greatest of the European Powers are engaged, each pursuing its own course, in its own way, of its own lines, with apparently very little heed on the work of, or sympathy with the others. I have sometimes felt that the safety of the African lies in the antagonism among themselves of the invaders of his country! but I have also felt that the European traders and other agencies on the Coast would be able to accomplish more for uniform and permanent progress if there were more of mutual sympathy and trust among them. Notwithstanding the alleged partition of Africa, those who travel along the West Coast can detect little of practical occupation. Hundreds of miles sometimes intervene between individual Europeans, and these individuals often of different nationalities. It is difficult to see how, under such circumstances, i.e. the constant striving for ascendency or precedence in trade or politics on the part of restless and divergent individualities, and the absence of any concurrent interest, there can be any sustained, any concentrated, influence, upon the African or his country.

41

Some Problems of West Africa

An Address delivered before the Africa Society, London, June 26th, 1903;
West Africa Before Europe, London, 1905, 100–122

TWO PRINCIPLES FOR PROGRESSIVE IMPERIAL RULE

Two principles, it seems to me, should guide the policy of the Imperial Powers which have taken upon themselves to partition Africa.

First, to encourage the development of the natives along the lines of their own idiosyncrasies as revealed in their institutions. No people can profit by or be helpful under institutions which are not the outcome of their own character. The sudden and wholesale imposition of European ideas and methods upon the African has been like the investing of David in Saul's armour. He is falling before the Goliath of progress. . . .

The next principle which, it appears to me, governors and administrators in West Africa should pursue, and which I am glad to know they are conscientiously endeavouring to pursue, is to give to the African taken under British rule all the advantages, in their spirit and effect, which as individuals or communities, as rulers or people, they would have enjoyed under native conditions. Do not deprive them of rights and advantages which they valued and enjoyed before you came, and which were in accordance with justice and equity, without making it clear to them that you give them their equivalent. The sense of justice is as keen in the African as in any one else. For example, if, for the necessities or convenience of European enterprise or for more effective administration, you close one door, which for generations they have prized, open another, which the native will feel is an adequate substitute for the one he has been induced to surrender. . . . I believe that the future of Africa will rest with that Power which will establish its authority upon the basis of the two principles I have just enumerated. . . .

LUGARD AND NORTHERN NIGERIA

Referring to the new acquisitions in Northern Nigeria, it is encouraging to know that General Lugard has exhibited so much mildness in conquest, and so much wisdom and moderation in policy, that, as far as I can learn, he has won the respect and esteem not only of the people who have come under his sway, but also of the officers who assist in administration. He has, I may venture to say, a splendid field before him. The new subjects he has brought within the Empire are among the greatest of the African tribes, and will be the most intelligent and more effective co-workers with England in the regeneration of the Continent. Their leaders— the Almamis, the Sheiks, the Kadis—are, as a rule, a respectable and useful class of men who have great influence, not only among their own co-religionists, but also among Pagans; and the High Commissioner is pursuing the enlightened policy of attaching them firmly to the Government, and endeavouring to procure the exertion of their influence to give effect to the far-seeing schemes of his administration. He would gladly, as he has several times informed me, appoint political agents from among them, if there were any sufficiently educated in Western learning to be made available for this work as expounders of the British spirit and policy.

MUSLIM AFRICAN EDUCATION

Growing out of this necessity, another problem before the Government and British people is the training of co-workers and leaders from among these followers of the Prophet. Here, the French, from their longer dealings with African Mohammedans, are far ahead of the English. I visited last year, in my capacity of Director of Mohammedan Education at Sierra Leone, with the consent and approval of Sir C. A. King-Harman, the Governor, the Colony of Senegal to study the French system of education for their vast Mohammedan population. Their chief instrument for this purpose is the College for the Education of Sons of Chiefs and of Interpreters, founded at St. Louis, by that enlightened statesman, General Faidherbe, fifty years ago.

It is a most interesting Institution which, the Governor-General, M. Roume, informed me, was admirably fulfilling its purpose. I learn that, since my visit, the buildings I saw have been taken down as not adapted to the increasing necessities, and a magnificent up-to-date structure is now in course of erection. They have also endowed schools in all the towns. So that with all the vast preparation they are making for material improvements—for railroads, and docks, and wharves—they do not neglect the fundamental necessity of the people—education. These are the high-minded uses which the French in that part of Africa are making of Imperial power, so that whatever their faults they must command the respect and confidence of their Mohammedan subjects. The precise problem of the education of the African is to develop his powers as an African—a strange man to the European—in the way he should go; a way not known to his foreign guide, who is a stranger endeavouring to develop a strange man in a strange direction. The method which has been generally pursued in the training of the African has been absurd—superficial in its results—because it has been carried on without the study of the man and his intellectual possibilities, and, of course, producing, as a rule, only caricatures of alien manners, who copy the most obvious peculiarities of their teachers, with all their drawbacks and defects.

The British are only now entering upon the policy of educating Mohammedans. They have elementary schools for Muslims at Sierra Leone and Lagos. At Sierra Leone, the Governor is particularly anxious to promote this enterprise in the Colony for which he is responsible; but it is a very small part of the work that any Colony can do by itself. The question is one of Imperial interest and requires for its success the patronage and stimulus of Imperial resources. I hope that Sir Frederick Lugard, who is now in England, will be able to induce the Government to provide either out of Imperial funds, or by contributions from the various colonies interested, for the establishment of a Central Institution on the highlands of Sierra Leone for the education in English and Arabic of Mohammedan youth from Northern Nigeria and the Colonies on the Coast.

In the interior there are thousands of Mohammedans who when such a movement becomes generally understood, will give it their earnest support. Intellectual culture, when it is known that such culture is not intended to interfere with their religion, is highly prized among them. I venture to say that the love of learning, for its own sake, is as general among African Mohammedans as it is in Europe. . . .

We learn English, they say, or the language of the white man, to succeed in this world; we learn Arabic to prosper in the next. There is constant communication, epistolary and personal, between Mecca and the Mohammedans in West and Central Africa. Very few incidents occur in West Africa, affecting Mohammedans, which are not in a very short time known in Mecca and at Constantinople. There was a rumour some time last year that Messrs. Elder, Dempster & Co. would probably put a steamer on the Coast at stated times to take pilgrims to Mecca. This report was hailed with great joy all through the interior of Senegal, Gambia, Sierra Leone, the Gold Coast and Lagos. News of it reached Mecca, and I saw Arabic letters written from that Holy City to Mohammedans at Freetown, congratulating them on the prospect of greater facilities for reaching Mecca and sending the orthodox itinerary for the fulfilment of the requirements of the pilgrimage after landing at Alexandria. Sir Frederick Lugard was communicated with on the probability of pilgrims going from Northern Nigeria. He thought that the movement would be possible and useful after the country was settled.

Considering the importance attached to the pilgrimage in all parts of the Muslim world, this is another enterprise of Imperial interest, and will, no doubt, be looked upon not without sympathy by the Imperial Government.

I see reports in the papers of a probable rising by the people of Northern Nigeria against their recent conquerors, but I feel sure that the people of Kano and Sokoto—that is, the indigenous Mohammedans—having laid down their hostility, it will never be necessary hereafter, if the policy of Sir Frederick Lugard is persevered in, for England to maintain her ascendancy in those countries by force of arms.

You will be surprised to learn that you have in Liverpool an element, an apparently trifling element it may be, but, nevertheless, an element, of the security of British Administration in those countries. Whatever view you, as Englishmen and Christians, may take of one of your countrymen who embraces Islam, I would like to assure you that the fact of there being among you such a pervert, as you would designate him, or a convert, as the Mohammedans would call him, he being an Englishman [William H. Abdullah Quilliam] and the head of a mosque in the greatest commercial city of the Empire, produces in the mind of the African Muslim the deepest possible impression and the most favourable conception as to the friendship and tolerance of the British nation. I have been surprised at the extensive knowledge among West African Mohammedans of this man and his work. I was, as I have just told you, on a visit to French Guinea last year, and travelled by rail from Dakar to St. Louis, a distance of nearly two hundred miles, and at nearly every station I met with Mohammedans who enquired about Quilliam; so when going along the coast on British steamers I have encountered traders from the interior, who, as soon as they found me out, would address me in the following manner :

"Do you know Quilliam?" On my answering in the affirmative, they would proceed : "Do you believe that a white man, an Englishman, can be a true Muslim?" On being assured of the confidence reposed in him by the Sultan of Turkey, the Ameer of Afghanistan, and the Shah of Persia, whose Consul in Liverpool he is, they would exclaim with evident emotion, *Allahu akbar*—"God is Great"—a phrase common among them when expressing surprise or admiration. In this case it meant "God can do anything—He has even made an Englishman a devout Muslim". Mr. Quilliam himself hardly understands the unique character and importance of his position here. He is a silent, perhaps a suppressed, certainly an unconscious, element of British Imperial influence in the Muslim world.

It is a curious thing that the two English names extensively known among the West and Central African Mohammedans are those of Liverpool men. During the journey, to which I have referred, on the Senegal railway, I was introduced by Momodu Wakka, a Mandingo Mohammedan, who accompanied me as interpreter from Sierra Leone, to the private secretary of the celebrated African warrior, Samory, or Samadu, whom we met at one of the stations. He inquired of the gentleman, named Jones,[1] who sent, in 1892, a magnificently bound copy of the Koran to his royal master, the name of the donor having been inscribed on the back of the book. He asked me if Jones was still alive; I said, "Rather!" The book, he said, was still in the possession of the family of Samudu. I told him that Mr. Jones was not only alive, but interested in the pilgrimage to Mecca from West Africa, and one of these days he might be able to provide facilities for making the journey to Mecca shorter and easier for West African Mohammedans. He could not suppress his delight at this piece of information. He grasped my right hand in his two hands, exclaiming, *Alhamdu lillahi Allahu akbara; In sha Allah*—"Thank God; God is great; if it please God." An Empire builder, like the Empire itself, must take within his cognizance and sympathy all races and creeds.

GREATER COMMUNICATION NEEDED

Another problem before Great Britain is the establishment of adequate means of communication between the different portions of their possessions in West and Central Africa, which, though increasing in productive power, are practically inaccessible to each other and to the coast.

It is a source of not a little gratification to every one acquainted with past and present conditions, to see the importance now being attached to the construction of railways in West Africa. If this

[1] Sir Alfred Jones, the Liverpool shipping magnate and trader.

question has come within the range of practical politics in England, it is entirely owing to the persistent representations and irrepressible energy of Liverpool. It is not very long ago since it was a matter of the utmost difficulty to make the British public understand the important advantages to be derived from railways in West Africa, independently of their immediate pecuniary return.

During a succession of years a railway was earnestly recommended between Sierra Leone and its hinterland, but without effect. After more than a generation of discussion and hesitation, the lines for railways at Sierra Leone and Lagos were at length surveyed, and eventually railways were built; and nothing can be more promising than the reports we hear from time to time of their excellent effects upon the country through which they pass.

The African Section of the Liverpool Chamber of Commerce is now diligently listened to by those in Downing Street, who hold in the hollow of their hands the destinies of that important part of the Empire. . . .

Many years ago, the French foresaw the exigencies of the present, and planned for the construction of railways, and in considering the question they did not confine their deliberations to the single point which often influences business men, viz., the amount of profit which might be looked for on the line as an ordinary speculation. There are cases, no doubt, in which the immediate question of profit and loss is everything. But a nation is sometimes called upon to deal with matters from a different point of view. There are occasions which demand somewhat of generous enterprise, far-sighted wisdom, and, it may be, of immediate self-sacrifice. While England hesitated, France was covering her West African possessions with a network of high roads, in the first instance, and now she is extending her railways in every direction, linking together French Guinea and Dahomey and the Ivory Coast, with a view, probably, of eventually connecting French Congo with her possessions in North Africa. And it cannot be said that France has not splendid *ex post facto* justification for all her expenditures and sacrifices thus far.

If England does not keep her eyes open, her aspiring, energetic and far-sighted neighbour will command all the traffic between the Soudan and the Mediterranean, and divert it to the Atlantic through French Guinea and Senegal. . . .

BRITISH-FRENCH RAPPROCHEMENT

The *entente cordiale* between England and France is hailed with delight by all Africans and workers for Africa; and I believe that Africa has largely contributed to this *rapprochement*. Moved by the same impulse towards that country during the last twenty years, and eager about the responsibilities they have there assumed before the whole world, the sympathy and cordiality which now distinguish their relations should not be considered strange.

For the first time in the history of the two nations in West Africa, an event occurred a few months ago which surprised and delighted everybody. An English Admiral's ship not only visited Dakar, the chief port of Senegal, but the Admiral landed with his suite, and proceeded by railway to Saint Louis, the capital, a distance of 180 miles, on a friendly visit to His Excellency, M. Roume, Governor General of French West Africa. At all the railway stations—which were beautifully decorated, and there are about sixteen of them—between Dakar and Saint Louis, Admiral Moore was greeted with the greatest enthusiasm by enormous crowds of natives.

If Africans are delighted at the present happy state of things between the two great nations, it is because they feel that, owning larger stakes in Africa than any other foreign Power, and ruling over the mightiest populations of that continent, there could be no better guarantee for the peace, the freedom, and the prosperity of the natives, than in the harmony and co-operation of France and Great Britain. It is of the utmost importance that these two nations should, by union and co-operation, impress a wholesome direction upon what must be regarded as the most critical period in the modern history of Africa.

I have heard of a railway to be constructed to Baghdad by international co-operation. I believe that the most important railway yet to be constructed in the cause of Africa and humanity, is that to be built by Great Britain and France, conjointly, from Algiers to the Cape of Good Hope, the terminus on one side being in French territory, and on the other in English. Such an enterprise would make for the permanent peace, not only of Africa, but of Europe. The united interests of England and France would be a guarantee for the easy and successful arbitration in any difficulties arising out of commercial or political rivalries. On the other hand, the railway would furnish facilities for most effective police supervision of the continent, which is almost equally divided between the two nations, France, perhaps, having the larger share.

But to keep up railways, and practically justify their existence, they must be fed. The next problem, therefore, which must be solved, is that of enlarged and scientific agriculture. I am glad to see that the new Cotton Growing Association has set before itself the work of promoting this industry in West Africa, where, it is to be regretted, it is almost non-existent. If the philanthropic agencies, which have for nearly a hundred years been in operation in that country, had sown in the hearts of the natives the seeds of industry, and busied themselves in bringing those seeds to maturity, they would indeed have opened to the West African a career of usefulness which would have enabled him now to come forward as an effective co-worker and valuable contributor to the cause of the general progress of his country.

West Africa and England are mutually dependent upon each other. The work of England in that country would of course be far easier if Englishmen could colonize it, and England could send human labour to cultivate those fertile regions; but this is not possible.

The Lancashire manufacturer is indebted to West Africa at once for cheap cotton and for a customer. It must be, for you, both farm and shop, plantation and market, and it must also supply the necessary labour. Everything, except the material capital, must be found on the spot. The human intellectual capital which you can supply from this country, is most expensive and most uncertain, and must in the course of time disappear. . . .

Well, as a market for your products, it is well known that West and Central Africa are unsurpassable, not simply for their geographical or territorial importance. Without the men it would be as valuable to you only as the Arctic regions are valuable as a place for scientific expeditions or for sport. Equatorial Africa must be for the African or for nobody. Therefore, you must foster the native—not coddle him—but don't kill him; study him, and teach him how to make the best use of his country. With your superior intelligence and experience, with your large scientific attainments, you must find out ways and means for energizing the industry of the people. They are, Sir Alfred Jones has said, the assets of this nation, and you are our assets. It is your part by judicious methods to create in the natives wholesome wants. Don't stimulate in them a desire for luxury, for that will defeat the end you have in view. The love of luxury will effeminate them and convert them into ambitious idlers, anxious to exploit the labour of others—always plotting and scheming, not to eat bread by the sweat of their own face but by the sweat of the face of others. . . .

Bibliography

SELECTED PUBLISHED WRITINGS OF EDWARD WILMOT BLYDEN CHRONOLOGICALLY ARRANGED.

Asterisks indicate which items were not used in this volume. In the case of articles which appeared in several publications, the original source and at least one other accessible source are given.

A Voice from Bleeding Africa on Behalf of Her Exiled Children, Monrovia: G. Killian, 1856. 33 pp.

A Vindication of the African Race, Monrovia: G. Killian, 1857. *Liberia's Offering* (1862), 31–64.

Liberia as She is, and the Present Duty of her Citizens, Monrovia: G. Killian, 1857. 21 pp.
African Repository (1857), 326–36.

A Eulogy pronounced on Rev. John Day, Monrovia: G. Killian, 1859.
Liberia's Offering (1862), 127–49.

"A Chapter in the History of the African Slave Trade", *Anglo-African Magazine* (June, 1859).
Liberia's Offering (1862), 151–67.

Hope for Africa, American Colonization Society: Washington, 1861. 18 pp.
African Repository (1861), 258–71.
Liberia's Offering (1862), 4–29.

"Inaugural Address at the Inauguration of Liberia College at Monrovia, January 23rd, 1862", *African Repository* (1862), 332–49.
Liberia's Offering (1862), 95–123.

The Call of Providence to the Descendants of Africa in America, New York, 1862.
Liberia's Offering (1862), 67–91.

African Colonization, Portland, Maine, 1862. 4 pp.
New York Colonization Journal (July, 1862).

Liberia's Offering, New York: John A. Gray, 1862. 167 pp.

335

Our Origin, Dangers and Duties, New York: John A. Gray, 1865. 42 pp.

The Pastor's Work, London: Dalton and Lucy, 1866. 24 pp.*

Liberia: Past, Present and Future, African Repository (1866), 353–70; Washington: McGill and Witherow, 1869. 27 pp.*

"Africa's Types and Promises", *African Repository* (1867), 289–97*

"Liberia as a Means, not an End", *African Repository* (1867), 321–41.

"The Negro in Ancient History", *Methodist Quarterly Review* (1869), 71–93.

The People of Africa, New York: Anson D. R. Randolph, 1871, 1–34.

"Mohammedanism in Western Africa", *Methodist Quarterly Review* (1871), 133–48.

The People of Africa (1871), 74–98.

Christianity, Islam and the Negro Race (1887), 173–88.

"Mixed Races in Liberia", *Smithsonian Institute Annual Report*, Washington, 1871, 386–8.

"The Boporo Country", *African Repository* (1871), 199–203; 236–42; 258–62; 321–37.

"Africa for the Africans", *African Repository* (1872), 14–20*

"The Republic of Liberia—its Status and its Field", *Methodist Quarterly Review* (1872), 466–90.

African Repository (1872), 257–69; 287–97.

The West African University: Correspondence between Edward W. Blyden . . . and His Excellency, J. Pope-Hennessy. . . . Freetown: "Negro" Printing Press, 1872. 17 pp,

"Report on the Expedition to Falaba (January to March, 1872)", *Journal of the Royal Geographic Society* (1873), 117–33.†

Report on the Timbo Expedition, 1873, London: Government Printer 1873. 18 pp.†

From West Africa to Palestine, Freetown: T. J. Sawyerr; Manchester: John Heywood, 1873. 201 pp.

† The original manuscripts of these two reports plus letters of Blyden while on these expeditions will appear in another volume entitled *Selected Letters and Manuscripts of Edward W. Blyden.*

"The Problems Before Liberia", *African Repository* (1874), 228–39.*

"The Prospects of the African", *African Repository* (1874), 295–307.*

"Mohammedanism and the Negro Race", *Fraser's Magazine* (1875), 598–615.
Christianity, Islam and the Negro Race (1887), 1–24.

"Christianity and the Negro Race", *Fraser's Magazine* (1876), 554–68.
Christianity, Islam and the Negro Race (1887), 25–45.

"Christian Missions in West Africa", *Fraser's Magazine* (1876), 504–22.
Christianity, Islam and the Negro Race (1887), 46–70.

"Islam and Race Distinctions", *Fraser's Magazine* (1876).
Christianity, Islam and the Negro Race (1887), 241–59.

"Liberia at the American Centennial", *Methodist Quarterly Review* (1877).*

"Africa and the Africans", *Fraser's Magazine* (1878), 178–96.*
Christianity, Islam and the Negro Race (1887), 260–83.

"Echoes from Africa", *The American Missionary*, December 1878, January and February 1879.
Christianity, Islam and the Negro Race (1887), 130–51.

"Africa's Service to the World", *African Repository* (1881), 109–25.
Christianity, Islam and the Negro Race (1887), 113–29.

The Aims and Methods of a Liberal Education for Africans, Cambridge, Mass.: John Wilson, 1882. 30 pp.
Christianity, Islam and the Negro Race (1887), 71–93. New York: George Young, 1920.

Report of the President of Liberia College to the Board of Trustees Cambridge, Mass.: John Wilson, 1882. 26 pp.

Christianity and the Negro Races, Washington: Union Bethel Literary and Historic Association, 1883. 12 pp.*

"The Origin and Purpose of African Colonization", *African Repository* (1883), 69–89.
Christianity, Islam and the Negro Race (1887), 94–112.

The Instruments and Methods of African Evangelization, Cambridge, Mass.: J. Wilson, 1883. 30 pp.*
African Repository (1884), 1–12; 50–9.
Christianity, Islam and the Negro Race (1887), 152–72.

Sierra Leone and Liberia; their Origin, Work and Destiny, London: John Heywood, 1884.
Christianity, Islam and the Negro Race, 189–240.

"The Mohammedans of Nigritia", *A.M.E. Church Review* (1887), 237–49; 411–18; 533–6.
Christianity, Islam and the Negro Race (1887), 306–36.

Christianity, Islam and the Negro Race, London: W. B. Whittingham, 1887. 373 pp. Second Edition, 1888. 432 pp.

"Latrobe's 'Maryland in Africa' ", *African Repository* (1887), 65–88.*

"The Historical Representation of Sierra Leone" (play) and "Centenary Ode", *Memorial of the Celebration of the Jubilee of Her Majesty's Reign and of the Centenary of Sierra Leone,* London: W. H. Whittingham, 1887, Appendix, 93–108.*

"The African Problem and the Method of its Solution", *African Repository* (1890), 65–80.

The African Problem and other discourses delivered in America in 1890, London: W. B. Whittingham, 1890. 104 pp.

The Elements of Permanent Influence, Washington: R. L. Pendleton, 1890. 18 pp.*

The Return of the Exiles and the West African Church, London: W. B. Whittingham, 1891. 39 pp.
African Repository (1892), 1–18.

England and the Black Race, Liverpool: The Geographic Society, 1892. 23 pp.*

A Chapter in the History of Liberia, Freetown: T. J. Sawyerr, 1892.
A.M.E. Church Review (1892), 48–72.

"Study and Race", *Sierra Leone Times,* May 27th, 1893.

"The African Problem", *North American Review* (1895), 327–39.

Lagos Training College and Industrial Institute, Lagos. *Correspondence between Edward W. Blyden*, L.L.D. [*sic*] *and His Excellency Sir Gilbert Carter*, K.C.M.G., Lagos: "Lagos Standard" Printing Office, 1896. 21 pp.

The Jewish Question, Liverpool, 1898. 24 pp.

"The Negro in the United States", *A.M.E. Church Review* (1900), 308–31.

"The Liberian Scholar", *Liberian Bulletin* (November, 1900), 11–22.

"Islam in the Western Soudan", *Journal of African Society* (October, 1902), 11–37.

Africa and the Africans. Proceedings on the Occasion of a Banquet . . . for Edward W. Blyden . . . by West Africans in London, London: C. M. Phillips, 1903. 69 pp.*

"The Native African—His Life and Work", *Liberia Bulletin* (February, 1904), 61–72.*

West Africa Before Europe and other Addresses, London: C. M. Phillips, 1905. 104 pp.

"The Koran in Africa", *Journal of the African Society* (January, 1905), 157–71.

Proceedings at the Banquet in Honour of E. W. Blyden . . . on the Occasion of his Retirement from his Official Labours in the Colony of Sierra Leone, London: C. M. Phillips, 1907. 64 pp.*

The Three Needs of Liberia, London: C. M. Phillips, 1908. 36 pp.

African Life and Customs, London: C. M. Phillips, 1908. 91 pp.

The Problems Before Liberia, London: C. M. Phillips, 1909. 32 pp.*

The Arabic Bible in the Soudan: A Plea for Transliteration, London: C. M. Phillips, 1910.*

Index

Abdul Hamid Khan, 304
Abomey, 318
Abu Abdallah, 308–9
Abu Ishak Assabi, 291
Abu'l Aswad, 300
Abyssinia, 281
Across Africa (Cameron), 169
Adams, 146, 147
*An Address before the Maine State
    Colonization Society, 1862* (Bly-
    den), 11–20
Afghanistan, 331
Africa, *see* Central Africa; North
    Africa; South Africa; West Africa
Africa and the Africans (Blyden),
    xxin.
"Africa's Service to the World", *see*
    "Ethiopia stretching out her hands
    unto God; or Africa's Service to
    the World" (Blyden)
African Life and Customs (Blyden),
    xxv, xxvii, xxxvi, 129, 163–81
"The African Problem" (Blyden),
    317–21
"The African Problem and the
    Method of its Solution" (Blyden),
    45–52
African Repository, 45, 63, 81, 85, 93
African Sketch Book (Reade), 285n.
African Society (London), xxxii, 327
Agbebi Mojola, 260n.
Ahmad Gouray, 304
Ahmadu Samadu, 284, 296–9, 331
Ahmadu Sofala, 298
*The Aims and Methods of a Liberal
    Education for Africans* (Blyden),
    231–45
Akbah, 281
Aku Tribe, 283
Alabama, 208
Alexander the Great, 145, 291
Alexander High School, xii, xv, 188,
    217, 248
Alexandria, 145–7, 157, 275, 276, 330
Alfiyeh (Ibn Malik), 300
Algeria, 224
Algiers, 333
Alkitab, see Koran

Allen, Samuel, xxxii
America, *see* Central America; South
    America; United States of America
American Bible Society, 277
American Civil War, *see* United
    States of America
American Colonization Society, xivn.,
    xxixn., xxxiii, xxxiv, 18, 19, 39, 42,
    45, 48, 50, 100–2, 108–9, 111, 115,
    135–6
*American Methodist Episcopal
    Church Review*, 53, 99
American Missionary Association,
    159
American Negro Academy, xxxii
American Philological Association,
    xxxii
American Revolution, *see* United
    States of America
American Society of Comparative
    Religion, xxxii
Anderson, Benjamin, 188n., 248, 279,
    295, *see also Narrative of a
    Journey to Musadu*
Anderson, W. Spencer, 95, 96
Anglo-African, 135
Antarah, 308
Anti-Lynching Committee (England),
    208
*Apology for African Methodism in
    the United States* (Tanner), 289n.
Appomattox, 46
Arabia, 36, 147, 279, 281, 284, 286,
    300, 305, 308–10
Aragon, 177
Arctic Ocean, 334
Aristotle, 267, 277
Armistead, 188
Arnold, Dr Mühleisen, 283n.
Ashantee, 176, 281, 285n., 296
Ashantee Wars, 286, 319
Ashmun, Jehudi, 101–2, 107–8, 136
The Assemblies of Al-Hariri (trans.
    Chenery), *see Makamat*
The Assemblies of Al-Hariri (trans.
    Steinglass), *see Makamat*
Athenaeum Club, xxxii
Athens, 198

Atlantic Ocean, 10, 17, 36, 83, 120, 154, 170, 186, 256, 281, 296, 299, 304, 310, 319, 332
Atterbury, Olivia Phelps, 250
Augustus, 188
Augustus, Emperor, 177
Australia, 82, 145
Austria, 83
Ayres, Dr Eli, 100, 101
Azikiwe, Dr Nnamdi, xxxiv, 61, 272, 316, *see also Liberia in World Politics*; *Renascent Africa*

Back-to-Africa Movement, xxxiv, 5, 61
Bacon, 200
Bagdad, 276, 291, 305, 333
Baird, Professor, 250
Bakai Ba, 305
Baker, Samuel, 159
Baltimore, 101
Bamah, *see* Boporo
Bantu Philosophy (Tempel), xxvii
Barbados, xiv
Barbary States, 142, 281
Barclay, Arthur, xvi, xviii, 123, 248
Barline Tribe, 95–6
Barrows, Dr J. H., 206
Barth, Dr Heinrich, 30, 237, 277, 279, 293, 295, 300–1, 303, *see also Collection of Central African Vocabularies*
Basle, 211
Bassa Cove, 105, 109–12, 114
Bassa Tribe, 41, 95, 96, 114, 116, 249
Beaconsfield, Lord, 197, 243
Beecher, Rev. T. K., 205
Beethoven, 197
"Behaviour Book" (Leslie), 14
Beirut, 157, 249
Belgian Congo, 47&n., 320
Bendu, 181
Benin, 176, 319
Benin, Bight of, 295
Benjamin, Judah P., 209
Benson, James (father of Stephen Allen Benson), 104, 108
Benson, James (brother of Stephen Allen Benson), 107
Benson, Joseph, 104
Benson, Stephen Allen, 8, 99, 104, 106–7, 112, 113, 117

Berlin, xx, 241
Berlin Conference (1884–5), 317, 318
Beyrout, *see* Beirut
Biafra, Bay of, 81
Bible, the, 178, 194, 206, 211, 242, 249, 259, 283n., 299
Bickersteth, E., 260n.
Big Boumba, 298
Bilah, 278n., 291
Bilâl, 299
Biographies of Ibn Khallikan (trans. Slane), 291n., 300n.
"Bishop Turner's African Dream" (Redkey), 4n.
Bismarck, 241, 323
Blackstone, 267
Blaize, R. B., 260n., 261
Blyden, the African Educationalist (Deniga), 218
Blyden of Liberia. An Account of the Life and Labors of Edward Wilmot Blyden, LL-D. As Recorded in Letters and Print (Holden), xin.
Boatswain, King, 85–6, 88
Bokma, *see* Boporo
Bokoma, *see* Boporo
Bombay, University of, 255
Bonaparte, Napoleon, 197, 267
Bonny, 319
Booth, William, 173
Boporo, xiii, 62, 82, 85–92, 241, 271, 276–9
"The Boporo Country" (Blyden), 85–92, 276n.
Bornou, 281, 282
Boston, 267n.
Boston University Papers on Africa (ed. Butler), 4n.
Bowen, Thomas J., 131–2, *see also Central Africa*
Bowrah, King, 85
Brass, 319
Brassey, Captain H., 105
Brazil, 36, 41, 100
Britain, and jurisdiction over Sierra Leone, xv, xix–xxi, 83, 112, 218, 224, 307, 319, 321, 323, 329, 332; and jurisdiction over Lagos, xv, 319, 321, 329, 330, 332; Blyden as ambassador to, xv, xvii–xviii; and

West African nationalism, xix–xxi, 315, 318–21, 323–5, 327–34; and jurisdiction over Gambia, xxi, 319; exploitation of African labour by, 35, 165; and trade with Liberia, 41, 111–12; exploration of Africa by, 47, 81, 317; and foundation of Liberia, 105–6, 111–12, 114, 119; political economy in, 121, 168, 170; and diplomatic relations with Liberia, 124, 137, 252; Constitution of, 125; and abolition of slave trade, 135, 319, 323; and *Regina Coeli* dispute, 138; penal system in, 175; and West African Church, 194, 227; Anti-Lynching Committee in, 208; and West African education, 218, 223–9, 250, 253–64, 272, 329; and jurisdiction over Western Soudan, 303, 319; and jurisdiction over Gold Coast, 319, 330; and Ashantee Wars, 319; and Niger Coast Protectorate, 319–20; and jurisdiction over Nigeria, 327–30; mentioned, xiv, xxiii, xxix, xxxiii, 209, 252, 297, 308
British East Africa Company, 320
Bromley, Peter, 107
Browne, Hugh Mason, 40n.
Brumskine, Walker, 99
Brussels Conference (1890), 317
Bryant, 197
Buchanan, 71
Buchanan, Thomas, 110–12
Bundo Society, 164–5, 181
Burns, Rev. Francis, 8
Burton, Richard, xxix
Bushrod Island, 102
Butaw, 106
Butler Bill, 47n.
Butler, Jeffrey, *see Boston University Papers on Africa*
Buxton, Sir Thomas Fowell, 197
Byron, Lord, 197
Byzantium, 293

Caillié, Réné, 292–3, 295
Cairo, 145–8, 150, 154–7, 276, 299, 305, 309
Calabar, *see* New Calabar; Old Calabar

Calcutta, University of, 255
The Call of Providence to the Descendants of Africa in America (Blyden), 25–33
Cambridge, University of, xxviii
Cameron, Lieutenant, 169–70, 237, *see also Across Africa*
Cameroon, 320
Canada, 29
Cape Coast, xxv, 105
Cape of Good Hope, 333
Cape Mesurado, 143
Cape Montserrado, 101, 107, 135
Cape Mount, 138
Cape Mount River, 89
Cape Palmas, 8
Capitein, J. E. J., xxvi
Cardew, Colonel Frederic, 321
Carib Tribe, 82
Carlyle, 277, *see also Heroes and Hero Worship*
Carter, Sir Gilbert T., xxiv&n., 253–64, 304, 321
Cary, Lott, 4, 103
Castile, 177
Caulcrick, H. A., 260n.
Cavalla River, 96
Central Africa, 19, 141, 273–4, 277–8, 281, 284, 286–7, 295, 301, 329, 331, 334
Central Africa (Bowen), 131n.
Central America, 18, 71, 100, 167
Césaire, Aimé, 186
Ceylon, 41, 100
Chad, Lake, xxi
Chamberlain, Joseph, 323–4
Chambers, J. T., 188
"A Chapter in the History of the African Slave-Trade" (Blyden), 135–9
"A Chapter in the History of Liberia" (Blyden), 99–117
Chatham, 114
Cheeseman, Rev. John H., 99, 113
Chenery, Thomas, *see The Assemblies of Al-Hariri*
Chicago, xxxvi
Chicago, University of, 206
China, 36, 145, 283, 285n.
Chitty, 267
Christian Advocate, 206
Christianity, Islam and the Negro Race (Blyden), xi, xvn., xxn.,

xxviin., xxviii, xxxn., xxxin.,
xxxivn., 35, 39, 129, 159, 231, 273,
281, 295
Church Missionary Society, xxiii–
xxiv, 143, 253
Cicero, 37, 176, 177
Clapperton, 295
Clay, 267
Clopton, Rev., 69
Coker, Daniel, 4
Cole, Julius Ojo, see Dr Edward
Wilmot Blyden, an Interpretation
Coleman, 265
Collection of Central African
Vocabularies (Barth), 279n.
College for the Education of Sons
of Chiefs and of Interpreters, 328
College of William and Mary, 221
Colophon, 290n.
Colston, 188
Comdo Tribe, 85&n.
Congo, Belgian, see Belgian Congo
Congo River, 310
Congo Tribe, 249, 285n.
Constantine, Emperor, 193
Constantinople, 193, 286, 329
Coppinger, xxixn.
Cornell University, 247
Cotton Growing Association, 334
Cresson, Elliot, 109
Crisis, xxxiv
Crowther, Bishop Samuel, xxiii–
xxiv, 192, 197, 299
Crummell, Rev. Alexander, xxviii–
xxix, xxxiii, 9
Cuffee, Paul, 4

Dahomey, 91, 176, 296, 318, 332
Dakar, 330, 333
Dales, 147
Damascus, 281
Darfur, 282
Darmesteter, James, see Selected
Essays
Dartmouth University, 247
Davies, Aaron P., 99
Davies, J. L., xxivn.
Davis, Jennie E., 41
Day, Rev. John, 6k, 67–75, 99,
111–13
De Tocqueville, see Democracy in
America

Decazes, 305
Decline and Fall of the Holy Roman
Empire (Gibbon), 276, 281n.
Delany, Martin R., 4
Democracy in America (De Tocque-
ville), 221&n.
Denham, 295
Deniga, A., see Blyden the African
Educationalist
Denmark, 83, 176, 209
Deutsch, Emmanuel, 276n.
Dey Tribe, 95
D'Lyon, Samuel, 188
Dostoevsky, Fyodor, xxx
Douglass, Frederick, xxvi–xxvii,
xxxiii, 9, 53–4
Dr Edward Wilmot Blyden, an
Interpretation (Cole), 218
Draper, Araminta, 103, 104
Dress Reform Society (Freetown),
xxv
Dring, Captain, 112
Dubois, Felix, 303, 305, 308–9, see
also Timbuctoo the Mysterious
DuBois, Dr William E. B., xxxiii–
xxxiv
Dumas, Alexander, 8
Durham, University of, xxiii

East Indies, 29
Eastern Church (Stanley), 293n.
Eaton, Hon. John, 250
Eboe Tribe, 55&n.
Ebute Metta, 255, 257, 262
"Echoes from Africa" (Blyden),
159–61
Edina, 109, 110, 116
Edinburgh, 109
The Edinburgh Review, 317
Edward Wilmot Blyden, Pan-Negro
Patriot 1832–1912 (Lynch), xin.,
xxxivn., 316n.
Egypt, xxvii, 27, 37, 47, 129, 142,
145–57, 167, 200, 227, 267, 271,
275, 278–9, 281, 286, 296, 309–10
El-Medineh, 147
England, see Britain
Essays on Eastern Questions (Pal-
grave), 292, 293n.
Essays on the Inequality of the
Races (Gobineau), xxix
Essays and Reviews (Hodge), 294n.

Ethiopia, xvii, 20, 35–7, 278n.
"Ethiopia stretching out her hands unto God; or Africa's Service to the World" (Blyden), xxvii, 35–7
Ethiopian, xxv
Euclid, 152
A Eulogy pronounced on the Reverend John Day (Blyden), 67–75
Euphrates River, 317
Evangelical Alliance, 147
Evans, James H., 188

Factory Island, 108, 116
Fahqueh-queh, 241
Faidherbe, General, 328
Falaba, xx, 272, 297–9
Fanfidoreh, 241
Fanti Customary Laws (Sarbah), xxv, 129
Fanti National Constitution (Sarbah), 129
Fenian Movement, 79
Fez, 301, 305, 309
Fichte, xxx
Finley, Josiah P., 110, 111
Fish War (1838), *see* Liberia
Fishmen, 110–12
Fishtown, 110, 114
Fleming, 200
Florida, 208
Fostat, 156
Foulah-town, 285
Foulah Tribe, 41, 95, 274, 277, 283, 287, 297, 300, 304, 305
Fourah Bay 100
Fourah Bay College, xxiii
Fra Angelico, 289
France, Blyden as diplomatic envoy to, xviii; and jurisdiction over Guinea, xviii, 330, 332; and jurisdiction over Ivory Coast, xviii, 324, 332; diplomatic relations with Liberia, xviii, 83, 114, 124, 129, 137–8, 324; and expansion in the Sudan, xxi, 165, 318; and jurisdiction over Senegal, xxi, 81, 304, 305, 318, 328–9, 332, 333; and imperialist policies in Africa, xxi, 36, 81, 124n., 318, 324–5, 332–3; mentioned, 8, 94, 119, 303
Franco-Liberian Treaty (1892), 324

Fraser's Magazine, 281
Frederick Douglass' Paper, 206
Freeman, Professor Martin H., 187&n.
Freetown, xx, xxiii–xxv, xxxi, 100, 145, 223, 226, 298, 330
French Revolution, 239
From West Africa to Palestine (Blyden), 145–57, 210
Froude, 239
Fryzon, 188
Fulindiyah, 297
Fuller, T. C., 248
Futah, 227, 282, 286
Futah Jallo, 282, 308
Futah Toro, 284, 296

Gaboon, 100
Galilee, 178
Gallagher, Rev. Thomas, 250
Gallinas, 94, 95
Gambetta, 241
Gambia, xxi, 277, 319, 329
Gando, 303
Gardner, A. W., 113, 252
Garibaldi, 79
Garnet, Henry Highland, 4
Garvey, Marcus, xxxiv&n., 5, 61, 185, *see also A Talk with Afro-West Indians: The Negro Race and Its Problems*
Gebeh, 89
Georgia, 119, 123, 208
Germany, nationalism in, xxx, 79; and expansion in Africa, 36, 47, 318, 320, 325; and diplomatic relations with Liberia, 41, 119, 124
Ghana, xxi, 129, 186, 316, *see also* Gold Coast
Gibbon, 239, 276, *see also Decline and Fall of the Holy Roman Empire*
Gibraltar, 27
Gibson, 252
Giotto, 289
Gladstone, 197, 241
Gobineau, Count Arthur de, *see Essays on the Inequality of the Races; the Moral and Intellectual Diversity of Races*
Gogommah, Chief, 88
Golah Tribe, 85, 88, 244

Gold Coast, xxi, 201n., 319, 325, 330, *see also* Ghana
Gold Coast Institutions (Hayford), xxv, 129
Gordon, Midshipman, 105, 106
Granada, 305
Grand Bassa, 62, 71, 72, 95, 99, 100, 108–16, 119
Grand Cape Mount, 95
Grand Sesters, 96
Grant, William, xx, xxi, 218, 223–5
Granville, Lord, 252
Grebo Tribe, 41, 96
Greece, Ancient, 151, 152, 198–200, 203, 239–41, 267, 283
Green, 239
Greener, Richard T., xxxiii
Grimke, Dr Francis, xxxiii, 205
Guiana, 167
Guinea, xviii, 330, 332
Gurley, *see Life of Ashmun*

Haiti, xv, xxvi, 8, 18, 68, 83, 286&n.
Al-Hajj Ahmed Sek, 305
Al-Hajj Omaru, 271, 284–5, 296&n.
Hale, 146
Hallam, 239, 276, *see also Middle Ages*
Hamd-Allahi, 284
Hamilton, 47
Hampton Roads, 102
Hamzah, 308
Hankinson, Edward Y., 109, 110
Hanson, John, 99, 113
Al-Hariri, *see Makamat*
Harlem, xxxiv
Harris, J. H., 188
Harris, Joseph, 109
Harris, Nathaniel, 111
Harris, Peter, 109
Harrisburg, xv
Harvard University, xxxiii, 247
Hausa, 281, 282
Hausa Tribe, 283, 286, 304
Hawaii, 197
Haweis, 292, *see also Music and Morals*
Hawkins, Ann, 103–4
Hawkins, Daniel, 104
Hayes, 241
Hayford, J. E. Casely, xxxiv, 316, *see also Gold Coast Institutions*

Heber, Bishop, 294n.
Heddle, Charles, 112
Hegel, xxx, xxxii
Hennessey, John Pope, 218, 226–9, 254, 263
Henrico, University of, 221
Henry, Charles, 99
Henry, John, 188
Henry, Patrick, 22, 47, 68
Herder, xxx
Herodotus, 151, 152, 154, 281
Heroes and Hero Worship (Carlyle), 277n.
Herring, Rev. Amos, 113
Herring, S. S., 99
Herzl, Theodor, 211
Hibbert Lectures (Renan), 37n.
Hippocrates, 277
Historical Society of Pennsylvania, xxxvi
History of Liberia (Johnston), 120
History of the Saracens (Ockley), 291n.
Hodge, Dr Charles, 294n., *see also Essays and Reviews*
Holden, Edith, *see Blyden of Liberia. An Account of the Life and Labors of Edward Wilmot Blyden, LL-D. As Recorded in Letters and Print*
Homer, 151, 152
Horace, 177
Hose, Samuel, 53
Houdas, Professor, 303
Howard University, xxxvi
Hugo, Victor, 35
Hungary, 79
Hunt, James, xxix, *see also On the Negro's Place in History*
Hussey Charity, 263

Ibn Batoutah, 281–2, 292, 303
Ibn Khallikan, 284, 291, *see also Biographies of Ibn Khallikan* (trans. Slane)
Ibn Malik, *see Alfiyeh*
Ibn Muslimeh, 292
Ibo Tribe, *see* Eboe Tribe
Ibrahima Sisi, 97
Idrisu, 303
Illorin, 295

"Inaugural Address at the Inauguration of Liberia College at Monrovia, January 23, 1862" (Blyden), 219-22
India, Indians, 21, 36, 145, 189, 255, 285n., 294n., 308
Infalli, 299
Inquisition the Spanish, 177
International Review, 250
Ireland, 243
Irving, *see Successors of Mahomet*
"Islam in the Western Soudan" (Blyden), 303-6
Ita, Eyo, xxxiv
Italy, xxx, 47, 79
Ivory Coast, xviii, 324, 332

Jackson, Captain, 111
Jackson, John P., 260n.
Jalof Tribe, 274, 277, 300, 304, 305
Jamaica, xxxiv, 61
James, Frederick, 101
Japan, 36, 145, 180, 197
Jefferson, 47, 68
Jenne, 284
Jerusalem, 156, 178, 210, 278n.
Jeter, Rev. J. B., 69
The Jewish Question (Blyden), xxxi-xxxii, 209-14
Johnson, Elijah, xvii, 4
Johnson, Hilary R. W., xvii
Johnson, James, 192, 260n.
Johnson, Henry, 260n.
Johnson, Dr Wesley, 110, 116
Johnston, Sir Henry, *see History of Liberia*
Jolloff Tribe, 164
Jones, Sir Alfred, 331&n., 334
Josephus, 289
Journal of the African Society, 124, 303, 307
Journal of American History, 4n.
Julius Caesar, 175, 176

Kairawan, 318
Kalish, Dr Isidor, 210
Kankan, 241, 276, 277, 289, 295
Kanó, 279, 285, 287, 295, 301, 330
Karamazin, xxx
Kent, 267
Kimberley, Lord, 254, 263

King-Harman, Sir C. A., 305, 328
Kingsley, Mary, 124&n., 324-5, *see also Travels in West Africa; West African Studies*
Kishnieff, 176
Knight, 253
Koelle, Rev. S. W., 95&n., 143, *see also Polyglotta Africana*
Kohn, Hans, *see Prophets and Peoples: Studies in Nineteenth-century Nationalism*
Konia, 297
Koran, the, 87, 170, 271, 275-8, 282-3, 287-9, 297, 299, 301, 304-5, 307-11, 331
"The Koran in Africa" (Blyden), 307-11
Kordofan, 282
Kossuth, 79
Kroo Tribe, 41, 95, 96, 105, 106, 109, 110, 114, 244, 249
Kuka, 287

Lafayette, General, 115
Lagos, British jurisdiction over, xv, 319, 321, 329; Blyden's residence in, xv, xxii, xxiv, xxv, 217, 253-64, 271, 304; education in, xvi, xxiv, 217, 253-64, 271, 329; cultural nationalism, in xxv; Muslim influence in, 271, 274, 304, 310, 329, 330; internal communications in, 332; mentioned, 218, 299
Lagos Echo, 263
Lagos Standard, 263
The Lagos Training College and Industrial Institute (Blyden), 253-64
Lagos Weekly Record, xxv, 263
Lagrange, 250
Laing, Captain, 105, 106, 295
Lancashire, 35, 334
Lander, John, 47, 295, 317
Lander, Richard, 47, 295, 317
Lansing, Rev., 147
Lasanna, Chief, 88
Lawson, Thomas G., 298
Lecky, 239
Leigh, J. S., 260n.
Leist, 320
Leo Africanus, 303

Leone, J. W., 188
Leslie, see "Behaviour Book"
A Letter to Booker T. Washington (Blyden), 205–8
"A Letter to the *Liberia Herald*, New York, July 5, 1862" (Blyden), 21–3
Levant, 281
Lewis, Samuel, xxi, 196
Liberia, Blyden's career in, xi–xix, xxii, xxiv, 3, 61–2, 130, 153, 209–10, 217–18; foundation of, xii, 11–13, 99–111; becomes independent Republic, xii, 61, 72–3, 111–17; black American emigration to, xii–xiii, xix, xx, xxvi, xxxii, xxxiii, xxxv, 3–5, 21–3, 25n.,29, 30, 33, 39, 42–3, 45–52, 100–2, 110–11, 119–25, 132–3, 135–6, 187–9, 210, 237, 315; boundary dispute with Sierra Leone, xiv, xvi, 83&n.; boundary dispute with Guinea, xviii; boundary dispute with Ivory Coast, xviii, 324; role in West Africa of, xix–xxi, 3–5, 79; and pan-Africanism, xx–xxi, 3–5, 61; racial divisions in, xxviii–xxix, 17, 185, 187–9; Whig party in, xxviii; Republican party in, xxviii; and suppression of the slave trade, 7–10, 97–8, 129, 135–9; Christian influence in, 19, 48, 82, 86–7, 98, 115, 116, 122–3, 143, 286; indigenous inhabitants of, 40, 48, 61–2, 81–2, 85–92, 94–8, 100–17, 119–25, 136–9, 187; education in, 40–1, 48, 115, 116, 187–9, 217–22, 231–45, 247–52, 265–8; natural resources of, 41, 48; trade of, 41, 48, 99–100, 111–12; Muslim influence in, 62, 271, 276, 277, 279, 307; position of foreigners in, 63–5, 82; the Rev. John Day's career in, 67–75; Constitution of, 77–9, 93–4, 113, 115, 123–5; and international relations, 82–4, 124, 138; *Regina Coeli* dispute with France, 83, 138; and Padee War (1861), 106; and Fish War (1838), 110; method of government in, 115–17; adoption of African principles of life in, 119–25; agricultural system in, 121–2; modern cultural developments in, 142–3, 152; and

Franco-Liberian Treaty (1892), 324; mentioned, 295, 296
Liberia Bulletin, 265
Liberia College, xiii, xv–xvi, xxiv, 40–1, 187–8, 210, 217–22, 231–45, 247–52, 265–8, 271
Liberia Herald, xii, xxv, 21, 115
"Liberia as a Means, Not an End" (Blyden), 81–4
Liberia as She is; and the Present Duty of her Citizens (Blyden), 63–5
Liberia in World Politics (Azikiwe), 61
"The Liberian Scholar" (Blyden), 265–8
Liberia's Offering (Blyden), xiiin., 25, 131, 135, 219
Libya, 148, 156
Life of Ashmun (Gurley), 136n.
Life of Heber (Taylor), 294n.
Life of Mahomet (Muir), 291n.
Liles, Edward, 113
Limba, 298
Lincoln, Abraham, 47, 83, 120, 323
Lincoln University, xxxii
Little Cape Mount, 94, 95
Little Popo, 325
Liverpool, xxxi, 105, 209, 320–1, 323, 330–2
Livingstone, Dr, 47, 197, 207, 237, 317
Lome, 325
London, Blyden's residence in, xvii–xviii, xxxii; *Quarterly Review* published in, 276n.; Chambers of Commerce in, 321; African Society of, xxxii, 327; mentioned, xxviii, xxxiii, 112, 143, 146–7, 156, 159, 163, 191, 201n., 207, 231, 241, 273, 281, 285–6, 291, 295, 323
Longfellow, 197, see also *St Augustine's Ladder*
L'Ouverture, Toussaint, xv, xxvi, 8, 197
Lowell, 197, 206
Lower Buchanan, 119
Lowrie, xvn.
Lugard, Sir Frederick, 317, 327–30
Lumpkin, C. J., 260n.
Lynch, Hollis R., see *Edward Wilmot Blyden, Pan-Negro Patriot*,

1832–1912; "Pan-Negro Nationalism in the New World Before 1862"

Macaulay, Herbert, xxxiv, 272, 316
Macaulay, Lord, 197, 198, 200, 225, 239
Macaulay, Zachary, 253, 254
McClellan, 15
Macdonald, Sir Claude, 319
McDowell, Dr, 110
McGill, George R., 88
McGill, Hon. J. B., 88
Madras, University of, 255
Madrid, 83
Mage, Lieutenant, see Voyage d'Exploration dans le Soudan Occidental
Mahmudi Daranii, 298, 299
Maine, 11, 21, 25n.
Makamat (Hariri trans. Chenery), 277, 292n., 300, 308n.
Makamat (Hariri trans. Steinglass), 308n.
Manchester, 145, 321
Manding, 244
Mandingo Tribe, 41, 85–9, 91, 94–7, 143, 244, 249, 274, 277–9, 283, 285n., 287, 289, 296–7, 300, 304–5, 331
Manna, 138
Mano-Salija, 180
Marcus Aurelius, 167
Marfah Bay, 181
Marmora, 22
Martinique, 186, 318
Marvi, Chief, 88
Marvo, 90
Maryland, 106
Masina, 282, 284
Maxwell, Joseph Renner, 201n., see also The Negro Question or Hints for the Physical Improvement of the Negro Race
Mazzini, xxx, 79
Mecca, 156, 279, 284, 286, 296, 304, 305, 329–31
Mechlin, Joseph, 108
Medina, 97, 241, 276, 308
Mediterranean Sea, 145, 281, 296, 304, 310, 332

Melville, 188
Mendi Tribe, 95
Mesurado River, 249
The Methodist Quarterly Review, xxvii, 141, 273
Mexico, 36, 79
Michelangelo, 197
Middle Ages (Hallam), 276n.
Miller, 188
Milton, John, 197, 239
Mischat ul-Masabih, 289n.
Missouri, 250
"Mixed Races in Liberia" (Blyden), 187–9
Mohammed Ali, 155–7
Mohammed Sanusi, 305
Mohammed and Mohammedanism (Smith), 285n.
"Mohammedanism and the Negro Race" (Blyden), 272, 281–94
"Mohammedanism in Western Africa" (Blyden), 271–9
"The Mohammedans of Nigritia" (Blyden), 295–301
Momodu Wakka, 305, 331
Momoru Sou, 85–92
Monrovia, xii, xv, xxvi, 7, 63, 67, 77, 81, 86, 95, 97, 101–11, 119, 122, 138, 143, 187, 219, 231, 250, 276n., 279
Montserrado, 101, 105, 109, 110, 112
Montserrado River, 100
Montserrado Roads, 138
Moore, Admiral, 333
Moore, Gabriel, 248
Moore, James, 99, 113
Moore, Richard, xxxiv
The Moral and Intellectual Diversity of Races (Gobineau), xxixn.
Morocco, 286, 287, 292, 301, 309
Morris, Edward S., xvii-xviii
Mount of Beatitudes, 178
Mount Zion, 210
Mozambique, 156
Mozart, Wolfgang Amadeus, 197
Muallakat, the, 293, 299–300, 308
Muhammed Wakka, 249n.
Muir, see Life of Mahomet
Musadoreh, 89
Musadu, 82, 241, 248, 249, 276, 277, 279, 295
Museilama, 308
Music and Morals (Haweis), 292n.

Narrative of a Journey to Musadu (Anderson), 188n.
Natal, 100
Nation, 250
Nazareth, 178
Negro, xxv, 225
"The Negro in Ancient History" (Blyden), xxvii, 141–3
The Negro Question or Hints for the Physical Improvement of the Negro Race (Maxwell), 201n.
"The Negro in the United States" (Blyden), 53–7
New Calabar, 319
New-Cess, 137
New England, 146, 221, 251
New York, xxxvi, 21, 25, 77, 131, 135, 141, 188n., 250, 267n., 290
New York Age, xxxv, 205
New York Colonization Journal, 11, 21
New York Colonization Society 186n., 248
New Zealand, 82
Newton, Commander, 112
Nicene Council, 193
Niger Coast Protectorate, 319–20
Niger River, xxiii–xxiv, 47, 81, 192, 224, 244, 272, 287, 295, 296, 303, 317, 319
Nigeria, xxi, 55n., 61, 272, 306, 316, 327, 329, 330
Nigritia, 281, 284, 295–301
Nile River, 146–8, 156, 317, 319
Nkrumah, Kwame, xxx, xxxiv, 186, 316
North Africa, 281–2, 284, 296, 318, 332
North American Review, 317
North Carolina, 68
Northern Baptist Board of Missions, 71
Northwestern University, xxxvi
Norway, 83
Nubia, 281
Nupe, 301

Ockley, *see History of the Saracens*
Official Journal, 286n.
Ohud, Battle of, 308
Old Calabar, 319
On the Negro's Place in History (Hunt), xxixn.

Opobo, 319
"The Origin and Purpose of African Colonization" (Blyden), 39–43
Osiut, 147
Our Origin, Dangers and Duties (Blyden), 77–9
Overweg, 295
Oxford, University of, 198

P. & O. Company, 145
Padee War (1861), *see* Liberia
Padmore, George, xxxiv
Paine, Thomas, 283n.
Pakroyah, Chief, 88
Palaka, 96
Palestine, 213
Palgrave, Gifford, 147, 292, 293n., *see also Essays on Eastern Questions*
Pan-African Conference (1900), xxxiii–xxxiv
"Pan-Negro Nationalism in the New World Before 1862" (Lynch), 4n.
Panofsky, Hans, xxxvi
Paris, xviii, 115, 241
Park, Mungo, 47, 160, 273–4, 295, *see also Travels*
Payne, Edmund J., 188
Payne, J. A. Otunba, 260n.
Payne, James S., xvii, 9
Pennington, Rev. J. W. C., 9
The People of Africa (Blyden), 141
Perseverance Island, 86, 100
Persia, xviii, 36, 156, 283, 331
Pesseh Tribe, 95, 244
Petion, 8
Philadelphia, 21
Phoenicia, Phoenicians, 281
Plato, xvii, 151, 267, 277, *see also The Republic*
Plymouth, 221
Poland, 79
Polyglotta Africana (Koelle), 95n., 284
Porroh Society, 165, 181
Porter, Dorothy, xxxv
Portland, 11, 21, 25n.
Portugal, 141
Pre-Adamite Man (Winchell), 237n.
Presbyterian Board of Foreign Missions, xvn.
Princeton Review, 250

Princeton Theological College, xii, 217, 294
Prophets and Peoples: Studies in Nineteenth-century Nationalism (Kohn), xxxn.
Puskin, Alexander, 8
Pythagoras, 151, 267

Qualu Creek, 181
Quarterly Review, 276n.
Quilliam, William H. Abdullah, 304, 330–1

Rand, Matthew A., 99, 113
Randolph, 68
Raphael, 197, 289
Reade, Winwood, 295, *see also African Sketch Book*
Red Sea, 295, 304, 310
Redkey, Edwin S., *see* "Bishop Turner's African Dream"
Renan, *see Hibbert Lectures*
Renascent Africa (Azikiwe), 61
Report of the President of Liberia College to the Board of Trustees (Blyden), 247–52
The Republic (Plato), 199
"The Republic of Liberia—its Status and its Field" (Blyden), 93–8
Republican Party (Liberia), xxviii
Republican Party (United States of America), xxviii
The Return of the Exiles and the West African Church (Blyden), 191–4
Richardson, N. A., 86
Richardson, N. R., 188
Richardson, Rev. Robert B., 248
Richmond, 15, 69, 122
Ripon, Lord, 323
Roberts, James H., 188
Roberts, Joseph J., xxviii, 8, 93, 111, 114, 116–17
Roberts, J. J. jr., 188
Rocky Mountains, 50
Rogers, Col. W. K., 250
Rome, Ancient, 37, 167, 177, 178, 193, 203, 239–41, 267, 283
Roosevelt University, xxxvi
Roumania, 224
Roume, 305, 328, 333

Royal Niger Company, 320
Roye, Edward James, xiv
Russell, Beverly, 188
Russia, xxx, 8, 83, 176, 177, 293, 317
Russwurm, John B., 4, 8, 115

Sabsu, *see* Boatswain, King
Sahara Desert, 281, 299
St Augustine's Ladder (Longfellow), 149&n.
St John River, 95, 108, 110
St Louis (Senegal), 304, 328, 330, 333
St Paul River, xv, 87, 89, 107, 249
St Thomas, xii, 3, 209, 210
Salvation Army, 173n.
Samadu, *see* Ahmadu Samadu
Samori Toure, 271, 272
Samory, *see* Samadu
Sanankodu, 297
Santo Domingo, 79
Sarbah, John Mensah, *see Fanti Customary Laws; Fanti National Constitution*
Sartre, Jean-Paul, xxxii
Savage, J. A., 260n.
Schmettau, Rev., 147
Scotland, 251
Sego, 241, 284, 295
Seka Ahmadu, 271
Selected Essays (Darmesteter), 212
Senaar, 282
Senegal, xxi, 81, 186, 274, 277, 279, 303–5, 318, 328–9, 331–3
Sengkor, Leopold, 186
Seville, 177
Sewah, King, 298
Seymour, George L., 295
Shakespeare, William, 197, 239
Sherbro, 100
Sheridan, Louis, 111
Sherman, R. A., 248
Sierra Leone, and diplomatic relations with Liberia, xiv, xvi, 100, 101, 105, 112; British jurisdiction over, xv, xix–xxi, 83, 112, 319, 321, 323, 329; Blyden's residence in, xv, xix–xx, xxii, xxiii, xxxi, 208, 217, 223–9, 254, 271–2, 328; education in, xvi, xxii, xxiv, 217, 218, 223–9, 249&n., 253–4, 263,

271–2, 328, 329; Porroh Society in, 165; Young Men's Literary Association in, 195; Muslim communities in, 272, 282, 285&n., 286, 307, 310, 329; internal communications in, 332; mentioned, 71, 95, 143, 295, 297–9, 305, 324, 331
Sierra Leone Times, xxxv, 195
Sierra Leone Weekly News, xxv, 263
Simms, James L., 96, 295
Simoro, 241
Sinai, 150
Sinidudu, King, 297
Sinoe, 106, 110, 112
Sissi, Abrahima, 241
Skinner, Dr Ezekial, 110
Slane, Baron de, *see Biographies of Ibn Khallikan*
Smith, Bosworth, 285–6, *see also Mohammed and Mohammedanism*
Smith, Dr J. S., 99
Smithsonian Institute, 23, 187, 250
Smyth, Hon. John H., 250
Society of Sciences and Letters of Bengal, xxxii
Socrates, 267
Sokoto, 279, 284n., 295, 330
Solon, 151
Some Problems of West Africa (Blyden), 327–34
Soolima, 297, 298
Soosoo Tribe, 283
Soudan, xxi, 35, 97, 165, 281, 296, 298, 303–6, 308–10, 318, 319, 332
South Africa, 203
South America, 18, 29, 167, 234, 286
South Carolina, 119, 123, 208
Southern Baptist Convention, 71
Southern Workman, 205
Spain, 83, 177, 180
Spencer, Herbert, 235
Spinn, Thomas, 104
Spurgeon, 21
Stanley, Dean, 289n., 293, *see also Eastern Church*
Stanley, H. M., 47, 159–61, 170, 207, 237
Steinglass, *see The Assemblies of Al-Hariri*
Stewart, Thomas McCants, 40n.
Stowe, Harriet Beecher, 17
Strang, David, 147–8, 155
Stubbs, 239

"Study and Race" (Blyden), xxxi, xxxv, 195–204
Sublung, 88
Successors of Mahomet (Irving), 278n.
Sudan, *see* Soudan
Sugary, 181
Suluku, 298
Suna Society, 164
Sweden, 83, 176
Swinburne, 197, 251
Syria, 156, 278, 279, 286

A Talk with Afro-West Indians: The Negro Race and Its Problems (Garvey), xxxivn.
Talmud, the, 210
Tanganyika, Lake, 160
Tanner, *see Apology for African Methodism in the United States*
Tarik e Soudan, 303
Tarplan, 114
Taylor, *see Life of Heber*
Tchad, 81, 281
Tchad, Lake, 295, 303
Teage, Hilary, 8, 152, 153
Temne, 310
Tempel, Rev. Placide, *see Bantu Philosophy*
Tennyson, Alfred, Lord, 197
Thales, 151
Thomas, J. J., 260n.
The Three Needs of Liberia (Blyden), 119–25
Tijani, Sheikh, 284
Timbo, xx, 272, 285n., 295
Timbuctoo, 227, 281, 284, 287, 292, 295, 305
Timbuctoo the Mysterious (Dubois), 303n., 305n., 309n.
Times, 207
Tines, Mary, 104
Titian, 197
Titler, Ephraim, 113
Togoland, 325
Toledo, 177
Torquemada, 177
Tosoru, Chief, 88
Toto-Coreh, 279
Toto-Korie, 91
"Toussaint L'Ouverture, the Emancipator of Haiti" (Blyden), xv

Trade Town, 105, 115
Traditions of Bochari, 301
Travels (Park), 160&n., 274n., 295
Travels in West Africa (Kingsley), 124n.
Tripoli, 299
Trollope, Anthony, 17, 18
Tunis, 309
Turkey, 145, 275, 283, 308, 331
Turner, Bishop Henry McNeil, xxxiii, 4, 53–6, 206
Turner, Nathaniel, 68
Tuskegee, 208
Tyre, 145

Uganda, 181
United States of America, Blyden's influence in, xi, xxviii, xxxii, xxxiv, 3–5, 185; Blyden's residence in, xii, xiv, xxix, 185, 209; and black American emigration to Liberia, xii–xiii, xix, xx, xxvi, xxxii, xxxiii, xxxv, 3–5, 21–3, 25n., 29, 30, 33, 39, 41–3, 45–52, 100–2, 110–11, 119–25, 132–3, 135–6, 187–9, 210, 237, 315; Civil War in, xiii, 4, 57; abolition of slavery in, xiii, 45–7, 120, 189, 197, 323; Blyden's visits to, xv, xxvii, xxxii, xxxiii, 3, 21–3, 25n., 35n., 211; and connections with Liberia College, xv–xvi, 217, 218, 222, 233, 247, 249, 250, 252, 266, 267; Booker T. Washington's work in, xviii, xxxiii, xxxv, 57, 185, 205–8; exploitation of Negroes in, xxvii, xxviii, 3–4, 9–33, 35–6, 53–7, 123, 141–2, 234, 236; evangelism among Negroes in, xxviii, 272, 286, 290; Back-to-Africa Movement in, xxxiv, 5, 61; Revolution in, 22, 68; and trade with Liberia, 41; position of American Indians in, 82, 221; and diplomatic relations with Liberia, 83, 114, 124; circulation of Liberia Herald in, 115; literature in, 197; size of Negro population in, 203; mentioned, 113, 116, 146, 147, 171, 194, 224, 244, 274, 296, 325
Usuman dan Fodio, 271, 284&n.

Van Dyck, 151
Venezuela, xii, 3, 36
Venn, Rev. Henry, 253
Vey Tribe, 41, 94–5, 142–3, 170, 180, 244
Vienna, 211
A Vindication of the African Race (Blyden), xxvii, 131–3
Virgil, 16, 152, 177
Virgin Islands, xii, 3
Virginia (Liberia), 107
Virginia (United States of America), 68, 69, 119, 122, 123, 221
Vogel, 295
A Voice from Bleeding Africa on Behalf of Her Exiled Children (Blyden), xxvi–xxvii, 7–10
Voice of Missions, 56
Voltaire, 283n.
Vonswah, 86, 249
Voyage d'Exploration dans le Soudan Occidental (Mage), 296n.

Waday, 282
Wahshi, 308
Wakora, see Grand Cape Mount
Walters, Bishop Alexander, xxxiv
Ward, Rev. Samuel R., 9
Waring, 188
Warner, Daniel Bashiel, xiv, 8
Warsaw, 176
Washington, Booker T., xviii, xxxiii, xxxv, 57, 185, 205–8
Washington, George, 47
Washington, Portia, xviii
Washington D.C., 21–3, 25n., 45, 54, 205, 211, 241
Wasulu, 297
Weaver, William L., 99, 111, 113
Webster, 267
West Africa, Blyden's influence in, xii, xiv–xvi, xix–xxvi, xxxii, xxxiv, xxxv, 209; Muslim influence in, xix, xxii, xxxv, 271–311, 328–31; Christian influence in, xix, xxii, xxxv, 123, 179–81, 191–4, 214, 227; cultural nationalism in, xix, xxii–xxvi, xxxiv, 218, 316; and pan-Africanism, xx–xxi, xxvi–xxx, xxxiii–xxxv; role of newspapers in, xxiv–xxvi, 179, 263; European imperialism in, xxxv, 179, 315–34; trade in, 99–100, 173; history of

people of, 129, 141–3, 153, 179–81, 185; higher education in, 218–29, 231–45, 247–68, 328–9; mentioned, xviii, 4, 50, 95, 96, 119, 202, 208

West Africa (Blyden), 323–6

West Africa Before Europe (Blyden), 323, 327

West African Conference (1884–5), xxi

West African Reporter, xxn., xxv, 298

West African Studies (Kingsley), 124n.

The West African University (Blyden), 223–9, 254n.

West Indies, Blyden's birth in, xi, 3, 209; emigration to Liberia from, xiv, 29; and slave trade, 9–10, 36; mentioned, 129, 209, 210, 234, 286

Whig Party (Liberia), xxviii

Whitfield, Henry B., 113

Whittier, 197

Wilberforce, William, 135, 197

Wilkinson, Sir J. S., 151

Williams, G. A., 260n.

Wilson, Rev. D. A., xii, 217

Wiltberger, 101

Winchell, Dr Alexander, 236–7, *see also Pre-Adamite Man*

Wirth, Otto, xxxvi

Wordsworth, William, 197

"Work and Destiny of the Races" (Blyden), 211

Wurukud, 297

Xenophanes, 290n.

Yale University, 247

Yoruba, 224, 281, 310

Yoruba Tribe, 304

Yosemite Valley, 50

Yumna, 291

Zionist Movement, xxxi, 210–14

Zontomy, 180–1

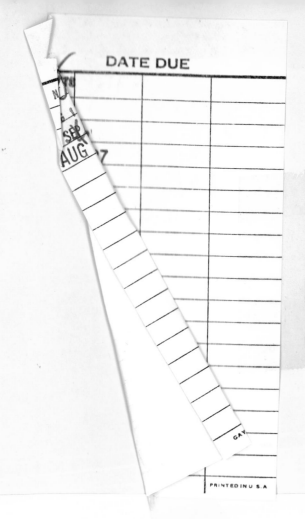

DATE DUE